Surplus Citi

Surplus Citizens

Struggle and Nationalism in the Greek Crisis

Dimitra Kotouza

First published 2019 by Pluto Press
345 Archway Road, London N6 5AA

www.plutobooks.com

Copyright © Dimitra Kotouza 2019

The right of Dimitra Kotouza to be identified as the author of this work has been asserted by her in accordance with the Copyright, Designs and Patents Act 1988.

British Library Cataloguing in Publication Data
A catalogue record for this book is available from the British Library

ISBN   978 0 7453 3779 1   Hardback
ISBN   978 0 7453 3778 4   Paperback
ISBN   978 1 7868 0366 5   PDF eBook
ISBN   978 1 7868 0368 9   Kindle eBook
ISBN   978 1 7868 0367 2   EPUB eBook

Typeset by Stanford DTP Services, Northampton, England

Simultaneously printed in the United Kingdom and United States of America

Contents

Acknowledgements

The manuscript of this book went through a long seven-year journey and many transformations before reaching its current form, shaped by the input of several individuals, collectives and institutions.

The very subject of the book – social struggles in Greece – could not exist without the collective praxis that took place in the crisis and I am thankful to those who gave their time to talk with me about their experiences. My ideas were continually and fruitfully challenged by the critical exchanges among self-organised collectives and networks, not all of which are currently still in existence. I thank all of the friends from reading groups, discussion groups and self-published journals, for the time, engagement, research and theoretical work they have shared, whose influence has been defining. I am especially indebted to the *Endnotes* journal collective who inspired my thinking, among other things, on 'surplus population' and the psychoanalysis of political groups; my friends from the late Feminist Reading Group for creating a nurturing space for open reflection on gender; as well as the contributors to the now-discontinued journal *Blaumachen* for the stimulating discussions on social struggles in Greece between 2011 and 2013. Heartfelt thanks also to Andreas Serifis for his enthusiasm in discussing my work with others and communicating feedback, as well as for providing advice and introducing me to people with long-running experience in important movements and projects.

I completed the earliest version of this work as a doctoral thesis for the school of Politics and International Relations at the University of Kent, where I received the kind support – intellectual, emotional and practical – of my supervisor Iain MacKenzie. I am grateful to him for encouraging critical exploration and creativity beyond the often restrictive confines of academia and its disciplinary boundaries. The thesis manuscript received extremely useful commentaries from my two examiners who graciously demanded no corrections, Donatella Alessandrini and Alberto Toscano. I am especially grateful to the latter for his impressively detailed and thoughtful notes spanning the entire manuscript, which fed into significant revisions. The research for the thesis would not have been possible without the funding, in the first three years, of the Economic and Social Research Council, for which I am very fortunate. I am also thankful to friends who offered feedback on that early text: Themis Katsoulis, whose substantial knowledge and experience provided invaluable information and a unique perspective on Greek history; Zacharias Zoubir, Sam Clodd and Simon Bull, who picked out weaknesses in my early analysis of migration, racism and biopolitics; and Larne Abse Gogarty, for her attentive comments on my approach to history.

For always encouraging my writing, providing an avenue to publish early versions of it and offering thoughtful feedback and a formative space for critical reflection over the many years of working together, I owe a great deal to my colleagues of the *Mute* editorial collective: Pauline van Mourik Broekman, Simon Worthington, Josephine Berry, Benedict Seymour, Anthony Iles, Matthew Hyland, Mira Mattar and Stefan Szczelkun. For his appreciation of this work and for motivating me to complete the book manuscript I am thankful to David Schulman of Pluto Press, as well as to Dan Harding for painstakingly copy-editing the text in a short space of time.

Finally, my deepest gratitude goes to my husband Dimitris, who, in addition to his love and his daily emotional generosity, has provided care and material support during the difficult time of trying to combine writing, navigating the frustrations of the academic labour market and becoming a mother. Not only this, but he continues to help me grow intellectually and emotionally in more ways than he knows.

Note on Transliteration

All transliterations use the ISO 843 system, which allows full reversibility, to assist the reader in locating original Greek titles. Please see: https:// en.wikipedia.org/wiki/ISO_843.

List of Abbreviations

AK	Astikós Kōdikas (Civil Code)
ANTARSYA	Antikapitalistikī Aristerī Synergasía gia tīn Anatropī (Anticapitalist Left Cooperation for the Overthrow)
ASOEE	Anōtátī Scholī Oikonomikōn kai Emporikōn Epistīmōn (Athens University of Economics and Business)
DIMAR	Dīmokratikī Aristerá (Democratic Left)
EAM	Ethnikó Apeleutherōtikó Métōpo (National Liberation Front)
EC	European Commission
ECB	European Central Bank
EEC	European Economic Community
EL.STAT	Ellīnikī Statistikī Archī (Greek Statistical Authority)
ELAS	Ethnikós Laïkós Apeleutherōtikós Stratós (National Popular Liberation Army)
EMU	Economic and Monetary Union
ERT	Ellīnikī Radiofōnía kai Tīleórasī (Greek Radio and Television)
EU	European Union
FEK	Fyllo Efīmerídas tīs Kyvernīseōs (Official Government Gazette)
GD	Golden Dawn (Chrysī Augī)
GSEE	Genikī Synomospondīa Ergatōn Elládos (General Confederation of Workers of Greece)
IKA	Ídryma Koinōnikōn Asfalíseōn (Institute of Social Security)
IME GSEVEE	Institoúto Mikrōn Epicheirīseōn – Genikī Synomospondía Epaggelmatiōn Viotechnōn Empórōn Elládas (Small Enterprises Institute of the Hellenic Confederation of Professionals, Craftspersons, and Merchants)
IMF	International Monetary Fund
INE-GSEE	Institoúto Ergasías GSEE (Labour Institute of GSEE)
KKE	Kommounistikó Kómma Elládas (Communist Party of Greece)

LAOS	Laïkós Orthódoxos Synagermós (Popular Orthodox Rally)
N	Nomos (Law or Statute)
ND	Néa Dīmokratía (New Democracy)
OVES	Omospondía Viomīchanikōn kai Ergostasiakōn Sōmateíōn (Federation for Industrial and Factory Trade Unions)
PAME	Panergatikó Agōnistikó Métōpo (All Workers Militant Front)
PASOK	Panellīnio Sosialistikó Kínīma (Panhellenic Socialist Movement)
SEK	Sosialistikó Ergatikó Kómma (Socialist Workers' Party)
SKYA	Synéleusī gia tīn Kykloforía tōn Agōnōn (Assembly for the Circulation of Struggles)
SYRIZA	Synaspismós Rizospastikīs Aristerás (Coalition of the Radical Left)

Introduction: Squares and Frontiers

After the global financial crisis broke out in 2008, new forms of struggle and uprisings began to spread, reinvigorating discussions around social transformation and left-wing political avenues out of the crisis. But by 2011, it was clear the new sequence of struggles did not have the recognisable form of class struggle: it was not primarily located in workplaces or led by a re-empowered labour movement. New movements occupied public spaces, demanded democracy, practised self-organisation and broke out in riots. In the case of Greece, the most indebted country of the European Union (EU) periphery where the most severe austerity was imposed, social struggles drew attention for their intensity and the graveness of what was at stake each time: supervisory institutions and governments claimed that if protests succeeded in their demands against austerity, then the country would default, and that would be even more catastrophic. Yet, over the years of austerity, which struggles failed to hinder, unemployment rose to over 25 per cent, and, from 2010 to 2013, the average wage purchasing power fell by 21 per cent.[1]

In this context, with little room to move within the shackles of debt, the Eurozone project and the imperatives of capitalist reproduction in the crisis, the struggles resisting austerity in Greece displayed similar characteristics as elsewhere. In the 'Aganaktisménoi' movement of public square occupations, which was inspired by the occupation of Tahrir Square and Spain's Indignados and lasted for over two months, party mediation was unwelcome. In the squares there was an attempt to self-organise daily and develop the movement's own language. In the large demonstrations resisting new austerity measures, ferocious riots expanded spatially, numerically and compositionally. After these struggles peaked in early 2012, and a new right-wing-led coalition government was formed to counter the unprecedented electoral rise of the left, international headlines were made by the smaller, but significant, empowerment of the neo-Nazi party Golden Dawn (GD), and by the racist violence it perpetrated. There was an anti-fascist response, yet the energy of 2011 had disappeared, and the prior movement seemed

---

1. INE-GSEE, *Í Ellinikí Oikonomía kai í Apaschólisí* (Athens: 2014), 143.

to have been split along political lines. The broader left found itself in a defensive position, reduced to fighting against the drive to legitimise racist victimisation and murder. Political parties were again dominating public discourse, each offering its own solution to the crisis and the management of capitalist reproduction. It is out of this situation that SYRIZA (Coalition of the Radical Left) won the 2015 elections.

SYRIZA's victories, and the failed negotiations in the EU with Greece's creditors, invited both optimism for recreating a space for the return of social democracy, and pessimism around the possibility of transforming the EU, leading to demands for reinstating 'full national sovereignty'. The Anglophone discussion on the Greek situation has been dominated by these concerns. It has addressed in depth the causes of debt in the Greek state,[2] the merits and downsides of Eurozone and EU membership, theories of dependency and economic imbalances among European countries,[3] questions of left leadership and the handling of negotiations over Greece's debt bailouts.[4] Writing on social struggle in the crisis has tended to reproduce the same concerns, and either to focus on the rise of SYRIZA,[5] or to describe social struggle by focusing on its conflict with outside adversaries,[6] without drawing out internal conflicts, contradictions, dilemmas and debates. While there are some exceptions to this, for example in the work of critical anthropologists on migrant solidarity,[7] they have not received very much exposure.

Surplus Citizens aims to problematise the principles taken for granted in the mainstream debate: sovereignty, citizenship, democracy and economic growth, accepted as preconditions or even as ends in themselves, and used as yardsticks to evaluate and understand social struggle. It raises often-neglected questions that emerged through the

---

2. John Milios and Dimitris Sotiropoulos, 'Crisis of Greece or Crisis of the Euro?', *Journal of Balkan and Near Eastern Studies* 12, no. 3 (2010): 223–40.

3. Costas Lapavitsas, *Crisis in the Eurozone* (London: Verso, 2012); Stavros Mavroudeas, 'Greece and the EU' (First International Conference on Political Economy, Rethymno, 2010); Christos Laskos and Euclid Tsakalotos, *Crucible of Resistance* (London: Pluto, 2013).

4. Laskos and Tsakalotos, *Crucible of Resistance*; Kevin Ovenden, *Syriza* (London: Pluto, 2015); Yanis Varoufakis, *Adults in the Room* (New York: Vintage, 2018).

5. Costas Douzinas, *Syriza in Power* (Cambridge: Polity, 2017); Ovenden, *Syriza*.

6. E.g. Costas Douzinas, *Philosophy and Resistance in the Crisis* (Cambridge: Polity, 2013); Dimitris Dalakoglou and Giorgos Poulimenakos, 'Hetero-Utopias', in *Critical Times in Greece*, ed. Dimitris Dalakoglou and Giōrgos Angelopulos (London: Routledge, 2018).

7. Katerina Rozakou, 'Socialities of Solidarity', *Social Anthropology* 24, no. 2 (2016): 185–99; Euthýmios Papataxiárchīs, 'Mia Megalī Anatropī', *Sýgchrona Thémata*, no. 132–3 (2016): 7–28.

practices of movements: how movements have dealt with the antinomies of crisis, precarity and extreme levels of unemployment; the role of nationalism and notions of citizenship; their impact on gendered and racialised relations. It communicates critical perspectives elaborated through confronting these problems, and challenges the dominant portrayal of struggles as the democratic protests of Greek citizens against international institutions imposing upon their government – that is, in terms that understand class as nationally circumscribed. It is urgent now to deconstruct the common-sense ethno-national unities expressed when non-European migrants crossed Europe's borders via Greece en masse in 2015–16.

Throughout this crisis period, plenty of commentary talked about 'Greeks' either as a subject of struggle resisting austerity,[8] or as a corrupt and decadent people who cannot manage their finances.[9] The assumption that these 'people' are, or should be, unified, colours dominant analyses of the 'Greek crisis' and of social struggles in Greece, which have reproduced ethnocentric narratives of Greek history, linked to anti-imperialist frameworks of understanding the crisis. These frameworks, despite their critique of 'Empire', reproduce a Eurocentric philosophy of history and an attachment to national production against the international level of finance. This simple opposition between the nation, its people and its territory and deterritorialised globalisation, often identified with 'cosmopolitan elites', is at the root of contemporary nationalist reactions to the crisis.

This has implications not only for understanding relations of class, both in Greece and beyond, which are overshadowed by the focus on power relations between nation-states, but also for racialised relations. The victims of neoliberal crisis management are not the 'Greek citizens', but the subordinate classes in Greece, not all of whom are citizens. These subordinate classes are differentially affected by the racialised management of borders and populations, as they have been since the Greek state's establishment. The nation and citizen-centred lens also has gendered implications. It only registers the gendered impacts of crisis through reproducing the naturalisation of family and patriarchal household as spaces of safety and relations to be protected from social disintegration. Those who do not find safety in this hetero/cis-normative

---

8. Stathis Kouvelakis, 'The Greek Cauldron', *New Left Review*, no. 72 (2011).
9. E.g. Jeremy Bulow and Kenneth Rogoff, 'Don't Blame Germany for Greece's Profligacy', *Wall Street Journal*, 16/4/2015.

and patriarchal notion of shelter were soon to not find safety in the Greek streets either, as nationalist oppositional discourses were used violently to reaffirm the male 'head of family' as the sole signified of the 'citizen'.

The figure of the citizen in movements with democratic demands, as it has been mobilised in squares and citizens' assemblies, is thus a central concern of *Surplus Citizens*. I interrogate the 'antinomies' and exclusions of citizenship (of class, race, gender), in the sense proposed by Etienne Balibar, exploring the ability of different movements to question them.[10] These antinomies, of course, are not static or inherited in any direct way from the original constitution of the Greek state. There is a continual dialectic of insurrection and constitution involved in the formation of citizenship, the meaning of 'the citizen' and the rights this entails. But we should not limit our conception to struggles for 'inclusion' into an already given regime of rights, especially a regime founded on and delimited by national belonging and the nation-state. This approach highlights not only the forms of domination and exclusion enshrouded by the notion of a unified 'people'. In line with a long lineage of feminist and anti-racist critique, it also shows that political unity cannot be an end in itself. On the contrary, a unity founded on a supposed neutrality and universality – in reality dominated by the white male figure – had better be dismantled before a new kind of collectivity and universality can emerge, one that recognises and addresses these forms of oppression.

Part I thus examines the historical formation, transformation and reproduction of class, racialised-ethnic and gendered social relations in Greece through social struggle, alongside the constitution of these divisions in citizenship and in law. To analyse nation and race in Greece's specific capitalist formation, I foreground the country's material and symbolic position within postcolonial international hierarchies. The analysis also serves as a response to theories of dependency and under-development of the Greek economy and society, according to which Greece 'lags behind' in developments that began in capitalist 'core' countries. Two phases of neoliberal transformation and social struggle against it come to light – the second being the ordoliberal management of crisis pursued by the EU – with different effects on class identity and forms of collective action, as well as on the concept of citizenship. The latter phase has led struggles, especially the movement of the squares, to

---

10. Etienne Balibar, 'The "Impossible" Community of the Citizens', *Environment and Planning D: Society and Space* 30, no. 3 (2012): 437–49.

fight against what appears to be at stake: national sovereignty in a crisis of sovereign debt, democracy in the context of neoliberal dedemocratisation and depoliticisation.[11]

But beyond reading neoliberalisation as an instance of cruelty delivered 'from above' – by bankers, capitalists and political leaders conspiring against 'us' – I take seriously the contradictions of social citizenship in what Balibar calls the 'national-social state',[12] as well as the contradictions and limits of political community encountered by the multiple subjects involved in struggle. It would thus be too simple to analyse neoliberalisation as a question of utilitarianism versus equality, linked, correspondingly, to neoliberal versus social democratic governmentality and social ethics. Neoliberalism promotes its own sense of 'equality', based on a biopolitical rationality that manages and sorts populations impersonally based on their market value. The racialised and gendered (not only class) dimensions of market forces are often left unquestioned because of the market's apparent 'blindness' and its contribution to a 'common good': a strong national economy that creates more 'job opportunities'. The social democratic critique of neoliberalism, promoting more regulation of finance and redistribution via welfare based on Keynesian economic principles, does not sufficiently challenge this market principle and thus teeters at the brink of a contradiction: it wants to maintain market capitalism, yet it constantly undermines the market definition of equality and fairness, as well as the right to property and the commodification of labour. It aims to level economic hierarchies and was even thought, at the apex of its success, to have overcome material concerns,[13] yet its combination of full employment and inflationary tendencies is partly what led to the class war waged by the neoliberal turn. Today, governance with a social democratic orientation like that of SYRIZA resorts to creating funds for minimal welfare and advancing a liberal humanitarian discourse, which it cannot but combine with 'attracting investment', a priority incompatible with labour rights in the current international context.

We lack the theoretical tools to understand and question inequalities or exclusions unless we recognise the misery of crisis as caused not

---

11. Werner Bonefeld, 'European Integration', *Capital & Class* 26, no. 2 (2002): 117–42; Wendy Brown, 'American Nightmare', *Political Theory*, no. 34 (2006): 690–714; Peter Burnham, 'Depoliticisation', *Policy & Politics* 42, no. 2 (2014): 189–206.

12. Balibar, '"Impossible" Community', 437.

13. Ronald Inglehart, *The Silent Revolution* (Princeton: Princeton University Press, 1977).

merely by lack of democracy and redistributive social policies, but by the very fact that, for proletarians,[14] subsistence depends on the wage and the continuation of exploitation – the production and expansion of surplus value, accumulation. In the Great Recession, when this capacity for expanding accumulation has reached a limit, we cannot afford to take our capitalist world system for granted. Dependence on wages under conditions of 28 per cent unemployment and 'conditional' or absent social security is founded on the premise that the production of value (business, investment, productivity) is what human life *must* depend on, and, thus, the life of populations not fully integrated into that system is a matter of indifference, or, worse, an abject social burden.

Superfluity is not conceived here in the Malthusian sense (too many people, too few resources), but rather from the point of view of capitalist reproduction and of integration into the formal labour market. The 'surplus population' is not simply workless, but its activity remains outside the core circuit of capitalist reproduction. There is evidence of an expanding surplus population worldwide, if it is carefully conceptualised. This population is unevenly distributed, relative to the creation of a stratified global labour market reinforced by heavily policed national borders.[15] Thus the meaning of the title, *Surplus Citizens*, is not that the superfluity of Greek citizens is the primary condition around which our politics ought to concentrate. That a great number of citizens of subordinate classes have become surplus, i.e. thrown out of what was previously thought to be a 'normal' wage relation or relatively safe small business ownership, is only part of the picture. Instead, I draw attention to *how* this superfluity of citizens generated identifications with nation, class and, often, masculinity, in the political discourse and identities of movements. This enabled crisis management ideology to externalise social conflict into international relations (the EU, immigrants and refugees), and perceived threats to patriarchal roles and identities.

Equally, it is misleading to see class as in opposition to national unity, since workers' identity has been historically nationally circumscribed as well as often aligning its interests with those of capitalist employers. To explore this, I adopt the critique of labour and the notion of mutual

---

14. I use the term 'proletarian' throughout in its plain material sense: one who does not have any source for subsistence other than selling one's labour-power.

15. Stephen Castles, 'Migration, Crisis, and the Global Labour Market', *Globalizations* 8, no. 3 (2011): 311–24.

implication between capital and labour.[16] The affirmation of labour in class struggle, which, in this crisis, has translated into the demand for and the defence of jobs, welcomes and supports capitalist investment and accumulation with all that it entails. Proletarian dependence upon capitalist reproduction itself should then be the object of critique, although that poses difficult questions as to what practices of struggle might enact such a critique. As I describe in Part II, this opposition has led to community conflict in Chalkidiki, northern Greece, where flexibly employed mine workers have supported the destruction of a forest in opposition to its local defenders. We see multiple similar struggles and contradictions elsewhere in the world, and, in these contexts, also a special role for women, a role whose ambiguous implications I also explore.[17] Beyond this case, the majority of workers' struggles faced this contradiction in the form of internal hierarchies and a distance between the practices of workplace protest, blockade, strike and self-management.

In spite of this proliferation of social divisions, the idea of a 'commons' is an imaginary that has inspired radical collectives in Greece to construct alternative economic communities of solidarity in the crisis. Emerging from an autonomist-Marxist analysis, this perspective suggests that the crisis is capital's opportunity to appropriate everything that is 'common' – welfare, publicly owned enterprises and land.[18] The future of struggles thus depends on their ability to reclaim those 'commons' and expand communities where the development of non-capitalist social relations would flourish.[19] Yet how the space of the commons can become and remain 'anti-capitalist', as opposed to merely an informal economy for survival, remains a question. George Caffentzis and Silvia Federici assert that a 'common' equally accessible space or resource is not capitalist, as long as it is communal, is regulated through egalitarian decision

16. Moishe Postone, *Time, Labor, and Social Domination* (Cambridge: Cambridge University Press, 1996); Werner Bonefeld, *Critical Theory and the Critique of Political Economy* (New York: Bloomsbury, 2014), 29–43; Théorie Communiste, 'Communization in the Present Tense', in *Communization and Its Discontents*, ed. Benjamin Noys (New York: Autonomedia, 2012), 41–60.
17. Some examples are the resistance of Zapatista and other agricultural communities in Mexico, rural conflicts in China over industrial pollution, the NoTav campaign in Italy and anti-airport protests in France.
18. Midnight Notes Collective and Friends, *Promissory Notes*, 2009.
19. George Caffentzis and Silvia Federici, 'Commons Against and Beyond Capitalism', *Upping the Anti*, no. 15 (2013): 83–97; Michael Hardt, 'The Common in Communism', in *The Idea of Communism*, ed. Costas Douzinas and Slavoj Žižek (London: Verso, 2010), 131–44.

making, and is not used for commercial purposes,[20] warning against its co-optation by a capitalist outside.[21] But problems become evident when we examine the practices of solidarity economies, the self-organisation of work, the Occupy movements, struggles to prevent privatisation.[22] Celebratory accounts often do not extend to a critical analysis of movements' compositions and social relations within them, their relationship with their outside and whether they live up to these theoretical aspirations or reproduce the very relations they aim to fight against. In Part II, I examine local assemblies and alternative economies by asking these questions.

Social struggles in the crisis, dominated by the discourse, composition and imaginaries of the squares, took place amid heightened and purposely cultivated national and identitarian insecurity. By mid-2012, governments openly attempted to exploit this insecurity through policing internal and external 'threats', the spectacular criminalisation of immigrants and sex workers. GD's vigilantism was permitted and often praised as an instrument of social control. I explore this conjuncture in Part III. Seen through the lens of biopolitics, reinforcing sovereignty and the relationship between the national citizen and the national state in the crisis came to concern the separation of a 'healthy' political body from a racialised and gendered, 'diseased' and abject marginal body. In this context, the separateness of immigrants' movements, often also from the anti-fascist movement, has been a symptom of the deep racialised divisions in Greek society, and a precondition of ethnocentrism in citizen mobilisations. This normalised social segregation, especially of those visibly distinguished by skin colour, posed a great challenge to movements when GD began to gain popular support.

SYRIZA won the 2015 elections with a nationalist language, but also with the opening of detention camps written in its manifesto, a significant act that was soon reversed. The so-called migrant crisis that peaked in 2015–16 raised vital questions about the possibilities and meanings of solidarity beyond national belonging. It brought an important shift in migrant struggles and the practices and scale of migrant solidarity. Extending transnationally, these movements are the most hopeful developments after the end of the 2010–14 wave of struggles, and stand against

---

20. Caffentzis and Federici, 'Commons'.
21. George Caffentzis, 'The Future of "The Commons"', *New Formations* 69, no. 1 (2010): 23–41.
22. Caffentzis and Federici, 'Commons', 92–6.

anti-immigration trends in Europe, strengthened structures of border security and incarceration, humanitarian population management by non-governmental organisations (NGOs) and everyday racism. Yet movements and migrant subjects can still reproduce the hierarchies and subjectivities cultivated by border regimes. Based on interviews with activists, Part III explores what conditions and initiatives might enable a questioning of such hierarchies.

Surplus Citizens addresses the central question of how the citizens of subordinate classes might avoid entrenchment in national belonging and rigid racialised and gendered identities. This concerns both Europeans and non-European migrants, who frequently organise on a national, ethnic or gender-exclusive basis. Asking this question is the opposite of holding an abstract principle of internationalism or of transcending identity in a voluntaristic fashion and joining a privileged elite of globe-trotting 'social justice warriors' – as populist neo-reactionaries would have it. Instead, it demands a self-critical theory and collective practice that eschews the easy answers of fixed collective identities and the supposed 'shelter' of the nation-state and traditional patriarchal family. These not only fail to protect from the ravages of financialised capitalism, but reproduce deeper forms of brutality, in which immiserated citizens are invited to participate. While struggles cannot transcend these social relations and dynamics at will, they can and do often challenge them, as I hope to show in this book.

A Note on Method, Sources and Presentation

Aiming for an analysis that would document the most important movements in the crisis and bring them into theoretical conversation has demanded both empirical and theoretical research. *Surplus Citizens* is based on participant observation, interviews and analysis of documentary material (websites, posters, self-publishing, self-critical analyses, ideological pronouncements, etc.), which aimed to detect the limits, points of conflict and tensions in the experience of movements. These limits were encountered collectively, and movement groups have been driven to reflect upon them, organising discussions and producing critical texts. Such experiences and reflection were the focus of eight months of participant observation in group discussions (grassroots unions, organisations of the unemployed, alternative economy collectives, anti-fascist groups, prisoner solidarity, social centres), assemblies (neighbourhood assemblies, the movement of the squares), small protests and large demonstrations in Athens and Thessaloniki. Documentary research looked at movement communications (websites, posters, leaflets, newsletters, self-publishing, self-critical analyses, ideological pronouncements), first-person accounts and opinion pieces by participants in movements.

However, because of its broader perspective, *Surplus Citizens* does not offer the details of social interactions and personal or collective stories that would typically accompany ethnographic work on movements. In doing so, it deviates from common practices and modes of presentation in critical social movement research, which valorises experiences of struggle and the co-production of knowledge. Instead it offers not only less, but also more than would have been otherwise possible: it brings together theory and practice, and micro and macro levels of analysis. Through examining the practices, imaginaries and dilemmas of movements as expressed in their debates, and linking them to a broader historical, geographic and sociopolitical context, it explores the relationship between social action, social reproduction and notions of emancipation in the crisis. Debates within movements and encounters between their practices and the conditions of crisis impinge upon questions of value, exchange relations and the meanings of solidarity; the strength and limits of self-organisation; and the relationships between the 'popular', nationalism, class and racialised and gendered dynamics, in this *specific* historical conjuncture and geopolitical space. This approach is able to detect ambivalence and contradiction in social action and imaginaries, as well as distance and conflict between different forms of practice, revealing new avenues for social transformation and new obstacles to be addressed. This is because the questions posed by struggles, which can ground immanent critique, are not only detectable in their critical discourse and self-awareness, but also in the relation between their practices and the broader capitalist, patriarchal and racialised social relations of their historical context.

PART I

Histories: Undead and Invisible Conflicts, Transformations, Crisis

1

The Making of Greek Capitalism through Race, Gender and Class

The phrase 'undead conflicts' in Greece typically evokes the haunting of political culture by collective traumas of the Axis occupation, the civil war and the colonels' dictatorship. After having been seemingly laid to rest between the 1980s and 2008, these memories were reawakened in the crisis, by both the role of Germany and the intense polarisation between right and left. Given these associations, the title's prioritisation of race and gender may seem incongruous. Yet race and gender invisibly also haunt the history of class and political struggle in Greece, along with political discourses, experiences and imaginaries in the crisis. The 'return' and political mobilisation of war traumas staged a conflict over competing nationalisms (German and Greek, left and right), which obscured from view, both in historical narrative and in narratives of the present, the racialised, gendered and class dimensions of these conflicts. This chapter aims to reorient our vision towards these dimensions.

'Race' is first in order, because the most invisible. Any literature review of the Greek social sciences will discover minimal mention of its role in the construction of 'Greece' and Greek national identity, let alone in the current crisis. Even though Greek 'whiteness' is not racialised in a straightforward way, the epistemic impact of this ambiguity is profound. It affects not only who is automatically taken to belong to national and class history, but also the seemingly objective economic question of Greece's place within global capitalism. The responses are typically as racialised as the concept of 'capitalist development' itself.

Relations of race and their inter-articulation with nationalism are little engaged with by the Greek left. We are usually presented with the opposition between racist far-right nationalisms and noble, anti-racist left-wing nationalisms, the latter essential for 'hegemonizing the very concept of "the people" that constitute the living substance of the nation to transform it into an inclusive, multiracial, multicultural, welcoming, and sovereign body politic.[1] The vision turns away from how national unity, in the history of left strategy as well, silenced class antagonisms at critical moments, and has been founded on the hegemonic figure of the Greek man.

'Gender' is the second least visible, but an essential 'filter' for the circumscription of what nation, class, labour, citizenship, democracy, security and 'exit from crisis' might mean in the current context. This is because, if the history of class struggle fails to register gendered unpaid labour, if the fraternal meanings of democracy and nation are taken for granted, then we fail to imagine the exit from crisis as anything other than immunising the national-fraternal-patriarchal-class community from internal and external threats. It is unsurprising that the politics of securing the domestic (understood in both its meanings as nation and household) were successfully appropriated by the far right during the crisis.[2]

Finally, class: the concept in whose place the term 'popular' often stands nonchalantly. I ask what may be revealed if we disentangle class from the popular, that is, from nation, while avoiding assumptions about the political subjectivity of different types of workers, peasants or small business owners, to consider how different class alliances played a role in significant historical moments.

Greek political culture and polity has been historically constituted by these three dimensions, located within international and intra-European hierarchies.

Capitalist Development, Eurocentrism, Race

Within Greek Marxist historiography, the debate of how Greece's capitalism relates to that of Western Europe is far from resolved. Two polarised positions have persisted in the past three decades. The first, most traditional and dominant position argues that Greece's capitalism, and Greece as a nation-state, has always been in a relation of dependency on the imperialist capitalisms of the West, a relation that has caused and reproduced Greece's underdevelopment. This has been the official position of the Communist Party of Greece (KKE) and of many Marxist academics,[3] but it is a view that also draws on the long history of theories

---

1. Kouvelakis, 'An Open Letter'.
2. See also Angela Mitropoulos, *Contract and Contagion* (New York: Minor Compositions, 2012).
3. The most influential proponents of this view have been Vergopoulos and Mouzelis. See Kôstas Vergópoulos, Níkos Mouzélis, et al., *To Krátos ston Perifereiakó Kapitalismó* (Athens: Exántas, 1985).

of imperialism and dependency that use the centre–periphery model, from Luxemburg to Wallerstein.[4] The second perspective minimises the different characteristics and differential timing of the development of the productive forces in Greece and insists on a conception of class struggle that remains within the boundaries of every 'social formation'.[5] The political debate behind this polarisation is one between the nationalist anti-imperialism of traditional Greek communism and an anti-nationalist critique that emphasises the power of Greek capital over the domestic working class, as well as its expansion in the Balkans and the Mediterranean.

The peculiarities of class structure in the country are similarly unresolved, entangled as they are in political debates, many of which concern the restructuring under way since 2009. Theoretical models of dependency tend to present Greek capitalism as suffering from under-development and a weak bourgeoisie that is unable to drive development forward, because of 'pre-capitalist', 'patrimonial' and 'clientelist' forms of government,[6] as well as because of its 'dependency' on foreign capital. Underdevelopment is also attributed to strong state intervention in the economy and to an 'extensive' rather than 'intensive' mode of development that has tended to spawn a large number of small capitals instead of a few large ones.[7] An alternative view is given by the work of Milios,[8] which places more emphasis on the internal class struggle within the country. Still, even Milios and Sotiropoulos refrain from doing away with oppositions between 'developed' and 'undeveloped' social formations that are taken to contain 'pre-capitalist modes of production'.[9]

These analyses are unsatisfactory for a number of reasons. First, they remain within ontologies of social relations between entities that are defined by the boundaries of states or national communities as if

---

4. See Rosa Luxemburg, *The Accumulation of Capital* (London: Routledge, 1971); Immanuel Wallerstein, *The Modern World-System* (New York: Academic, 1974); Samir Amin, *Unequal Development* (Sussex: Harvester, 1976).

5. John Milios and Dimitris Sotiropoulos, *Rethinking Imperialism* (New York: Palgrave Macmillan, 2009), 199–203.

6. Nicos Mouzelis, *Politics in the Semi-Periphery* (New York: St. Martin's, 1986). For a critique of the explanatory use of 'clientelism' see Giánnis Mīliós, 'Ī Ypanáptyxī (tīs Theōrías) ōs Apologītikī́', *Théseis*, no. 45 (1993).

7. Michális Mállios, *Ī Sýgchronī Fásī Anáptyxīs tou Kapitalismoú stīn Elláda* (Athens: Sýgchronī Epochī́, 1979); Giánnis Samarás, *Krátos kai Kefálaio stīn Elláda* (Athens: Sýgchronī Epochī́, 1982).

8. Milios, *Ellīnikós Koinōnikós Schīmatismós*.

9. Milios and Sotiropoulos, *Rethinking Imperialism*, 199–203.

these are transhistorically given. Key power relationships either take place between states or between classes within states, and it becomes impossible to see how, for example, class conflict can transcend state boundaries in forms other than the model of a national struggle against imperial domination. Second, both accounts understand capitalism within a linear Western European model of development as the norm, and as the measure against which other economies are compared. Third, and this is especially true of mainstream Greek anti-imperialism, they fail to reflect upon the cultural and racialised dimensions of international hierarchies, and thus reproduce orientalist modernisation discourses of 'clientelism', 'corruption' and 'patrimony'. These weaknesses carry implications not only for the analysis of class relations in the region, but also for understanding their racialised and gendered dimensions, which are often invisible or at least underexplored in these accounts.

The problem with a developmentalist perspective has long been highlighted by postcolonial critics. Despite many episodes of conflict between Marxist and postcolonial thinkers,[10] authors such as Dipesh Chakrabarty and Massimiliano Tomba have worked on combining the critical insights of Marxism and postcolonial critique. Drawing upon Ernst Bloch's conception of non-simultaneity, they emphasise the different coexisting temporalities of capitalism,[11] beyond a Eurocentric progressivist teleology that periodises capitalism on the basis of concepts of absolute and relative surplus value or formal and real subsumption.[12] Tomba's work on multiple temporalities shows that capitalism is compatible with different forms of labour, including (racialised) slavery and (gendered) non-waged labour.[13] These do not merely co-exist with one another, but are reciprocally implicated within networks of trade and relations of competition that establish a variety of exploitative forms. 'Exceptions' and differentials in the forms of exploitation are constitutive of capitalist

---

10. A recent example is Vivek Chibber, *Postcolonial Theory and the Specter of Capital* (London: Verso, 2013), and the response by Gayatri Chakravorty Spivak, 'Postcolonial Theory and the Specter of Capital', *Cambridge Review of International Affairs* 27, no. 1 (2014): 184–98.

11. Ernst Bloch, *The Heritage of Our Times* (Berkeley: University of California Press, 1991).

12. Such an approach is exemplified by Robert Brenner's critique of dependency theories. Brenner takes his critique too far, confining an enormous part of the (ex-)colonised world to 'residual' forms of development that, he suggests, have had little if any impact upon the formation of world capitalism. Robert Brenner, 'The Origins of Capitalist Development', *New Left Review* I, no. 104 (1977): 25–92.

13. See Marcel Van der Linden, *Workers of the World* (Leiden : Brill, 2008).

competition and the international hierarchy of the division of labour: global capitalism by definition cannot be homogeneous. Tomba quotes George Caffentzis' argument that "'new enclosures" in the country-side must accompany the rise of "automatic processes" in industry, the computer requires the sweat shop, and the cyborg's existence is premised on the slave'.[14] These 'exceptions', such as the contemporary existence of slavery, pockets of subsistence agriculture and workshops using antiquated technologies are not peripheral to the dynamic of capitalist expansion but are necessary parts of it.

Yet, the labour of developing a viewpoint beyond Eurocentrism without magnifying cultural difference in a way that reproduces orientalist imaginings can be a treacherous task. Chakrabarty promotes a 'subaltern historiography' against 'universalist narratives of capital', which assume that 'capitalism necessarily brings bourgeois relations of power to a position of hegemony'.[15] He is interested in how 'non-rational' political and cultural forms survive in global capitalism, arguing that there is a living experience, a 'history 2', a 'politics of human belonging and diversity' that coexists with capital's logic but is not subsumed by it. This 'history 2' of lived experience exists within the time of capital but disrupts its unity. Thus, Chakrabarty criticises as 'historicist' E. P. Thompson's argument that time-discipline would be internalised in the 'developing world' sooner or later.[16] Indeed, the 'protestant work ethic' may be best understood as a culturally and historically specific phenomenon and not as the universal cultural essence of capitalism worldwide. But we should also be wary of repurposing orientalist stereotypes of 'laziness' as instances of anti-capitalist resistance in the peripheries. The notion of an unsubsumed cultural-temporal experience, which can even be thought of as a site of resistance, can potentially conceal the power relations at play. As we will see in the case of Greek workers in the current crisis, the charge of a culture of 'laziness' preceded the act of resistance, and was not used to cultivate a work ethic, but, more materially, to forcibly impose time-discipline through workforce rationalisation, flexibilisation and wage cuts. In turn, the resistance itself often adopted the logic of hard work, through the creation of co-operative self-employment structures,

14. George Caffentzis, *In Letters of Blood and Fire* (Oakland, CA: PM, 2013), 79.
15. Dipesh Chakrabarty, *Provincializing Europe* (Princeton: Princeton University Press, 2000), 14.
16. Chakrabarty, ibid., 48; E. P. Thompson, 'Time, Work-Discipline, and Industrial Capitalism', *Past and Present* 38, no. 1 (1967): 56–97.

in which the self-imposition and internalisation of time-discipline is required for market survival. It is important to note that the imposition of time-discipline can be far more rigorous under conditions where absolute surplus value has to be extracted in small non-industrialised businesses and workshops, particularly under conditions of high unemployment. Time-discipline here is not primarily a matter of culture and ethics, nor is it a matter of the absolute subsumption of human subjectivity under capital, but a matter of local modes of value production and values of labour power.

At the same time, attempting to locate resistances to capitalism in the authenticity of ethnic or national culture can awaken the racist colonial imaginaries embedded in the historical construction of Greek national identity, which are both racialising of non-European others and self-racialising. The stereotype of the 'lazy [modern] Greek' is of course not new and did not come alone. It has persisted through and beyond the process by which Western European Philhellenes constructed 'Greece' as the 'cradle of European civilisation', separating its heritage from the influence it received from Africa and the Middle East. In this act of separation, contemporary 'Greeks' were never seen as able to live up to the idealised ancients. This encounter produced the contemporaries as a degenerate version of a romanticised past, attributed especially to the historical mediation of Ottoman culture.[17] That allowed Western European racial theorists to claim a more direct inheritance of Ancient Greek civilisation than they would admit to the Greek-speaking inhabitants of the eastern Mediterranean, who failed to resemble the 'Venus of Melos'.[18] Modern Greeks were too disappointingly oriental. The Greek nation-building and modernising project thereby incorporated as its nemesis orientalist constructions of laziness, pre-modern habits, corruption, patrimonial culture and 'oriental' cultural elements in art and everyday life,[19] along with narratives of ethnic diversity and mixing in the region, seeking to produce a culturally and racially purified and truly European 'Greece'.

---

17. Stathis Gourgouris, *Dream Nation* (Stanford: Stanford University Press, 1996).

18. The most well known are the Austrian historian Jakob Philipp Fallmerayer (1790–1861), the Scottish anatomist Robert Knox (1791–1862) and the French racial theorist Arthur de Gobineau (1816–82). See Nina Athanassoglou-Kallmyer, 'Excavating Greece', *Nineteenth-Century Art Worldwide* 7, no. 2 (Autumn 2008).

19. See also Dimitra Kotouza, 'Music Is the Crime that Contains All Others', *Mute* 3, no. 1 (2010): 70–81.

The same orientalist tropes have persisted in the ideologies promoting the neoliberal restructuring during the current crisis.[20] Similar to the nationals of (at least formally) decolonised states, the Greek is continually constructed as in a state of lack or failure vis-à-vis the 'developed West'. In contrast to the former, however, the Greek can continue to make claims to Europeanness and white Christianity, as well as participate in military violence and practices of exclusion against all those other Others. Greece's membership in the EU, and its belonging in 'Europe', thus has a contradictory symbolic and affective dynamic. The desire to belong in the club of white modern Europeanness and to participate in its neocolonial role in the world brings nationals continually into conflict with Western European constructions of who they are. The attempt to provide a coherent nationalist narrative, for example the use of the Byzantium as the missing link between antiquity and modernity,[21] continually collides with historical evidence, cultural experience and, most importantly, the power relations upon which Western European contempt is founded. Thus, it should not come as a surprise that nationalist, socialist, anti-imperialist and racist ideologies have found historically a fertile ground for cross-pollination in Greece.[22]

The charge of 'corruption', a ubiquitous element in common-sense explanations of the 'Greek crisis', is part of these relations. The Greek state is accused of not following the rules of the bourgeois separation of public and private interests. To that is attributed the failure of the Greek economy, notwithstanding the fact that the economies of states involved in mafia networks and extrajudicial killings, such as that of Mexico, appear to be thriving in growth statistics and state finances. But we should also question what 'corruption' means exactly, and how it is that, in comparative measures of corruption, the vague geographical and discursive construction of 'the West' consistently comes up as the most politically noble. Could this have anything to do with the fact that most measures of corruption are founded on 'perceptions' as, for example, the Corruption Perceptions Index? We may also question how US institutions come up

---

20. Johanna Hanink, *The Classical Debt* (Cambridge, MA: Belknap, 2017).
21. This was the highly influential project of the historian Constantinos Paparrigopoulos, which still structures popular understandings of national history (1815–91). Gourgouris, *Dream Nation*, 145.
22. A significant example is the prominent political thinker and diplomat Ion Dragoumis (1878–1920), who developed a racial anti-imperialist strategy for Greece and later came to admire the Bolsheviks and advocate socialism.

in such indices as 'less corrupt' than those of Greece, when in the USA it is legal to donate to politicians through the 'lobbying system' while in Greece this is completely illegal.[23] If we look into it further, we may find, with Peter Bratsis,[24] that anti-corruption laws are arbitrary, as in the US example, allowing a significant degree of violation of the normative bourgeois separation between public and private, so 'corruption' is detected only through minor violations of the law. Thus, '[the] purity of the public is specular and illusionary, a performative gesture, a product of a series of rules designed to cloak the fetishistic nature of the public/ private split'.[25] The fact that Greek law does not recognise any level of lobbying or gifts to public servants as an acceptable endeavour allows 'perceptions of corruption' to flourish; but it also reveals the inflexibility with which bourgeois ideals – taken in their idealised, pure, 'Western' form – are imposed in Greece. With all these complexities disguised under spurious statistical measurements, the supposed deviations of the peripheries from the 'model' liberal democratic state are all too easily explained away as symptoms of 'backwardness' and not as alternative forms of state rationality adapted to the interaction between local and international contexts marked by social, cultural and political histories.

Another problematic assumption is the notion that capitalism was 'imported' into the region that became Greece by imperialist powers, because the region lacked an 'indigenous capitalism'. Such theories of transition only recognise the development from feudalism to capitalism as an endogenous process, viewing 'asiatic' pre-capitalist societies as recipients of exported capitalist relations. It is only possible to touch on this far-from-settled debate here, by mentioning the important historical and theoretical work of Jairus Banaji, which most radically challenges this view, while also questioning the supposed homogeneity of the 'asiatic' modes of production.[26] The narrative of capitalism as only indigenous to Western Europe can be problematic if it comes to paint 'Western Powers' as the purveyors of capitalism and 'Greeks' (or, more broadly, 'Balkan peoples') as its mere victims, erasing historical class distinctions in the region. The notion also seems erroneous when

---

23. Article 159 of the Criminal Code. 'Lobbying' is unknown in the Greek legal system and in public practice and discourse.
24. Peter Bratsis, 'The Construction of Corruption', *Social Text* 21, no. 4 (Winter 2003): 9–33.
25. Ibid., 26.
26. Jairus Banaji, *Theory as History* (Leiden: Brill, 2010).

one considers that powerful Greek merchant and shipping-shipbuilding capitals were operating in the region at least a century before the uprising against the Ottoman Empire (1821), which, particularly in the Peloponnese and the islands, had subsumed local production in imposing the demands of international trade.[27] A clear bourgeois-enlightenment expansionist-nationalist character was embedded in the ideology and demands of the Greek revolution, which was developed by a Greek middle class of intellectuals and merchant capitalists in the Ottoman Empire. This milieu had strong cultural and economic connections with the Western European bourgeoisie, and economic interests to defend from the tributary system of the Ottoman state.[28]

While the existence of capitalist forms of exploitation does not indicate a fully formed capitalism, it did entail the emergence of early forms of proletarian class struggle (in shipbuilding on Aegean islands, 1800–15), as well as a war for a territory that would allow the establishment of a liberal bourgeois state.[29] It is indicative of the emergence of capitalist class relations that labour organisations appeared before the turn of the twentieth century, not only within the newly formed Greek state, but also within the territories that still belonged to the Ottoman Empire (centred around the major port of Thessaloniki that had undergone an industrial boom in the 1870s). Yet the fact that there was an indigenous, ethnically Greek merchant capitalism in the area of the Balkans and Asia Minor, and that capitalism was not merely 'imported' into the area, in no way belies the uneven power relations and competition, as well as collaboration, between Western European and Greek capitalisms (both economic and political). This relationship gave shape to a particular type of capitalist development, while interacting with the dynamics of class and ethnic relations in the region.

In the aftermath of empire, not only Greece, but also other newly formed Balkan nations strove to produce ethnic homogeneity within the territories they had gained, through racial discourses, ethnic cleansing, imposed homogenisation and irredentism. In Greece, this included ethnic conflicts, the repression of Slavic and Aromanian languages (1912–36), pressure on Jewish communities to assimilate and population exchanges with Bulgaria (1920) and Turkey (1923). As noted by Calotychos,[30] the

---

27. Giánnīs Mīliós, *O Ellīnikós Koinōnikós Schīmatismós* (Athens: Kritikī, 2000), 133.
28. Ibid., 123.
29. Ibid., 132.
30. Vangelis Calotychos, *Balkan Prospect* (Basingstoke: Palgrave Macmillan, 2016).

narrative of Greek superiority constructed its Balkan neighbours in the north and Turkey in the east as uncultured 'barbarians' – a racial discourse that does not differ much from long-running Western constructions, and which is central to the Greek national imaginary that is strengthened every time the modern Greek state's belonging to Europe is put into question.

The question of 'capitalist development' in Greece is thus not simply an economic matter, but also a matter invested with anxieties around race and ethnic identity. Locating Greece's place in a developmental teleology of more or less 'developed' regions, who differ with regard to their 'advanced' or 'backward' position along a linearly progressive time, also locates it within a racialised geopolitical configuration. We can only get beyond the reproduction of this racialisation by attempting to see beyond its developmental schemas, which tend both to idealise 'Western Europe' and to construct the resistance against it as a local culture that is somehow authentically non-capitalist. Thus, if the expansion of capitalism through the world can be said to entail a kind of universalism, this does not necessarily have to mean a blanket imposition of protestant culture. Instead, we have to investigate the precise ways in which the becoming-universal of capitalism does not produce sameness but multiple particularities – economic, political and cultural – which are, nevertheless, still capitalist. These particularities should not be understood as exceptions to a dominant form of capitalism, but as themselves part of the definition of what capitalism is today.

Gender, Class, Nation

The mainstream progressivist understanding of capitalist history also has gendered implications, which remain invisible unless we take a feminist materialist perspective on what constitutes labour. If capitalism is only to be found where free labour and the wage contract exists, women's dependent and unpaid labour in the domestic sphere becomes an exception, a space of pre-capitalist relations, or worse, a space where work is naturalised as a spontaneous female activity. The latter is the assumption that pervades most of the historiography of labour in Greece, in which women's work often only begins to be mentioned when it starts to take place in mass agricultural production and factories, that is, when it begins to be market mediated and waged.[31] There is

---

31. Éfi Avdelá, 'I Istoría tou Fýlou stīn Elláda', in *Fylo kai Koinōnikes Epistîmes stī Sygchronī*

insufficient research on women's (and, typically, also children's) agricultural work as unpaid employees of their husbands or fathers in small family production units, which, for a long time, formed the majority of employment in Greece. It is beyond the capacity of this book to make up for these gaps, which historians of gender are currently addressing. However, it is possible to say a few things about how this social structure affected the gendered constitution of Greek civil society, its articulation with capitalist relations and the role of nationalism.

The Greek constitution of 1864, notable for reaffirming the principle of popular sovereignty after an uprising against King Otto's constitutional monarchy, granted civil rights and suffrage to all men regardless of class and property ownership earlier than in other countries. Historians and anthropologists attribute this development to the high proportion of small ownership in rural and urban areas, which formed the social basis of the uprising, a dominant social model further associated to the social status and economic independence, both from the state and from waged labour, of male heads of household.[32] According to the feminist historian Efi Avdela, this structure reproduced a domestic hierarchy of a gendered division of labour, as well as gender inequality in the public sphere and in law.[33] Thus, the constitution did not even have to indicate the sex of citizens – they were 'naturally' assumed to be male.[34] Here we have a construction proclaiming universality but, unspokenly, excluding women from its concept of citizenship. As elsewhere, the male-headed household was taken to be the individual unit of humanity, with marriage granting him full power over all household members and property. Based on a composite of existing Roman, Byzantine and customary law, while women could independently own property, they could not enter legal contracts, and when married they had no right to manage their property. While they were subject to criminal laws and taxation, they had no right to be witness or jury in courts. At the same time, the universal vote for men was threatened by women's exclusion. Conservatives, who questioned universal suffrage, argued that uneducated men

Elláda, ed. Venetia Kantsa, Vasilikī Moutafī-Galanī and Euthymios Papataxiarchīs (Athens: Alexandreia, 2010), 89–117.

32. Efi Avdela, 'Genere, Famiglia e Strategie del Lavoro in Grecia', *Passato e Presente* 15, no. 41 (1997): 145–63.

33. Ibid.

34. Elénī Fournarákī, 'Epi Tini Lógō Apostereín Autīn Psīfou?', *Mnīmōn* 24, no. 2 (2002): 179.

were no better qualified to vote than women, taking advantage of this blindspot in the notion of the vote as a natural individual right.[35] Thus, in that moment, a political discourse emerged that actively excluded women by arguing that the female body is antinomical to public life and politics. This was accompanied by a feminine ideal of motherhood, domesticity, the education of future citizens and service to the nation, which responded to the needs of the upcoming bourgeois classes and the Greek nationalist project.[36] The first feminists of the upper classes, in the second half of the nineteenth century, justified their argument by reference to patriotic motherhood, promoting women's education on the basis of their social role as mothers and hostesses, while women's right to a level of independence through paid work was again framed as a service to the nation.[37]

It was only in the mid-war period when feminists began to demand suffrage, to develop arguments based on a logic of equality and to include welfare for mothers and children in their demands. Educated women over 30 years old (only 9.6 per cent of women at the time) gained the right to vote in municipal elections in 1930.[38] Mid-war feminists also had some partial success in claiming social rights on the basis of motherhood as a 'service' of women to society, through notions of social solidarity, prevention of social problems and welfare. Yet, their demand for political rights was consistently undermined both by conservative politicians, who either thought it to be an irrelevance or a 'communist threat' to the reproduction of the Greek 'race'.[39] Despite the support of a small number of politicians, the political context was not favourable for women, so much so that, after the end of World War II, the legal power of husbands over married women, which had not been codified in law until then, was reaffirmed in the Civil Code of 1946.

---

35. Ibid.
36. Eléni Fournaráki, 'Perí Morfôseôs "Chrīstôn Mītérôn" kai Ekpaideúseôs "Mellóntôn Politôn"', in *To Paidí stī Neoellīnikī Koinōnía, 190s-200s Aiōnas*, ed. Vásō Theodōrou and Vasilikī Kontogiánnī (Athens: Dīmokríteio Panepistīmio Thrákīs, 1999), 73–120; Demetra Tzanaki, *Women and Nationalism in the Making of Modern Greece* (Basingstoke: Palgrave Macmillan, 2009).
37. Eléni Varíka, *Ī Exégersī tōn Kyriōn* (Athens: Ídryma Éreunas kai Paideías Emporikís Trápezas, 1987), 140.
38. Efi Avdela, 'Between Duties and Rights', in *Citizenship and the Nation-State in Greece and Turkey*, ed. Faruk Birtek and Thalia Dragonas (London: Routledge, 2009), 117–43.
39. Stylianós V. Prôtonários, *Ai Gynaíkes kai oi Anílikoi ōs Egklīmatíai* (Athens: Týpois Foínikos, 1925).

This was despite – or perhaps because of – the active role women played in the National Liberation Front and National Popular Liberation Army (EAM-ELAS) led by the KKE, and their participation in its 1944 elections of the 'Government of the Mountains', the 'Political Committee of National Liberation'.[40] According to Avdela and other historians,[41] this participation did not constitute a significant break in women's social role in Greece, because their participation in resistance and their inclusion in the 1944 vote was framed by the same nationalist discourse of 'patriotic motherhood', which mirrored the conservative valorisation of the family and of 'women's nature'. Nevertheless, there is plenty of evidence that the experience of war was transformative for women themselves. Oral history accounts and anonymous poetry produced by women at the time convey that, for many, participation in the war effort also meant liberation from the rule of men.[42] Yet, after the war, these women had to make difficult choices between family life and a politics that carried a severe risk of imprisonment, torture and a potential death sentence.[43] Additionally, the resurgence of Christian-conservative anti-communism, which imagined communists as sexually transgressive,[44] may have played a role in the reaffirmation of conservative gender roles in the 1946 Civil Code.

Subsequently, right-wing religious nationalism continued to go hand in hand both with the language of race and the oppression of women under the slogan of 'fatherland, religion, family'.[45] Feminism, associated as it was with the left, continued to be repressed until the end of the colonels' regime in 1973. But within the left too, taken-for-granted patriarchal norms, embedded as they have been in notions of class and patriotism, had to be continually challenged by feminists. These debates and conflicts

---

40. EAM (National Liberation Front) was the largest resistance organisation against the Axis occupation, after the Greek national army was defeated and the Tsouderos government exiled itself to Egypt. Politically led by KKE, which up to then had been illegal, EAM's stated aim was not only national liberation but also 'popular democracy'. ELAS (National Popular Liberation Army) was the guerrilla military arm of EAM. During the war, EAM was able to create an alternative state structure in the mountainous areas it controlled. Michális Lymperátos, 'Oi Organōseis tīs Antístasīs', in Istoría tīs Elládas tou 200u Aiōna, vol. 3, bk. 2, ed. Ch. Chatziiōsíf and P. Papastrátīs (Athens: Vivliórama, 2007).
41. Avdela, 'Between Duties'.
42. Angela Kastrinaki, Ī Logotechnía stīn Taragménī Dekaetía 1940–1950 (Athens: Polis, 2005), chapter 14.
43. Tassoula Vervenioti, 'Left-Wing Women between Politics and Family', in After the War Was Over, ed. Mark Mazower (Princeton: Princeton University Press, 2000), 105–21.
44. Effi Gazi, '"Fatherland, Religion, Family"', in Sex, Gender, and the Sacred, ed. Joanna De Groot (Oxford: Wiley Blackwell, 2014).
45. Ibid.

intensified in the 1970s and early 1980s, and made a contradictory return in the current crisis as we will see in the following chapters.

Capital, Classes and Social Relations

The question of classes in Greece is closely related to the debate on the 'underdeveloped' character of Greek capitalism and the problems of Marxist historicism. For traditional Marxists, it posed the conundrum of when the Greek working class would be sizeable enough and ready to lead a revolution. The existence of a sizeable 'petit bourgeois' class has been seen as an obstacle to that, and as a conservative element that holds back progressive politics. The issue has been complicated by the way in which these classes have been defined, as well as the anti-imperialist conceptualisations of the dominant class in Greece. These conceptualisations have been frequently used to understand the current crisis in terms which, as I have argued, contain Eurocentric, orientalist, productivist and nationalist assumptions: corruption of the elites, imperialist barriers to national economic development. For this reason, I aim to reconceptualise classes and class conflict in the Greek context, so that we can more clearly specify historical changes in relations of class over time and in the current crisis.

Before embarking on a class analysis, the contested definition of 'class' demands caution. Despite the problems of Marxist historicism mentioned above, I favour a Marxian notion of class, against a sociological classificatory one emerging from income differentials and levels of skilled employment, as well as against a Bourdieuian notion that focuses on the capacities afforded to the individual by access to cultural, social and economic 'capital'.[46] This is because, first, as E. P. Thompson has shown, classes are formations of collectivity and political subjectivity – they are not merely ways to group individuals based on information about their resources. Second – and this is Marx's most important insight – experiences of class are driven by socioeconomic *relations*, and not merely quantities of assets, whether they are economic, social or cultural. Elites' access to these forms of 'capital' cannot alone explain how class is reproduced without considering exploitation. Focusing *exclusively*, as many sociologists do, on the epiphenomena of systems of exploitation and accumulation, such as elites and financial power, globalisation,

---

46. Pierre Bourdieu, 'The Forms of Capital', in *Handbook of Theory and Research for the Sociology of Education*, ed. J. G. Richardson (Westport, CT: Greenwood, 1986), 241–58.

neoliberalism, deindustrialisation and discrimination against the poor, has grave political consequences. These consequences, as I will explain, are themselves implicated in the rise of nationalist anti-establishment discourse across 'the West'.

Marx's understanding of class, as Balibar has observed,[47] is not aimed at producing a map of stratification, but instead centres on a single class: that of those who are exploited. Proletarians are those who are 'doubly free': free from (that is, separated from) the means of production, and free to sell (that is, dependent on selling) their labour power to gain the means of subsistence. This notion of 'double freedom' Marx uses to illustrate ironically the simultaneous legal reality and material falsity of liberty in capitalism. It is also the condition and legal structure that enables exploitation. However, this abstraction can operate at a remove from historical experiences and political formations of class, often leading to the neglect of legal and normative structures that enable gendered and racialised forms of exploitation, and leaving open the long-running question of the middle strata.

The Open Marxism school has sought ways to overcome this question and retain the theoretical power of class as a relation. Richard Gunn has famously dismissed as a 'fetishism' any conception of classes as social groups.[48] Yet historical class formations are not the mere 'appearance' or 'manifestation' of an abstract 'essence' of a class relation.[49] Therefore we need a conceptualisation of class that allows us simultaneously to think of class as a relation and as *classes* in plural. Both of these aspects are necessary to understand how exploitation affects prole-tarian conditions in different historical moments, as well as how class identity shapes political ideologies, alliances and strategies. Besides, as Althusser has insisted, capitalist contradictions are never observed empirically in a 'pure form' but are always overdetermined, not only by politics and ideologies, but also by institutions, ethics, religion, culture

47. Étienne Balibar, 'From Class Struggle to Classless Struggle?', in *Race, Nation, Class*, ed. I. M. Wallerstein and É. Balibar (London: Verso, 1991), 153–84, 179.

48. Richard Gunn, 'Notes on Class', *Common Sense*, no. 2 (1987), 15–25.

49. The concept of objective appearance (*Schein*), which Marx inherits from Hegel, does not denote a false, but a real, socially produced appearance which is inseparable from its essence. Yet as Reichelt has pointed out, we do also find in Marx a conception of essence to be liberated from inverted forms of appearance. This is one of the roots of Marxist historicism. Helmut Reichelt, 'Social Reality as Appearance', in *Human Dignity: Social Autonomy and the Critique of Capitalism*, ed. Kosmas Psychopedis and Werner Bonefeld (Aldershot: Ashgate, 2005), 31–67.

and, of course, contingent historical events.[50] Such a conception of class relations and historical class formations makes it easier to see how class has been articulated with national identity, gender and racial constructions in particular historical conjunctures, shaping the meaning of class for future generations.

Greece's economic history forces us to think of classes in plural, in any case. As mentioned already, the wide spread of small property ownership troubles any attempt to speak about class struggle in Greece as if it had a singular meaning. It also troubles historicist conceptions that interpret this as the result of a delay in capitalist development. As Andreas Lytras' detailed study into the formation and reproduction of the petit bourgeoisie – the class of smallholding peasants and small urban businesses – has shown, this class cannot be understood as a mere pre-capitalist remnant. Instead, it was largely the outcome of post-revolutionary social struggle and deliberate policies of land redistribution instituted by the new Greek state.[51] Redistribution first took place in the Peloponnese and southern Greece (1821–8), and later in Thessaly, Macedonia and elsewhere, after these territories were annexed, in response to sharecroppers' movements. The process continued until 1925.[52] This distribution of landed property was instrumental in the establishment of universal male suffrage in the 1864 constitution. The reasons for these decisions of the Greek state combine concerns about political legitimacy, the international political conjuncture of World War I, the development of industry, and the escalation of struggle, both inside the country and internationally.[53] But land redistribution did not mean a good standard of living for its beneficiaries nor an escape from proletarianisation. The new smallholding peasants very soon became indebted to merchants and suffered extreme poverty.[54] Thus their struggles did not come to an end with land

---

50. Louis Althusser, 'Contradiction and Overdetermination', in *For Marx* (London: Verso, 2005), 87–129.

51. Andréas Lýtras, *Prolegómena stīn Theōría tīs Ellīnikīs Koinōnikīs Domīs* (Athens: Néa Sýnora-Livanī, 1993); Andréas Lýtras, *Mikró-Astikī Leitourgía kai Orgánōsī stīn Elláda* (Athens: Papazīsīs, 2010).

52. Sharecroppers and other landless agricultural workers in Thessaly and Macedonia rose up because the Greek investors who acquired large landed property after annexation imposed a regime of indebtedness, forced labour and social humiliation on sharecroppers. Most well known is the Kileler revolt in 1910, in which six peasants were shot dead by police forces. Giôrgos N. Alexátos, *Istorikó Lexikó tou Ellinikoú Ergatikoú Kinīmatos* (Athens: Geitoniés Tou Kósmou, 2008), 212.

53. Kōstas Vergópoulos, *To Agrotikó Zītīma stīn Elláda* (Athens: Exántas, 1992).

54. Seraphim Seferiades, 'Small Rural Ownership, Subsistence Agriculture, and Peasant

redistribution, but they continued with similar intensity, often armed, this time against merchants over the issue of prices.[55] These struggles may have provided the backdrop for the high levels of participation among the peasantry in EAM-ELAS during World War II, and later in the civil war. The governmental structures of EAM were instrumental in protecting harvests for peasants and organising agricultural production in the countryside.[56] After World War II, small land ownership formed the economic basis for small property and small family-scale business ownership in urban centres, as agricultural production was becoming less sustainable and the secondary and tertiary sectors of the economy grew.[57] This expanding urban petit bourgeois class, having formed its own political organisations, managed to reproduce itself by organising politically to gain state subsidies and market protections.

Although we began this discussion with the petit bourgeois class, it would be mistaken to present Greek capitalism as driven by a mass of small capitals, or, worse, small family businesses that subsist on revenue. It is commonplace, and part of the dominant discourse in Greece, both on the right and on the left, to underestimate the power of the Greek capitalist class, characterising it as 'parasitic' and 'unpatriotic'.[58] It is also frequently claimed that a 'national bourgeoisie' has never existed in Greece, but instead there is a 'comprador bourgeoisie' subject to foreign imperialist interests. Effectively, the dominant class of capitalist society is seen as falling short of the supposed criteria that would make it a real bourgeois class. According to this narrative, its failure lies in, first, not investing in real 'production' but only in 'compradorial' activities and in finance. Second, it lacks the necessary 'bourgeois ethic' and a unified bourgeois political formation. Many writers, including Lytras, tend to support similar views, influenced by a theory of dependency that understands the very existence of foreign investment in Greece as a form of 'colonialism',[59] analyses shipping capital and service sector firms

Protest in Interwar Greece', *Journal of Modern Greek Studies* 17, no. 2 (1999): 277–323.

55. An example is the armed uprising of the Peloponesian raisin producers in 1935. Dīmītrīs Livierátos, *Koinōnikoí Agōnes stīn Elláda (1932–1936)* (Athens: Enallaktikés, 1994).

56. Yannis Skalidakis, *Ī Eleútherī Elláda* (Athens: Asini, 2014).

57. Serafeím Polýzos, *Perifereiakī Anáptyxī* (Athens: Kritikī, 2011).

58. See, for example, James Petras, 'Sto Eisodīmatikó Kefálaio Ofeíletai ī Dynamikī Anáptyxī tīs Elládas kai ī Viomīchanikī tīs Ypanáptyxī', *Oikonomikós Tachydrómos*, 8/3/1984.

59. For a fuller criticism of this position see Giánnis Maúrīs and Thanásīs Tsekoúras, 'To Xéno Kefálaio kai ī Anáptyxī tou Ellīnikoú Kapitalismoú', *Théseis*, no. 2 (1983).

as 'unproductive'[60] and even sometimes makes the mistake of assessing the level of industrialisation by comparing the ratio of small to large businesses.[61]

If this perspective was based solely on an economic argument it could be easily refuted. In fact, the early pre-revolution Greek capitals operating from the Ottoman Empire were not only merchant capitals but were also involved in small industrial production, shipping and exports, mainly of textiles, to Western Europe.[62] Between 1850 and 1910 industrial areas grew in urban centres, attracting large concentrations of urban working populations in the cities of Athens, Pireaus, Thessaloniki, Volos and Ermoupoli.[63] By the early 1930s there had been rapid growth in industrial production (65 per cent, 1928–38), which had benefited from the 1929 crisis. The state contributed to this development, nationalising key industries and sectors (railways, infrastructure, banking) from as early as 1914.[64] After World War II, the state expanded its investments to facilitate business activity, and imposed a restructuring that entailed a wage freeze, very high unemployment (which, in combination with deep poverty in the countryside, contributed to the largest emigration wave the country had seen, after that of 1900–20) and currency devaluation. A new boom period began in the 1960s and lasted until the crisis of 1973. In this 'golden' period of Greek capitalism, Greece's gross domestic product (GDP) growth rates topped Organisation for Economic Co-operation and Development (OECD) rankings. The construction industry expanded its activities to the Middle East and North Africa, while the tourism industry also began to expand rapidly internationally (in addition to the shipping industry, whose activities have been expansive throughout its long history).[65] In the 1990s another

---

60. According to the Marxian definition, productivity is the valorisation of capital, which is independent of whether the commodities produced are material goods or 'immaterial' services. Karl Marx, 'Results of the Direct Production Process', in *Collected Works of Marx and Engels*, vol. 34 (New York: Lawrence and Wishart, 1994), 355–466, 448.

61. Lytras, in *Prolegomena*, notes that in 1920s Greece only 10 per cent of industries employed more than ten workers. But consider that, in 2007–11, this statistic was 10 per cent in the UK and 18 per cent in Germany, the highest in the EU. Eurostat, *Business Demography by Size Class (2004 Onwards)*.

62. Serafeím Máximos, *I Augi tou Ellinikoú Kapitalismoú* (Athens: Stochastís, 1973).

63. Líla Leontídou, *Póleis tis Siópis* (Athens: Cultural Technological Institute ETVA, 1989). The industries mentioned are gas, mining, concrete, chemicals.

64. Staúros Mauroudéas and A. Iōannídis, *Stádia tis Kapitalistikís Anáptyxis stin Elláda* (Athens: Ídryma Sákī Karágiōrga, 1999), 17–22.

65. Ibid.

phase of expansion of Greek capital took place (banking, construction, industrial production), this time outwardly into the Balkans, where it continued to be relatively dominant.[66] This history certainly does not indicate a compradorial character for Greek capital.

The popularity of this perspective, however, does not lie in an economic argument but in an ethical and political one. The notion of the 'bourgeois ethic' that the Greek bourgeoisie supposedly lacks and the comprador/national bourgeoisie distinction have their origins in the discourse of anti-colonial struggles, which is taken up by theories of dependency. This discourse supposes that a proper national bourgeois class would not merely exploit the country's proletariat, but it also ought to take upon itself the responsibility for national economic development and 'independence'. Even though the Greek war of independence was led by a class akin to such a bourgeoisie, it is thought to have been powerless, because it welcomed British loans in the war (1824, 1825), and had King Otto of Bavaria imposed as king along with an additional loan. The Greek state declared bankruptcy in 1893 and, after its defeat in the Greco-Turkish war, it was placed under International Financial Control. These, along with later incidents of bankruptcy, are used as evidence of the weakness and dependency of Greek capital and its dominant class.

This narrative, originally, did not stop here, for it concluded with the traditional revolutionary vision of the communist movements of the twentieth century: it was not the 'decadent' bourgeoisie, but the working class that could manage the national economy effectively and drive out the 'foreign imperialist powers'. Today, with this revolutionary narrative having lost its appeal, the criticism of the comprador bourgeoisie refrains from reaching such subversive conclusions – all that is left is the question of economic management alone. It is no wonder that in the current crisis this argument has even been utilised by the neoliberal press in order to promote the strengthening of capital, the consolidation of its political power, and the acceleration of the restructuring.[67]

As for the political power of the Greek bourgeoisie, the historical outcomes of class struggle in Greece and the political forms of the first two-thirds of the twentieth century reveal a dominance imposed by

---

66. Anéstis Tarpágkos, 'Ī Valkanikī Dieísdysī tou Ellīnikoú Kapitalismoú', *Théseis*, no. 50 (1995).

67. For example, Páschos Mandravélis, 'Ta Elleímmata tīs Astikīs Táxīs stīn Elláda', *Kathīmerinī*, 5/8/2012.

force. This is evidenced by the anti-communism of successive governments and dictatorships from 1929 onwards, when Venizelos' Liberal
Party government criminalised strikes, demonstrations and syndical-
ism along with the 'subversive ideas' of communists, anarchists and the
labour movement, with the *Idiónymo* law ('*idiónymo*' stands for 'special
offence'). Anti-communist laws took a number of different forms, and
led to the mass imprisonment, exile and torture of political activists – not
to mention over 5,000 executions after the civil war – until their repeal
in 1974. Generally, we might say that up until the 1980s the dominant
bourgeois political ideology in Greece has tended to range between
liberalism and the conservative far right, both of which subscribed to a
nationalist and anti-communist common sense.[68]

Did these laws respond to a powerful working class and labour
movement? It is hard to determine whether, prior to the civil war, the
labour movement posed a significant threat of 'subversion', or whether
these responses overreacted to the ethnic diversity of the labour
movement (its Jewish leadership and its internationalism) and to international events (the October Revolution and later the Cold War). The
structurally defined working class was a minority through the first half
of the twentieth century. However, significant struggles began to be
staged earlier than that. The first notable strike demanding wage rises
and the reduction of the working day to ten hours dates back to 1879,
by shipbuilding workers in the port of Syros. The first labour unions
were formed from 1886 onwards, and the first Labour May Day took
place in 1894. Literally explosive struggles took place since the 1890s:
Lavrio miners blew up a dynamite warehouse and took over a factory
in 1896.[69] The first labour confederations were formed in 1908 (the
Association of the Working Classes of Greece in Volos), 1909 (the multiethnic Fédération in Thessaloniki, a predecessor of the KKE), and 1910
(Workers' Centre of Athens).[70]

By the 1910s, socialist ideologies had been formed, and, in the
context of Greece's expansion into Macedonia, the nation and ethnicity
of workers was posed as a *question*, which was also linked explicitly to

---

68. See Spýros Markétos, *Pōs Fílisa ton Mousolíni*, vol. 1 (Athens: Vivliórama, 2006); Ilías
Nikolakópoulos, *I Kachektikí Dīmokratía* (Athens: Patákīs, 2001); Déspoina Papadīmītríou,
Apó ton Laó tōn Nomimofrónōn sto Éthnos tōn Ethnikofrónōn (Athens: Savválas, 2006).
69. Dīmītrīs Katsorídas, *Vasikoí Stathmoí tou Ergatikoú-Syndikalistikoú Kinīmatos stīn
Elláda* (Athens: Aristos/GSEE, 2008), 31–3.
70. Ibid., 34–6.

that of gender. These questions emerged centrally in the 1914 multi-ethnic strike of tobacco workers in Macedonia (mostly Thessaloniki and Kavala), whose events are worth describing, because they mark the formation of a more openly nationalised and gendered labour movement in the region, as well as the early shaping of anti-communist and antisemitic discourse. A century later, the same discourses continue to haunt both contemporary nationalist socialism and the national socialisms of the far right. I follow the incisive analysis of the events by the feminist historian Efî Avdela.[71]

In 1914, Greece had annexed the multiethnic region of southern Macedonia from the Ottoman Empire. Most tobacco workers were concentrated in Kavala, largely male and Greek in their majority but with significant numbers of Jewish and Muslim workers. They were organised in the 'International Association of Kavala Tobacco Workers, Eudaimonia', which was divided into ethnic subunions. In Thessaloniki, the second largest centre, tobacco workers were mostly women, two-thirds Jewish and the rest Muslim. The strike, which lasted for 20 days and involved around 30,000 workers across Macedonia, was initiated by Fédération, which was multiethnic but mostly Jewish at the time, reflecting the majority of the city's population. Yet despite Thessaloniki workers being mostly female, they were not allowed to join the union as equal members or participate in assemblies. Moreover, along with demands to increase wages and reduce working hours, another core demand of the strike was to forbid women from taking jobs in the most senior tobacco selection specialism. The maleness of the job and male privileges within it were being actively defended.

While it is known for being a multiethnic strike that won its demands and led to the signing of the first collective contract in Greece, the events that took place in the streets of Thessaloniki during those days reveal multiple complexities and tensions. Overlooking the strike demand against their interests and their exclusion from the union, Jewish women took part in the strike en masse. On the contrary, Muslim women, many of whom were also part of a broader wave of war refugees on their way out of Greece, broke the strike. This provoked street clashes between Jewish female strikers, Muslim female strike breakers, and the police. Avdela notes that, despite the diversity of ideological press responses to the events (defending either the strike or the 'right to work'), there was

---

71. Efî Avdelá, 'O Sosialismós tōn "Állōn"', *Ta Istoriká* 10, no. 18–19 (1993): 171–204.

a common expectation that male community leaders and union leaders ought to 'collect' the women from the streets. This was followed by warnings that women's 'instability' may come to threaten male workers' interests.[72]

The meaning of 'socialism' was also at stake in relation to the question of national belonging – more so, it would appear, than to workers' rights. Both the press and the Liberal Venizelos government openly supported the workers' 'just' demands. Indeed, labour protections were expanded during this period, up into the mid-1930s. The General Governor of Macedonia, Themistoklis Sofoulis, even stated that 'the Greek state follows a policy whose aim is socialism, true socialism'.[73] But there were provisos. 'True socialism' was a state socialism that put national interests first, as opposed to the 'false' internationalist socialism of Fédération. Indeed, Fédération was a potential threat to Greek nationalists, rejecting, as it did, the ethnic nationalisms of the Balkan wars and later supporting, for a while, autonomy for Macedonia. This was not unrelated to its majority Jewish membership, a majority that had now become the only ethnic minority in Greece with no new nation-state to emigrate to. Thus the conservative press used the episodes between Jewish and Muslim female workers to accuse Fédération and its leaders of leading 'foreign workers' to cause disorder and ethnic conflict, promoting 'suffragettism' and engaging in anti-Hellenic agitation by provoking the Greek police forces and collaborating with Bulgarian guerillas. In contrast, they showed support for the Greek Kavala strikers, whom they advised to keep a distance from the 'a-national' and 'uncontrollable' – implicitly but clearly feminised – Jewish workers.[74]

Elements of this proto-fascist antisemitic ideology in the conservative press grew over time to persist in contemporary far-right discourse. Yet, more revealing is the fact that this ideology tapped into an existing common sense that the workers themselves were not prepared to challenge. Thus the Jewish workers denied all accusations of collaboration with Bulgarians, while Greek workers affirmed their patriotic credentials. Fédération leaders prevented women from demonstrating and picketing workplaces for the rest of the strike. But protestations and

---

72. Ibid., 190–1, referring to the newspapers *Néa Alīhia, Makedonia, Fōs* and *Estía* in the dates between 31 March and 6 April 1914.
73. *Makedonia*, 16/6/1914 cited in ibid.
74. Ibid., 190–1, referring to the newspapers *Néa Alīhia, Proïa* and *Patrís*, from April to June 2014.

precautions read as admissions of guilt. After the events, the conservative press eventually came to completely reject socialism, while the more liberal Thessaloniki newspapers became increasingly antisemitic. The government's 'socialism' did not prevent them from exiling Benaroya and two other Jewish strike leaders to Naxos for being 'bad socialists'.[75] In such terms thus began the long history of anti-communist persecution by the Greek state.

Things continued to escalate in the following two decades. In the period of rapid capitalist development (1928–32), conditions for workers worsened. New Asia Minor immigrants were heavily exploited, newly instituted labour rights were disregarded, and the proportion of children in the workforce increased. The Thessaloniki rebellion of May 1936, involving a paralysing ten-day general strike and pitched battles with the police in which twelve demonstrators were killed, prompted Ioannis Metaxas, the authoritarian, royally appointed prime minister, to declare a state of emergency against 'the communist threat'. His dictatorship on 4 August 1936 further raised the level of repression and sent even more labour activists to exile.[76]

These historical episodes give us an insight into the processes through which a workers' identity was formed through struggle, and established as Greek and dominantly male in a context of heightened nationalism. Fédération, under Benaroya's leadership, later evolved into the Socialist Workers' Party of Greece, the predecessor of the KKE. In his memoirs, Benaroya reframed Fédération as part of the history of the 'Greek proletariat'.[77] During World War II, the workers' movement went a long way, from its early class-based anti-nationalism – which was very fragile, amid multiple nationalisms – to embracing the national struggle, becoming the main patriotic force in Greece and following a strategy of national unity.[78] Women became included in unions and the national struggle in ways that avoided threatening the dominance and identity of the male worker and the patriarchal family. The elimination of the Jewish community of Thessaloniki contributed to forgetting the multiethnic past of the workers' movement, which became replaced by an anti-imperialist common sense of a unified national 'people'.

---

75. *Makedonia*, 15/6/2014 cited in ibid.
76. Katsorídas, *Vasikoí Stathmoí*, 83–8.
77. Avraám Mpenarógia, *Ī Prōtī Stadiodromia tou Ellīnikou Proletariatou* (Athens: Olkós, 1975 [1931]).
78. Giōrgos Margarítīs, 'Politikes Prooptikes kai Dynatotītes kata tīn Apeleutherōsī', *Mnīmōn* 9 (1984): 174.

Thus, in the following decades, and up until today, political conflict between left and right has taken place at two levels. First, both sides have persistently challenged one another on their patriotic credentials. Second – and especially prior to the neoliberal transformation of the 1980s – they promoted opposed strategies for workers. Right-wing factions within labour unions promoted conciliatory strategies and were supported by the state. The conflicts of 1956–65, a period of rapid development of the industrial and construction sectors, are characteristic. At that time when the General Confederation of Workers of Greece (GSEE) was controlled by the state and had an anti-communist agenda,[79] the mass of workers formed alternative organisations, leading to a strike wave in the industries of construction, mining, tobacco, electricity, rail, press, mail, education, banking and a variety of others. In 1961–2, several categories of public sector workers carried out coordinated strikes lasting several days. The state's response was to ban the strikes and prosecute their participants. Still, the alternative labour organisations grew stronger and more coordinated, forming the SEO-115, an association of 115 unions expelled from GSEE, which achieved several demands (wage rises of 31.6 per cent on average, paid leave, benefits for dangerous occupations, the 1 May holiday).[80] The movement's climax was in 1964–5, when Greece reached a record high level of strikes worldwide, and Enosi Kentrou was voted into power, promising to reinstate political liberties. Once more, the establishment responded with a royal coup (1965), soon to be followed by the colonels' junta in 1967, which was not received negatively by NATO powers in the context of the Cold War.[81] For the left, the junta was associated with 'American interests' and they agitated against its 'imperialist' motivations.

There is thus a history through which the nation was articulated with working-class interests, though in different ways, by the right and the left. Did the size of the working class – defined as wage-dependent workers – determine such an outcome? Can we attribute the strength of nationalism to the size of the petit bourgeoisie? This argument is considered to be common sense within the history of Greek socialist and communist

---

79. Successive governments and right-wing parties had attempted, and frequently managed, to control GSEE internally, ever since its foundation in 1918. Katsorídas, *Vasikoí Stathmoí.*

80. Ibid., 120–4.

81. Konstantina Maragkou, 'Favouritism in NATO's Southeastern Flank', *Cold War History* 9, no. 3 (2009): 347–66.

thought,[82] and it is true that the proportion of waged workers in the workforce has been smaller than in Western Europe, while the proportion of 'own-account' workers has been higher. Yet there is little evidence to support any obvious correlation between the numbers of waged workers versus petit bourgois small business owners and dominant political and ideological tendencies in the country. Moreover, as already discussed, many authors, including sociologists like Lytras, underestimate the size of Greek industry, and by extension its employment. Waged labour expanded significantly through the twentieth century: from 36.8 in 1951, the percentage of waged workers had increased to 51.4 by 1981 and to 65 by 2008. Meanwhile, the percentage of own-account workers has fluctuated between 28 and 38 through the twentieth century, reaching the lowest point of 21 per cent in 2008.[83] It should be noted, however, that self-employment did not have the same meaning in the middle of the twentieth century as it does today. In the 1950s, own-account workers were employed in trades that could be carried out by lone individuals, for example as traders of a variety of goods, independent skilled tradespersons (electricians, tailors, etc.), doctors and accountants. To an extent this is still the case, but a growing proportion of 'self-employed' workers are in fact employees without insurance and employment rights. In 2008, about one-third of those who declared themselves as self-employed were office workers, unskilled labourers and industrial workers.[84] These statistics indicate that, through the latter half of the twentieth century, waged labour became, quantitatively, the dominant production relation, despite the simultaneous reproduction of the petit bourgeois class. Yet, over this period, we do not see a similar growth of class-based ideologies that *oppose* nationalist ideologies. On the contrary, that was a characteristic of the early workers' movement when ethnic diversity had not yet been streamlined into a dominant Greek identity. We cannot attribute the dominance of nationalism on the number of waged workers in Greece.

At the same time, it is worth considering certain special characteristics of the majority working-class experience in Greece, such as increased access to landed property (which does not necessarily entail access to means of production but may translate into lower wage demands) and

---

82. The theme reappears throughout the 100-year survey of socialist thought in Greece by Panagiōtīs Noútsos, *Ī Sosialistikī Skepsī stīn Elláda 1875–1974* (Athens: Gnōsī, 1990).
83. EL.STAT., *Population Census 7/4/1951* (Athens: EL.STAT, 1951); EL.STAT. *Population Census 5/4/1981* (Athens: EL.STAT, 1981); employment data available for 2008, EL.STAT.
84. EL.STAT, 'Employment Data by Employment Position and Occupation', 2008.

fragmentation into a large number of small workplaces. Lytras argues that these features thwarted possibilities for collective organising and bargaining.[85] Additional factors are institutional characteristics of labour unions in Greece such as the degree to which unions have historically succumbed to state interference, their financial dependence on parties and the state, the embedding of political parties within unions, and the divergence and differentiation between public sector and private sector unions.[86] The final division is important, given that the state has offered the most stable employment since the permanence of public sector employees was instituted in the constitution of 1911. 'Permanence' has meant that employees cannot be laid off except in cases of severe misconduct. In other words, the state offered jobs for life, a situation that created a kind of 'labour aristocracy' with strong unions tied to governmental political parties, placing a significant section of the labour force under state control.

Socioeconomic struggle and its ideological manifestations in Greece must then be grasped in its historical specificity, in the context of international and local conjunctures. Marxist theoreticians of class have tended to apply pre-existing theoretical models on the Greek case and have continually found reality lacking. This 'lack' is tied to Eurocentric and historicist notions of capitalist development, according to which the petit bourgeoisie and the comprador bourgeoisie are blamed for 'weaknesses' and 'delays'. These narratives tend to lose sight of how social relations of class, gender and ethnicity/race, mediated by nationalist and socialist ideologies, have been articulated with one another and have been challenged and shaped historically. Attention to what has been at stake in specific conjunctures not only troubles the concepts and assumptions of traditional Marxist strategic scenarios, but also helps us understand how social conflicts and the political ideologies that mediate them have developed to this day.

The Nation-State as a Limit of Struggle

According to Michel Foucault, the liberal bourgeois state emerged as the type of sovereign whose raison d'être was no longer itself,[87] but the

---

85. Lýtras, *Prolegómena*, 215–24.

86. Giánnīs Kouzīs, *Ta Charaktīristika tou Ellīnikou Syndikalistikoú Kinīmatos* (Athens: Gutenberg, 2007).

87. Michel Foucault, *The Birth of Biopolitics* (Basingstoke: Palgrave Macmillan, 2008), 318.

management of the capitalist economy and of a population within a given territory. This aim becomes the 'common' (national) good, a universalist discourse, which again was only realised by social struggles for rights, and in reality was constituted by exclusions (in the case of Greece, the female – especially when she acted outside her gender role – the Muslim, the Jew, the Slav, the peasant, the communist). Balibar usefully develops the notion of the 'trace of equaliberty' to refer to this dialectic of struggle and constitution, and uses Rancière's concept of 'la part des sans-part, or the share of those who are deprived of a share in the common good' to emphasise the incompleteness of 'the people' as a body politic.[88] While this 'common good' and the unification of the social into the national formation is a near fiction, considering that it is riddled with power struggles, this is still the core discourse of state power and its practice.

In Greece, to the degree that social struggles achieved their aims, over the early twentieth century they effected (at least partially or temporarily) shifts in the character of the state and the meaning of the citizen, and sometimes even challenged them as institutions. In their most dangerous moments, they resisted proletarianisation, questioned the state's monopoly of violence and disconnected class from nationhood and race, 'womanhood' from motherhood and the reproduction of the nation. But in their moments of reintegration or constitution, they returned to precisely those divisions: they reassured established national leaders of their movements' patriotism, produced national narratives of class by forgetting the ethnic diversity of its history and present, sought recognition for women's 'special social contribution' and put national unity above everything else. If the state was treated as a tool for emancipation, it was also the state that, after failed uprisings, reimposed the principles of patriotic collaboration between state, employers and workers and of 'fatherland, religion, family'.

Regardless of the long-running and very deep divisions between left and right in Greece, there is also a commonality that has prevented a clear *break* between them, and has tended to bring uprisings back into line. This is national belonging, and the taken-for-granted notions that the nation-state, its standing in the world and the growth of its economy must take priority over internal 'divisions' of class: that to be called a 'patriot' is synonymous to workers' solidarity and that the 'patriot' is of course a man who sacrifices himself for the people of this fatherland,

88. Balibar, '"Impossible" Community', 438.

surrounded by women lamenting his death. The most conservative left nationalist cultural representation descends into a fantasy of male patriotic heroism characteristic of the traditional songs and poetry of the left, especially those set to music by Mikis Theodorakis. Here, similar to the typical nationalist fantasy described by Yuval-Davis and Anthias' analysis of nationalism and gender,[89] songs figure the nation and community as 'a loved woman in danger' or 'a mother who lost her sons in battles': 'sons', young men, whose heroic virtue ought to set an example. Even though this conservative militaristic narrative, as shown in this chapter, does not correspond to the actual histories of struggle, it has tended to re-embed struggle into a hegemonic collective national memory that has passed down generations, including through schooling after PASOK (Panhellenic Socialist Movement) came to power in 1982. But despite its dominance, this discourse, its cultural norms and the party organisations that disseminated it were also seriously challenged in the 1970s and in the decades that followed.

---

89. Nira Yuval-Davis, Floya Anthias and Jo Campling, *Woman-Nation-State* (New York: St. Martin's, 1989), 9.

2

Victories, Defeats and Neoliberal Transformation, 1973–2008

Post-Dictatorship Struggles and Metapoliteusi, 1973–1989

Much of the mainstream post-crisis discourse on the period of 'Metapoliteusi', that is, the democratic period that succeeded the colonels' dictatorship from 1974 onwards, has been one of contempt. It is hard for the generations who came of age after the 1970s to see PASOK, the party that symbolically represents Metapoliteusi, as anything but a party of the establishment, especially considering that PASOK was the first to impose austerity and repress demonstrations in the recent crisis. It was only seemingly a paradox that the right-wing propaganda *in support of* the restructuring showed a similar contempt for Metapoliteusi, not for representing political passivity, but, on the contrary, for being dominated by the 'ideological hegemony of the left' – embodied by strong labour unions, recalcitrant workers and left intellectuals – which is said to have strangled the Greek economy. The latter argumentation has been shared among the 2012–14 New Democracy (ND)-led coalition government, the 'national-socialist' GD, and financial services firms such as J. P. Morgan.[1]

Yet looking carefully at the history from 1974 until the current crisis presents a very different picture, which is hard to homogenise under the concept of Metapoliteusi.[2] If anything, the word merely means 'regime change' (similar to the Spanish *transición*). Instead of this generalisation, the term here will be reserved for (a) the fall of the dictatorship in 1974, and (b) the victory of PASOK in 1981, which went a long way towards expanding political freedoms for the left.

---

1. Arís Ravanós, 'Ī Ideologikī Īgemonía tīs Aristerás, o Néos Echthrós tou Samará', *Vīma*, 29/02/2012; Nikólaos Michaloliákos, 'Wikileaks gia to 1974', Xryshaygh.com, 12/08/2013; David Mackie et al., 'The Euro Area Adjustment' (London: J.P. Morgan, 28/05/2013).

2. Although there are disagreements between historians in this respect. See Mános Augerídīs, Éfī Gazī and Kōstīs Kornétīs, eds, *Metapolíteusī* (Athens: Themélio, 2015).

Most distorting in both of the critical narratives of Metapoliteusi has been the missing history of social struggle from 1974 to the mid-1980s, replaced by the mainstream account of this period as one of PASOK's ascent to power through its charismatic populist leader, Andreas Papandreou. Even when this history is remembered, it is typically represented as the co-optation of movements by PASOK.[3] Yet, these movements had transformative effects on Greek society, as well as contributing to the ideology and political dynamic that brought PASOK to power: this represented a victory of these movements, and soon later, their defeat, as the first phase of neoliberal restructuring began.

The colonels' regime fell in 1974 as the result of the Turkish invasion of Cyprus, the student uprising of November 1973, the first strikes after a long period of relative quiet[4] and the international crisis that had begun to affect Greece with high levels of inflation and low profit rates. It was smoothly succeeded by a junta-approved right-wing government under Konstantinos Karamanlis. Karamanlis' government began a transition to democratic rule by legalising the KKE, releasing political prisoners, and prosecuting the core members of the junta regime. However, at the same time, the state apparatus of the old regime (most notoriously, the torturers of political prisoners) either remained in their positions, or received very lenient sentences, while neo-fascist organisations began to terrorise the social movements of the left.[5] The government remained authoritarian, intimidating police practices continued to oppress demonstrators, and the GSEE remained under government control.

Contemporary commemorations of Metapoliteusi tend to focus on the student movement. But while it played an important role in the November uprising and continued to be active in the years that followed – fighting for the conviction of those responsible for the deaths in the uprising and the expulsion of junta collaborators from key university positions, and expressing solidarity with workers' and peasants' struggles – its role was not as central as that of the other movements that emerged in the wake of regime change.[6]

In this repressive and crisis-ridden but hopeful context, a self-organised factory-based movement emerged in the industrial sector, a sector that

---

3. Autónomī Prōtovoulía Politōn, *Noémvris 1973: O Agōnas Synechízetai* (Athens, 1983). This publication is an exhaustive chronicle of struggles in 1973–80, from the perspective of an 'autonomous' contingent. It includes flyers, newspaper cuttings and polemical essays.

4. Katsorídas, *Vasikoí Stathmoí*, 125–6.

5. For more on these organisations, see Part III.

6. Autónomī Prōtovoulía, *Noémvris 1973*, 99–100.

had grown very significantly in the previous decade. The movement began a power struggle for the self-representation of factory workers as opposed to sectoral union and party-led representation, establishing OVES, the Federation for Industrial and Factory Trade Unions, in 1979.[7] It launched forceful strikes for higher wages (which had been dwarfed by high inflation) and better working conditions. As the movement grew, it established forms of democratic self-organisation of workers in the factories, and the demand for self-management began to emerge, in a context of a European discourse of self-management, especially in France. This evolved, in some cases, into factory occupations.[8] The discourse of self-management became dominant within OVES, when a large number of loss-making enterprises were threatened with closure. Alongside factories, there were mobilisations in several other sectors (transport, electricity, telephony, construction, shipping, education, etc.) where there was a large concentration of workers. A second wave of action (1979–81) was driven by the more secure workers in the public sector.[9] Overall, this period saw the highest number of days lost in strikes thus far in Greek history.[10]

At the same time, indebted smallholding farmers began to fight for price protection and financial support from the state, as the low prices for which their products were sold to merchants and the industries were only sufficient to sustain a life of deep poverty in the countryside. Many villages had no infrastructure such as electricity or water supply, and small farms had no irrigation. This condition had led previously to a large emigration wave from the countryside into urban areas and abroad in the 1950s, 1960s and into the early 1970s. There were also demands by landless peasants for the redistribution of the remaining large landed estates belonging to monasteries, private landowners and the state.[11] Similar to the workers' organisations, farmers' organisations (the Agricultural Societies), which had been very active in the 1960–7 wave of protest, had been entirely dissolved by the dictatorship.[12] The

---

7. Spýros Sakellarópoulos, *Ī Elláda stī Metapolíteusī* (Athens: Livánīs, 2001), 61–7.
8. Katsorídas, *Vasikoí Stathmoí*, 131.
9. Sakellarópoulos, *Ī Elláda stī Metapolíteusī*, 68–74.
10. Chrīstos Iōánnou, *Misthōtī Apaschólīsī kai Syndikalismós stīn Elláda* (Idryma Mesogeiakōn Meletōn, 1989), 102.
11. Tásos Trigónīs, 'To Agrotikó Syndikalistikó Kínīma stīn Elláda, 1974–1981' (Panteion University, Athens, 2010).
12. Andréas Lýtras, *Mikro-Astikī Leitourgía kai Orgánōsī stīn Elláda* (Athens: Papazīsīs, 2010), 237–44.

few protests that took place during the dictatorship against compulsory land purchases by the state for development projects had been heavily repressed.[13] However, from 1974, with the impetus of wider social radicalisation, Agricultural Societies began to be re-established, and launched campaigns involving strikes (the non-distribution of agricultural products), road closures, large demonstrations that confronted the police and land occupations.[14] This questioning of the use of landed property also encouraged slum dwellers to demand rights to land intended for development.[15]

A new and very significant feminist movement also emerged from 1975 onwards through the formation of new feminist organisations and groups, alongside, but also separately from, women workers who organised themselves in the female-dominated sectors. Such women workers' organisations had been first established in 1954–67.[16] Metapoliteusi allowed the re-emergence of feminist organisations allied to political parties, such as the Federation of Women of Greece (KKE), the Movement of Democratic Women (KKE Interior)[17] and the Association of Women of Greece (PASOK). But the Metapoliteusi feminist movement went far beyond both the bourgeois feminist movement of the first half of the century and women's labour struggles in the 1950s and 1960s. Inspired by feminism abroad, it brought into the public sphere issues of the private sphere, as well as challenging patriarchal culture and the common sense of the neutrality of the male point of view. Institutionally, it targeted patriarchal family law (the dowry system, the unequal rights to property of married and divorced women), laws against abortion and rape legislation. The female body came to be the centre of many discussions of sexuality (including compulsory heterosexuality) and identity, particularly in the 'autonomous' women's groups, which grew from 1975 onwards and separated themselves from the party-based women's organisations that focused on economic matters

---

13. See the documentary *Megara* (1973) by Sakis Maniatis and Giorgos Tsemberopoulos on the movement in Megara against compulsory purchases for an oil refinery.

14. Trigōnis, 'To Agrotikó Syndikalistikó Kínīma stīn Elláda, 1974–1981'; Autónomī Prōtovoulía, *Noémvrīs 1973*, documents monthly incidents of unrest in rural areas in 1973–80.

15. Autónomī Prōtovoulía, *Noémvrīs 1973*, 99–100.

16. Archives of women workers' organisations 1951–1967 are held in the Gender Studies Department of Panteion University in Athens.

17. The KKE Interior was formed by a Eurocommunist faction of KKE that split off in 1968, following the invasion of Czechoslovakia.

and legislative change.[18] These groups addressed all of the same issues, but went further in questioning marriage and the family, deconstructing the social meanings of motherhood imposed on women and reproduced through medical authorities, and sharing their personal experiences in order to politicise them. But feminists also came into conflict with their comrades by intervening within left-wing organisations. For example, in EKON-Rīgas Feraíos, the youth organisation of KKE Interior, women questioned patriarchal hierarchies and ideologies within the organisation.[19] They also sought to bring new feminist ideas into the party's official statements and practice, ensuring that separate women's organisations allied to the party promoted women's liberation as opposed to simply recruiting women to a socialist cause. Their intervention provoked splits and accusations of 'bourgeois ideology', and they were unable to significantly alter male-dominated leadership structures. However, they were able to embed a feminist agenda and opened a discussion over a theory of the 'double contradiction' of class and gender.[20]

Autonomous groups were part of a broader rebirth of anarchist and anti-authoritarian ideologies towards the end of the dictatorship period, inspired to a great extent by the May 1968 movements in France.[21] An anarchist/anti-authoritarian milieu grew associated with a militant counterculture, and found its centre in the area of Exarchia in Athens – a long-established intellectual centre of the metropolis, where a large number of radical publishers, bookshops and social centres are still located today. These militant groups (whose positions varied and overlapped, ranging from ultra-leftists, anarchists and situationists to supporters of violent vanguardism and armed struggle) had been active in dynamic demonstrations and clashes with the police, solidarity action in support of arrestees, university occupations, militant workers' action and anti-fascism.

Meanwhile, the organisations of small business owners also put forward demands that matched the wider movement's anti-imperialist,

18. 'Autónomes Gynaikeíes Omádes', *Sfígga*, no. 1 (1980): 21–30; No Woman's Land, 'Syzītīsī me tīn G.: To Vivliopōleío Gynkaikōn kai to gynaikeío kínīma stīn Elláda', *Mītra*, no. 2 (2005). More is available in the archive of feminist magazines and journals of this period held at Panteion University.
19. María Repoúsi, "'To Deútero Fýlo" stīn Aristerá', *Ellīnikī Epitheōrīsī Politikīs Epistīmīs* 8, no. 1 (2017): 121.
20. Aggélika Psarrá, Ínta Florentín and Éfī Avdelá, 'To Gynaikeío Zītīma kai to Kómma', *Augī*, 19/3/1978.
21. Alexátos, *Istorikó lexikó*, 34–5.

anti-European Economic Community (EEC) stance.[22] As already mentioned, small family-based businesses objected to the opening of the Greek market, fearing competition from stronger European capitals, and preferring a protectionist regime of controlled markets and subsidies. Even though this movement was clearly petit bourgeois in its demands, it formed an integral part of this period's movements, precisely because of the latter's understanding of the Greek economy, and by extension the 'Greek people', as the dependent victim(s) of imperialism. The movement's dominant discourse was patriotic socialist and anti-imperialist, in that it promoted the advancement of the national economy for the good of the 'Greek people', both ideals that the bourgeois class, in collaboration with foreign capitalist superpowers, particularly the USA, had supposedly betrayed.[23]

The movements of this period thus were not only class based but put forward diverse social, political and cultural demands. Yet, across the left-wing political spectrum, including autonomous groups, these demands were framed around patriotic anti-imperialism, and the notion that socialist-inclined policies would bring forth national economic development and independence. Feminist groups were the only exception to this nationalist trend, by questioning the meaning of motherhood and its naturalised association with marriage and family, criticising the nationalist justifications for preventing abortions (the 'demographic problem of Greece')[24] and campaigning against proposals for female military service, without, however, engaging with the nationalism of the left.[25]

The Karamanlis government heavily repressed these movements, especially those of workers and students, expanding the police force and introducing new riot police units and armoured vehicles for crowd control. The suspicious death of Alekos Panagoulis (1 May 1976), a leading anti-dictatorship activist who objected to the inclusion of junta sympathisers in the government, seemed to send the message that not that much had changed. In response, many of the demonstrations of the period culminated in rioting. According to contemporary accounts of the autonomous groups, this rioting was not acceptable to the left party

---

22. Lytras, 'Mikro-Astikī Leitourgía', 259–64.
23. Autónomī Prōtovoulía, *Noémvrīs 1973*.
24. For example, 'Mītrótīta', *Skoúpa*, no. 1 (1979): 49–53.
25. Ánna Karapánou, ed., *O Feminismós sta Chrónia tīs Metapolíteusīs, 1974–1990* (Athens: Ídryma tīs Voulīs tōn Ellīnōn, 2017), 62.

organisations of KKE and PASOK, which favoured more disciplined forms of action, and typically condemned rioting as the result of 'infiltration by provocateurs'.[26] It does seem that, since the Polytechnic uprising, left parties struggled to keep up with the dynamism of grassroots action, and often strategically acted as a pacifying force in order to regain control.[27]

Despite the intensity of the conflict over modes of action between autonomous and party-controlled organisations, the rerouting of grassroots protest into high levels of active participation in political parties was successful.[28] It would be mistaken, however, to understand party participation and its influence on the social movements as a 'capturing' and misleading of movements into a reformist path, as was argued at the time by the supporters of autonomous organising and of a non-parliamentary revolutionary route.[29] The fact that the movements were so easily 'captured' was an expression of the very content of the movement's demands (so long as they exceeded immediate concerns), including those of autonomous organisations: political liberties, social equality, social welfare, the redistribution of wealth, the socialisation of production through a combination of state ownership and self-management[30] and the creation of an independent national state and economy outside the EEC and free from American 'imperialist control' (given that the theory of dependency was the dominant understanding of Greece's position in international power relations).[31] Besides, mass active participation in political parties was, with the exception of KKE, a new phenomenon of the post-dictatorship period. The representative authoritarian hierarchy of the older party form, whose members were mere voters, was no longer sustainable in a period of mass mobilisation.[32] These demands, as well as significant sections of these movements' organisations, were then integrated, albeit using different discourses, within the

---

26. Ibid., quoting several newspapers and political statements of PASOK and KKE.
27. Christóforos Vernardákīs and Giánnīs Maurīs, 'Oi Taxikoí Agōnes stī Metapolíteusī, Méros 1', *Théseis*, no. 14 (1986); Sakellarópoulos, *Ī Elláda stī Metapolíteusī*, 61–7. Autónomī Prōtovoulía, *Noémvrīs 1973*.
28. Christóforos Vernardákīs and Giánnīs Maurīs, 'Oi Taxikoí Agōnes stī Metapolíteusī. Méros 2' *Théseis*, no. 16 (1986).
29. Autónomī Prōtovoulía, *Noémvrīs 1973*.
30. It is probably not coincidental that the discourse of self-management was also used in the parallel electoral campaign and 1981 victory of François Mitterrand in France.
31. Sakellarópoulos, *Ī Elláda stī Metapolíteusī*.
32. Vernardákīs and Maurīs, 'Oi Taxikoí Agōnes 2'.

agendas of PASOK, KKE and KKE Interior, the three main party forces in the movements. PASOK was then not merely a 'populist' party led by a 'demagogue' aiming to gain power and control social movements,[33] but it was also the political expression of movements whose demands already presupposed a form of state and a government that would put them into practice. Yet PASOK, unlike the communist parties, while supporting radical reform in favour of 'the people', including increasing the role of the state in proletarian reproduction through nationalisations, did not employ an anti-capitalist discourse.

Although some authors refer to a 'defeat' of the workers' movement of this period due to a decrease in the number of strikes from 1978 onwards,[34] it is important not to underestimate the social transformations effected by this wave of struggle, in which workers played a hegemonic role. We may even speak of a victory, however partial, of this movement, expressed in the radical, in relation to Greece's authoritarian history up until that point, social and economic transformations from the fall of the dictatorship to the end of the first PASOK government. Politically, this was a momentous shift towards the legitimisation of the left, and, temporarily, of workers' demands. PASOK's measures in the first three years satisfied many of these demands. For workers, this included wage increases (a 40 per cent increase on the minimum wage, translating into an average real annual wage increase of 2.2 per cent, including a 4.1 per cent increase in the industrial sector),[35] and the introduction of the automatic readjustment of wages with inflation.[36] The right to unionise was safeguarded, lockouts were banned and the existing government-installed right-wing leadership of GSEE was fired. PASOK's labour organisation, PASKE, immediately became dominant within GSEE.[37] For small producers, there were significant increases in subsidies.[38] PASOK originally resisted EEC economic policies, shifted

---

33. This is the dominant view in the literature, even though it has been subjected to some criticism. See, e.g., Ággelos Elefántīs, *Ston Asterismó tou Laïkismoú* (Athens: Polítīs, 1991) and for criticisms Vernardákīs and Maurīs, 'Oi Taxikoí Agōnes 2'; Sakellarópoulos, *Ī Elláda stī Metapolíteusī*, 204–27.

34. Sakellarópoulos, *Ī Elláda stī Metapolíteusī*, 70–3.

35. Giánnīs Voúlgarīs, *Ī Elláda tīs Metapolíteusīs 1974–1990* (Athens: Themélio, 2008), 161–2. However, statistics on wages and income in 1981–85 vary. According to Bank of Greece data, the average annual wage increase was only 1.1 per cent. Sakellarópoulos, *Ī Elláda stī Metapolíteusī*.

36. N. 1264/82 A.K.

37. Ibid.

38. Sakellarópoulos, *Ī Elláda stī Metapolíteusī*, 359–69.

the balance in public spending in favour of social welfare and carried out a long series of nationalisations. Many of these nationalisations responded to workers' demands in loss-making enterprises, including several mines, shipbuilding firms, concrete production firms, the largest textiles industry, paper mills, a steel firm and a multinational oil firm.[39] The state sector was enlarged so much that the size of its capital exceeded that of the private.[40] PASOK's government also took symbolic action to signal the end of persecution for the left. It disbanded the gendarmerie, removed remaining military influence from state television, officially recognised EAM and ELAS as part of the national resistance movement, provided pensions for veterans and encouraged the repatriation of political refugees. PASOK also decentralised state power, and it enacted laws on academic freedom, the university asylum and the democratic participation of students in the management of universities.[41] Under strong pressure from women's movements, the dowry and the legal privileges of men in marriage were abolished, adultery was decriminalised, abortions were legalised and new legislation was introduced to safeguard equal pay for women.[42]

It is often claimed that PASOK's attempt at socialist/social democratic transformation was 'out of phase',[43] given that much of the West was entering a phase of neoliberal restructuring, having already gone through a social democratic or 'Keynesian' phase of accumulation that had reached a point of crisis. Yet this apparent exception was not unique to Greece.[44] In other Southern European countries (Spain and Portugal)

---

39. Many large loss-making corporations were already nationalised under the prior ND government, notably Olympic Airways (owned by Aristotelis Onassis) and several enterprises owned by Stratis Andreadis (four banks, five insurance firms, a pesticides firm, two ship-building firms, several ships, the Hilton Hotel). Níkos Trántas, 'Politikí kai Oikonomía tī Dekaetía tou '80', in *Oikonomía kai Politikí stīn Sýgchronī Elláda*, ed. Theódōros Sakellarópoulos (Athens: Diónikos, 2004).

40. Geōrgios Provópoulos, *Oi Dīmósies Epicheirīseis kai Organismoí*, Eidikés Melétes 11 (Athens: IOVE., 1982).

41. The university asylum, which protected campuses from police raids, has been part of customary law since the nineteenth century, and was not introduced in the Metapoliteusi as is sometimes claimed. Students have appealed to it during protests since 1897, though its significance increased after the 1973 Polytechnic uprising, and the first PASOK government formalised it into law. Chrīstos D. Lázos, *Ellīnikó Foitītikó Kínīma 1821–1973* (Athens: Gnōsī, 1987).

42. Vasilikī Chálaza, 'Oi Gynaíkes stī Metapolíteusī (1975–1987)' (postgraduate dissertation, University of Thessaly, 2008).

43. Voúlgaris, *Ī Elláda tīs Metapolíteusīs 1974–1990*, 149.

44. Alain Lipietz, *Mirages and Miracles* (London: Verso, 1987), 113–30.

that had undergone dictatorships in their period of rapid industrial-isation that climaxed in the 1960s, the fall of dictatorial regimes was typically followed by socialist governments. This shaky socialism was not even unique to Southern Europe, in that France also elected a 'socialist' president in 1981, François Mitterrand. The attempt to persist with social democratic policies in the early 1980s, when the paradigm had already shifted towards neoliberalism in the USA, the UK and Germany, is then perhaps not such a great anomaly.

Despite this favourable political conjuncture, PASOK's social democratic policies were hard to sustain at a time when Greek capital was weakened by the international oil crisis, and quickly came up against a limit. Most of these policies were funded by government debt, and it soon became clear that increasing aggregate demand and the 'socialisation of production' could not translate into a 'lever for devel-opment' in this instance.[45] Instead, a significant bulk of the industrial sector that had driven the boom of the 1960s was making losses, but the nationalisation of those industries was not helping to turn them around. Soon, the slowdown would lead to a fall in the proportion of employment in the industries, although the absolute size of industrial employment still remained stable.[46] Meanwhile, the international crisis created a deficit in the national balance of payments, because of losses of income from the shipping industry, tourism and emigrant transfers. Business organisations then pressed the state to control wages, and an economic restructuring aimed at increasing productivity via policies that controlled wages and labour activism was in order.[47] Still, PASOK attempted to introduce this restructuring through the very discourse of the socialisation of production and workers' self-management. In 1983, it introduced the legal framework for socialisation, including the notorious Article 4, which limited the right to strike by making its legality conditional on a majority vote. This was presented as a 'new quality' of unionism, which would no longer remain stuck in 'economism' but would recognise its new 'responsibilities'.[48] Disagreement over the new

45. PASOK. 'To PASOK stīn Kyvérnīsī, o Laós stīn Exousía', Government Policy Announcement, 4/10/1981.
46. Dīmītrīs Oikonómou, 'Sýgchrones Táseis stī Chōrotaxikī Orgánōsī tīs Ellīnikīs Viomīchanías', *The Greek Review of Social Research*, no. 76 (1990): 3–39.
47. Trántas, 'Politikī kai oikonomía', 7.
48. Stéfanos Vamiedákīs, 'Ergasiakés Schéseis kai Syndikalistikó Kínīma metá tī Metapolíteusī' (doctoral thesis, University of Crete, 2009), 145.

law within GSEE drove the KKE unionists to leave the confederation. In the same year, PASOK attempted to institute workers' 'committees' and workers' 'supervisory councils' that would manage issues of labour and production jointly with employers and managers. In this way, 'socialisation' would truly become compatible with 'development': workers would be involved in management and in disciplining their own productivity. Within OVES, this move was welcomed as a step towards the ideal of the democratic management of production, despite voices that warned against the undermining of unions by management committees.[49]

Indeed, the undermining of unions was soon a fact, as the restructuring ('stabilisation programme') essentially involved undoing many of the measures introduced in the first years, alongside the devaluation of the drachma. This involved the gradual withdrawal of automatic inflation readjustment, a reduction in the minimum prices of agricultural products, the reduction of employment in public sector firms, the non-safeguarding of the new laws on trade unions' freedoms, state intervention and economic dependency of the GSEE, and a series of spending cuts. In the years 1986–7, real wages fell by 8.9 per cent and 4.4 per cent respectively, while the profit rate improved. Inflation and the external deficit also fell, even though the pressure to improve 'competitiveness' and to get rid of labour market 'rigidities' continued. State subsidies of private investment also tripled from 12 billion drachmas in 1986 to 36.5 billion drachmas in 1988.[50] PASOK's dissenting activists were attacked by their governing party; the PASKE leadership of GSEE who disagreed with the restructuring was removed via the same legal act that had been previously used to democratise GSEE. The government was again installing its preferred leadership.[51] These developments encouraged employers to go on the counter-attack as the factories movement had lost its strength, by gradually establishing managerial and governmental party control over factory unions, distorting internal democratic procedures and isolating committed labour activists, so that, by the 1990s, many factory unions had been transformed into tools for controlling workers.

49. On the contemporary debate over workers' committees see Anéstīs Tarpágkos, 'Epitropés Ergazoménōn stis Epicheirīseis', *Théseis*, no. 10 (1985).
50. Kéntro Programmatismoú kai Oikonomikōn Ereunōn, *Ī Anáptyxī tīs Elládas* (Athens: KEPE, 1990), 103.
51. Voúlgarīs, *Ī Elláda tīs Metapolíteusīs 1974–1990*, 363.

PASOK's swift transition to policies that went against the movements that had brought it to power was not only a compromise or a betrayal, but also the outcome of the combined aims of 'socialisation' and 'growth' demanded by the movements of Metapoliteusi. The contradiction between these aims came to the surface before long. As soon as there was a crisis of profitability, deepening the exploitation of labour was the obvious route to recovery. In this context, PASOK's so-called 'capturing' and 'pacification' of the movement was in fact the realisation of the limits of the movement's demands: the nationalisation and 'self-management' of production entailed the involvement of labour in the management of the capitalist 'national economy'. This involvement ended up validating the policing of struggles that became an obstacle to capitalist 'development'.

The defeat of labour struggles in this period is epitomised by the left's inability to speak on behalf of 'society', 'the nation' and the 'national economy', because of the contradiction between labour demands and the neoliberal accumulation strategy that responded to the 1970s crisis in Western Europe. The interests of the national economy – the return to profitability – contradicted the interests of labour in the clearest possible way, since profitability was no longer founded on domestic consumption and was impeded by wage growth. The new model, in the face of crisis, recognised the problems that inflation caused to international markets and the limits of protectionism. Deintegrating labour and pushing down wages (both direct and indirect) would be a way not only to increase profits (and surplus value) but also to ward off inflation and allow for more freedom in international trade. Finance would then play the important role of flexibly distributing investments to Greece and around the world, allowing for more accurate projections of profitability, secured by greater price stability.[52] Greece had been affected by these restructuring trends since joining the EEC in 1981, even though political developments held back their adoption until five years later.

The period of the first two PASOK governments ended with the 1989 scandals which forced it out of power.[53] The left parties formed a coalition with the right-wing ND, in the name of 'purging corruption'.

---

52. See Dimitris Sotiropoulos, John Milios and Spyros Lapatsioras, *A Political Economy of Contemporary Capitalism and its Crisis: Demystifying Finance* (London: Routledge, 2013).
53. According to Sakellarópoulos (*I Elláda stī Metapolíteusī*, 490), the government's support for a new generation of entrepreneurs like Georgios Koskotas, whom it saw as more willing to make investments than established industrialists, contributed to the 'corrupt' enmeshment of state and private finances.

This was another blow to the left, as after its alliance with the right it became irretrievably fragmented between KKE, the Left Coalition (the predecessor of today's SYRIZA) and several other small parties. This reflected the fragmentation of the labour movement, which continued to weaken with ongoing deindustrialisation and the increasing alignment of state policies with those of the rest of the EEC.

Greece's non-alignment and realignment with the dominant trends in socioeconomic management and modalities of accumulation is then related to the level and outcomes of class struggle in the country, as well as its geographical proximity to the countries of the Eastern bloc and prior episodes of intense struggle, namely the civil war. Prior to the Metapoliteusi, the labour movement was not integrated into the state, regardless of the political cost, because of the perceived threat that a stronger labour movement and KKE could push Greece into an alliance with the Eastern bloc. Given this economic and geopolitical risk, authoritarian control of labour and social resistance was a key ingredient in Greece's local mode of accumulation through the twentieth century,[54] up until 1981, and explains Western 'tolerance' for the violent dissolution of democracy and political persecution of the left in the country.[55] The differently timed shift to a weak social democracy was thus not a 'delay' but was enabled by a crisis of that model of accumulation and of the Eastern bloc itself. This permitted the development of struggles and a more liberal social deal, which soon also met its limits, unable to resolve the economic crisis.

The Continuing Restructuring and Struggles against It, 1990–2008

The series of governments from 1991 onwards (alternating between PASOK and ND) aimed to impose neoliberal-style reforms, prompted by the fiscal targets demanded by the EU as a condition for adopting the common currency. While the progress of this restructuring was slowed down somewhat by the resistance of movements, it was also accelerated by the fall of socialist regimes in Eastern Europe. The latter opened up opportunities for Greek capital to expand to those regions in banking, construction and industrial production. The state also contributed to

---

54. Spýros Sakellarópoulos, *Ta Aítia tou Aprilianoú Praxikopímatos 1949–1967* (Athens: Néa Sýnora, 1998).
55. Konstantina Maragkou, 'The Foreign Factor and the Greek Colonels' Coming to Power on 21 April 1967', *Southeast European and Black Sea Studies* 6, no. 4 (2006): 427–43.

grow with a number of important infrastructural projects (the Athens Metro, the Venizelos airport, the bridge linking Rio and Antirio, the Olympic Stadium for the 2004 games). After the introduction of the euro, Greek capital was further empowered and its growth continued, based not only on access to new markets and the adoption of new information technologies but also on the expansion of a precarious labour force. Continuing deindustrialisation compounded this, as many productive units were transferred to Eastern Europe, striking the last blow to what remained of the industrial labour movement. Labour was also weakened by privatisations, flexibilisation,[56] the expansion of the informal labour market[57] and, correspondingly, the size of the unorganised labour force. The collapse of the Eastern bloc also brought a series of splits in the Greek left, further disempowering it, while union membership declined and increasing labour precariousness made organising more difficult. Under such conditions, the wages for precarious workers and young labour market entrants continued to be very low, and wage rises overall failed to correspond to inflation, prompting more women to enter the labour market and support household incomes.[58]

At the same time, significant numbers of immigrants arrived from Eastern Europe and, after 2005, from South Asia and Africa. Eastern European immigrants were exploited in extremely low-paid and precarious work at the bottom ranks of the labour force (construction, clothing and textiles, care work, agricultural work, cleaning and catering). Over the 1990s, it became commonplace for Greek households to employ low-paid Eastern European women as cleaners and carers. Small businesses would casually employ immigrant men for agricultural, construction and other manual jobs, and women typically as sewing machine operators.[59] Cheap migrant labour was also used for the 2004 Olympics construction projects.[60] In those informal employment

---

56. Mauroudéas and Iōannídīs, *Stádia.*
57. Undeclared labour increased rapidly after the 1970s crisis. V. N. Geōrgakopoúlou, 'Átypa Morfōmata kai Paraoikonomía', *The Greek Review of Social Research*, no. 63 (1986): 3–29.
58. Sakellarópoulos, *Ī Elláda stī Metapolíteusī*, 456.
59. Ntína Vaïou and Kōstīs Chatzīmichálīs, *Me tī Raptomīchanī stīn Kouzína kai tous Polōnoús stous Agroús* (Athens: Exántas, 1997).
60. Thousands of non-European immigrants were informally employed in construction for the 2004 Athens Olympics under life-threatening conditions. Daniel Howden, Nikolaos Zirganos and Nikolaos Leontopoulos, 'Thirteen Workers Die as Safety Standards Are Ignored in Race to Build Olympic Sites', *Independent*, 3/4/2004.

encounters, everyday racism became a tool for the legitimation of degradingly low wages, at levels inconceivable for Greek workers.

South Asian and African immigrants were even less fortunate than Eastern Europeans, who, after a decade or so, managed, to some extent, to be integrated into the Greek economy in a period of economic growth and to 'mix' more easily with the Greek population owing to their whiteness. With Greece one of the main entry routes into the EU, and the only entry route by land, the EU Dublin II regulation of 2003 effectively trapped these immigrants in Greece, by assigning responsibility for processing asylum applications to the first EU country of entry. This meant that Greece would have to become a major site of EU border policing. As the economy began to slow down, African and Asian migrants became surplus to the requirements of agriculture and construction. In response to these demands, the Greek state followed a policy of discouragement by intensifying the policing of borders and existing immigrants, making it almost impossible to make asylum applications,[61] with near-zero chances of success for those who managed to submit one.[62] This created a marginalised class of people trapped in the country without papers, many employed under slave-like conditions, while others resorted to unlicensed street trading, as well as the drug trade and sex work, resulting in them being constantly persecuted by the police. Continual references to the 'decline of the Athens city centre' in the mainstream press implicitly or explicitly meant that marginalised immigrants had no place there and that it had to be 'cleansed'.[63]

As for the stance of unions, GSEE shifted its position over the 1990s, from failed efforts to create a tripartite committee for the regulation of immigration, to a more positive stance, demanding equal labour and welfare rights for migrant workers and straightforward regularisation. This positive attitude translated to offering advice to migrant workers regardless of immigration status and providing spaces for immigrants' labour organisations, but there was very limited campaigning for migrant workers' rights or to increase membership in unions in proportion to the migrant population. Besides, GSEE's campaigning for workers' rights in

---

61. Paul Mason, 'Greece Asylum', *BBC News*, 19/02/2013.
62. Greece's first instance asylum recognition rate in 2012 was only 0.84 per cent. Alexandros Bitoulas, 'Asylum Applicants and First Instance Decisions on Asylum Applications: 2012', *Eurostat: Data in Focus*, May 2013.
63. Giôrgos Kandýlis, 'O Chōros kai o Chrónos tīs Apórripsīs tōn Metanastōn sto Kéntro tīs Athīnas', in *To Kéntro tīs Athīnas ōs Politikó Diakýveuma*, ed. Thōmás Maloútas et al. (Athens: National Centre for Social Research, 2013), 257–79.

general was limited by governing parties' co-optation and state funding. An exception were unions in construction and textiles, sectors with high numbers of irregular migrant workers, 20–30 per cent of whom participated.[64]

Cuts were perpetually on the agenda over the 1990s and 2000s, and a prime target were pensions and social security. Already since the late 1980s, the government declared that the system was in deficit because of increased spending on pensions and the health service under the first PASOK government.[65] The neoliberal argument, according to which extreme state generosity and an ageing population caused the deficit, is contestable, at least in the case of Greek social security funds. The Institute of Social Security's (IKA) deficit was not so much caused by increased spending but by reduced income. IKA funds had been held in the Bank of Greece in the post-war period, providing an interest rate below the market average. Employers were also able to avoid paying social security contributions for increasing numbers of undeclared workers. Yet IKA renegotiated employer debts with terms favourable to employers. This lost income was assessed to comprise 15–20 per cent of IKA's total income. To cover the resulting deficit, IKA took private loans with interest rates in the range of 32 to 35 per cent.[66] Through successive legislations,[67] governments then increased the pension age and the number of years of work required to obtain a full pension, changed the rules of pension calculation so as to cut pensions, increased workers' pension contributions and restricted incapacity pensions to recipients at more advanced levels of disability. IKA's primary healthcare also remained underfunded, involving long queues and very little regulation of the quality of service. Meanwhile, the contribution of beneficiaries to the cost of medicines increased, and the right to a free health service became conditional on a higher level of social security contributions. This situation gradually led those with relatively higher incomes to use private sector services. In 2008, IKA wrote off another enormous amount of debt owed by non-compliant employers.[68] Clearly, this was a restructuring policy that redistributed social costs downwards.

---

64. Apóstolos Kapsális, *Adīlótī Apascholīsī kai 'Nomimopoiīsī' tōn Metanastōn* (Athens: INE-GSEE, 2007), 262–328.
65. The Greek national health system depends on individual workers' social security contributions, for a part of whose disbursement employers are responsible.
66. INE-GSEE, *Ī Koinōnikī Asfálisī stīn Elláda* (Athens: INE-GSEE, 1993).
67. N. 1902/1990 AK; N. 2084/1992 AK.; N. 3029/2002 AK; N. 3655/2008 AK.
68. N. 3655/2008 AK, Ar. 137.

Last to be touched by reforms were public sector workers, whose privileges consisted of wages higher than average, a shorter working day and better pension and social security arrangements. Along with deepening the associated labour market segmentation, this encouraged resentment among workers in the private sector. Compounded by the universally despised byzantine state bureaucracy that public sector workers have been accused of maintaining, this discontent was and has continued to be used ideologically to gain public support for privatisations and other public sector reforms (mostly in health and education). While the privileges of permanent public sector workers were not removed during this period, a parallel, precarious labour stratum was created in the public sector, by employing workers paid by the hour with temporary low-wage contracts, as well as outsourcing positions via subcontracting agencies.

Similar to transformations across Europe, this policy was complemented by an upwards redistribution of profits. State spending was increasingly diverted away from welfare and towards infrastructural projects, carried out by state-supported private capital, as well as towards privatisations (of airports, ports, telecommunications, banks, undeveloped public land including beaches and forest areas, etc.) and the opening of state-monopolised markets to the private sector (health, college-level education, the radio and television industries) with beneficial terms and subsidies for the new owners and entrepreneurs. Overall, the state's intervention in the distribution of incomes favoured the immediate interests of capital over those of workers, while unions were gradually disempowered. These changes disproportionately affected the younger generation – the entrants to the labour market – and perpetuated the marginalised status of immigrant workers. From the mid-1990s onwards, households began to supplement their incomes with consumer debt (via mortgages, loans and credit cards), which had become available cheaply.

The initial response to the restructuring was strong. In 1990, under an ND government, a significant strike wave – the largest of this decade – fought against the abolition of automatic inflation readjustment, a pension reform and the reprivatisation of previously nationalised loss-making enterprises (Peiraïkī Patraïkī, Olympic Catering, Euvoia Mines, VELKA and others). After 234 strikes across many sectors and 20 million hours of work lost, they were unsuccessful.[69] Policies of low-level

---

69. Dīmītrīs Katsorídas and Sofía Lampousákī, 'Oi Apergíes to 2011', in *Eidikī Ékdosī: Tetrádia tou INE*, ed. Giánnīs Kouzīs (Athens: INE-GSEE, 2012).

austerity continued through the 1990s, without any significant workers' resistance. In 2001, a renewed pension and social security reform, now introduced by PASOK, faced particularly strong resistance, with very high levels of strike participation (75 per cent in the private sector) and broad social support, including the support of small business associations.[70] Although the mobilisation was able to halt the reform, a similar pension reform was approved the next year,[71] and no further significant strike waves took place until the sovereign debt crisis.

From 2000 onwards, in response to the difficulty of representation via larger unions and the GSEE, small self-organised unions began to be set up, mostly in the urban service sectors where flexible and insecure employment was normalised (shop assistants, catering workers), or sectors created through public sector outsourcing (couriers, hospital cleaners). These unions cannot be compared with the grassroots industrial unions in the 1970s in terms of their strength. They are rarely recognised by the larger unions or employers, so they have had little negotiating power. Since they cannot offer security, they often cannot attract the majority of workers in their sector or workplace to organise strikes, and have thus engaged in labour activism (blockades and demonstrations) outside their workplaces. Grassroots-level unionism continued to be active through to the crisis period. Beyond grassroots labour organising, there were, of course, also ad hoc labour disputes in the informal sector, notably by immigrant agricultural workers, who were usually not supported by unions or any political organisations, and faced extremely violent and openly racist repression by employers, police and local communities.[72]

While labour struggles weakened, a new oppositional social category emerged, that of the 'youth'. In 1990–1, high-school pupils occupied thousands of schools across the country against reforms that would not only cut the education budget but also reinstate a more conservative school discipline and culture: school uniforms, nationalist and religious observances, lower tolerance of absences and surveillance of students' conduct outside school. The occupations lasted for several months despite heavy police repression and right-wing vigilante attacks. In one such attack, a teacher was murdered by a member of the ND party youth

---

70. Ibid., 87.

71. N. 3029/2002 AK.

72. Mákis Nodarou, 'N. Manōláda: Típota Den Állaxe sta Fraoulochōrafa tīs Ntropīs', *Eleutherotypía*, 23/3/2009.

in Patras.[73] The incident inflamed the protests and forced the government to withdraw the reform. But there is also a lot of truth in the observation that the occupations expressed a desire that went beyond what was circumscribed by their demands: resistance against the daily routine of schoolwork.[74] In the following years – 1993, 1996–2000 and 2005–8 – mass school occupations became annual events, gradually moving from demands for better education and a lighter study load, to expressions of revolt in the face of a quickly vanishing future (particularly in 2008).

University students also carried out a series of significant mobilisations, with occupations as their main bargaining tool, in 1991, 1998, 2001 and 2006–7. These responded to a series of gradual reforms that aimed to align Greek higher education with the Bologna Declaration, by authorising private universities, privatising university property and transforming assessment. In 2006 a reform to university asylum was proposed to defend the 'rights to work and education', reframing protests, occupations and strikes as *violations* of asylum.[75] These reforms, as part of the overall economic and social restructuring introduced over this period, were in line with the general trend of minimising the state's contribution in the reproduction of labour power, while enhancing its facilitation of private investment. The restructuring, of course, also had a political aspect. The university reforms have been aimed at controlling student activism and the influence of the left in university campuses.

The strikes and occupations in education of 2006–7 were among the strongest responses to the restructuring over these two decades, managing to force a withdrawal of the reform for private universities, while many of the other reforms (intensifying studies by shortening their length, introducing forms of funding that are conditional on low-paid or unpaid academic work, stopping the provision of free textbooks, university asylum reform, making university funding conditional upon assessment of academic performance, internal regulations containing a series of disciplinary rules affecting students) were eventually only partially enforced due to the resistance of tutors and students. University occupations and mobilisations began in May 2006 and continued, after the summer break, from October 2006 to March 2007. A strike by lecturers from May to June 2006 joining forces with students in large and disruptive demonstrations escalated the situation. The number of occu-

---

73. 'To Chronikó tīs Dolofonías tou Níkou Temponéra', *TVXS.gr*, 27/7/2011.
74. Lacenaire, 'Diagōgī Epímemptos', *Ta Paidiá Tīs Galarías*, no. 2 (1991): 4–45.
75. Prionistírio 'to Chrysó Chéri', *O Néos Nómos-Plaísio*, brochure (Athens, 2006).

pations reached 420 nationwide (out of 448 university departments),[76] and the government was forced to withdraw the reforms temporarily. In September, schoolteachers went on an impressive six-week-long strike demanding better pay and job security. In October, up to 467 high schools were occupied across the country. In 2007, the reforms were resubmitted and a renewed wave of occupations began, accompanied by extremely well-attended weekly demonstrations from January through March, which frequently ended in clashes with the police with dozens of demonstrators badly injured. In February 2007, PASOK withdrew from the discussion on the constitutional reform that would open the way for private universities. Yet, on 8 March, PASOK approved the rest of the reforms, which soon brought the end of the movement.

Certain characteristics of this movement anticipated the riots that took place a year and a half later. The role of 'active minorities' greatly expanded,[77] questioning the dominant role of political parties in student politics. Broader than usual participation in the assemblies by students who did not belong to political parties made them less controllable by organised left party activists, and their traditional methods of functioning – focusing on producing carefully worded ideological texts, defining strict march routes, aiming for ideological hegemony among students – were to some degree undermined.[78] This situation allowed militant minorities to be formed, to gain influence and to define the combativeness of the student movement overall.[79] While the great mass of students did not actively participate in occupations or their coordinating discussions, they took part in assemblies and demonstrations in large numbers, and supported confrontations with the police, to the extent that the mainstream press began to consider whether this reflected 'the rage of an entire generation'.[80] It may not be so far-fetched to suggest that the frequency and intensity of demonstrations around this movement legitimised the act of confronting the police, mostly on the grounds of

---

76. Aiōnioi Katalīpsíes kai Ametanóītoi Apergoí, *Foitītikés Katalīpseis, Apergía Daskálōn* (Athens, 2008), 36.

77. Ibid., 9.

78. Ibid., 34.

79. Examples are: radio station interventions, locking oppositional professors into their offices, blocking research activity, publicising the university's financial data found in hard disks, blockading rail stations and highways, interventions in call centres where students were employed, neighbourhood demonstrations, demonstrations at GSEE headquarters to demand a general strike and more. Ibid.

80. O Ios, 'Autóptīs Mártys: To Krátos tīs Fysoúnas', *Eleutherotypía*, 9/3/2007.

responding to police violence. This was in light of instances of undercover or uniformed police heavily assaulting and teargassing handcuffed or otherwise trapped protesters, arresting them without charges and refusing them access to lawyers.[81]

At the time, 25.5 per cent in youth unemployment and the minimum wage of €700 were already considered to be causing significant hardship.[82] It was commonplace for the younger generation to depend on family incomes throughout their twenties.[83] Yet conditions were to become far worse very soon, and perhaps the militancy of these student mobilisations betrayed a premonition of that possibility, in response to accelerated restructuring, heightened police repression and new legislation that set limits on the right to protest.[84] This militancy would escalate further in December 2008, though in a manner rather different from that of the student movement.

The Riots of December 2008 and Their Aftermath

On 6 December 2008, a police officer shot and killed the 16-year-old Alexis Grigoropoulos in the neighbourhood of Exarchia, for allegedly cursing at him and throwing a plastic bottle. The event was followed by furious demonstrations and riots of an unprecedented scale that lasted several days. The suddenness, spread and duration of the riots were surprising even for the anti-authoritarian milieu, whose presence in the area and its long-running feud with the police was directly linked with the incident. Everything began before anti-authoritarians could make any decisions for a strategic reaction to the event,[85] and the riots spread very quickly across the country, lasting for at least four days, with thousands of participants. From Monday the 8 December, the riots spread among high-school students throughout Greece, who left their

---

81. One significant incident was the 'flower box case' ('ypóthesī zarntiniéra'). A student was heavily beaten by undercover police, arrested without charges and left without medical treatment. The official police report stated he had accidentally fallen into a flower box, disregarding widely publicised video evidence. Amnesty International, *Police Violence in Greece* (London: Amnesty International, 2012), 45–6.

82. 'Prōtiá metaxý tōn 27 stīn Anergía tōn Néōn', *Eleutherotypía*, 4/5/2007.

83. This trend began in the 1980s. Sakellarópoulos, *Ī Elláda stī Metapolíteusī*, 436–7.

84. 'Efarmózetai o Periorismós Diadīlōseōn', *Kathīmerinī*, 3/1/2007.

85. This is evident in several anti-authoritarian publications, blogs and oral accounts, e.g. Cognord, 'Énas Chrónos kai Káti me tous Pigkouínous', neucognord.wordpress.com, 4/3/2010;

Woland, 'Dekémvrīs 2008', *Blaumachen*, no. 3 (2009).

schools to go and attack police stations and anti-riot units. Few of the actions were prearranged or organised: participants met in the street and rallied alongside strangers.[86]

The December riots, despite taking place in the end of 2008, when the shockwaves of the global financial crisis had already reached the USA and the EU, cannot be easily classified as an event that *belongs* to the period of crisis, although it did take place in a context of anxiety about its outcome.[87] In late 2008, 'Greek consumers' were said to express deep worries regarding future developments in unemployment and their personal incomes.[88] The crisis had begun to impact negatively on the construction and tourism sectors, and interior demand had begun to fall by the first quarter of 2009.[89] Yet the discussions of the time, referring to an uprising of the '700-euro generation' (even if sometimes reduced to '600' or '500'),[90] appear very distant from the attack on the wage and the mass unemployment unleashed by the restructuring in response to the crisis, as will become obvious in the following chapters. Still, this was certainly not a time of prosperity. The pressure of over 20 years of neoliberal-style restructuring had begun to be clearly felt among a younger generation whose future prospects already looked worse than those of their parents. Policing, as we have seen, had also become increasingly repressive in prior years as part of the attempt to accelerate this restructuring.

The murder of Grigoropoulos not only showed that the state no longer negotiated, but that it was cultivating a repressive apparatus that would not hesitate to terrorise and kill using any excuse. The riots in response to this did not articulate any specific demands, such as the prosecution of the officer, or a better social deal. They responded with acts of destruction, which were not merely a revenge on police violence, but also included the vandalising of government buildings, bank burning and destroying and looting shops. Looting – expropriating any commodity

---

86. Cognord, 'Énas Chrónos'.
87. My argument is contrary to the reading that locates the riots in the same cycle as the movements of 2010–14, proposed by Georgios Agelopoulos, Dimitris Dalakoglou and Giorgos Poulimenakos, 'De Te Fabula Narratur?', in *Critical Times in Greece*, ed. Dimitris Dalakoglou and Giōrgos B. Angelopulos (London: Routledge, 2018).
88. 'Oi Ellīnes Eínai oi Pio Apaisiódoxoi', *Kathīmerinī*, 7/12/2008.
89. 'Provlépseis tīs Komisión gia tīn Ellīnikī Oikonomía', *Enīmérōsī: Athens Chamber of Tradesmen Bulletin*, April 2009.
90. Eirīnī Chiōtákī-Poúlou and Aléxandros Sakellaríou, 'Ī Koinōnikī Kataskeuī tīs "Genias tōn 700 Eurō" kai ī Anádysī tīs ston Īmerīsio Typo', *The Greek Review of Social Research*, no. 131 (2010): 3–32.

from food and basic items to luxury goods – was not merely an 'opportunistic' activity that took advantage of the meaning of the riots, but it was part of that meaning. The riots pointed at a stifling social situation in a broader sense, which encompassed unobtainable commodities as well as the loci of state power. Their duration over four days, often continuing through the night, temporarily denaturalised the normality of going to work, of shopping, of circumscribed and hierarchical politics, as well as the state's monopoly on violence.[91]

The rioting crowds were composed mainly of young people and teenagers, including many 'second-generation immigrants',[92] a smaller proportion of middle-aged people and groups of the anarchist/anti-authoritarian milieu. The last group were, for the first time, outnumbered in violent street practice.[93] Groups of the broader left participated in demonstrations, but tended to distance themselves from the riots. The looters tended to be immigrants of various ages and high-school and university students. Immigrants also took part in anti-police clashes in the inner-city neighbourhoods where they lived, attacking the Omonoia Police Station, known for systematic racist abuse. Communiqués issued and analyses developed by groups in the left and anti-authoritarian milieus referred to the subject of the uprising as young 'proletarians'.[94] But, contrary to riots like those of the French *banlieues* in 2005, these riots were not led by the most socially oppressed sections of Greek society: immigrants participated, but did not lead or dominate the riots. At the same time, contrary to previous smaller riots at demonstrations, here the rioters rarely acted *as* students, immigrants, workers or even citizens. Crowds came together against the police, but they had little collective control of the situation. Political groups were unable to either represent or control the rioters when the latter acted against their

---

91. Hara Kouki, 'Short Voyage to the Land of Ourselves', in *Revolt and Crisis in Greece*, ed. Antonis Vradis and Dimitris Dalakoglou (London: AK, 2011).
92. The pamphlet issued by the Albanian Immigrants' Social Centre, *Autés oi Méres Eínai kai Dikés Mas*, is characteristic in making links between the murder of Grigoropoulos, the riots by high-school students, and the 'mass participation of second-generation immigrants', cataloguing the racism, abuse and deaths suffered by immigrants in Greece in 'eighteen years of [accumulating] rage'. (Republished in 'Dekémvris 2008: Chronológio', *Blaumachen*, no. 3 (2009): 29–81, 54.)
93. Ibid., 37.
94. For example, Proletárioi apó tīn kateilimménī ASOEE, 'Katastréfoume to Parón Giatí Erchómaste apó to Méllon', katalipsiasoee.blogspot.com/2008/12/, 14/12/2008; Ta Paidiá tīs Galarías, 'Chronikó Enós Makrósyrtou Dekémvrī', *Ta Paidiá tīs Galarías*, no. 14 (2009): 4–45; Blaumachen, 'Dekémvris 2008'.

political principles. Those who condemned the looting or the destruction of 'small shops' were unable to stop such practices.

The political language that accompanied the riots repudiated the entirety of a murderous social system. The main political voice came from the anti-authoritarian milieu and the left, some of whom participated in the riots, while others organised large daily rallies of sizes similar to those of the peak of the 2006–7 student movement. These groups also initiated the occupations of universities and public buildings around the country, to create spaces for reflection and facilitate the 'continuation of the uprising' beyond the streets. The occupation of public buildings other than universities as a tactic of struggle, which was unprecedented in December 2008, probably influenced the ease with which this practice spread in 2012. This tactic also led to large numbers of youth joining anti-authoritarian networks and later creating their own new groups, expanding that political milieu significantly.

The December riots were felt by many of the participants as a qualitative break from the student movement of 2006–7 and the period of social struggles that had preceded it.[95] Their practices went far beyond the usual forms of protest, without positing a specified subject and without formulating demands.[96] Events escaped the control and imagination of political organisations, whose vanguardism was seriously challenged. But with the lack of a workers' subject, the desire for political initiatives towards creating a social uprising that would invade workplaces would not be fulfilled. The occupation of GSEE offices in Athens, which was a reaction to GSEE cancelling a pre-planned 24-hour strike that had happened to coincide with the riots, did not evolve in that direction. The occupation itself followed the demand-less character of the riots and did not aim at a dialogue with GSEE,[97] which meant that the occupation became an end in itself. This caused a conflict with grassroots unionists who, used to acting with clear political aims, could not see the point of the occupation unless it related to a specific workers' struggle. Despite thousands passing through the five-day occupation and hundreds participating in its assemblies, few actions emerged from it that would affect workplaces.[98] In every case, it is clear that even though December could perhaps

95. A. G. Schwarz, Tasos Sagris and Void Network, *We Are an Image from the Future* (Edinburgh: AK, 2010).
96. Woland, 'Dekémvris'.
97. The only demand posed was the freeing of riot arrestees.
98. Ta Paidiá tīs Galarías, 'Chronikó', 21.

legitimately be called an 'uprising by young proletarians', especially given the participation of young immigrants, it was not a workers' uprising, and it could not become one through political agitation. In fact, this was a social explosion that took place *away* from the spaces of work, targeting instead the spaces where the obstacles to proletarian reproduction are immediately experienced, those of consumption, exchange and policing.

Yet it is difficult to disentangle the events of the riots from their political articulation given the highly politicised nature of social relationships and everyday life in Greece. Large numbers of young people who participated in the riots had also participated in the student movement and school occupations, and their memory of confrontation with the police and increased police violence was fresh. While Grigoropoulos was not killed for being a proletarian but for questioning the power of the police, and while the riots and demonstrations did not carry any class-related slogans, his death showed how far the increasingly violent and provocative policing of social resistance could go. The police represented, for this young population, first, a state that showed contempt for their generation and its future, and second, for those who were immigrants, repeated racist police abuse. The fight against the police became an end in itself: an expression of alarm and anger about the murder; joy in overpowering the police by numbers, and finding one another in this collective act of transgression and empowerment, supported by widespread social condemnation of the police. This much is evident in accounts of the riot by high-school and first-year university students from Exarchia:[99] 'I felt depressed because I hang out with my friends in this exact place, and I realised it could have been me.' 'I also saw that the neighbours in Exarchia were speaking with the demonstrators and that was good ... We were welcomed' (Thodoris, high-school student). 'And all the kids felt so much power yelling at the cops, and throwing rotten fruit at them, those wild oranges that are all over the street in the winter' (Alexander, high-school student). 'It was the first time that we saw so many people of different ages attacking the cops with such limitless determination and hatred' (Vlasis, university student). 'During the funeral ... the police provoked people ... singing a humiliating song ... going "Where is Alexis? Tralala!"' It was a spark that made the whole thing explode' (Kostas, university student). 'I am an Albanian immigrant

99. Quotes are from interviews in A. G. Schwarz et al., *We Are an Image from the Future*, 144–52.

... We have big problems with the copocracy [*sic*] because the cops and many normal people treat us like shit, like we are nothing. If the cops ask for your papers you'll have big problems. ... they treat you like you're already a criminal' (Thodoris).

While everything stopped during December, it was not an uprising that attacked all forms of social domination embedded in the everyday, as it has been idealised in the collective memory of the anti-authoritarian milieu. It was directed primarily against state violence and, other than this, the motivations of crowds and individuals in them were hard to interpret. The lack of future prospects, whose closing down was also expressed by the defeat of the student movement, have figured most prominently as interpretations,[100] along with social discontent about the state failure in stopping forest fires in the summer of 2007. Some have even attributed the riots to a culture of 'revolutionary fetishism', which idealises the 17 November Polytechnic uprising, and encourages mimetic action by younger generations,[101] while others refer to this historical legacy to explain the social conflict between a far-right police force and the left.[102] But while the uprising did not have any coherent ideological content or demand, and, as most riots, it was also male dominated,[103] it was able to bring large numbers of a younger generation into deeper involvement with long-running radical movements outside political parties. If December did not alter existing relations, it certainly created new relations – it legitimised new social practices and opened up new social spaces. The political and social networks that these events brought together were central to mobilisations that took place later in 2009. Through organising local assemblies, new spaces for social bonds and self-organisation were created, a legacy that would be revived after the movement of the squares in 2011. December also injected youthful energy into the vanguardism of 'urban guerilla' organisations such as the Cells of Fire Conspiracy and Revolutionary Struggle. These groups, many members of which were arrested over the following years, have

100. John Karamichas, 'The December 2008 Riots in Greece', *Social Movement Studies* 8, no. 3 (2009): 289–93; Théorie Communiste, 'Le Plancher De Verre', in *Les Émeutes en Grèce* (Marseille: Senonevero, 2009).

101. Karamichas, 'The December 2008 Riots in Greece', 291–2.

102. Antonis Vradis, 'Greece's Winter of Discontent', *City* 13, no. 1 (2009): 146–49.

103. This issue was raised by feminists who also objected to the sexist language used in anti-police slogans. Môv Kafeneío, 'Synénteuxī me to Periodikó Z', Mwvkafeneio.squat.gr, 18/2/2014.

continued to receive support within the anarchist/anti-authoritarian milieu.[104]

Above all, particularly because of their unusual generalisation and partial social legitimation,[105] the events of December generated a sense of oppositional strength, which was expressed in the protests and mobilisations that succeeded it. Significantly, the participation of immigrants in the riots was a precedent for the clash between Muslim protesters and police on 21 and 22 May 2009,[106] when, during another police raid into one of the many makeshift mosques used by Muslim immigrants in Athens, a police officer tore into pieces a Quran study notebook. Immigrants rioted against the police and vandalised cars, shops and banks. The 2009 movement of solidarity to Konstantina Kouneva, the Bulgarian secretary of the Pan-Attica Union of Cleaners, who had been a victim of an acid attack for her labour activism, also had additional energy inspired by December, and extended to occupations, demonstrations and non-payment campaigns in Metro stations around Athens. The cleaners' precarious work conditions and the attack were brought to the surface, condemned and linked to broader issues of precarity for workers, although this did not spark a deeper critique of the gendered and racialised basis of the treatment the cleaners had to face.[107]

Greek Neoliberalism in Context

Greece is thus not a state that suddenly awoke from its cosy socialist/ Keynesian slumber in 2009. It is also not merely the dominated 'weak link' in the EU, but has also been a key geopolitical and economic player in the Balkan region and a destination for economic immigrants from Eastern Europe, the Middle East, Africa and Asia. The long passage from authoritarianism to a short-lived period of social democratic policies in the 1970s (Metapoliteusi), from the autonomous factory movement of the 1970s to the student movement of 2006–7 and the riots of December

---

104. See also Part III on the nationalist turn of some of these tendencies.

105. As discussed by Poúlou and Sakellaríou, 'Ī Koinōnikī Kataskeuī', governmental discourse attempted to contain the riots by reducing them to the 'healthy rebelliousness' of Greek youth, while racialising the attacks on property by attributing them to immigrants. This attempt at appeasement also led to the very rapid sentencing of the police officer, Epameinondas Korkoneas, to life.

106. Giannis Souliotis, 'Ī Prōtī Anoichtī Sýgkrousī EL.AS. – Metanastōn', *Kathīmerinī*, 24/5/2009.

107. Éfī Avdelá, 'To Fýlo stīn (se) Krísī', *Sýgchrona Thémata*, no. 115 (2011): 8–17, 14.

2008, reflect the progress of the neoliberal restructuring, the internationalisation of Greek capital and the actively devalued social status of immigrants and their descendants.

This first phase of neoliberal restructuring came in parallel with a passage from struggles organised or hegemonised by the labour movement, concerning the direct wage, the rights of workers and their autonomy in organising their labour, to struggles in spheres outside production, concerning indirect wages (pensions, education, welfare) and policing. The shift took place through a process of deindustrialisation, as well as government policy, including the policing of immigration, that created an ever-expanding section of the labour force that was flexible and precarious, and, because of this, structurally fragmented. This was not a merely political shift, but a shift that synchronised Greece with international tendencies in the mode of accumulation. Capitalist competition pushed towards a mode of accumulation that would no longer depend on a national working class that produced and consumed commodities. The advances in finance, shipping and transportation, and the opening up of nearby Eastern European economies offering cheap labour and new consumers, pushed those capitals that survived the competition towards increasing internationalisation and outsourcing. This is the context in which the crisis took place.

3

Symptoms of Crisis

The global financial crisis that broke out in 2008 radically halted the growth of the Greek economy, and the developments that took place in its wake were rapid. During 2009, Greek banks were already making losses and reducing the availability of credit to small and medium-sized businesses, despite having received a €28 billion government support package. After the elections of November 2009, the country attracted an official rebuke by the European Commission, when the new centre-left PASOK government revealed the country's deficit to be reaching 12.5 per cent of GDP, with public debt rising to 111 per cent of GDP. Over the following months, pressures rose on the newly elected government – which had promised to turn Greece into a social democratic 'Denmark of the South'[1] – to impose austerity and restructuring measures and come closer in line with the EU stability pact. Meanwhile, interest rates on government bonds rose rapidly, making it increasingly difficult for the country to service its debt and raising market fears of a default. The wrangling between Eurozone members over the possibility of International Monetary Fund (IMF) intervention and a bailout for Greece, particularly Germany's disagreement, heightened the market panic. Eventually, in April 2010, an agreement was reached between the Greek government and the European Central Bank (ECB)–European Commission (EC)–IMF 'Troika' on a bailout, on the condition that an agreed programme of economic restructuring would be implemented. This was ratified in May 2010 by the Greek parliament, amid a massive general strike demonstration and riots against the police, bank branches and the parliament building itself.

The economic and fiscal adjustment programme proposed 'internal devaluation' through labour market deregulation,[2] layoffs, pay cuts, pension cuts, regressive tax rises and privatisation, removing 'privileges'

---

1. 'Olóklīrī ī Omilía tou G. Papandréou stī DETh', *Imerisia*, 13/9/2009.
2. International Monetary Fund. *Greece: Staff Report on Request for Stand-By Arrangement* (Washington: IMF, 2010).

from public sector workers and prosecuting tax evaders. Under the close guidance and scrutiny of the Troika, the government would vote on more austerity and restructuring measures every few months over the following eight years, under the constant threat of a default, as bailout funds were conditional on each vote. Deep cuts on pay, pensions, benefits and the health service were implemented most readily. The scale of these cuts and the impact they and the labour deregulation have had on the Greek economy and society cannot be overstated.

These were the broad events that set the context of social struggles in the crisis. However, the impact of events and facts on social struggles is not immediate, but mediated by interpretations and feelings. This chapter looks at events, EU policies and structures, influential analyses of the crisis and their implications on collective action and ideology. I show that the forms of critique that fixate on finance and the EU are theoretically limited, with troubling implications for the ideologies that mediate collective action.

The Logic of Destruction: Ordoliberalism and the EU

The impetus to prevent the collapse of the financial system did not on its own determine the particular form of restructuring that has been imposed on the Eurozone periphery, and on Greece in particular. The Memorandum of Economic and Financial Policies contained measures based on a diagnosis of the sovereign debt crisis that exclusively attributed Greece's economic problems to the supposedly excessive incomes and protections for workers and small businesses. The weak external competitiveness of the Greek economy was thought to be caused by wages rising faster than productivity in 2000–9 and by rising levels of consumption. Fiscal imbalances were thought to be caused by state overspending, the 6 per cent growth of the state sector which 'crowded out' the private sector, and the 'unreformed' health and pension systems. Finally, growth was thought to be stifled by 'rigid' product and labour markets.[3] Corporate tax evasion was also identified as a problem, but it was not on the list of priorities for intervention. The main idea seems to have been that this form of structural adjustment would eventually create favourable conditions for investment.

---

3. European Commission, and Directorate-General for Economic and Financial Affairs, *The Economic Adjustment Programme for Greece* (Luxembourg: EU, 2010).

Accordingly, the measures included deep cuts to public sector wages, pensions, unemployment benefits and employment, and *flat* tax rises on the lowest incomes, VAT, fuel, cigarettes, alcohol, gaming and property. As for reforms, the Memorandum first of all urged a pension reform aimed at raising the pensionable age to 65 and unifying all the different sectors' pension funds into a single fund. Second, it pushed a 'product market' reform that would deregulate all the professions protected via licences and trade associations (such as lawyers, pharmacists, taxi drivers), as well as liberalise the sectors of services, energy and transport, and cut 'bureaucratic burdens'. This entailed a systematic privatisation programme to be carried out by a new specialised agency.[4] Finally, and importantly, it necessitated labour market deregulation that would 'curb undue wage pressures' and 'spur job creation and increase wage flexibility'.[5]

The economists and politicians who made these decisions, along with conservative media commentators, asserted that this was a 'necessary adjustment' responding to 'excessive wage rises' and 'privileges'.[6] But it became increasingly obvious that these assertions were not based on data but were instead part of a power struggle, dressed in 'objective' economic language, over who would pay for the losses of the financial crisis – a struggle in which workers did not have much leverage. The rate of wage rises had been below productivity gains from 1985 onwards,[7] reflecting the imposition of the first phase of neoliberal restructuring, and average wages were at 81 per cent of the European average in 2009. There are also strong and convincing arguments against the scenario of excessive welfare spending. Maniatis, in an extensive study, shows that Greece's state spending as a percentage of GDP over the previous 30 years had been close to the European average, but it had lower than average revenue. However, whatever tax revenue there was, most of it came consistently from waged workers, while only a small proportion of that tax was returned to them in the form of indirect wages or welfare.

---

4. See the mission statement and history of *The Hellenic Asset Development Fund*, Hradf. com.

5. European Commission, *Economic Adjustment Programme*, 20, 22.

6. The influential conservative German newspaper *Bild* has promoted an image of 'Greeks' living it large and robbing 'German taxpayers'. E.g., D. Hören. 'Multi-billion Euro Aid to Greece: German Anger at Paying for Luxury Greek Pensions', *Bild*, 30/4/2010.

7. Thanasis Maniatis and Costas Passas, 'Explaining the Rising Wage–Productivity Gap in the Greek Economy', in *Greek Capitalism in Crisis*, ed. Stavros Mavroudeas (New York: Routledge, 2014), 51–66.

This means that the state's redistributive policies already benefited high incomes and capital, not workers.[8]

The restructuring sought to accelerate this trend. After the 'adjustment', wages fell to 65 per cent of the European average,[9] and from 2010 to 2013 the purchasing power of the average wage fell by 21 per cent.[10] Collective contracts were invalidated, which, in combination with the net minimum wage falling to €495 and to €431 for under 25s, meant that even professionals' wages suddenly fell to that level. As if the wage cuts were not enough, around a million workers were left unpaid, without serious consequences for employers, for periods from one to over five months, both in the private and in the public sector.[11] Meanwhile, the deregulation of collective dismissals and compensations allowed mass public sector layoffs,[12] and contributed to the steep rise in unemployment. From 2012 to 2017, unemployment has ranged between 24 and 27 per cent, rising to a peak of 57.1 per cent for those under 25, and to 31.6 per cent for women.[13] Young women from 20 to 29 years old have faced the highest rates of unemployment, reflecting a long-running pattern in the Greek labour market. Meanwhile, more and more women sought work in the crisis regardless of age and family demands.[14]

This situation was worsened by unemployment benefit cuts, which limited payments to €460 per month and reduced their duration,[15] hitting 70 per cent of the unemployed, who had been out of work for over a year.[16] As health coverage by the Greek national insurance system was dependent upon employment, the vast number of unemployed also lost access to free health services. Uninsured and migrant pregnant women now had to pay thousands of euros for childbirth.[17] At the same time,

---

8. Thanasis Maniatis, 'The Fiscal Crisis in Greece', in ibid., 33–50.

9. INE-GSEE, *Ī Ellīnikī Oikonomía*, 144.

10. Ibid., 143.

11. Īlías Geōrgákīs, 'Ena Ekatommýrio Ergazómenoi Aplīrōtoi éōs kai 5 Mīnes', *Néa*, 25/4/2015. The article quotes data provided by the Ministry of Labour.

12. Dīmītrīs Nikolakópoulos, 'Me Vásī Perigrámmata Théseōn oi Apolýseis 150.000 Dīmósiōn Ypallīlōn', *Vīma*, 12/5/2012.

13. EL.STAT, Labour Force Survey: 3rd Quarter, 2014.

14. EL.STAT, Labour Force Survey. Annual Time Series Since 1981: Population, Education, Employment Status, 2018.

15. From 1 January 2013, unemployment benefits were reduced or removed depending on the number of days the benefit had been received previously, up to a maximum of 450 days in four years (N. 3986/2011).

16. INE-GSEE, *Ī Ellīnikī Oikonomía*, 204.

17. Giánnarou, *Kathīmeriní*, 9/7/2014.

basic commodity prices continued to rise, with the inflation rate falling at a very slow pace from 4.4 per cent in 2010, only reversing in 2013, reaching 1.7 per cent in 2015, and then rising again.[18] This means that there has been no uniform 'internal devaluation', but rather a *massive devaluation of labour power*.[19]

In addition to encumbering workers, the combination of crisis and austerity proletarianised a large section of the petit bourgeoisie – the artisans and small business owners who constituted about 30 per cent of the working population.[20] Indicatively, in the first quarter of 2012, 53.3 per cent of small businesses considered themselves likely or very likely to close down, while 54 per cent had difficulties paying their employees. Profits decreased by 35 per cent between 2011 and 2012, as businesses faced low consumption and lack of credit for raw materials.[21] Small and medium-sized enterprises employed 85 per cent of the labour force in 2009. By 2014, one-fourth had closed down, and employment in the sector had shrunk by 27 per cent.[22]

Grave indicators of these policies' social impact are the 25 per cent estimated increase in homelessness from 2009 to 2013,[23] and the 55.8 per cent rise of suicide rates between 2007 and 2011.[24] This was not only caused by unemployment, poverty and debt, but also by the closure of numerous mental health centres and three major psychiatric hospitals.[25] Public hospital provision suffered from shortages in staff, medical supplies, salary arrears and closures, after a 30 per cent healthcare budget cut coinciding with a 24 per cent rise in hospital admissions.[26] The closure of drug rehabilitation centres also resulted in rising HIV

---

18. EL.STAT, Annual changes to the Consumer Price Index, 1959–2018.

19. For a critique of internal devaluation as economic strategy see Ilías Iōakeímoglou, *Esōterikí Ypotímīsī kai Syssōreusī Kefalaíou* (Athens: INE-GSEE, 2012).

20. Sofia Lampousaki, 'Greece: Self-Employed Workers', EurWORK Observatory (Eurofound, 23 February 2009).

21. IME GSEVEE, *Estimation of Economic Climate* [in Greek], January 2012.

22. IME GSEVEE, *Economic Climate Trends*, July 2014.

23. UN High Commissioner for Human Rights, 'End-of-Mission Statement' (New York: OHCHR, 2013).

24. Michael G. Madianos et al., 'Suicide, Unemployment and Other Socioeconomic Factors', *The European Journal of Psychiatry* 28, no. 1 (2014): 39–49.

25. Sofia Neta, 'Kleínoun ī Mía metá tīn Állī Domés Psychikīs Ygeías', *Eleutherotypía*, 19/9/2011; Elena Fyntanidou, 'Ta Psychiatreía Kleínoun, ta Nosokomeía Stenázoun', *Vīma*, 2/11/2014.

26. Effie Simou and Eleni Koutsogeorgou, 'Effects of the Economic Crisis on Health and Healthcare in Greece in the Literature from 2009 to 2013', *Health Policy* 115, no. 2–3 (2014): 111–19.

infections among injecting drug users, hundreds of whom became homeless.[27] In schools and kindergartens, free meals were reintroduced after numerous cases of children passing out from malnutrition.[28]

This retraction of social and health services placed, as would have been expected, an increased burden on women to perform domestic care work, in addition to them undertaking more paid work outside the home. This took place in enlarged households, as more family members tended to share each home to reduce costs.[29] The pressure to perform this double burden at a time of high unemployment also worsened conditions for women in domestic violence situations. In some cases, this was because unemployment increased their economic dependence on their male partner – when the Greek state still does not oblige divorced fathers to support their family; in other cases, because male unemployment and business failure increased anger about emasculation and loss of status.[30]

As for privatisations, at least until 2015, when SYRIZA began to systematically attract Chinese capital, those mostly benefited Greek mega-companies and their owners, who have enormous political and economic leverage. As an example, the core bidder in the privatisation of the state lottery business, OPAP, was the oil magnate and owner of football club AEK Athens, Dimitris Melissanidis. Melissanidis competed for the deal against Intralot, a subsidiary of Intracom, a multinational technology and defence communications group, owned by the billion-aire Sokratis Kokkalis, who also owns the football club Olympiacos. Melissanidis made the news for trying to use his political connections to bypass the open bidding process,[31] but Kokkalis himself had also been prosecuted in 2011 for similar activities.[32]

Clearly, these measures have redistributed wealth upwards to the detriment of lower social strata. From a Marxian perspective, the attack on direct and indirect wages produced a deeper disconnection between

---

27. Eirīnī Andriopoúlou, Fōtīs Papadópoulos and Pános Tsaklóglou, *Ftōcheia kai Koinōnikós Apokleismós stīn Elláda* (Athens: INE-GSEE, 2013).
28. Márny Papamatthaíou, 'Ta Syssítia Epistréfoun sta Scholeía', *Vīma*, 11/12/2011.
29. María Karamesíni, 'Ī Krísī ōs Próklīsī gia tis Feminístries', *Fýlo Sykīs*, 16/10/2012.
30. Euaggelía Kakleidákī, 'Endooikogeneiakī Vía katá tōn Gynaikōn tīn Epochī tīs Oikonomikīs Krísīs stīn Elláda' (postgraduate dissertation, University of the Aegean, 2012); Christína Karakiouláfi et al., *Anergía kai Ergasiakī Episfáleia* (Athens: INE-GSEE, 2014).
31. Kerin Hope, 'Greece Faces Collapse of Second Key Privatisation', *Financial Times*, 27/6/2013.
32. Gianna Papadakou. 'Diōxeis gia Symváseis OPAP-Intralót tīs Periódou 2005–2007', *Vīma*, 30/5/2011.

the reproduction of capital and proletarian reproduction. What the state instead 'offered' to proletarians was aimed at keeping them in their place: increasingly oppressive policing, accompanied by more stringent legislation against protests and higher penalties for those arrested.[33] All this then effected the second and deeper stage of neoliberal restructuring in Greece, in which labour and its organisations were demoted to the status of social pariahs, with labour power now even more openly treated as superfluous. The capitals that could do so took advantage of a labour market rigged in their favour: a large unemployed population prepared to work for very low wages, or even unpaid. The elusiveness of the wage became a theme in mainstream television: comedy sketches of the unemployed begging to work unpaid, programmes on how to make a living from small patches of land. The media message encouraged a make-do attitude and the acceptance of ever more exploitative conditions, in tune with the state's new workfare programmes.[34]

Still, it would be simplistic to understand such measures as a response to Greek capitalists' demands. In fact, the EC's 'adjustment programme' mentions that Greek industrialists were not primarily interested in wage cuts but in the easing of bureaucracy.[35] Rather than simply pander to groups of industrialists, the policy followed a specific economic logic that aimed to secure the reproduction of the capitalist economy in the EU and in Greece as a whole. Yet, over a period of eight years, these policies struggled to restore the 'reliability' and 'competitiveness' of the Greek economy, or to ensure its capacity to repay debts and reborrow on capital markets. Instead, public debt rose to 178 per cent of GDP, alongside an abrupt shrinking of the economy.[36] As originally intended, austerity policies reduced domestic consumption, which had been thought to stifle international competitiveness, but that had a negative impact on the state's tax revenue from capitals that depended on this consumption.[37] Economic sufferings translated politically to the instability of governments and the weakening of the parties that supported these

---

33. 'Mpaínei "Fréno" stīn Omīría tīs Pólis apó Mikrés Diadīlōseis', *Kathīmerinī*, 29/5/2013.
34. These programmes (N. 3845/2010 AK) essentially subsidised unpaid labour for businesses and NGOs, as elsewhere.
35. European Commission, *Economic Adjustment Programme*, 21.
36. EL.STAT., Annual Budget data, 2018.
37. George Economakis, George Androulakis and Maria Markaki, 'Profitability and Crisis in the Greek Economy (1960–2012)', in *Greek Capitalism in Crisis*, ed. Stavros Mavroudeas (New York: Routledge, 2014).

policies, bringing on a left government that promised to halt or reverse restructuring measures.

Despite these seemingly self-defeating consequences, it is possible to show that the restructuring, while devastating on multiple levels, was not a mere mistake, but followed the dominant strategy of accumulation and economic restructuring of the pre-crisis period, which is also a *political* strategy. That this particular form of restructuring, including its consequences, was not a mistake but a conscious strategy is evident in the most overt way by the zeal with which it has been defended by Eurozone officials and ministers, particularly those from Germany, but also by all the governments of Greece up until 2015. When anti-austerity SYRIZA came to power, statements reacting to SYRIZA's rejection of austerity revealed that the reforms themselves were considered more important than solving the problem of Greece's sovereign debt – let alone responding to citizen needs and demands – and that debt was used to justify the forced implementation of austerity reforms across Europe. A statement by a 'senior German official' quoted in the *Financial Times* in February 2015 makes this clear: 'Germany wants Greece to stay in the eurozone, but not at any price. "If we go deeper into the [debt] discount debate, there will be no more reforms in Europe … There will be joyful celebrations in the Elysée and probably in Rome, too, if we go down this path."'[38]

To understand the logic of such statements and of the type of restructuring they continue to support, we need to take a step back and consider the structure and intent of European Economic and Monetary Union (EMU) in both political and economic terms. The content of the restructuring imposed on Greece is not an innovation but a deepening and acceleration of all the measures Greek governments were already imposing since the 1990s. PASOK's decision not to leave the European Community, as it had promised before the 1981 elections, meant that it had to follow the roadmap towards monetary integration, which began most decisively from 1996 onwards by the (PASOK) government of Kostas Simitis.[39] This roadmap had the typical characteristics of neoliberal restructuring: privatisations, pension reforms, local authority cuts, public–private partnerships and outsourcing in the public sector, liberalisation of labour contracts, wage cuts to overtime work and the

---

38. Alex Barker and Kerin Hope. 'Gap Still Yawns Between Greece and Its Creditors', *Financial Times*, 16/2/2015.
39. See also Laskos and Tsakalotos, *Crucible*, 22–6.

institutionalisation of flexible and part-time work.[40] Why were such measures promoted by the EU, and why were they the condition for joining the EMU? Was this merely an ideological shift following the collapse of the Eastern bloc?

A revealing way to analyse these policies is by looking at the development of ordoliberal thought in Germany and its influence on the European Community, as Werner Bonefeld has done.[41] Tracing the history of neoliberal thought from the 1930s onwards, he has insisted that the logic of European integration has been both economic and political. The shift towards neoliberalism in the 1970s cannot therefore be understood either as solely an economic response to the crisis or as the mere rise to dominance of an ideological project. In the 1930s, ordoliberals criticised not only the Weimar Republic's inability to facilitate a liberal economy, but also its 'weak' state, that is, a state that did not have the monopoly of violence and could not draw the locus of politics back into the state. Influenced by Carl Schmitt's authoritarian criticism of the Weimar Republic, ordoliberals like Alexander Rüstow and Wilhelm Röpke advocated a 'dictatorship within the bounds of democracy',[42] while Alfred Müller-Armack explicitly supported a strong state that resolves socioeconomic difficulties and frees the initiative of individuals (*Vitalpolitik*) by suppressing 'the class struggle'.[43]

There is thus a continuity between the ordoliberal conception of the free economy as political practice whose operation depends on the 'market police', in Bonefeld's words,[44] and the project of European integration, especially given the influential role of Alfred Müller-Armack in shaping this project. In both cases, the problem these liberal interventions wished to address was not a state that was too strong or too interventionist, but rather a state that was too weak, so that it gave in to the demands of 'special interests' – that is, to social demands that increased the cost

40. Ibid. 27.

41. Werner Bonefeld, 'European Integration', *Capital & Class* 26, no. 2 (2002): 117–42; Werner Bonefeld,, 'Human Economy and Social Policy', *History of the Human Sciences* 26, no. 2 (2013): 106–25.

42. Alexander Rüstow, 'Diktatur Innerhalb der Grenzen der Demokratie', *Vierteljahreshefte für Zeitgeschichte*, no. 7 (1959): 87–111; Wilhelm Röpke, *International Economic Disintegration* (London: Hodge, 1942), 246–7. Both cited in Bonefeld, 'Human Economy and Social Policy', 109.

43. Alfred Müller-Armack, *Staatsidea und Wirtschaftsordnung im Neuen Reich* (Berlin: Junker & Dünnhaupt, 1933), 41. Cited Bonefeld, 'Human Economy and Social Policy', 110.

44. Alexander Rüstow, 'General Social Laws of the Economic Disintegration and Possibilities of Reconstruction', in Röpke, *International Economic Disintegration*, 267–83.

of labour power – while allowing the politicisation of society beyond the supposedly objective rules of economic management. Bonefeld also refers to Hayek's 1930s vision of a supranational Europe that would encourage competitiveness as opposed to national economic protectionism, and would allow the free movement of capital, labour and commodities. Most relevant and central to Hayek's vision is that monetary policy would be centralised and national states would not be able to pursue monetary policies independently in order to satisfy popular demands. A Keynesian response to social conflict would no longer be possible, thus guaranteeing the freedom and stability of the markets, on the basis of a rule-based, centralised monetary policy, which shields central banks from political interference. Thus, national fiscal policies that veer away from a prudent fiscal discipline of surpluses in their current accounts would be punished by market forces. While Hayek's work was written in the 1930s, its logic directly applies to common analyses of the 1970s crisis: the inflationary pressures of labour demands, the exorbitant price of welfare, recalcitrant unproductive workers.[45] Thus the response, from the 1970s onwards, to these pressures was what political theorists of the Open Marxism school have called 'depoliticisation': the establishment of new 'independent' technocratic institutions, and especially independent national banks, which would manage fiscal matters independently from democratic processes.[46]

These principles of European economic integration and ordoliberal governance have become extremely clear in the case of Greece, as well as the cases of Spain, Portugal, Ireland and Italy. In contrast to vague understandings of neoliberalism as advocating a small, weak and non-interventionist state, this analysis shows that the neoliberal state is, above all, one that does not yield to social demands, and entails the 'harsh and disciplinarian control of the labour market'.[47] It is also clear that monetary integration strategically functions to separate and externalise an important branch of the state's powers, that which concerns monetary policy and could potentially allow currency devaluation to accommodate credit expansion and inflationary tendencies, so as to

---

45. Claus Offe, 'Some Contradictions of the Modern Welfare State', *Critical Social Policy* 2, no. 5 (1982): 7–16.
46. Peter Burnham, 'Depoliticisation: Economic Crisis and Political Management', *Policy & Politics* 42, no. 2 (2014): 189–206. Also Wendy Brown, 'American Nightmare', *Political Theory*, no. 34 (2006): 690–714.
47. Bonefeld, 'European Integration', 128.

make it impervious to mass democracy and the 'excessive expectations' this democracy generates.[48] In Greece we have seen this 'mass democracy' being treated as a major threat, not only in the form of social mobilisation, but also in electoral participation itself. In 2012, EU leaders issued public statements warning Greek voters against electing parties that did not support the restructuring measures, threatening that this would cause Greece's exit from the Eurozone and an economic collapse.

Within the scope of these structures and principles, then, dealing with high levels of sovereign debt within the monetary union created a dilemma between the ECB refinancing the member state in some way, which would generate 'moral hazard' (that is, the possibility that other member states will expect to be let off the hook) or forcing the member to leave the EU, which would jeopardise the entire Euro project. The solution was found in the way the IMF has previously dealt with debt in developing countries: bailing out Greece's national debt could not be permitted without demanding something similar to a 'structural adjustment programme', because if the debt was bailed out without such demands, the whole mechanism of imposing fiscal discipline and neoliberal reforms in the Eurozone would be defunct. Of course, the same does not apply in the case of bailouts for private financial institutions, except some minor reforms, since the free functioning of the latter is what the mechanism was set up to protect in the first place. Thus it was preferable to honour Greece's obligations to investors in public debt via bailouts to Greece, and effectively transfer losses to workers and devalued assets to the ECB, instead of allowing losses for those investors.

We see then that European monetary integration puts pressure on the sovereignty of European states. Yet this pressure is not merely external, but becomes internalised by national states. As Bonefeld observes, the monetary union does not simply make 'democratically unaccountable what previously had been democratically accountable', nor does it simply constrain state power, but instead 'national states, *on their own initiative*, will no longer be able to accommodate class conflict through credit expansion or currency devaluation'.[49] Drawing on Foucault, the Greek Marxist economists Sotiropoulos, Milios and Lapatsioras name this internalisation of fiscal discipline by governments a 'technique

---

48. Samuel Brittan, *The Economic Consequences of Democracy* (London: Temple Smith, 1977), 248. Cited in Bonefeld, 'European Integration', 125.
49. Bonefeld, 'European Integration', 132, my italics.

of financial governmentality'.[50] The reinforcement of a rule-based monetary policy in the Eurozone runs parallel to the functioning of financialised debt and the assessment of risk. When currency devaluation is no longer possible, unsustainable national debt runs a higher risk of defaulting in a disorderly way. High risk entails high interest rates, creating a vicious circle where debt becomes unserviceable.

The valuation of capital assets through financial markets ultimately plays a role in the organisation of social power. Sotiropoulos and his colleagues show how the assessment of risk by financial markets, even when it appears dysfunctional, is a technology of power which, through valuation, shapes and reinforces the forms of the exploitation of labour. Financial markets permanently oversee other markets and the collective social events and processes that affect them, reacting with assessments of risk, which they objectify in statistical terms. In doing so, their power does not reside in imposing an abstract norm by direct force, but instead they reinforce or punish the activities of capitals, states, workers or other social groups that respectively contribute or pose obstacles to the valorisation of capital.

Indeed, from 2009 to 2016 we have seen how the risk valuation and interest rate of Greece's sovereign debt has fluctuated wildly in response to Eurogroup discussions, parliament decisions, large demonstrations and election predictions and outcomes. At the level of individual capitals, the possibility of insufficient profits translates almost immediately to reduced access to credit. Lastly, at the level of workers' experience, the pressure translates into the message that if too much is demanded, or, more likely, if wage cuts and labour market reforms are resisted, the capital that mobilises their labour power will be devalued, and they could find themselves without jobs. The mediated immediacy of this type of market supervision is a specific characteristic of contemporary highly financialised capitalism.

The restructuring was then imposed on the Greek economy and society, and on the lower classes most directly, both via the structure of the EMU, whose very premise was to impose fiscal discipline through the removal of monetary control from participating states, and via the governmental technology of finance, which reinforces that discipline on all whose power (states), existence (capitals) or subsistence (proletarians) depends on the expanded reproduction of capital. 'On the basis of

---

50. Sotiropoulos et al., *Demystifying Finance*, 154.

this "material" blackmailing the most significant social consensus in the logic of capital is usually organized.'[51]

Greek Sovereign Debt, the World Crisis and Surplus Population

If the sovereign debt crisis was not caused by high public sector wages, pensions and welfare spending, then how did it come about? We may start by pointing to the €28 billion government support package that was paid to loss-making Greek banks in 2009, but why did banks make such losses? We know that the Greek government was allowing high rates of tax evasion among big businesses, and that most of its revenue came from workers. According to the neoliberal logic, that should have increased competitiveness and attracted investment.

Indeed, although Greece's current account deficit and its large external debt represent weaknesses, they were not seen as problems until 2009. As Sotiropoulos, Milios and Lapatsioras have observed,[52] the size of debt as a proportion of GDP had remained more or less stable since 2000 and up until the crisis, without triggering a rise in interest rates. On the contrary, high levels of debt were considered to be evidence for the peripheral countries' successful adjustment process in the Eurozone. Even though Greek capital and households were not as heavily finan-cialised as those in the USA and Western Europe,[53] the Greek state was heavily dependent on finance, that is, on the issuing of treasury bonds (selling sovereign debt) to capital markets, similar to other states in the Eurozone periphery. The low interest rates of the pre-crisis period powered not only Greece's long-running current account deficit and external debt, but also its rapid economic growth in the 2000s.[54] It was only the financial crisis of 2008 that reframed the debt as representing the high risk of sovereign default at a time of generalised market panic, which made it impossible for the Greek state to continue borrowing in capital markets. So this is not merely a 'Greek' crisis but one that is linked to the world financial crisis that started in 2008, and the ways in which it affected the Eurozone.

A significant proportion of Greek Marxists use the theoretical tools of dependency theory to understand Greece's integration in the world crisis.

---

51. Ibid.
52. Ibid.
53. Stavros Mavroudeas and Dimitris Paitaridis, 'The Greek Saga' (draft paper), 1st World Keynes Conference, Izmir, Turkey, 2013.
54. Economakis et al., 'Profitability and Crisis'.

They criticise what they call 'imperialist exploitation' within the EU,[55] aiming to show that European integration has caused a fall in competitiveness for the Greek economy because its government no longer had control over the monetary and fiscal instruments of economic policy, and that the competition among economies with differential levels of development causes 'value transfers' from less developed to more developed capitals. Lapavitsas's work similarly points to trade imbalances within the Eurozone, which, he argues, have benefited exporting economies with strong prior currencies such as Germany.[56]

This type of argument, however, suffers from conceptual weaknesses. First, it advocates a protectionist approach, arguing that Greek capital was only harmed by joining the EU. One then wonders why Greek capitals and the country's establishment have so enthusiastically supported and continue to support their participation in the Eurozone. In fact, the Greek economy grew more rapidly after entering the Eurozone, even if this was accompanied by high external deficits reflecting relatively low competitiveness and a high ratio of imports, associated with increasing demand.[57] There was also an influx of savings and low-interest credit into Greece after joining.[58] All of the 'peripheral' economies of the Eurozone grew more rapidly than the 'central' ones after accession.[59] This means that the effect was contradictory and should not be viewed one-sidedly. Second, the unbalanced relationship between the value of imports and the value of exports of an economy is conceptualised as *exploitation*, suggesting that the losers in capitalist competition are not the real exploiters of their workers, as if value travels directly from domestic to 'foreign' capitals in this way. Third, this view's anti-imperialism acknowledges but underestimates the hegemonic role of Greek capital in the Balkan region after 1990, especially in Romania, Bulgaria, Serbia and North Macedonia.[60]

While the fact of these trade imbalances cannot be denied, the political and theoretical thrust of these arguments can be questioned.

55. Stavros Mavroudeas and Dimitris Paitaridis, 'The Greek Crisis', in *Greek Capitalism in Crisis*, ed. Stavros Mavroudeas (New York: Routledge, 2014).
56. Lapavitsas, *Crisis*.
57. Economakis et al., 'Profitability and Crisis'.
58. Giánnis Milios, 'Ī Ellīnikī Krísī ōs Ekdochī tīs Pagkósmias Oikonomikīs Krísīs kai tīs Krísīs tīs ONE', conference paper (Nicos Poulantzas Institute, 2011).
59. Ibid.
60. Jens Bastian, '"Knowing Your Way in the Balkans"', *Southeast European and Black Sea Studies* 4, no. 3 (2004): 458–90.

These contributions suggest that it is in the interests of the Greek economy and Greek capital to exit the Eurozone. While, then, insisting on the 'Marxian' character of their contributions, they end up developing a criticism of capitalism that only questions exploitation through the relationship between different national capitals, with the implication that the interests of labour are aligned with the success of the capitals of 'their' nation. The veteran enemies of this view in the Greek discussion, Milios and Sotiropoulos, argue that it fails to understand the international market as not simply an area for international transactions, but as the framework for global capitalist competition.[61] International competition reproduces international differences in labour productivity and national profit rates, but it does not eliminate the capitals of less competitive economies. Instead, it produces pressures towards the *internal restructuring* of those economies to increase the competitiveness of their capitals through the continuing reorganisation of labour. The common European market was created in order to perform this precise role. It is then no wonder that the less competitive country is continually blamed of having fallen behind in carrying out neoliberal reforms.[62]

Yet it is clear that the crisis in Greece was expressed as excessive levels of debt, as elsewhere in the world. But if debt was not caused merely by bad economic management, how was it created? According to the most prevalent Marxist account, of which there exist several variations by well-respected scholars such as Robert Brenner,[63] Andrew Kliman,[64] David McNally[65] and Paul Mattick Jr.,[66] the classic Marxian 'tendency of the rate of profit to fall' is at the root of the crisis. Accompanied by a wealth of data (long-term rates of world GDP in the case of Brenner, devised measures that are meant to correspond to Marxian categories in the case of Kliman), the main thrust of this account is that, since the peak of the 1960s, the rate of profit in the world economy has entered a period of stagnation or decline. This is attributed to the high organic composition of capital in production, which led to strong productivity increases and rising real wages in the 'Golden Age' of capitalism (up to the end of the 1960s). But these productivity increases, based on the proportional rise

61. Milios and Sotiropoulos, *Rethinking Imperialism*, 145–83.
62. E.g. Pános Kazákos, *Apó ton Atelī Eksygchronismó stīn Krísī* (Athens: Patákīs, 2010).
63. Robert Brenner, *The Economics of Global Turbulence* (New York: Verso Books, 2005).
64. Andrew Kliman, *The Failure of Capitalist Production* (Pluto, 2011).
65. David McNally, *Global Slump* (Oakland, CA: PM, 2014).
66. Paul Mattick, *Business as Usual* (London: Reaktion, 2011).

of the value of fixed capital in relation to variable capital in production, and given an inability of the rise in relative surplus value to exceed rising production costs, have as a long-term effect the falling rate of profit.[67] According to Kliman, the crisis of the 1970s, which was a crisis of over-accumulation caused by rising organic composition, was not overcome, because not enough capital was devalued. For Brenner, escalating global competition over the adoption of innovative technologies and the use of cheap labour allowed the cheaper production of goods in the world market, but also caused growing overcapacity and a downward squeeze on profits – and, in turn, wages and jobs – in the world manufacturing industries.[68] This 'long downturn' was, however, countervailed, over the period since the 1970s, by financial deregulation and the supply of credit to states, companies and households. This situation created bubbles in the property and stock markets, which underwent consecutive crashes in the 1990s and 2000s, culminating in the credit crash of 2008.[69]

Many attribute the financialisation of the world economy to the replacement of the Bretton Woods gold standard arrangement by the dollar as principal reserve currency. According to Richard Duncan,[70] this allowed the USA to expand its sovereign debt without the type of market corrections that the gold standard would have imposed. US trade and current account deficits increased as the country took on the role of the world's largest consumer, pushing the economy forward and benefiting especially the export-oriented economies of Germany, Japan and later China. Japan and China in particular tended to amass dollars from these exchanges, which they reinvested in US assets in order to maintain artificially low US interest rates, a low dollar price and high levels of US debt-fuelled consumption for their exports. Debt and financialisation are then understood as alternative methods of boosting demand to counteract a long-term tendency of low profit rates, suppressed wages and increasing unemployment.

This is also a common interpretation among Greek Marxist economists, who argue that the crisis in Greece is not the conjunctural result of policy mistakes but a structural feature of capitalism. This structural feature is

---

67. This does not mean that absolute profits fall, but that their rhythm of increase becomes slower.
68. Brenner, *Global Turbulence*, 27–40.
69. Robert Brenner, 'Los Orígenes de la Crisis Actual', in *La Economía de la Turbulencia Global* (Tres Cantos: Akal, 2009), 23–101.
70. Richard Duncan, *The Dollar Crisis* (Hoboken, NJ: Wiley, 2005).

sought in production, not in distribution or circulation, and specifically in the movement of the rate of profit. Maniatis and Passas, for example, have examined econometric data, constructing Marxist variables to assess the profit rate, and have demonstrated trends that are very similar to the pattern identified by Kliman and Brenner.[71] After high profit rates in the 'Golden Age' of 1958–72, the profit rate declined sharply with the crisis until 1984. Then the profit rate slightly recovered and showed no significant rise or decline until 2007. Like Kliman, Maniatis and Passas argue that profit rates have not returned to pre-1972 levels because not enough capital was devalued during the 1970s crisis. They contend that growth after 1995 was effected by excessive financial expansion, on the basis of data that, while financial profit rates were close to or lower than the profit rates in the non-financial sector in 1980–90, afterwards they rose at levels comparatively much higher. They then attribute the crisis also to what they consider to be an increasing ratio of unproductive to productive labour, and an increasing proportion of financial profits among total profits.

Brenner, among others,[72] understands the fall of the rate of profit as a *secular* tendency of the capitalist mode of production, rather than merely a cyclical tendency of periodic crises. He associates this long-term decline with rising inequality and stagnant real wages,[73] as well as the growth of surplus populations that are thrown out of the production process due to increased mechanisation and correspondingly high labour productivity. Endnotes and Aaron Benanav, in their article 'Misery and Debt',[74] also make this argument, following the Marxian 'General Law of Capitalist Accumulation':[75] this crisis has not produced merely a reserve army of labour, but the historical development of the means of production has produced an ever-growing surplus population that is not integratable into the wage relation.

Profit rate accounts of global crisis such as those of Kliman, Brenner and others are compelling, providing a wealth of data to demonstrate

71. Thanasis Maniatis and Costas Passas, 'The Law of the Falling Rate of Profit in the Post-war Greek Economy', in *Greek Capitalism in Crisis*, ed. Stavros Mavroudeas (New York: Routledge, 2014).

72. This view is also supported by Robert Kurz, who predicts capitalism's collapse. Robert Kurz, 'On the Current Global Economic Crisis', in *Marxism and the Critique of Value*, ed. Neil Larsen et al. (Chicago: MCM, 2014), 331–56.

73. Brenner, 'Los orígenes'.

74. Aaron Benanav and Endnotes, 'Misery and Debt', *Endnotes*, no. 2, Misery and the Value Form (2010).

75. Karl Marx, *Capital*, vol. 1 (London: Penguin, 1990), 781–802.

their arguments, and satisfying the Marxian demand for a systemic explanation of crisis that is founded on capitalism's contradictions. These analyses also correspond to the widespread pre-crisis experience in developed countries of low wages, high indebtedness and unemployment in ex-industrial regions. These data convincingly evidence a world economy that since the 1970s has not been able to reach 1960s levels of growth.

We may wish to be cautious, however, about the notion that the period since the 1970s was one of stagnation or of a 'long downturn'. A lower profit rate does not suggest a stagnant economy, but one that is expanding at a slower pace. Stagnant wages and a widening income gap are also no indicators of a lack of growth of accumulation, precisely because the capitalist motivation is profits, not the improvement of the conditions of life. Besides, stagnant wages, disconnected from rates of productivity, was the very paradigm of growth in the period after the 1973 crisis, rather than a sign of economic weakness. It combined the extraction of relative surplus value (through technological development) and absolute surplus value (through falling wages and extending the working day). This model was functional, over these decades, with the supplementation of wages by credit, and it did produce growth. If the rate of profit failed to reach post-war heights in the post-1973 period, then, it may be an exaggeration to draw conclusions of secular decline. Such conclusions can leave open a deterministic reading that rejects the possibility of capitalism entering a new phase of growth after the current crisis. In combination with a theory of secular surplus population growth due to this decline, this can favour dystopian end-of-world scenarios or, conversely, the notion of the impending collapse of capitalism.

A rigid interpretation of the Marxian 'tendency of the rate of profit to fall' as a historically determining 'law' even belies Marx's text, which qualifies the theory with a number of counter-tendencies (increase in the rate of surplus value, wage cuts, fall in the prices of constant capital), leaving a lot of room for a cyclical, or even a more contingent (i.e. dependent on a larger number of identifiable but unpredictable factors) interpretation, which would mean that the 'law' is indeed all too often offset by the counter-tendencies.[76] Moreover, the relationship between the Marxian tendency of the profit rate to fall and historical profit

---

76. This is the case according to Riccardo Bellofiore, who agrees with this criticism and the monetary approach to value. Riccardo Bellofiore, 'Which Crisis, of Which Capitalism?', conference presentation (Izmir University of Economics, 2014).

tendencies measured in currency is far from simple, since Marx's general rate of profit is a ratio between amounts of value, that is, of abstract socially necessary labour time. The empirical monetary profit rate (in currency) thus does not behave in the same way as the Marxian general profit rate when mechanisation makes labour savings in the production process, because necessary and surplus labour time do not factor into its calculation as they do in the Marxian formula. Mechanisation also means that the monetary profit rate, as a ratio between prices, can increase even if labour time is minimised in the production process.[77] To make the theory even more precarious, Michael Heinrich's closer analysis of Marx's work, based on the evolution of his manuscripts,[78] has questioned whether the falling rate of profit was convincing as a 'law-as-such' even to Marx himself.[79]

Why is this important? Because we ought to distinguish between a critical analysis of capitalist exploitation – Marx's critique of political economy – from an economic theory that seeks to fix the capitalist economy, but also we ought to move away from a kind of Marxism whose argumentation is dependent on a determinism of collapse. Marx's critical analysis identifies not a trend that is of use to mainstream economics, but an antithesis between capitalism's dependency on the exploitation of labour and its tendency to expel labour from the production process: a fully automated capitalism freed from its dependence on labour power and waged labour would cancel capitalism's own foundations. But this insight is more useful as a conceptualisation of capitalism's contradictions, rather than as a law that proves capitalism's coming demise.

It is certain, however, that expanding numbers of the subordinate classes across the world have been facing increased barriers to their subsistence, especially after the Great Recession. Despite all the caveats, a surplus population has indeed expanded worldwide, if it is carefully conceptualised as a population not excluded from the wage relation, work and economic activity in any absolute sense. In other words, this is not a condition of absolute exclusion or permanent unemployment

---

77. Geoff Hodgson, 'The Theory of the Falling Rate of Profit', *New Left Review* I, no. 84 (1974).

78. This is a collective project organised around the first German edition of *Marx-Engels Gesamtausgabe*, the complete writings of Marx and Engels. It has become a significant tool for problematising the orthodox Engelsian interpretation of volumes I and II of *Capital*.

79. Michael Heinrich, 'Crisis Theory, the Law of the Tendency of the Profit Rate to Fall, and Marx's Studies in the 1870s', *Monthly Review* 64, no. 11 (2013).

but a socially marginalised form of economic *integration*. An increasing section of the global population has been in insecure and low-waged employment (without contracts, part-time, temporary, informal and unpaid), concentrated in economic sectors that are peripheral to capitalist development, such as highly labour intensive informal trade and services.[80] This has taken place alongside a decline in world agricultural and industrial employment since 1992.[81] This surplus population is not evenly distributed across the world. Informal employment, which is a correlate of poverty levels, is most prevalent in low-GDP per capita countries ranging from 42.2 per cent of non-agricultural employment in Brazil to 83.6 in India. Informal employment has also increased in Africa, Latin America and South Asia since the 1970s and 1980s.[82] In many so-called 'periphery' regions that were rapidly industrialised over the past decades, this surplus population was produced through the privatisation and concentration of land that proletarianised former peasants, forcing them either to work in factories or to end up in vast urban slums.[83] The turning of those regions (particularly South and South East Asia) into a global productive powerhouse thus produced populations that could not be formally integrated and at the same time were separated from the land which may have previously provided them with a basic means of subsistence. Struggles around this process are ongoing in places like China and India.[84] A section of these populations has constituted the waves of African and Asian immigration towards Europe in recent decades, amid the war refugees from Afghanistan and Iraq, Libya and most recently Syria. In the same period we have seen the strengthening of border controls, and especially those that separate 'centres' from 'peripheries',

---

80. There has been a decline in world employment growth since the beginning of the Great Recession, especially in the most developed countries. Part-time and own-account jobs growth has outpaced growth in full time and permanent contract jobs, while everywhere but in high-income countries around half of all waged workers are employed without contracts or informally. ILO, *World Employment and Social Outlook 2015* (Geneva: Brookings Institution, 2015), 17–28.

81. Ibid., 31.

82. ILO Department of Statistics, *Statistical Update on Employment in the Informal Economy* (Geneva: ILO, 2012); Jacques Charmes, 'The Informal Economy Worldwide', *Margin* 6, no. 2 (2012): 103–32.

83. For an analysis of these processes of proletarianisation and the production of a surplus population see Mike Davis, *Planet of Slums* (London: Verso, 2006).

84. Julia Chuang, 'China's Rural Land Politics', *The China Quarterly* 219 (2014): 649–69; M. Levien, 'The Politics of Dispossession', *Politics & Society* 41, no. 3 (2013): 351–94.

but also of walls and gated communities internal to states,[85] all of which reproduce a stratified global labour market.[86] These walls and borders, marked by a history of colonial racialisation, are maintained through increasingly lethal militarised forms of border control, and prevent the global mobility of surplus populations who are trapped in these forms of poverty.

Greece, located in a border region and assigned the task of protecting Europe's racial and 'civilisational' integrity, has become itself the locus of a surplus population. Already between 1970 and 2009, while rates of employment were stable or rising and more women continued to join the labour market,[87] the increasingly neoliberal growth model produced a mostly young population segment that was integrated into the wage relation informally and insecurely, always at risk of unemployment. This condition aggravated competition in the labour market and was another factor conducive to stagnant wages.[88] In the crisis the unemployed surplus population grew alongside the expansion of informal labour, while the formal labour market itself came to resemble the informal in contract terms (insecurity, low wages). At the same time, the internal segregation of this surplus population deepened, as migrants became more systematically racialised and their movement and employment heavily policed.[89] Thus the figure of the 'surplus citizen' has become implicated in protecting itself – economically, symbolically, racially – from the 'surplus migrant'. As Part III will demonstrate, this popular response to the conditions of crisis and global superfluity is not solely materially determined, and is complicated by the ambiguous way in which Greece is embedded in global power relations and racialised hierarchies.

Finance and the Capital Fetish

The surplus citizen is thus not only an economic reality but also a discursive construction with ideological uses. In much European popular and academic discourse, impoverished or 'working-class'

---

85. Wendy Brown, *Walled States, Waning Sovereignty*, (New York: Zone Books, 2014).
86. Castles, 'Migration, Crisis'; ILO, *Wages and Equitable Growth*, Global Wage Report 2012/13 (Geneva: ILO, 2013), 7–40.
87. Ibid.; OECD, *Dataset: Labour Force Statistics—Sex and Age Indicators*, data extracted on 10/8/2015 from OECD.Stat.; OECD, *Historical Statistics, 1970–2000* (Washington, DC: OECD, 2002).
88. Maniatis and Passas, 'Falling Rate of Profit'.
89. See Part III.

citizens are talked about as facing a series of supposedly objective threats. These threats, most of the time, are not discussed as emerging from the depth of exploitation that neoliberal transformations have effected, but rather as the triple problem of globalisation, financialisation and immigration.

Most accounts of the world crisis – orthodox, neo-Keynesian or Marxist – have pointed to processes of financialisation in order to explain the crisis, at the same time as treating it as inherently an element of instability and speculative bubbles. The deregulation of finance and its profuse convolution into derivatives which themselves became traded as commodities is often seen as caused by the power of speculators who could make easy money by betting on markets instead of investing in productive business. This type of reading is especially prevalent among neo-Keynesian accounts, which demand more financial regulation and a boost to welfare and wages to treat underconsumption. But Marxist analyses become implicated in this discourse as well when they become a Marxist economics as opposed to a critique of exploitation. Their focus on the falling rate of profit, mechanisation and automation, instead of leading to a critique of all the ways in which humanity is dependent on capitalist valorisation – not to mention its destruction of the natural resources that enable life – often trains attention on what they see as a dynamic between productive and unproductive labour and industries. This is the narrative of financialisation and finance as superfluous and predatory in relation to the productive sectors of the economy – and especially the industrial sector – neatly 'covering up' a lack of growth. The logic goes that, if banks were to be controlled by the state, then industries would flourish, workers would find jobs and we would overcome the crisis.

This view oversimplifies the relationship between the profit rate and the development of finance, and tends towards a form of productivism. But this oversimplification is based on a traditional understanding of value in Marx and not on a misreading.[90] Marx inherited a Ricardian notion of value through his engagement with classical political economy, which remains influential among orthodox understandings of the labour theory of value and especially Marxist economics. In its most extreme form, it does not distinguish between concrete and abstract labour, in that it assumes that value is produced *by labour* independently of

---

90. Sotiropoulos et al., *Demystifying Finance*.

the equalisation of different commodities and labours via a universal equivalent, money. Value, measured in labour time, is assumed to exist as a *substance* in the products of labour whether these are commodities or not. This definition of value entails a conception of finance as mere air.

Against this view, the 'monetary' interpretation of Marx's theory of value, in which the work of Georg Backhaus was central, argues against the substantialisation of labour into the product,[91] and against the understanding of value as a quantifiable essence that can exist separately from its form, money. Backhaus has argued that Marx's critique of political economy was not aimed at revealing labour time as the hidden magnitude of value (the principle upon which most Marxist economics is based), but instead it was a critique of value that analysed its genesis, the transformation of social activity into something that can be accumulated.[92] The value-form is here understood as a historically specific *social relation* that is established through the generalisation of production for the market, commodity exchange and its mediation by money in capitalism. It is only the generalised exchange of the products of labour as commodities, mediated by money, that brings value into existence, equalising different quantities and qualities of concrete labour. This understanding of the value-form is not entirely new – the work of Isaak Rubin in the 1920s contains such insights[93] – but has re-emerged in contemporary debates because of increasing interest in the German discussion on the value-form, which has been based on the renewed study of Marx's complete manuscripts.[94]

This understanding of value first of all puts into question the orthodox categorisation of service sectors, particularly those in the sphere of circulation, as by definition 'unproductive'. Indeed, if value is understood as embodied in the material commodity and not as a social relation, the service commodities of advertising, research and development, transportation and logistics would only be understood as revenue expenditure,

91. Michael Heinrich, *An Introduction to the Three Volumes of Karl Marx's Capital* (New York: Monthly Review Press, 2012), 49.

92. Hans-Georg Backhaus, 'On the Dialectics of the Value-Form', *Thesis Eleven* 1, no. 1 (1980): 99–120, 104.

93. Isaak Illich Rubin, *Essays on Marx's Theory of Value* (Montréal: Black Rose Books, 1996).

94. The analyses of Hans-Georg Backhaus and Helmut Reichelt have been particularly influential in this respect, proposing a monetary approach to the theory of value, even though few of their works have been translated into English. See Backhaus, 'Dialectics'; Reichelt, 'Social Reality as Appearance'.

and the labour processes associated with them as income transfers from industrial production. However, following Marx's definition that 'such labour is productive as is *consumed* directly in the production process for the purpose of valorising capital', means that the material or 'immaterial' nature of the commodities is no criterion for distinction.[95] Only unsocialised private labour (for example, production for consumption within a household), and labour that does not produce commodities (for example, services offered for free by the state) is unproductive of surplus value by definition.

On the basis of such an understanding of the monetary theory of value, Sotiropoulos, Milios and Lapatsioras mount one of the strongest criticisms against conceptions of finance as predatory and superfluous. Their criticism is not only relevant to analysing the crisis but also the forms of resistance to the restructuring. First, they argue that, if the process of circulation is not separated from the circuit of social capital but is instead a moment of the valorisation process, then we also cannot theorise separate 'fractions' of capital (financial/rentier, productive capitalist and commercial capitalist) as if they are independent from one another.[96] The notion of financial capital as a 'fraction' has led to voluntarist political understandings of the crisis, according to which the hegemony of the financial class has managed to control state policies and impose the neoliberal restructuring of the economy, causing a chronic shortage of investment and misallocations of capital, as well as imposing a widening of income differentials and increasing the indebtedness of working populations.[97] Opposed to this view, Sotiropoulos et al. recognise 'fractions' as *personifications* of capital.

Most interestingly for understanding the crisis, the restructuring and the forms of resistance to it, Sotiropoulos et al. discuss finance and credit based on the theory of the *fetishism of capital*. The capital fetish consists in the invisibility of exploitation as a necessary mediation in the production of value. Capital invested into the production process appears to beget an expanded value in money capital through the sole

95. Marx, 'Results', 442.

96. The separation originates in Thorstein Veblen's interpretation of Marx's 'metamorphoses' of capital in vol. II. Thorstein Veblen, *The Theory of Business Enterprise*, 1904 reprint (Eastford, CT: Martino Fine Books, 2013). Quoted in Sotiropoulos, Milios and Lapatsioras, *Demystifying Finance*, 47.

97. For example see Gerard Duménil and Dominique Levy, *Capital Resurgent* (Cambridge, MA: Harvard University Press, 2004).

acumen or luck of the capitalist: exploitation is not immediately visible in the process. This fetishism reaches a higher level in the case of finance capital. Financial capital (circulating claims to value, securities, stocks and derivatives), as a form of interest-bearing capital, the most general and developed form of capital according to Marx, is (only) 'fictitious' in the sense that the expansion of capital that takes place through its process, and the value produced, is based on assessments of the probability of future profits (process of capitalisation). In this process, the place of capital is occupied both by the money capitalist (finance) and the 'functioning capitalist' who manages the productive enterprise: the distinction of the former as parasitical upon the latter does not hold. Capital as finance is a forward-looking claim on the future production of surplus value.[98] According to Sotiropoulos et al., this makes capital in this 'most developed' form itself a financial 'derivative': its valuation derives from the performance of firms. In this sense, the most complex form of this function, the commodification of risk in the form of derivative products, is also at the heart of the capital circuit. Finance, following the explosion of innovations over the last 30 years, has represented and enabled the increasing worldwide speed and flexibility of the movement of capital. The *fetishism* of capital is then produced by the process that expands capital as finance as if it were unmediated by the production process. Financial capital is the ultimate capital fetish, because the mediation of its expansion by the production process becomes completely invisible – capital appears as what it really is: *self-valorising value*.[99]

But fetishism does not imply unreality. The critical power of the theory of fetishism is to denaturalise abstractions and point towards their paradoxical character, the mediations of capital's apparently autonomous self-expansion, as opposed to presenting the more concrete mediations (concrete labour, industrial capital) as the true reality of capitalism that needs to be liberated from the abstract 'illusory' forms. The attempt by many economists to discover the 'real productive economy' underneath the 'appearance' of finance neglects the fact that finance has a practical social validity *as capital*, and has a significant function in accelerating the international circulation of capital, which cannot be done away with unless the capital relation itself is dissolved. Treating 'fictitious' finance

---

98. Similar arguments are made by Heinrich, *Three Volumes of Karl Marx's Capital*, 155–68.
99. For a detailed exposition of the capital fetish, also see Jacques Rancière, 'The Concept of "Critique" and the "Critique of Political Economy" (from the 1844 Manuscript to Capital)', *Economy and Society* 5, no. 3 (1976): 352–76.

capital as false capital, excluding its movements from an analysis of the pre-crisis dynamic of accumulation and the current crisis except as a parasitical factor on the 'real' economy, is, effectively, a refetishisation, instead of a defetishisation, of finance. It affirms finance capital's 'ficti-tiousness' instead of paying attention to its mediation by the production process and the latter's dependence upon it: the value of financial capital, once more, appears to come out of thin air; it multiplies of its own accord, it is purely a bubble that steals value from production.

The non-correspondence between financial claims to future value and the realised value of investments is the rule, not the exception. Valuations of firms and assets fluctuate daily in stock markets, with enormous amounts of capital being destroyed and created rapidly. Yet, in this crisis, the value of inordinate amounts of capital was put in question: only in the cases of the USA and Greece, vast amounts in the form of mortgage-backed securities (USA) and treasury bonds (Greece) have either been devalued, or have been at a high risk of becoming devalued. In the case of Greece, the risk of a sovereign default on external debt has corresponded to the devaluation of capital invested in Greek treasury bonds, as the 'virtuous circle' of high external debt/high GDP growth turned into a vicious circle.

We could say that the crisis was also a form of capital fetishism. In the USA (but also in other countries like the UK and Spain) the value of a specific form of capital – housing property – was expected to continue expanding indefinitely regardless of any correspondence to the expansion of value from exploitation. In fact, investment in consumer property essentially invested in wage rises that have an *inverse* relation-ship to exploitation. High interest rates could not make up for the risk that borrowers could at some point be unable to pay. But if housing property was the only culprit and everywhere else profits were growing at the rate invested in, it would have been easier to contain the crash. It *is* important that profit growth was static as well and that other sectors were vulnerable to this financial shock.

To help interbank lending and thus liquidity, many national central banks, along with the ECB, purchased devalued long-term assets and securities held by private banks. Thus, sovereign debt rose during the crisis, in the attempt to prevent the collapse of banks, while servicing that debt became far more difficult and expensive because of low demand for government securities, which have longer maturity. Given their already higher levels of debt, peripheral countries were hit worse. This triggered further insecurity, with increased speculation on possible defaults in the credit default swaps market.[100] The virtuous circle had clearly become vicious, through the process by which states and the ECB helped prevent the abrupt devaluation of assets and the threatened collapse of the financial system. Meanwhile private banks, in their attempt to deleverage, continued to restrict their supply of credit to the economy.

While financial capital, then, cannot be seen as an extraneous, predatory level of the capitalist economy, the central structural role that financial markets play in the currently dominant model of capitalist accumulation and in the organisation of the Eurozone has coincided with *political* interventions that have prevented losses in private financial institutions, that is, the rapid wipeout of devalued assets, securities and, in the case of Greece, government debt. Instead, the strategy followed now transferred the debt burden from states to the subordinate classes through austerity and wage suppression. This strategy essentially puts exploitation back into the centre of value production and growth, attempting to make it somehow match the expectations of financial investment. This, so far, has not been successful. However, artificially maintaining the value of sovereign debts that ought to have been devalued is strategically useful precisely for pushing towards the types of 'reform' that will deepen exploitation.

Lost Sovereignty, the Surplus Citizen and Nationalism

The presentation of the restructuring on the Greek political scene as an 'external' material blackmailing, imposed either by the institutions that monitored it (the IMF, the ECB and the EC) or by the anonymous agency of 'banks' and 'financiers', was another instance of the fetishism of capital. This fetishism has entailed a particular understanding of the crisis, one affected by the distance and apparent disconnection of finance capital from labour and the process of valorisation. The increased exploitation, the pauperisation, the particular reconfiguration of class relations effected by the restructuring then appeared as the domination of an international elite of powerful politicians and financiers upon the nation-state and its 'people' – its surplus citizens. Via international institutions, it appeared to be this elite that eroded national sovereignty and intervened into and invalidated democratic processes. The demands

---

100. As recounted more analytically in Lapavitsas, *Crisis*, 51–8.

for democracy, the retrenchment into xenophobia and anti-imperialist nationalism and the subject of the national citizen dominant in the discourses of many movements mirrored the manifestation of the restructuring in the political scene.

The relationship between these political tendencies and the fetishism of capital becomes clear when we consider how the 'metamorphoses' of capital are concretised, not only by laypeople and journalists, but by Marxist theorists as well, into particular capitalist fractions. If taken further, this concretisation becomes personification, when financial capital is not seen as merely a sector but as a clique of powerful capitalists who alone control developments in the global and local scenes.[101] The abstract, collective, decentred operation of financial markets is then personified into individuals. An extreme case of this type of personification has been antisemitism, whose mid-war ideology, according to Moishe Postone, can be understood as a fetishistic form of anti-capitalism that targeted only the *abstract* forms of capital and opposed to them the land and *concrete* industrial capital.[102] The opposition to abstract capital in the form of finance, Postone observed, extends also to the concept of the mobile 'abstract' cosmopolitan citizen, without ethnic roots or national attachments, personified by the Jew. It is no wonder that antisemitic conspiracy theories have been rising in popularity, in Greece and elsewhere, in the midst of this 'financial' crisis.[103] But a parallel and broader discourse to antisemitism has also emerged, expressed in the continuum 'globalisation-finance-immigration = capitalism' and the strengthening of anti-immigration sentiment alongside anti-globalisation and anti-elite discourses across Europe and the USA – all of which figured in the neo-Nazi propaganda of GD. The success of fetishistic anti-capitalism materialised in the movement of many voters from the left to the far right and in emboldened racist commentary and violence in public spaces, now reframed as a form of resistance.

But Marxist economists and political theorists of the left have not been particularly consistent in countering this narrative either. The majority

101. Duménil and Levy, *Capital Resurgent*.
102. Moishe Postone, 'Anti-Semitism and National Socialism', in *Germans and Jews Since the Holocaust: The Changing Situation in West Germany*, ed. Anson Rabinbach and Jack D. Zipes (New York: Holmes & Meier, 1983), 302–14.
103. 'Why Is Greece the Most Anti-Semitic Country in Europe?', *Haaretz*, 20/5/2014; Stephen Pollard, 'Antisemitism in France', *The Telegraph*, 9/1/2015.

of Marxist analyses of the Greek crisis lay the blame on core–periphery relations within the Eurozone and place special importance on Greece's sovereignty and its nationally integrated economic development for overcoming the crisis.[104] The problem here is not only that the production of value itself is untouched by this critique in the name of the 'realism' of having to work within existing state institutions and economic variables. These approaches treat finance as an abstract level that can be dispensed with by choice, or which will go away as soon as Greece exits the EU and the common currency, so that concrete nationalised capitalist development can continue undisturbed. Yet even a nationalised capitalism, at least in the present configuration of international capitalist production and accumulation, can hardly exist without finance and cannot grow without competition.

The media presentation of the Troika as a group of individuals led by Angela Merkel, on the basis of Germany's political and economic power in the EU, validated a view of the restructuring not so much as a drive to restructure class relations and promote the economic model favoured by the founding ordoliberal ideology of the EU, but rather as German imperialist domination over Greece. What is not recognised in this narrative, which has also heavily influenced left politics and left economic analyses of the Eurozone as a structure that predominantly favours Germany,[105] is that Germany would never have been able to have the ideological dominance it does within the EU, and the depoliticised autonomy of monetary policy that the ECB represents would not function, had it not been for the far more diffuse discipline imposed by financial governmentality, which exceeds EU structures. This form of governmentality does not require the existence of the Eurozone to function, even though the Eurozone structures tighten its grip. Argentina, which is often mentioned as a positive example by anti-EU commentators, is, in fact, a case in point. Despite leaving the dollar peg, devaluing its currency and defaulting on its debts, its economy is still threatened, and its economic policy is still under the close scrutiny of impersonal financial markets.[106]

---

104. Stavros Mavroudeas and Dimitris Paitaridis, 'The Greek Crisis', in *Greek Capitalism in Crisis*, ed. Stavros Mavroudeas (New York: Routledge, 2014), 153–75, 170; Stathis Kouvelakis, Costas Lapavitsas, Kevin Featherstone, Peter Bratsis and Étienne Balibar, 'The Greek Crisis', *Journal of Modern Greek Studies* 28, no. 2 (2010): 303–6.

105. Lapavitsas, *Crisis*; Mavroudeas and Paitaridis, 'Greek Crisis'.

106. Elaine Moore and Philip Stafford, 'Argentina in Last-Ditch Manoeuvre to Pay Bondholders', *Financial Times*, 30/3/2015; Pan Kwan Yuk, 'Time to Cry for Holders of Argentina's 100-year Bond?', *Financial Times*, 30/4/2018.

The crisis revealed the degree to which financial governmentality and the ordoliberal structures of the EU together had dedemocratised the state's regulation of the national economy. Neither voting for the social democratic programme of George Papandreou nor the enormous demonstrations outside parliament had any impact upon the imposition of austerity. SYRIZA's defeated negotiations in 2015 solidified this fact. But demands for sovereignty and democracy could not be disconnected from an ethno-national discourse. Both left-wing and right-wing voices, as well as a large section of the crowds in demonstrations, branded as 'national traitors' the Greek politicians who signed the Memorandum agreements containing restructuring measures in return for bailout funds. The 'nation' and 'its people' or citizens were the unified classless mass confronting them. While this discourse of identifying proletarians and small business owners with the nation as a whole favours the strategic left-wing articulation of anti-austerity into a national-popular unity (the Gramscian recipe for a successful counter-hegemonic discourse),[107] this very discourse also legitimised far-right, not to say national-socialist articulations. This was to be expected in a country like Greece, where the 'national-popular' has a very weak history of being articulated with any ethno-racial identity other than that of the 'Greeks', and in which the left is rarely disquieted by the fact that their 'we' almost never includes immigrants.

National socialism was represented by the rise of GD, whose ideology combined anti-imperialism with a heightened discourse of betrayal and violent activist support for everything concrete: the Greek shipping industry against left unions (whose 'Jewish origins' became once more a discussion topic in the blogosphere); Greek 'blood', territory and 'health' against the corrupting invasion of 'clandestine immigrants'; the supposed existence of oil fields in the Aegean, which 'Jewish millionaire bankers' are said to be preventing the Greek state from investigating.[108] Not only in the blogosphere but also in city streets and means of transport I overheard discussions about betrayal, conspiracy and how 'we need a dictatorship' to get rid of corrupt politicians and put things in order. GD fashioned itself as the party to achieve this.

The other side of calls for a dictatorship was the rejection of the current form of non-functioning democracy and the valorisation of a more 'direct'

---

107. For the most recent articulation of this argument, see Chantal Mouffe, *For a Left Populism* (London: Verso, 2018).

108. 'Petrélaia', *Ellinokratia.blogspot.com*, 2/6/2012.

kind in the squares. The nationalist articulation of democracy with the ancient Athenian *polis* into which so much national pride is invested, again connoted the cultural and racial historical continuity and superiority of the *ethnos*, and equally fuelled a discourse of holding up the fort against invaders. The Troika *were*, in a way, invaders, but even though the ordoliberal ideology at the heart of the EU did create a structure that poses limits to 'mass democracy', the narratives of Greek democracy and national defence both racialised and obliterated from view the *class* dimension of this dedemocratisation. The core threat posed to market freedom by mass democracy is not the political rights of the national citizen as such, but rather the enabling of class struggle over the state's economic management. Still, it was democracy as such that appeared to be attacked by the restructuring. Its heavy effect upon a great section of the petit bourgeois stratum, combined with the long-lost hegemony of class-based politics, configured the pro-democratic resistance to the restructuring as a defence of the nation.

The Political Crisis

These nationalist narratives, while ubiquitous, were not dominant in all social spaces and struggles. Their popularity was, however, favourable for the two main parties of the Metapoliteusi – PASOK and ND – whose collapse, following the imposition of the restructuring, signalled a deep political crisis. Over 2011 and up to the May elections of 2012, the anti-political rejection of 'all politicians' manifested in forms of resistance that were autonomous from political parties and traditional forms of political organisation, and even in the regular humiliation of MPs in the streets.[109] But the nationalist content of this anti-politics allowed its gradual reintegration into traditional political structures when governments took advantage of and cultivated the xenophobic tendencies expressed by sections of movements against austerity.

Still, this 'return to politics' (elections and electoral discourse, the conflict between left and right, between human rights and xenophobia) from 2012 onwards was in no way stable. No party or government managed to gain enough support or to complete its term in the period until the end of 2014. Even oppositional parties of the left and right did

---

109. This included multiple incidents of yoghurt and tomato throwing, and similar kinds of attacks, against MPs.

not enjoy full support, because there had been no convincing economic answers, within the capitalist system, to the impasse posed by the crisis. Even the impressive rise of SYRIZA has not marked a return to the kind of mass politics characteristic of PASOK in the early 1980s. Its rise was relative, taking place in the context of broader political delegitimation. No party has enjoyed the kind of support that would suggest any wholesale return to the stable politics of the Metapoliteusi. The possibility of deep financial instability after SYRIZA's rise to power can only be followed by further political instability, which is likely to entail deep social upheaval and an even deeper crisis of politics.

If, however, the political crisis is to be understood in the sense of the autonomisation of civil society from the state, or the delegitimisation of the state by movements that do not address demands to the state, the crisis has been rather mild. Most of the mobilisations through the crisis have addressed themselves to the state, if not the executive certainly the courts, including in cases of defending self-management and self-organisation. Even riots, after 2009, were different from the December uprising's peculiar opposition to state authority itself. The legacies of December 2008 were subsumed under a more conservative anti-politics that criticised the government and politicians, not the state apparatus. This may not be paradoxical at a time when the state apparatus was crumbling under the pressures of debt: it may reflect the recognition that social reproduction – through healthcare, welfare and other forms of public service – is so closely tied to the state that attempts at autonomy and commoning immediately come face to face with their lack of resources, which so far only the state has been able to provide.

PART II

Becoming Surplus: Struggle and its Limits

4

Social Struggle, Non-Identity and Popular Democracy

In this book I analyse social struggles not by celebrating instances of effective resistance, but by developing the self-critical insights that emerged through these experiences. Doing so raises specific questions, some of which have long engaged critical thought. The first and most central concern is the problematics of identity. By 'identity' I refer not to what, in my view excessively loosely, has been called 'identity politics', but rather to the formation of group identities in the process of struggle, which are, usually, associated with subject positions within existing – but discursively and ideologically mediated – social power relationships. Thus the problem of identity is not only relevant to movements and politics of gender, race and sexuality, but also to labour, class and nation, and processes of self-identification and subjectivation are part of the material dimension of relations of domination.

The problematics of identity, as conceived here, is intimately linked with the ability of movements to effect social transformation, understood as something separate from the simple achievement of demands. While a degree of social transformation is, of course, achieved through winning demands, what is of primary concern here are not minor institutional adjustments but the transformation of the power relationships within which social struggles are embedded, and whose domination in everyday life drives us to participate in movements. Because subjects formed in struggle are not autonomous *ex nihilo* subjects, but are formed within the power relationships of which they are part, the possibility of social transformation is linked also to the transformation, and not the simple affirmation, of those subjects. This has practical implications, as I show through the analysis of specific struggles. This self-transformation is not merely something indeterminate, an abstract 'refusal of identity', but rather occurs through a process of self-critique that is not an organised or pre-scheduled process of deliberation, and is not enabled by the success of struggles; instead, it is enabled by their encounter with internal conflict, contradiction, splits, impasses and challenges to the movement's unity. Thus, I understand those *negative* moments, which appear as moments of defeat and disintegration, as simultaneously *productive* moments, which enable a self-critical process and, in turn, can potentially enable social struggles, at a later stage, to proceed to forms of practice that can effect deeper kinds of transformation.

Those 'negative' moments of conflict, contradiction and disunity were important in the conjuncture of the crisis in Greece, one producing a high degree of insecurity and precarity, as well as competitive individualisation and forms of relative exclusion (from the wage and secure employment; from citizenship and the idealised, gendered and racialised figure of the citizen). The analysis that follows shows, I hope, how those negative moments reveal the insufficiency of subjects that many struggles attempted to affirm in this conjuncture: among others, those of the national citizen as an embodiment of the 'people', of the classless 'neighbour', of community consisting of abstract individuals as economic units, of workers managing their own labour, of the unemployed as in need of jobs and investment, of women as carers, of anti-fascists as rescuers of migrants, of migrants as passive victims of racist violence and of 'struggle' as a matter of displaying masculine, physical strength in the street. I also wish to show that those negative moments were revealed through the challenge posed by alternative practices and deauthorised subjects, and that, where negative moments were able to produce critical reflection, they were also often able to produce, at a later stage, practices and forms of struggle that took into account a broader range of complexities, questioned their self-identification and were better able to address their own role in the reproduction of forms of social domination.

Finally, the problematics of identity, negative moments of conflict in struggle and the process of self-critique, are linked to the political question of democracy, as it emerged in the movement of the squares, in the practices of local assemblies and in the politics of referenda and the 'populist strategy' promoted by certain sections of the left. While there may appear to be some parallels of my focus on conflict and the questioning of unity with the politics of radical democracy as advanced by Laclau and Mouffe,[1] and as conceived by authors who have partly followed their lead like Judith Butler,[2] there is, here, both a difference of approach and

---

1. Ernesto Laclau and Chantal Mouffe, *Hegemony and Socialist Strategy* (Routledge, 1984).
2. Butler refers to radical democracy throughout her work, but see especially her contributions in Judith Butler, Ernesto Laclau and Slavoj Žižek, *Contingency, Hegemony, Universality* (London: Verso, 2000).

a critique of radical democratism. While I similarly problematise uni-versalisation, I doubt that political conflict and the rearticulation of a hegemonic left project that includes diverse identities dispenses with the problem. A radical democratic hegemonic project can be more nuanced than the often exclusive class politics of the 'old left', but, in attempting to produce a political unity-in-diversity, loses sight of the fact that we are not merely faced with internal 'difference', 'plurality' and 'diversity', but with relations of domination that have a material dimension, as well as with the constitutive exclusions of national democratic institutions. Radical democratism tends to reduce social conflict and power relations to the sphere of politics and its associated discursive processes, geared – more for Laclau and Mouffe than for Butler – towards the left-wing acquisition of state power. This leaves little space to consider what happens when a hegemonic populist project that embraces diverse demands, as was that of SYRIZA, actually wins elections and attempts to manage the state and a capitalist economy in crisis. Below, I expand on these points in a little more detail.

Capitalist Relations and Identity

The question of identity and the formation of subjects of struggle does not only concern gender, race and sexuality, as is typically assumed in left-wing debates, but also class. When we consider histories of class struggle in terms of identity we dispense with the notion of the working class, or the proletariat, as a (or 'the') universal subject that will liberate humanity, and are able, instead, to identify the contradictions in which this identity is immersed, as well as the divisions that have constituted it historically. As shown in Part I, class identity in Greece was consti-tuted as 'Greek' during the formation of the Greek state, a process that enmeshed it in the problem of 'patriotism' as posed by conservative political discourse.

But this story only tells us about the political dimensions of class struggle and little about how 'class' is constituted within the material relationship between capital and labour. While, as I have argued, historical class formations are not the mere manifestation of an abstract class relation, we still need to think of class as a relation too. The focus of authors like Moishe Postone and Werner Bonefeld on capital as an abstract relationship draws attention to a fact both structural and historical: that 'class struggle between the representatives of capital and the workers over working-time issues or the relationship of wages and profits ... are structurally intrinsic to capitalism, hence an important constitutive element of the dynamic of that system'.[3] Postone's critique argues that 'labour' is not the transhistorical essence of Man's relation with Nature but rather it is historically constituted, taking an abstract form – as quantified abstract labour – only in capitalist society. Political identities and organisations of struggle around labour as a misrecognised contingent social form have historically partaken in the reproduction of capitalist social relations through their affirmation of labour and industrial production, understood – erroneously, in orthodox Marxism and socialist political thought – as autonomous from capitalist reproduction. The workers' movement, even in its revolutionary moments, has sought to 'liberate' labour and industrial production from the 'fetters' of capital. In the Soviet Union and the Eastern bloc it promoted social formations in which value – and capital – continued to be produced and workers continued to be dominated by the results of their own activity (alienation), with the surplus now managed by 'their own' authoritarian workers' state.

Postone rightly argues that 'social domination in capitalism does not, on its most fundamental level, consist in the domination of people by other people, but in the domination of people by abstract social structures that people themselves constitute'.[4] Yet he goes too far in rejecting for this reason analyses based on class. It is possible, with Werner Bonefeld, to both reject an affirmative notion of the working class that 'perceives its position in production as an ontological privilege',[5] and recognise class as an objective social relation of *mutual presupposition and dependence* between capital and labour. The existence of waged labour, and of the class of workers, whether objectively or politically constituted, depends upon the reproduction of capital. In Bonefeld's formulation,

[h]er continuous access to subsistence rests on the profitability of her labour, that is, on the effective exploitation of her labouring existence by the buyer of labour power. Relating to each other as antagonistic members of opposing classes, each presupposes the other, and each produces the other, not by their own personal will but by means of an

---

3. Moishe Postone, *Time, Labor, and Social Domination* (Cambridge: Cambridge University Press, 1996), 36–7.
4. Ibid., 30.
5. Werner Bonefeld, *Critical Theory and the Critique of Political Economy* (New York: Bloomsbury, 2014), 104.

objective social process that prevails not only over them but also in and through them.[6]

Thus, '[a]ntagonism is not only a relationship of battle', as conceived in the Italian autonomist and post-autonomist Marxism of Tronti, Negri and associated theorists,[7] but 'it is also a relationship of mutual dependency'.[8] Class struggle and capitalist development cannot *originate* in workers' agency, since the worker is not ontologically primary or autonomous in the relation between labour and capital. The worker, and labour, is not the 'source of all wealth' but a by-product of, and embedded within, the historical constitution of capitalist relations of production, which are the source of wealth in capitalist society. 'Wealth' in capitalism only exists in the form of value, and is produced by the entire ensemble of production, consumption and the social, legal and cultural forms of capitalism.

Mutual dependency means 'social reproduction' is not something separate from the reproduction of all the social forms that compose the capitalist mode of production. Social reproduction is the reproduction of life mediated by its dependence on the reproduction of capital – a contradictory relation, because capital is both necessary for and hinders the reproduction of life. Mutual dependency also means that, when workers demand higher wages and labour rights, they simultaneously hinder capitalist reproduction by pushing individual capitals to cut their profits, and wish its continuation because their subsistence (their job) depends on it. The success of their struggle thus reproduces them as waged workers alongside capital's accumulation as the condition for subsistence.

To return to the question of identity, the workers' struggle has been limited by its specific, historically and geographically local, experience of work, in ways that have often led it to become a conservative social force. For the workers' struggle to move towards a more universal position – what Marxist revolutionary theory has imagined as the proletariat's ability to 'liberate humanity' – depends upon workers' ability to question their self-identity as producers, an identity constituted by the relationship of mutual dependence with capital. This dependence in turn ties workers to the concrete material and ideological forms of capitalist

6. Ibid., 109.
7. Two classic texts promoting this perspective are Mario Tronti, 'The Strategy of Refusal', *Autonomia III*, no. 3 (1980): 28–35, and Antonio Negri, 'Twenty Theses on Marx', in *Marxism beyond Marxism*, ed. Saree Makdisi and Cesare Casarino (Routledge, 1996).
8. Bonefeld, *Critical Theory*, 64.

reproduction in each historical conjuncture, shaped by the formation of nation-states, patriarchal social relationships and international racialised hierarchies of labour.

The resonances should now be obvious between the critique of the workers' identity and the feminist critique of 'woman' as subject, as well as the critique of 'race' and racial identity by critical theorists of race. Well-known examples are the work of Judith Butler, which I discuss below, and Paul Gilroy, who has criticised the politics of affirming distinct racial identities as a strategy of resistance.[9] In both instances, oppressed identities are not fetishised as loci of autonomy and agency, but are recognised as implicated in, and reproduced through, gendered and racialised relations of domination. A politics of affirming those identities thus affirms the relationships of domination that constitute them.

Identity and its Questioning: Social Struggle, Self-Critique and Group Psychic Processes

The problem of identity has been conceptualised by a variety of theoretical perspectives; philosophical, political, sociological, psychoanalytic and social psychological, with each discipline using a slightly different terminology. I draw on three relevant strands of the critique of identity: Adorno's philosophical critique of identity-thinking; the critique of the subject developed by Foucault and theorists who extended his work; and psychoanalytic approaches to subject formation, group relations and critical knowledge.

Adorno's negative dialectics – his critique of the positive and progressive element in Hegelian dialectics – asserts that the universal is always negative, because there is always a remainder, the 'non-identical remnant', an element that the universal denies.[10] Identity-thinking is the inability to acknowledge the existence of this element, to assert the universal as already complete and the concept as capable of exhausting its object.[11] Thus, the ideal of the reconciliation of all interests and conflict in the universal as an achieved identity would, for Adorno, 'not mean the identity of all as subsumed beneath a totality, a concept, an integrated society. A truly achieved identity would have to be the consciousness of non- identity'.[12] The recognition of non-identity is a precondition for

9. Paul Gilroy, *Against Race* (Cambridge, MA: Harvard University Press, 2001).

10. Theodor Adorno, *History and Freedom* (Cambridge: Polity, 2010), 97.

11. Theodor Adorno, *Negative Dialectics* (London: Routledge, 2010).

12. Adorno, *History and Freedom*, 55.

moving towards any kind of emancipated social unity, which is not the forced unification of interests under a hegemonic idea about human universals.

Adorno's critique directs us to conceive social struggle not as progressively reaching a higher, more universal unity and achieving its aims, but rather as continually being challenged *negatively* by elements – voices, internal contradictions, insights – previously denied in the course of constructing a collective identity and ideology of universality. Presumed or enforced unity and denial of internal difference and contradiction can appear to the collective as essential for action, but the reality of disunity cannot be avoided. Sooner or later it generates conflict, a negative moment in which what was denied demands to be accounted for.

The 'non-identical remnant' does not merely demand integration, so that it becomes intelligible in terms of the universal, nor is it identical with itself. It is not a moment of truth or authenticity. Its existence ought to produce further reflection on what Adorno has called a 'constellation' – its historical production through its relationship with other elements outside it.[13] For the purposes of analysing contemporary struggles, we can locate the non-identical in a contradiction denied. For example, the denial of interdependence between a subject of struggle and its 'adversary', the assumption of autonomy, is the denial of a non-identical element. Becoming conscious of non-identity would not entail the realisation of autonomy but rather exploring how interdependence is reproduced by both antagonistic sides, critical reflection on the constellation of relationships and social structures that reproduce this form of domination. The non-identical remnant can also be an internal difference that has been denied, or an exclusion that has been ignored.

It is not, however, easy to confront the non-identical. From the perspective of a psychoanalytic theory of thinking and learning, specifically that of Wilfred Bion,[14] a challenge to what is assumed to be known, which, in group situations, also challenges group identity, can be processed through either tolerating frustration and the risk of disintegration that the denied element is felt to pose, or through 'evacuation'. Evacuation pertains to what Melanie Klein has called the paranoid-schizoid position:[15] a

---

13. Theodor Adorno, *Gesammelte Schriften*, vol. 1 (Frankfurt: Suhrkamp, 1986), 359.

14. Wilfred Bion, *Experiences in Groups* (London: Tavistock, 1961); Wilfred Bion, *Learning from Experience* (London: William Heinemann, 1962).

15. Melanie Klein, 'Notes on Some Schizoid Mechanisms', in *Envy and Gratitude* (USA: Delacorte, 1946), 1–24.

persecutory reaction that, through a process of projective identification, evacuates all negative feelings to a vilified outside, to maintain a phantasy of goodness and coherence on the inside. Paranoid-schizoid processes in collectives and in movements – for example, the vilification of the 'common enemy', the anxiety to impose a 'line' that everyone must follow, the assumption of sameness and the need for uniformity, the strengthening of group boundaries in the definition of group identity, the circulation of conspiracy theories and 'rumours' – are forms of defence against the threatening non-identical. The paranoid-schizoid position is not a 'schizo' dissolution of identity but its protection in response to a perceived internal or external threat. We could say that in the most extreme cases, the paranoid-schizoid defence strategy produces a fascist group formation that strengthens collective identity in a delusional and violent manner, aiming to evacuate a threatening, collectively denied, non-identical element.[16]

Identity does not only signify unity and sameness but also a sovereign, autonomous subjectivity. Like Adorno, Michel Foucault and post-structuralist thinkers have questioned the notion of a subject with agency and sovereign will, capable of deciding, in an immediate and self-aware way, to act and to transcend its social conditions. There is a common thread here between the critique of existentialism and that of essentialist humanism.[17] Yet from this critique of agency it does not follow that transformation is impossible, or that the subject is animated by social structures and forces alone. Transformation does not require an ontology of autonomous agency or faith in its possibility. Rather, only by self-critically recognising the objective constraints imposed by oppressive social conditions may we begin to identify possibilities for transformation.

In certain post-structuralist tendencies, as in Deleuze and Guattari,[18] we find a more optimistic, positive moment that seeks to affirm the transgressive creativity of desire. While desire is recognised to be social,

---

16. Cf. The analysis of fascism as dissolution of individuality in a mass desiring its subjection to patriarchal authority, in Theodor W. Adorno, 'Freudian Theory and the Pattern of Fascist Propaganda', in *The Essential Frankfurt School Reader*, ed. Andrew Arato and Eike Gebhardt (New York: Continuum, 1982), and Gilles Deleuze and Félix Guattari, *Anti-Oedipus* (London: Continuum, 2004).

17. Theodor Adorno, *The Jargon of Authenticity* (Evanston, IL: Northwestern University Press, 1973); Michel Foucault, *Essential Works 1954–1984*, vol. 3 (London: Penguin, 2001), 246–52, 274–8.

18. Deleuze and Guattari, *Anti-Oedipus*.

shaped by language and domination, it also carries productive possibilities for resistance and liberation. Desire is split between a 'molecular', corporeal, unformed level composed of aimless and meaningless 'naked matter',[19] and a targeted, fascistic desire committed to reproducing the socius. The formulation is based on the Nietzschean notion that language and concepts oppress material differentiation. Desire, the id and material multiplicity become agents of freedom and transgression. Contrary to the Adornian view, what escapes the identity imposed by the concept and its universals is not conceived negatively as a 'lack' or a limit, but as a productive power whose generative capacity challenges the whole. 'Molecular desire', conceived as aimless multiplicity, intervenes at a purely material level and not at the level of thought, reflection or ideology.

Despite the energetic optimism that this view enables, its positivity can be limiting. Affirming a 'molecular' materiality and ontologising it as immediately transgressive takes as given the revolutionary content of unformed matter – itself an operation of identity. The negative moments of conflict and crisis are not ecstatic eruptions in which a corporeal, pre-discursive 'truth' or 'desire' is revealed. The risk is not a potential loss of identity and individuality (as Adorno might warn) but seeking unmediated authenticity in a corporeal interiority. The questioning of the subject and of an oppressive identity cannot be achieved through flight into a supposedly authentic pre-discursive state, which in a collective setting might be represented by the often ecstatic experience of togetherness and the breakdown of individual boundaries in collective action. This is not to undermine the importance of collective empowerment and what can be accomplished through collective force. However, collective empowerment is often transitory and meets internal limits, which are eventually experienced as disintegration, followed by attempts at recomposition. My core argument is that this subsequent disintegration – whether it is the disintegration of an organised or a chaotically produced identity – is not merely a moment of defeat but one that enables self-critique, because something is always denied for the collective identity to be formed, which needs to be addressed. While negative moments depend on the prior occurrence of positive ones, it is in the practice of self-critique, which takes place at both material and intellectual levels, that I would locate the ability of a movement, and

---

19. Ibid., 343.

of social transformation more broadly, to develop: a negative moment enables the next positive moment to take place.

This is not the affirmation of the different against a unifying universal, which would be too simple an opposition. With Adorno, what remains uncultured by the unifying concept (or the political identitarian unity) is not something already known or internally uniform, merely to be affirmed independently of the constellation of historical relations that have formed it. Put differently, there is nothing, whether a 'minor group' or a 'subaltern subject', whose identity is an autonomous carrier of unmediated truth. The affirmation of the particular would entail another level of repression of the non-identical, an essentialisation of 'minor' identities.

Could collective action be hindered by this degree of openness to the non-identical? Hoggett, for example, has argued that '[a]ction ... requires a capacity to use in a creative way what the Kleinians call the paranoid-schizoid position. ... Ideally activists need to be able to move back and forth between certainty and doubt, "black and white" and grey, if their commitment is to be free of dogmatism.'[20] Indeed, movements need not remain in constant indecision. Equally, action need not depend on the construction of a vilified 'enemy' and of the subject of struggle as given and coherent. Self-critique is not inaction, but suggests its own forms of action. It is not a process of self-dissolution but a necessary step for the subject of struggle to avoid reproducing the conditions of its own subjection, since its identity always contains something of its outside, even in the form of being denied.

Thus, if I struggle as a 'Black' subject or as a 'woman', as an oppressed 'indigenous national' or as a 'worker/proletarian', and I ground struggle on my identity, I freeze my becoming, because my identity was produced by the conditions of my oppression. I risk becoming static, fetishised, as well as exclusive of others who are similarly oppressed but do not fit in my identity. Equally, rejecting that identity and the historical experiences it is associated with may deprive me of tools for struggle. If I opt to redefine myself, 'resignify' who I am, as Butler suggests in her theory of performativity, again I imply a certainty that I am *already* liberated.[21] If my freedom depends on my ability to be anything, only limited by my corporeal capacities and the technological means to modify them,

20. Paul Hoggett, 'Climate Change and the Apocalyptic Imagination', *Psychoanalysis, Culture & Society* 16, no. 3 (2011): 261–75, 262.
21. Judith Butler, *Excitable Speech* (New York: Routledge, 1997).

I cannot simply declare such freedom, because I am both subjectively and structurally oppressed into a class, gender or race, which affects my imagination and desire of what I could be. Both in fact and in potential, I am more different from myself than I or others are yet capable of imagining. To *become* able to be anything would require a recognition of my current lack of freedom to do so, of my current oppressed identity as an imprint of the oppression I suffer, shaping on this basis my fight against the material and cultural dimensions of this oppression.

The focus here is thus on the *internal limits* produced by adopting a rigid identity, self-narrative and organisation, with a paranoid-schizoid psychic orientation to its interior and exterior. In such a situation, internal conflict within a group or between groups with common aims can produce a critical questioning of identity by revealing contradictions in the constellations of power relations and interdependence that constitute the subject of struggle. Beyond being a problem, disunity can provide opportunities for self-reflection, although it can also lead to new polarities, rigid identifications and impasses. What remains unreflected upon becomes a task for later critique.

Limits, Critique and Precarity

Social struggle and its limits are historically specific to the social tensions and contradictions reproduced in the present late capitalist world: the conditions of crisis and its forms of governmental management, labour superfluity, precarity and vulnerability.

Judith Butler has noted that, under conditions of crisis, precarity and vulnerability can generate both possibilities for movements and self-protective impulses.[22] Vulnerability, for Butler, is not merely weakness but also an opportunity to recognise our social interdependence. This parallels Klein's 'depressive position', in which, unlike paranoid-schizoid fantasies of omnipotence, dependence upon others as well as our inability to control them becomes accepted. It also has a gendered dimension, insofar as, for hegemonic masculinity, vulnerability is abject. We witness this in male public suicides in the crisis, which annihilate the abject vulnerable self and convert his 'victimhood' to a warning and a call for the empowerment of other men. Far from decrying

---

22. Judith Butler and Athena Athanasiou, *Dispossession* (Malden, MA: Polity, 2013); Judith Butler, *Precarious Life* (New York: Verso, 2006).

the loss of such a sovereign subjectivity, Butler suggests that recognition of interdependence and vulnerability has the potential to bring us closer to a universal ethics that accepts our common human fragility.

While Butler's ethical position is valuable, the normativity of her analysis seems disconnected from the way movements deal with these issues. She conceives the self-critique that vulnerability might produce at too abstract a level, from the perspective of an 'us', a 'First World' subject that had taken for granted its invulnerability.[23] It is not that Butler neglects those who were already vulnerable – she shows how they are produced as 'ungrievable' bodies, whose death typically goes unnoticed from this dominant perspective. But the 'other' remains 'other', suggesting a charitable attitude. Could the 'other', who was already vulnerable, also enter into a process of struggle, self-discovery and critique? While Butler acknowledges that 'precaritisation' reproduces contemporary economic hierarchies and the biopolitical sorting of bodies, she does not consider how the 'precarious', especially those whose lives 'don't matter', might overturn this condition materially, as opposed to promoting a universalist ethic of 'redistribution'. To imagine a solution through 'redistribution' is to assume that the global capitalist machine can be tamed democratically through good will, cooperation and inclusive institutions.

Here I do not so much use the concept of precarity but that of the 'surplus population', which highlights objective conditions in capitalist crisis: the wave of expulsion from the waged worker role as well as from self-employment and small business, a condition of non-integration into the formal economy. Superfluity is not a universal condition, nor has it, so far, emerged as a basis for a political unity – the category of the 'national people' has been far more dominant – but it has instead intensified intra-class hierarchies, competition and conflict. I am interested in the moments where the more insecure, economically marginalised and racialised challenge the self-protective attitude of the more secure sections. The former do not carry an authentic subjectivity; if their encounters open the possibility for insight, they equally produce possibilities for self-protective paranoid-schizoid reactions. As we will see, opportunities for temporary security can render the 'precarious' also into an army protecting 'investment' and 'jobs' indiscriminately despite destructive long-term consequences upon others and themselves.

---

23. See Butler, *Precarious Life*, 30.

Radical Democratism, the People and Nation

This brings me to the discussion of democracy, so prominent in recent movements, and, in turn, to that of 'radical democracy', which Butler is committed to and to which she and others have linked the performative dimensions of struggles in the squares, those of migrants and of non-conforming genders. Radical democracy is further connected to the resurgence of interest in left populist counter-hegemonic strategies, inspired by the theories of Laclau and Mouffe,[24] as a way to mount a response to the far right on the one hand and neoliberal hegemony on the other.

Butler, Athanasiou, as well as a series of writers on migrant struggles,[25] propose that the very presence of protesting bodies in public space redefines that space and expands the meaning of the 'public', 'citizenship' and 'democracy'. These are no mere *claims* for citizenship; as Butler rightly argues, even existing citizens, under conditions of undemocratically imposed austerity as in Greece, have needed to reclaim the meaning of citizenship and the public. Instead, these are *acts* of citizenship.[26] The acts themselves are thought to be transformative, producing rights that don't already exist. These views add a dimension to the historical process of 'equaliberty' as Balibar has described it – insofar as they also acknowledge the limits of inclusion in the liberal institutions of citizenship, rights and liberal democracy.

Within a democratic framework, however, the horizon is always one of broader inclusion into the political community. Political institutions themselves remain unquestioned, so that, to the extent that class, feminist, gender and migrant struggles have produced a series of exceptions to the principle of equivalence between abstract individuals embedded within liberal democracy (e.g. redistributive policies, maternity rights, multiculturalism, specific rights for new gender categories) the latter still figure as 'exceptions' and 'privileges', as the recent right-wing backlash against those rights has been asserting so forcefully. If the boundary problem

24. Most explicitly, their theory was actively used by Pablo Iglesias of Podemos, but similar perspectives have been used to comment upon SYRIZA and the value and strategy of a 'left populism' more broadly. Laclau and Mouffe, *Hegemony and Socialist Strategy*.
25. Butler and Athanasiou, *Dispossession*; Ilker Ataç, Kim Rygiel and Maurice Stierl, 'The Contentious Politics of Refugee and Migrant Protest and Solidarity Movements', *Citizenship Studies* 20, no. 5 (2016): 527–44.
26. Judith Butler, 'Bodies in Alliance and the Politics of the Street' (Venice: Office for Contemporary Art Norway, 2011).

of democracy is explored at all, it is only through processes of broader inclusion, not through questioning the basis of the territorial nation as the foundation of political community. Transnational and mobile constellations of struggle beyond national democratic institutions and territories then remain unintelligible and invisible, while territorialised – majority or minority – identities become fetishised.

These are the limitations of a democratic framework from the perspective of grassroots struggle. But from the perspective of a *hegemonic strategy* that aims to gain state power, these limitations are deepened. Laclau and Mouffe's position on hegemony provides, to a degree, a counter-model to that of traditional class-first politics. Yet their theory of 'empty signifiers' – words and phrases used knowingly and strategically in the absence of unity to produce constructed unities and universals – and Mouffe's rejection of transnational politics in favour of Gramscian 'national-popular' formations, not only fail to challenge the substantive limitations of liberal democracy, but also promote discursive strategies that accentuate paranoid-schizoid identitarianism (for example, the construction of a common 'enemy' or 'adversary'). It is an excellent theory of how populism *functions* – and especially of how fascism can mobilise masses – but, as a strategy, it undermines the possibility of self-critique. As Beasley-Murray has argued in his critique of Laclau, 'left populism' repeatedly fails to differentiate itself from the populism of the right.[27]

The limitations of left populist strategies for constructing political hegemonies towards gaining state power become even more obvious when they actually succeed. The case of SYRIZA shows that, despite its skilful ability to articulate diverse demands and claims inclusively, and even generate 'hope' – the empty signifier – among everyone, from Greek small business owners to migrants in detention camps, their political victory translated into very limited substantive transformation at the material everyday level. The limit was not only in complex international interests and politico-economic interdependence in global capitalism, but in the lack of 'strategy' that, instead of having state power as its ultimate aim, directly targets the reproduction of domination and exploitation at global and local levels.

---

27. Jon Beasley-Murray, *Posthegemony* (Minneapolis: University of Minnesota Press, 2010), 15–67.

5

Citizens from Democracy to Riot

One year before the onset of the debt crisis, the riots of December 2008 brought the youth to the forefront as a central figure of social unrest. The entrants into the labour market – then called the '700-euro generation', soon to become €400 in a matter of three years – were the first to feel the crisis, and the first to react to it. But December increased the social acceptability of acts of protest that the left previously viewed as destructive 'provocations', such as occupations and rioting. This was evident by 2010, the year Greece entered into the bailout agreement. On 5 May 2010, the day the first bailout's restructuring measures were being put to the vote, an enormous and furious crowd of the general strike demonstration overpowered the police guarding the parliament. Riots destroyed shops and banks, resulting in the death by fire of three employees who had been working in a shuttered branch of Marfin Bank. This event would be used politically against the escalation of protests and against the left as a whole. It took until the next year, May 2011, for large protests to resume, and they did so spectacularly with the 'Aganaktisménoi' movement of public square occupations.

In 2011, GSEE called six general strikes, accompanied by demonstrations of growing size and intensity. Yet the Aganaktisménoi movement, which began through calls on Facebook for daily demonstrations and assemblies in squares, and lasted until the end of July, has been the largest and most significant event to date of grassroots resistance to the austerity measures. The movement, inspired by the Indignados in Spain only weeks earlier, as well as the Tahrir Square occupation in Egypt, can be said to have expressed the deep legitimation crisis of parliamentary politics at that moment. Most importantly, it was also novel, as a form of struggle, in terms of its composition, its forms of practice, and for the unprecedented resilience that great numbers of people showed in the street.[1]

---

1. My account here is very condensed. For more details, see my daily blog of events in the squares: Break the Blackout, 'Updates from the Greek Squares and People's Assemblies', Metamute.org, 1/7/2011.

From the very beginning, the movement was split politically. There were two different types of Facebook calls to the protest. Some pages, filled with Greek flags, called on all 'indignant Greek citizens' to rise up, while others, following the Spanish example, called on everyone to unite under the demand for 'real democracy'. The difference in language is significant. 'Indignant citizens' (*aganaktisménoi polítes*), beyond merely a translation of the Spanish word *indignados*, is a self-appellation long adopted by far-right groups in their protests against or direct attacks on immigrants, Roma and squatters. Thus the more conservative wing of the movement preferred the term *aganaktisménoi*, while the left wing called it 'the movement of the squares' or used the slogan 'real/direct democracy now'. The division was most visible in the occupation of Syntagma Square in Athens, which was split between an upper part, on Amalias' Avenue facing the parliament, and a lower part, which formed the main part of the occupation and the square. The upper part was where nationalist organisations, such as the '300 Greeks' – a direct reference to the 480 BC battle of Thermopylae against a Persian invasion – had set up stalls.[2] It tended to attract crowds with Greek flags, ultra-masculine groups of young nationalists who shouted slogans the loudest and conspiracy theorists holding eccentric self-made banners. The lower part was where assemblies were held. It was dominated by a diversity of left-wing activists, who had hope that 'political fermentation' through discussion would generate new political subjectivities and unite the struggle.

The paradox was that, despite this obvious *political* split, the movement rejected 'politics' altogether. 'Burn the parliament', was one of the most popular slogans, and the movement was presented (with enthusiastic support from mainstream media, in the first few days) as one that rejected political parties and traditional forms of organisation such as unions: 'Greek citizens' were being peacefully united 'beyond political colours' against foreign political and economic control over the country and the 'traitor' politicians who allowed it. Thus no political affiliations were openly revealed, because one of the rules was for the protest to be 'party-less', 'colour-less' (in the sense of party colour, not skin colour) and 'flag-less' (with the exception of the Greek flag, of course). This opened the way to all kinds of party activists and newcomers with political

---

2. The '300 Greeks' attempted to summon patriotic pride against the humiliation of national debt and political corruption. Greek citizens ought to unite and re-empower their nation in a disciplined and lawful way, like an army.

ambitions to spread their ideas and become known, without attaching their ideology to a voting choice.

Which of the two sides was the most numerous is anyone's guess, but on the first day conservatism conspired with a rigid anti-political stance to boo out of Syntagma Square a trade union march of DEI (National Electricity Company) workers. The main reason was not so much a critique of unions but that they violated the call to come without flags or banners, as 'people', not as a group of workers making demands 'just' for themselves. Thus, at a time when wages were rapidly becoming unable to cover the cost of basic commodities like rent and heating for growing numbers of the subordinate classes, this movement began as radically separate from any labour struggle. Instead, the movement mobilised the subject of the *Greek citizen* – identifying as primarily democratic or primarily patriotic or both – towards the rejection of Greece's political system, combined, contradictorily, with a *demand* against austerity.

The language of citizenship, present in both the democratic and nationalist camps, contained an imaginary of destroying and rebuilding the national polity in this moment of crisis, and this required a form of national unity among those present, represented by national flags and the Greek cultural gesture of the *mountza*: the masses extended all fingers of their hands and presented their palms towards the parliament. The common-sense necessity of national unity was itself provoked by the way in which the crisis and restructuring appeared on the political scene: as an 'external' material blackmailing, imposed either by monitoring institutions (the IMF, the ECB and the EC) or by the anonymous agency of 'banks' and 'financiers',[3] but also as an event of internal 'corruption'. The corruption discourse was forcefully pursued by the creditors themselves, along with politicians on both sides of the debate, albeit with one core difference. Those who supported the restructuring maintained a concept of clientelistic corruption, epitomised by the infamous statement of PASOK politician Theodoros Pangalos, that 'we all ate together'.[4] Their opponents argued that corruption favoured the tax evasion of moneyed elites. Despite the class distinction, both versions counted on the orientalist stereotypes discussed in Part I: a narrative of decadence, and the notion of Greek inability to live up to 'European' standards of lawful state and citizen conduct.

---

3. For more on this see Chapter 3.
4. Pangalos even elaborated on this statement in a self-published book of the same title: Theódōros G. Págkalos, *Ta Fágame Óloi Mazí* (Athens: T. G. Págkalos, 2012).

The movement of the squares was thus contradictory. Parts of it were a pure conservative nationalist explosion, with the Greek citizen at its centre demanding the redisciplining of the political sphere – 'get rid of the fraudsters, the immoral, the thieves' – and, in some cases, rejecting democracy altogether in favour of a violent and dictatorial solution. This was represented by slogans like 'take the traitors to Goudi', referring to the 1922 execution of six politicians and army officers thought responsible for the 'Asia-Minor catastrophe'.[5] But others sought to self-organise, to participate in popular assemblies, and were critical of the central instrument of state politics, the parliament. Some spoke of direct democracy and others of reform. It was an important political moment, given the very wide, spontaneous and sustained participation by people who had never been involved in protests before. It was also a protest against austerity, which betrayed a certain class content to it, even though the latter was broad, given that, apart from cuts, labour market deregulation and layoffs, the mid-term programme of reforms also removed protections for small businesses, which had already suffered in the crisis.[6]

These characteristics attracted many on the left, from anarchists to left-wing party members, who wished to influence the assemblies and prevent anti-political fascistic tendencies from dominating the movement. This left and anarchist influence meant that the call for 'real democracy now' quickly changed to 'direct democracy now', and calls for self-organisation overshadowed the anti-corruption discourse, which had also dominated the Spanish Indignados assemblies. The call for 'direct democracy' rejected dominant avenues of representation, and worked to create structures of self-organisation – 'taking our lives into our own hands'. In the central assembly declaration, the movement's collective subject came to be described in terms of employment statuses and ages – 'we are workers, unemployed, pensioners, youth' – in an indirect reference to class. It also emphasised the collective process of 'co-shaping all our demands', and asserted a resoluteness inspired from

5. The massacre and mass displacement of Greek civilians in Anatolia and the Aegean coast by Turkish forces, after the Greek army's failed attempt to annex lands in the region.
6. The Mid-Term programme and the corresponding executive legal framework (N. 3986/2011 AK., FEK A' 152/01.07.2011) outlined cuts to services, wages, pensions and (what little remained of) benefits, and public sector layoffs, along with a long list of privatisations. It also aimed to deregulate protected industries and professions, for example, taxi companies and drivers. It further forecast that despite the scale of cuts, by 2015 Greece's external debt would only have been reduced by a tiny fraction.

the 2001 Argentinean movements: 'we will not leave the squares until those who have brought us here go away: governments, the Troika, banks, Memoranda and all those who exploit us. We send them the message that the debt is not ours'. It thus rejected, unreservedly, any notion that citizens were in any way implicated in, or responsible for, the accumulation of debt – the ideology upon which the imposition of austerity was based.

The 'direct democratic' imaginary envisioned a system of inclusive, bottom-up decision making, self-organised resistance and mutual support in neighbourhoods and workplaces, inspired, again, by Argentina, as well as building on local assemblies and actions that had existed since December 2008 across the country. The core advocates of 'direct democracy' in the assemblies were committed to the notion that a more 'decent' life would be possible, if only the citizens had the political power. The assemblies, ranging in numbers daily from a hundred to a few thousand people, were the central tool of decision making for the movement, in which anyone could speak, although for one minute only, after joining a queue. This meant that often there was not much of a dialogue, and many participants did not get the chance to speak, but proposals were made that were then put to the vote. The dominant force (inside the assembly organising committee, the only one whose members were not rotated) was that of SYRIZA members who hid their party identity. Later, 'thematic' groups were formed, in which discussions could actually be had, both face to face and online, which took on particular responsibilities (like food and cleaning, or art and making banners) or worked on collecting information on topics that concerned the protests, such as the sovereign debt. There was a group that offered free school support to children, one that advocated for workers and the unemployed, one for gender, one that discussed the meaning of direct democracy, a legal team, a medical team and more. A large number of new neighbourhood assemblies were added to those that had existed since December 2008 across the country, which reported back to assemblies and participated in the organising.

Amid all this activity, many tensions and debates came up, which indexed the antinomies that a united 'popular' movement in Greece would face in this particular conjuncture. Most obvious and intense was the question of nationalism and the movement's relation to non-citizen immigrants. A couple of left-wing speakers reminded the assembly, from the very first day, about the four-day anti-immigrant pogrom orchestrated by GD in the centre of Athens only a few days earlier, which had resulted in 25 hospitalisations and the murder of a young Bangladeshi man, Alim Abdul Manan.[7] A day against racism and xenophobia was also organised. In the daytime, migrants' groups set up information stalls and organised games for children. Teams of Pakistani immigrants took over Amalias Avenue – the space of nationalists – to play cricket, and Pakistani women made henna tattoos for demonstrators. There were talks from the African Women's Association, Action Congo, the Pakistani Community of Greece and Lahsan Karza, one of the 300 hunger strikers discussed in Part III. An open discussion followed, in which immigrants had to respond to a Greek man who, after denying he was racist, said that 'we don't want so many immigrants here [in Greece]'. They put forward multiple arguments: that Afghani immigrants are escaping wars to which Greece contributed, that Syrians are escaping a murderous regime, and they criticised with clarity, using stories and examples, the notion that immigrants are 'taking away jobs and money'. Some asked for class solidarity against the state and employers, describing how they are being exploited as workers and how impossible the Greek bureaucracy has made it for them to gain legal permits to stay. Many did not state their nationality to make a point about common humanity: 'I came from the earth'; 'I came from my mother's womb'.

It is hard, however, to interpret this day as much more than a gesture of friendship by a section of the movement to immigrants, who were taken by definition to be *external* to the movement. On the contrary, nationalist and far-right groups and individuals were thought to automatically 'harmlessly' belong, except in cases of racist violence. Not everyone liked the day against racism. The far-right 'Citizens' Movement', which had called on 'Greek citizens to protest in Syntagma with Greek flags', said on their website that those who 'have as point of reference the equality of "gender and race"' represent 'a circus of the political decay that has corrupted our society'. The left-dominated assembly simply waited for groups like them and the '300 Greeks' to decide on their own to leave.

But why would they leave? The movement took for granted as its subject the *unity of national citizens*, who organised democratically against a failed system of government – and not a unity of class or of any other social dimension that transcends national belonging. Given this

---

7. Used as an opportunity the mugging and murder of a Greek man by, according to the police, three Afghan men. Judith Sunderland et al., *Hate on the Streets* (New York: Human Rights Watch, 2012).

assumption, immigrants were excluded not just exceptionally, by racist individuals, but *by definition*, by the very concept of citizenship. The boundaries of the space were unspokenly – but unambiguously – national and racial. The self-policing of these boundaries by a rotating group of 'peacemakers' resulted, on one occasion, in them kicking immigrant street vendors out of the square, based on the assembly decision that no trading was allowed within the space. Despite the active criticism of racist statements that were occasionally made in the assemblies and the expulsion of violent racist groups from the occupation, the movement's national boundaries were rarely challenged. In such a context, the call for 'direct democracy' and self-institution itself also appealed to national pride, with evocations of ancient Athens.[8] Again, the democracy, while direct, was also to be exclusive: only Greek citizens would participate as a matter of course.

Thus, the lines of demarcation between the 'upper' and 'lower' parts of Syntagma were blurred, along with the political demarcation between 'left' and 'right', which anyhow the movement from the start claimed to have overcome. In one of the working groups, I met a young ship-building worker who supported communist workers' militancy and also had a visceral, unchallengeable hatred of 'Pakistanis'. Rather than interpreting his case as a mere exception, his seamless interactions with most people in the group exemplified the way in which the nationalisation of class brought together left-wing and far-right radical discourses to allow space for a kind of third-positionist fascism. Mikis Theodorakis, the 80-something anti-dictatorship activist and composer of songs for that struggle, was the only politician allowed to stage a rally for his third-positionist party, Spitha, not far from the square, while it was occupied, flooding it with his supporters. The rally was massive, and his speech was indicative: 'Our national wealth', he said, 'will be taken over by Turks and blacks from Timbuktu!' Later, groups of 'autonomous nationalists' demanding 'jobs for Greek workers' appeared in the square temporarily, before being asked to leave. The anti-political drive for autonomous citizens' organising and the discourse of 'beyond left and right' was then not so much of the liberal 'third way' kind than it was defined by national unity, and constant interventions had to be made to

---

8. This discourse often referred to Cornelius Castoriadis's work, particularly that which has valorised an idealised image of ancient Athenian democracy – a much-needed boost to the humiliated Greek national identity. See, Cornelius Castoriadis, *Philosophy, Politics, Autonomy* (New York: Oxford University Press, 1991).

stop the racism embedded in this national unity from expressing itself openly.

For the same reason, there was very little tension over what the class identity of the citizens was. Despite calls to expand the energy of the squares to workplaces, and the careful use of working-class-relevant words in the Syntagma Square declaration ('workers, unemployed, pensioners'), it could not be denied that participation included broader social strata of small business owners who were hurt severely by austerity. At the same time, insofar as the assembly and demonstrations reflected the composition of the population, the great majority would indeed have been waged workers. Thus this was probably more a question of identity and political hegemony than a question of composition: the subject of the worker was overshadowed by the citizen subject. Attempts by militants to establish a classic discourse of class conflict and exploitation were unsuccessful, and labour reforms and wages were discussed much less than issues of national debt, 'sell offs' of 'national assets', tax hikes and the devastation of public services. The assemblies placed 'democratic citizens' in the position of trying to solve these national economic problems, inviting experts to present economic analyses, as opposed to simply resisting cuts or demanding wages as past class-based movements would have done. While these national economic problems affected the lower economic strata most immediately, they were seen as predominantly related to a democratic deficit than to exploitation at work. Ideas like tax payment stoppages, and alternative currencies and economies, concerned the sphere of consumption. Despite the convergence in the street between the movement of the squares and two general strikes called by GSEE, on 15 and 29 June, there was no immediate connection or coordination between strikes and activities in the squares.

There was even less discussion of the gendered dimensions either of the crisis or of the commonplace male dominance in activism and politics, despite the creation of a thematic assembly for gender. The group organised discussions on gender violence and the impact of crisis on women and LGBTQI+, along with 'theatre of the oppressed' performances. They intervened in the general assembly, pointing out that all the 'expert' speakers invited to Syntagma had been male, that the audience was often only addressed in the male gender and that the repeatedly mentioned national ideal of 'Athenian democracy' was one that excluded women and immigrants. Their intervention highlighted the degree to which gender power relations were invisible at Syntagma and it did not seem to have a significant impact. Relations in the square reproduced everyday gendered relations outside it, since these were rarely openly questioned, other than by minorities like the assembly on gender.

Then again, the boundaries of the movement's self-organised practice against the elements of the social order it *did* oppose were perforated in many respects, continually brought back to face material realities in the social conditions of the crisis. The attempt to develop more immediate social relations within the square – through the rejection of money, a free collective kitchen, free lessons for homeless children – after a while met the limits of handling these social problems autonomously in any sustained way. Soon, we saw the return of money, and the closure of the kitchen, because it attracted too many homeless and addicted people. Besides, this inability to provide social care for the poor autonomously was already recognised in the movement's demands to the state – namely, the rejection of the mid-term austerity programme, which was one significant cause of immiseration.

Thus the language of material autonomy, 'taking our lives into our own hands', was mostly symbolic, in the face of a de facto heteronomy: the material dependence of each individual on the state, not only through benefits, pensions, wages and welfare, but at the most abstract economic level, its guarantee of money and currency, all of which fuelled the movement's protest against the new measures. Any discussion of actual opposition to the state, then, or the language of storming the parliament, was hyperbolic. While the assemblies made plans to surround the parliament on demonstration days, this was proven, in practice, to have been far from the agenda, as few people turned up on time to do so. This also demonstrated the limited authority that the Syntagma Square assembly had over the demonstrations that took place.

The movement's daily practice of organising, working, sharing, thinking and even living together, for those who had set up tents in Syntagma Square, provided to many participants a sense of solidarity and hope that a lot could be achieved by finding others who were hit by the crisis. Others were disappointed by the control over the assemblies by left-wing groups and departed at an early stage. Meanwhile, the daily demonstrations peaked and waned, and there was a lot of organising leading up to the day of the vote.

The general strike of 15 June, which had been called by GSEE before the movement had begun, was one of the most important events that escalated into extended riots in Syntagma Square. It was not so significant as a strike than it was as a massive and confrontational demonstration, which almost caused the prime minister to resign. The extreme police repression and extensive anti-police clashes and rioting that took place during the strike brought up renewed conflict within the assemblies, when the majority rejected a motion that condemned 'violence in all its forms'. This moment was a major turning point that brought to the surface an unresolved debate around protesters' violence.

The movement's relative tolerance of persistent clashes with the police was not so much indicative of an anarchist influence on demonstrations and assemblies, as of a wider social tendency towards the acceptability of violence against representatives of the state. Since 2009, the age range of those participating in riots broadened, as was also evident in the movement in Keratea a few months earlier. On 15 June, photos of rioting old-aged men and women were circulating on social media. Altogether, the rioters accounted for a significant subsection of the demonstration, to the extent that much of the assembly audience responded to hackneyed left-wing conspiracy theories about 'violent agent provocateurs' by declaring that 'the rioters are us'.

The next important event, around which the very life of the movement – and its core defensive demand – was constructed, was on 29 June, when the mid-term programme was being put to the vote. Once more the demonstration was extremely large, and, amid the news that the mid-term was being passed in parliament, rioting, as well as police repression of the demonstration, became exceptionally fierce. Riot police beat protesters ruthlessly, chased them into Metro platforms, attacked volunteer medical support teams and drove motorcycles indiscriminately into crowds that had been hiding in pedestrianised alleys. This convinced many more of those who had advocated peaceful protesting that police violence was not the result of provocation but of the state's extreme intolerance of demonstrations. But this did not put an end to the debate on violence. Those who took part in clashes and stayed to defend the square after everyone else had been chased away felt that their contribution was not recognised by everyone, and indeed some branded them as 'troublemakers'. This reflected partly the difficulty of political coexistence in Syntagma of anarchists and other leftists, and partly a split among those who did not belong to any of these groups. For some, the claims to superior knowledge by organised groups of activists presented a problem: 'I don't want the specialists of declarations, nor do I want the specialists of violence'.

Severely weakened by the defeat of its core demand, as well as its internal incongruences, combined with zero-tolerance policing of the square, the occupation at Syntagma and most other cities dragged on, with reduced participation, for one more month. Amid threats that the few remaining tents would be forcibly removed by the municipal police, the square was further depopulated, until the police made their surprise attack, ransacking the by now small occupation, on 30 July.

The movement of the squares was the locus of significant transformations in collective action: the expansion of popular participation in activities like mass demonstrations, assemblies and rioting; the multiplication of local assemblies and self-organised action against austerity; the creation of structures of solidarity and mutual support in the crisis; the social legitimation of public space occupations and refusing payment of new taxes or bills; the endurance of enormous numbers of people in the face of serious police violence and heavy use of teargas. These elements figured in the struggles of the following months and years.

Beyond a locus of transformation, however, the movement was also an index of what a 'popular movement' would look like in Greece, were it to establish itself. There, its limits, as well as the limits of 'popular unity' as a strategy in the current conjuncture, become very obvious. It is possible to claim that the internal distances within the movement – between extreme nationalism and a democratic anti-racism; between making demands and rejecting them in favour of self-organisation; between citizenism and class politics; between violence and non-violence – produced new discourses and practices among those who struggled. However, the shifts produced remained tied to a conservative imaginary. The discourse of democracy came to openly embrace the nation, despite internal criticism and challenges to overt racism, and it excluded 'foreign' non-citizens by definition. A community of struggle that would transcend a narrow national identity did not enter the political imagination, except when it was expressed by immigrants invited to the square for a day. A 'third' option was produced, beyond the opposition between demanding from a state unable or unwilling to deliver and turning to the self-management of poverty, that of the violent attack on politicians, instruments and symbols of the state. Rioting was the 'fighting back' at the violence of austerity, police oppression, and – for those who also broke into and looted a few high-end shops – against the barrier of poverty, which is a barrier of access to commodities. Yet the national framing of this violent practice meant that it did not at all entail a deepening criticism of social, economic and political structures. Everyday attacks on individual politicians limited social criticism to questions of individual responsibility and truly patriotic leadership, as became even more evident in subsequent events.

Relevant to the legacy of the movement of the squares were the angry interventions across the country against political celebrities at school and military parades for the 28 October national celebration.[9] Parading pupils turned their faces away from the President of the Republic, state officials were heckled and assaulted, and they were forced to abandon their platforms as crowds took them over. Military parades were cancelled, but some of the armed forces did parade in protest, amid cheers by the crowd. The dictator Metaxas' refusal to surrender to Mussolini's forces in 1940 is commemorated on 28 October, giving meaning to the protest as another popular expression of 'anti-establishment' authoritarian nationalism. The presence of parts of the left in the protests revealed its overlaps with such tendencies. Vague and still in flux at that moment, after the 2012 elections a clearer, anachronistic far-right narrative would emerge that was nostalgic of the Metaxas regime.

These events, despite their failure to achieve the slightest change in policy, demonstrated the depth of the political crisis.[10] The prime minister, George Papandreou, in an attempt to disassociate himself from the disintegration in his party over the mid-term vote, proposed a referendum on Greece's participation in the Eurozone in the first weeks of November.[11] This was rejected by the EU, most political parties, as well as members of his own party. Papandreou then resigned, claiming that he did so in the name of democracy.[12] A new technocratic coalition government was soon formed under Lucas Papademos, with the right-wing ND and far-right LAOS (Popular Orthodox Rally) joining PASOK in a promise to carry on with the restructuring.[13]

The stability this created was very fragile. Three months later, on 12 February 2012, the government had to vote on the second memorandum of reforms, which reduced the minimum wage by 22 per cent and 35 per

---

9. 'Mataiōseis kai Epeisódia stis Pareláseis se Ólī tī Chōra', *Vīma*, 28/10/2011.

10. Paúlos Papadópoulos, 'To Dramatikó Paraskīnio tōn Dýo Etōn tou Mnīmoníou', *Vīma*, 16/10/2011. This article claims to expose the backstage struggles within PASOK in the crisis, and their climax in October 2011.

11. 'Papandréou: Dīmopsīfisma stis 4 Dekemvríou me Erōtīma "Nai ī Óchi sto Eurō"', *Éthnos*, 3/11/2011.

12. Kerin Hope, 'Humiliating End to Greece's Social Reformer', *Financial Times*, 6/11/2011.

13. Kerin Hope, 'Papademos Named New Greek PM', *Financial Times*, 10/11/2011.

cent for those under 25, shortened the validity of collective bargaining agreements so that minimum wages could be paid after their expiry and prohibited wage rises until unemployment fell below 10 per cent.[14] This provoked the largest – and the last – truly mass event of the crisis period. The city centre burst with up to half a million people, after a 48-hour strike with low participation, probably because mass coordinated strikes had failed to gain results in October. The police forces on their part made sure demonstrators understood their insignificance by emptying Syntagma Square very early in the day. Insofar as the government, parliament and mainstream media were concerned, the square, where all the cameras were stationed, was empty, and the protests did not exist. But, in the invisible side streets, large-scale riots broke out – the most widespread since December 2008 – with broad participation in terms of age and social background. Rioters, whether it was the organised 'black bloc' or casual groups of demonstrators, were cheered on by the crowd.

The escalation of riots revealed not only the degree to which social demands had been rejected by that point, not only the fear that democracy had collapsed under the new technocratic government (would there be elections again?), but also the way in which social discontent had been repressed. The police was their core target, their rage having been built up over a year of increasingly violent policing. And it was no longer only immigrants, anarchists and leftists who were oppressed by the police, but 'regular citizens' as well.

Especially visible was a section of rioters, familiar from the movement of the squares, who saw the crisis as a conflict between 'the citizens of the nation' and 'traitor politicians'. Many of them likened the police to *germanotsoliádes*, the Greek paramilitary forces set up by German occupiers in World War II. This was part of the often startling political and ideological flux between left- and right-wing discourses that characterised the period just before the 2012 elections. Only two months later, in a demonstration for Dimitris Christoulas – a man who had committed a public suicide in protest against the bailout agreements and his own impoverishment – members of the '300 Greeks' patriotic organisation were shouting the anarchist slogan 'cops are not the workers' sons, they are the bosses' dogs'. While the rightist, patriotic strand of the Aganaktisménoi had questioned the democratic state in ways familiar to the history of the Greek far right, it had been unheard

---

14. N. 4046/2012 AK.

of for patriotic citizens' organisations to riot against the police and to use the discourse of 'workers' and 'bosses'. Conversely, a demonstration of pro-armed-struggle young anarchists protested Christoulas' death with slogans that placed themselves, as supporters of the terrorist organisation 'Cells of Fire Conspiracy', within a notional lineage of communist national liberation struggle: 'EAM, ELAS, Pyrīnes tīs Fōtiás'.

This apparent flux of political boundaries nonetheless did not produce a unification or a new collective subject, whether at the level of practice or ideology, as became clearer after the elections. On 12 February, while fighting against the police was accepted by almost everyone present, one would observe variations, even disputes in the street, as to what types of rioting were acceptable. A distance existed between those who only clashed with the police, those who also smashed and burnt banks, and those who went on to loot and burn shops and even entire buildings.

Despite the deaths at Marfin, the smashing or firebombing of banks had gained broader acceptance. Not only the generalisation of household debt in the crisis, but also the fetishism of finance explains this. When the crisis manifests itself as public debt, whose burden is then passed on indiscriminately to the lower strata, finance capital, represented by banks, immediately appears to be the beneficiary of widespread suffering. On the contrary, 'productive' capital and its employers, that which produces and distributes tangible commodities and 'provides' working-class jobs, is seen as a victim of the crisis, or, at least, as disconnected from any of its causes.

This can at least partially explain why the wider acceptance of bank burning did not extend to shop burning and looting, and why the reticence to violate private property only applied to shops, with some protesters intervening to protect them. The rejection of looting also reflects the wide distribution of small property and small business in Greece. While wider participation in the riots then was a violent criticism of the government, the police, and finance, the same actions saw the nation, its 'people' and its national 'productive' capital as what ought to be protected.

The looting and destruction of shops and buildings was thus the most minoritarian, condemned and exposed to the police. Its composition was most similar to that of December 2008, consisting of younger, unemployed or precariously employed, and immigrant rioters.[15] Their

---

15. 'To Profíl tōn Syllīfthéntōn', *Vīma*, 13/2/2012.

actions reflected a lack of future, in contrast to a certain hope that held onto the democratic or violent replacement of 'traitors' and the reaffirmation of national unity, national capital and liberation from 'foreign control'. But looting and shop destruction has not been unique to Greece during this crisis. In many contemporary riots, from London (August 2011), to Sweden (May 2013), to Argentina (December 2013), to Ferguson (August 2014), rioters expropriated goods and destroyed shops and other private property. Such rioters are often immigrants and people of colour, who face not just the limits of their proletarian condition, concretely experienced as lack of access to commodities, but also racialisation.

But despite the participation of immigrants in rioting, in contrast to December 2008, the general character of these riots was *national*. The composition of the demonstration, as well as its context, was associated with a demand, no matter how defunct, which presupposed the demanding subject of a citizen. This citizen faced not only the degradation of everyday life, but also the *national* question of Greece's sovereignty and economic dependence. The nation (and, with that, race) emerged as the focal point of social conflicts after the 2012 elections.

6

Labour and Superfluity

What happens to labour struggles in a context of extreme unemployment, amid a global capitalist crisis *and* a sovereign debt crisis that expands surplus populations? There is a precursor to the situation in Greece, albeit having taken place in a different international conjuncture: that of the crisis in Argentina. There, we saw the emergence of movements of self-management – takeovers of closing businesses by workers – and movements of the unemployed, the *piqueteros*, which evolved into expanded informal or 'popular' economies.[1] In the case of Greece, things were somewhat different: there were only a few initiatives for the self-management of closing businesses, but a large number of occupations. The social struggles of precarious workers, on the other hand, tended to use tactics of blockade and protest outside workplaces. Organisations of the unemployed, which were not particularly numerous, mostly focused on obtaining forms of welfare, and self-organised alternative economies and co-operatives also responded to the condition of unemployment, but these developed separately from labour movements.

Where it came to migrant workers, their established separation from citizens continued, although this has been less ideologically pronounced than in the movement of the squares. While, from 1990 onwards, unions developed a relatively supportive stance to migrant workers, they, at the same time, failed to advance a concerted strategy for integration, something that was made harder by the fact that the state dealt with migrant labour as a question of policing. Thus, despite their more internationalist attitude – at least on paper – than that of many unions in Western Europe who take an open stance against immigration, few unions in Greece can be said to have become inclusive and multiethnic in a way that reflects the working population, especially where it comes to the more recent immigrants from Asia, Africa and the Middle East. Thus, in the crisis, immigrant workers staged a number of small struggles separately, whose demands and outcomes are so intimately tied to the

---

1. Verónica Gago, *Neoliberalism from Below* (Durham, NC: Duke University Press, 2017).

question of race and the inclusive exclusion produced by the policing of immigration that I discuss them separately in Part III, focusing on this deepening social division in Greece.

Although there was a high number of strikes over 2010–14, those tended to be in the public sector and in the large unionised industries of the private sector.[2] In the remaining sectors and workplaces, grassroots unions attempted to stage resistance under extremely difficult conditions. These struggles were, in most cases, disconnected from each other, except when GSEE and ADEDY (the public sector unions confederation) launched one- or two-day general strikes, of which there were 32 between 2010 and 2014.[3] As to their demands, indicatively, in 2011 more than half of the strikes protested business closures or mass layoffs, and one of the top demands was to receive unpaid wages.[4] The restructuring produced these major issues with legislation that eased the process of company closures and mass layoffs, made it easier to justify delayed wages and enabled mass wage cuts – the third most common cause of strikes. After 2012, there was a steep decline in strikes as a practice of struggle, and an increase in demonstrations and protests, reflecting their lack of success, business closures and the rise in unemployment.[5]

A peak event of labour struggle was the 48-hour strike of 19–20 October 2011. Collective energies were directed to stage 'the mother of all strikes' and one of the largest demonstrations in decades, which many hoped could topple the government and halt or slow the progress of austerity. The government had announced measures that would invalidate existing collective bargaining agreements and impose mass layoffs and 30 per cent wage cuts in the public sector.[6] After a week of grassroots activism in workplaces to push for participation in the strike and for occupations in the public sector, including ministries,[7] GSEE was pushed to extend the strike to 48 hours.[8] Occupations are not a regular occurrence in the public sector, so their dynamism and perseverance was significant, especially in cases where they were met

2. Dīmítrīs Papanikolópoulos, 'Ī Syndikalistikī Dynamikī 2010–15', Enīmérōsī, no. 232 (2016): 2–28.

3. 'GSEE-ADEDY: Se Apergiakó Kloió ī Elláda', Īmerísía, 27/11/2014.

4. Katsorídas and Lampousákī, 'Apergíes 2011'.

5. Dimitra Kotouza, 'Practices of Labor Activism in Greece', Journal of Labor and Society 20, no. 3 (2017): 379–97.

6. N. 4024/2011 AK.

7. 'Me Katalīpseis Ypourgeíōn Apantoún oi Ergazómenoi', Nautemporikī, 4/10/2011.

8. 'Mparáz Katalīpseōn – 48ōrī ī Genikī Apergía', TVXS.gr, 13/10/2011.

with obfuscating resistance by managers or by sectoral unions. Athens waste collectors, despite their vilification by mass media for the impact on 'public hygiene', and the prefecture's attempt to break the strike though outsourcing, persisted and successfully blockaded private collection vans.[9] The week of mobilisations was also accompanied by a series of small demonstrations by local neighbourhood assemblies.[10] The massive scale of the general strike of 19–20 October, with increased participation from the private sector, added to the paralysis of the country's public services and infrastructure.[11]

The trend of escalating violence in demonstrations between 2010 and 2012 continued, but there was a difference. The street clashes were not between demonstrators and the police, but between the KKE union's PAME (All-Workers Militant Front) cadre and anarchists – including potentially others – who wanted to riot. This happened because PAME, contrary to its usual practice of marching separately from the main demonstration, decided on 20 October to take over the space in front of the parliament, effectively guarding it with its disciplined lines of men armed with thick flagpoles that could be used as weapons. The KKE's discourse justified such an action, since it has consistently branded all rioters as 'agent provocateurs', whose aim is to sabotage working-class struggle.[12] For anarchists and members of other unions, this was a provocation.[13] True to the machismo of left-wing displays of strength, anarchist demonstrators had also come carrying the same type of flagpoles, and the fight was on.

In all the significant demonstrations since May 2010, including that of the previous day, a large and diverse section of the crowd had aimed at pushing against the police lines that protected the parliament. In the aftermath of the movement of the squares, it had also become clear to demonstrators that police violence was unprovoked and part of their

9. 'POE-OTA: Klimákōsī me "Katalīpseis kai Apergiakés Frourés"', Vīma, 16/10/2011; 'Ī Periféreia Attikīs Éspase tīn Apergía!', blog thread, Indymedia Athens, 14 October 2011.

10. Examples: '15 Oktōvríou Óloi Mazí!', Syneleysipalaioyfaliroy.wordpress.com, 15/10/2011; 'Apofáseis tīs Laïkīs Synéleusīs Kallithéas 7/10/2011', Syneleysikallitheas.blogspot.com, 9/10/2011.

11. 'Evdomáda Kinītopoiīseōn', Vīma, 10/10/2011; 'Se Kloió Pallaïkoú "Óchi", ī Voulī tou "Nai"', Eleutherotypía, 20 October 2011.

12. An example is the reception of the December 2008 riots in Rizospástis, the official newspaper of KKE. Níkos Mpogiópoulos, 'Koukoulofóroi', Rizospástis, 10/12/2008.

13. Ian Delta, Michael Th, Filosofia Amos and JKL, 'Líga Lógia gia tīn 20/10', Eagainst, 22/10/2011; Pantelīs Authínos and Zétta Melampianákī, 'Gia ta Gegonóta stis 20 Oktōvríou 2011', Aformi, 24/10/2011.

strategy. Now that there were clashes, the police reaction was even stronger, and a PAME unionist died from the teargas.[14] The conflict was widely understood as a short-sighted sectarian clash and as a depressing instance of disunity at a very critical moment.[15] But its occurrence can also be interpreted symbolically.

At a time of persistent weakness for the labour movement, the KKE attempted to take advantage of this new spark of struggle and promote itself by showcasing its traditional leadership role: creating an orderly movement of workers who can in theory take over state power. Yet not only did the KKE's own power fail to correspond to this nostalgic ideal of the class, but it also rejected any emerging potential in contemporary struggles that did not correspond to this ideal. Its *performance* of that ideal – a strong and cohesive working class that is proud of its work and poses a threat to the state precisely by its numbers, hierarchical organisation and discipline – managed to turn into an obstacle. The anarchists' disorderly charge against the KKE bloc symbolised the fragility of this nostalgic act. Even at the highest point of labour struggles in this period, then, the ghost of workers' power was exorcised, not only by the state, but from within the movement itself.

Indeed, the restructuring left little space for this type of posturing, and the steep rise in unemployment that came with it made unionised workers – those whose union membership meant something – seem like a privileged class of a previous era. The restructured legal framework legitimised a type of work relation that was previously more typical under the precarious conditions of informal employment. Informal employment itself became more widespread, because, in addition to lack of labour protection, the lack of demand for labour forced workers to accept unlawful terms of employment.[16]

The long-term strike of the steelworkers is indicative. After over nine months of striking, occupying their factory and mobilising support from the left, the strike was crushed in August 2012, when riot police broke into the factory to let the management in. After the strikers agreed to

---

14. Dīmītrīs Galánīs, 'Enas Nekrós kai Dekádes Traumatíes sto Syllalītīrio sto Sýntagma', *Vīma*, 20/10/2011.

15. Ibid.

16. Roúla Salourou, 'Efialtikés Diastáseis Lamvánei ī Adīlótī Ergasía mésa stīn Krísī', *Kathīmerinī*, 29/3/2015. The payment of social security contributions is not automatic and depends on the lawfulness of the employer. In the crisis, the number of undeclared workers has risen, particularly in the hospitality sector.

return to work, the management fired six of them. Worse, 24 of the strikers were convicted and sentenced to between 21 and 23 months in prison for contravening a court decision against the strike and for 'illegal violence'.[17] Not only striking but also other forms of protest became criminalised, such as demonstrating outside workplaces and withdrawing labour when unpaid – wages could not be demanded if the employer had financial difficulties.[18] The dissolution of any form of labour 'justice' was comprehensive and even violated the most basic principle of the wage relation: getting paid.

Self-Management, Co-operatives and Unemployment

Within left-wing social media, much was made in recent years of self-management initiatives in Greece, in anticipation that a wave of takeovers would happen as in Argentina. In reality, there were very few such initiatives, even if workers did occupy many workplaces to prevent closures. Vio.Me. was the only case of a straightforward takeover of a factory. After being owed several months' wages by the company's absentee owners, Vio.Me. workers confiscated the machinery and materials of the factory and started production themselves. Helped by new legislation for co-operatives, they formed a new company, and in February 2013 they began producing eco-friendly cleaning products. Their choice was not only aimed at subsistence but was also politically motivated. They have long campaigned in the hope that company takeovers would spread: 'the message carried by our products is that workers and unemployed must take our lives into our own hands, fight decisively against the barbarism of contemporary reality, and to rid ourselves of centuries of exploitation and oppression'. The products also carry 'the message of a wholly different life, from the way we work to our relationship to the environment'.[19]

According to the workers, five years later the factory employs 24 workers who receive incomes that they do not yet consider 'decent' enough.[20] The legal wrangles with the previous owners over the company's bankruptcy and the auctioning of the land and buildings have not ended, threatening

17. 'Se 21 éōs 23 Mīnes Fylákisī Katadikástīkan oi Apergoí Chalyvourgoí', Augī, 9/4/2014.
18. Ar. 281 AK.
19. Vio.Me. Synergatiki, 'Arhiki Selída', Viomecoop.com.
20. Kóstas Papantoníou, 'Vio.Me: 5 Chrónia to Ergostásio Tōn Ergazoménōn', Interviews, 3PointMagazine.gr, 6/3/2018.

the continuation of the endeavour. Workers, along with their supporters, have been protesting in the courts and at the Ministry of Labor against this decision, where clashes with riot police have sometimes taken place as protesters set up tents outside the ministry.[21] Vio.Me. workers are also in direct conflict with the union representing over 200 workers left unpaid by the same parent company – Philkeram-Johnson – who look forward to the auctions so that they can receive compensation and unpaid wages owed since 2011–12. Beyond an economic conflict between two groups of workers fighting over company property, the conflict is also political, as is amply evident in the two groups' public statements against each other: Vio.Me. workers are called a 'travelling troupe of solidarians' and Philkeram-Johnson union leaders the 'faithful dogs of the employers'.[22] This reflects deep and long-running divisions between autonomous labour activists, politically on the anarchist and libertarian communist left, and union leaders embedded within GSEE, still dominated by established PASOK and ND networks.

By their actions, the workers of Vio.Me. have challenged the owners' property rights as well as the legal processes that liquidate the fixed capital of bankrupt companies. They have done this both by direct action (expropriation) and by petitioning SYRIZA's left-wing government to exempt the property from existing bankruptcy laws and processes. However, especially in the absence of a broad movement for such expropriation and the socialisation of production, their actions end up being more ideological than they are transformative, at best restricted to managing their appropriated capital and running a small business under precarious economic and legal conditions, while having a negative impact upon compensation processes for other ex-workers who, whether because of ideological disagreement or pragmatism, or because they are simply not interested in running factories, do not participate in their struggle.

Much has been written over the history of the labour and communist, anarchist and socialist movements about the contradictions of self-management as a revolutionary activity or strategy, from Bordiga to French and British post-ultra-left currents.[23] It is not my aim to review

---

21. Vio.Me. Supporters, 'Police Attacks Viome's "Caravan of Struggle and Solidarity"', VioMe.org, July 2016; Vio.Me. Assembly, 'Oloi sta dikastīria Thessalonikīs'. Biom-Metal. blogspot.com, January 2017.

22. Vio.Me. Assembly, 'Anakoínōsī tou Sōmateíou tīs Vio.Me.', Biom-Metal.blogspot.com, 23/1/2013; 'Anakoínōsī', Somateio-Philkeram.gr, 14/2/2018.

23. See Gilles Dauvé, *Eclipse and Re-Emergence of the Communist Movement* (Detroit: Black and Red, 1975); Jacques Camatte, *This World We Must Leave* (London: David Brown,

this history, but simply to highlight some of the critical observations that are relevant to the conjuncture in Greece, under conditions of a capitalist crisis and the production of surplus populations. The first is the critique of positing the central antagonism at the terrain of management, organisation and democracy and leaving work and production themselves unquestioned,[24] raising workers to the level of a subject that is always necessarily revolutionary and constructing work as a liberating activity.[25] The second, placing the same problematic in the context of crisis, notes the role of self-management in the state management of crisis and unemployment, and the conditions of deeper exploitation forced on self-managing workers under conditions of generalised unprofitability and company failure.[26]

These issues became evident not only in the case of Vio.Me., but also in other cases of workers' temporary self-organisation of production and of co-operatives created by unemployed workers. Most obvious, in cases of unpaid workers demanding wages and contesting closures, was their material inability to run production or services in the absence of capital investment and legal structures that at the very least would allow them to recover unpaid wages. Among a series of workers' struggles, occupations and temporary takeovers in the private media industry, the case of *Eleutherotypía*, a high-circulation left-leaning newspaper, was the most prolonged, involving a split among workers over the possibility – or unfulfilled promise – of job retention. After failing to pay wages for over a year in 2011, and workers going on strike to demand payment, the publishing company filed for bankruptcy under Article 99, along with a restructuring plan to lay off 70 per cent of the workforce, encompassing journalists, technical staff and managers. About a hundred workers who expected to be re-employed supported the bankruptcy, while the rest contested it and won. Continuing to demand their wages and compensations, the majority produced two 'strike issues' of *Eleutherotypía*, whose proceeds went towards their salaries owed.[27] Immediately after this, the employers restarted production of the newspaper with about

1976); International Communist Current, *The Italian Communist Left 1926–45* (London: ICC, 1992); Négation, *Lip and the Self-Managed Counter-Revolution* (Detroit: Black and Red, 1975). For an overview see Antagonism, *Bordiga versus Pannekoek* (London: Antagonism, 2001).

24. Dauvé, *Eclipse*.

25. Camatte, *This World We Must Leave*.

26. Négation, *Lip*; Antagonism, *Bordiga versus Pannekoek*.

27. 'Autodiacheírisī kai stīn "Eleutherotypía"?', Augī, 23/11/2012.

a hundred staff under a new company name and tax code, which they presented as a continuation of the 'strike issues', presumably to retain the newspaper title's left-wing credentials. The actual aim was to legally exclude the remaining workers from claiming compensations and wages from the proceeds of the new venture. Nevertheless, this attempt only lasted for about a year in 2013–14, amid a series of legal wrangles with the majority of workers, and with the 100 'faithful' workers remaining unpaid for a second time.[28] In the meantime, another small group of journalists started a new co-operative called *I Efimerída tōn Syntaktōn* (the editors' newspaper), which was sued by their prior employers for supposedly appropriating a copyrighted name. The latter is still in operation, benefiting to some extent from the market gap left behind by *Eleutherotypía* and other newspaper closures, and coming second in sales on Saturdays in 2018,[29] but without having avoided the risk of amassing debt and based on a lot of volunteer and low-paid labour.[30]

Alongside this high-profile case of a co-operative started after a closure and as part of a struggle, there have been many other collective business ventures initiated by unemployed workers. Some started with the explicit aim of the subsistence of their members, as, for example, Collective Courier, a company set up by ex-employees of private postal companies, and To Kazani Pou Vrazei a collectively managed small restaurant in Thessaloniki. Others were accompanied by a discourse of self-management as a radical or potentially revolutionary practice. Examples of the latter are To Pagkaki, a co-operative coffee shop; Oi Ekdóseis tōn Synadélfōn (the colleagues' editions), a publishing co-operative;[31] and Syn-Állois, a self-managed distribution network for products of 'alternative and solidarity markets'.[32] Most of these initiatives were created outside a context of direct labour struggle, and they overlap, in some cases, with 'alternative economy' initiatives. The most ideological of these see their practice as prefiguring a post-capitalist society where workers would decide what they produce, how they produce it and where they distribute it, in dialogue with the rest of society, to satisfy

---

28. O Ekdótīs, 'Anakoínōsī se Apántīsī tou Psīfísmatos tōn Ergazoménōn', *Eleutherotypía*, 21/11/2014.
29. Deltío Īmerīsiōn Efīmerídōn (Panelladikó), Argoscom.gr.
30. Efīmerída ton Syntaktōn, 'Etairikés Katastáseis' and 'H Istoría tīs Ef.Syn.', Efsyn.gr.
31. Ekdóseis tōn Synadélfōn, 'Líga Lógia gia Emás', Ekdoseisynadelfwn.wordpress.com.
32. Syn-Állois, 'Ti Eínai o Synetairismós Allīléggyas Oikonomías "Syn-Állois"', Synallois. org.

needs.[33] They argue that their practice, beyond simply being a solution for subsistence, opposes capitalist social relations, offering an alternative way of organising work. Workers try to break down internal hierarchies and to replace them with relations of solidarity. They make collective consensual decisions, they do not aim for profits – sharing out any profits or donating them to labour struggles and similar initiatives – and, most importantly for them, they prove that 'workers can work without bosses'. Oi Ekdóseis tōn Synadélfōn in particular insist that their practice separates itself from capitalist social relations. Their stated principle is that books must not be commodities but 'social goods', and that readers must not be consumers but 'book lovers'.[34] According to Pagaki, even though at present such initiatives cannot remain pure or separate from dominant social relations, their ideal is autonomy: networks of autonomous and anti-hierarchical forms of organising social life and production are, for them, the overcoming of capitalism.[35]

However, nobody can contest the fact that those who choose to set up new co-operatives also face the difficulty of business survival in a market characterised by mass closures for small businesses. According to Collective Courier workers, it took them a year of working unpaid until they started to have a basic income from their work.[36] Given that the success or failure of these businesses depends, as for every business, on capitalist competition within their sector, in order for them to be able to compete in the market under crisis conditions, a smaller or larger degree of devaluation of their members' labour power has to be imposed.

These issues have been much discussed through this period among supporters of self-management and their critics. Participants in such initiatives have often commented on their 'self-exploitation', explaining that they work very hard and carry increased responsibility considering what they earn.[37] This casual recognition that self-management maintains rather than challenges the core category of the capitalist mode of production – the exploitation of labour – shows that, at least in these

---

33. Ekdóseis tōn Synadélfōn, 'Preface', in *Autodiacheírisí*, ed. Guillaume Davranche (Athens: Ekdóseis tōn Synadélfōn, 2013).

34. Ekdóseis tōn Synadélfōn, 'Líga lógia'.

35. To pagaki, 'Liga Logia'.

36. Informal interview I conducted with workers at Collective Courier, Athens, February 2012.

37. Discussion on self-management entitled 'Synergatikés Morfés Ergasías ton Kairó tīs Krísīs' with members of self-management projects at Fabrica Yfanet, as part of the event Communismos 2.0, 26/5/2012.

cases, self-management is not the critique of the capital relation that it hoped to be. This recognition is often qualified with the defence that these initiatives are not part of a broader movement of self-management, which, if generalised, would end these forms of exploitation.[38] It is worth considering this question. What would the generalisation of self-management entail in the current context?

First, it is important to characterise precisely the kind of practice 'self-management' has been in the context of the current crisis in Greece. Contrary to the discourse of self-management that had emerged in the factory unions movement of the late 1970s, and contrary to the self-management movement in Argentina, this form of 'self-management' has not taken place in factories and has not been part of a struggle to expropriate constant capital from capitalist owners, with the exception of Vio.Me. This may have to do with the low organic composition of capitalist enterprise in Greece, which was further lowered with the flight of a number of industries from the 1990s onwards. Second, contrary to the 1980s wave of nationalisations under the PASOK government, and their temporary attempt to involve workers in factory management and the rationalisation of production, the role of the state vis-à-vis self-management is now very different. Nationalisation has not been on the agenda – quite the opposite – and instead co-operatives have been seen as a way to reduce unemployment statistics. This was clearly stated in the rationale for the new legal framework for setting up co-operatives (Social Co-operative Enterprises). Significantly, the framework was introduced in 2011 amid a barrage of onerous legislation for workers.[39] From the perspective of the state's social and economic management, co-operatives were a way to patch the benefit system amid massive unemployment and the radical curtailment of benefits.

To suggest that co-operatives necessarily fulfil this state agenda would be a functionalist argument. However, it is clear that they do not form part of workers' struggles but are instead *new enterprises*, fully capitalist in their functioning in the market aside from their principles of internal democratic organisation. The latter, in the best of cases, can facilitate better relationships and forms of emotional well-being at work, but under conditions of crisis and market pressure it also distributes to workers – who are now all also 'bosses' – responsibility for the rationali-

---

38. Workers' self-management archive, 'Gia Poia Autodiacheírisī Miláme', Autodiaxeirisi. espivblogs.net, June 2014.
39. N. 4019/2011, FEK A' 216/30.09.2011.

sation of production. What was previously externalised into the function of 'the boss' and expressed as class conflict is internalised, in a way that is not very different from small family enterprises. Members are not liberated from exploitation, they simply are themselves responsible for perpetuating it: it becomes a form of 'responsible' self-regulation. The generalisation of co-operatives in Greece could thus be a successful form of managing the crisis politically, and in fact it would be little different than the current promotion of small business ventures. The journal *Négation*'s assessment of self-management under crisis conditions, despite taking place in a different historical and regional-economic context (1970s France), is cogent:

> [s]elf-management is a way of having the work force control the contradiction between valorization and devalorization because all society would then be organized to lower the value of that living commodity, labor. It is a question of the population taking over activities previously run by Capital and which consequently increase the expense of the upkeep of the work force.[40]

Premised as it is upon *work* and *production* as the primary communal bond and social duty, and failing to question the production of value itself, self-management produces a semblance of democracy within a production unit still driven by imperatives of capitalist economic rationality and efficiency, which always entails the need to *reduce* labour and wages and increase profits. This much was already evident from the experience of self-management in the former Yugoslavia during the 1960s and 1970s. Rather than leading to workers' empowerment and the 'withering away of the state', it encouraged production units to function as businesses in a semi-free market. Self-managed workers rationalised production and cut costs with an overall effect of increasing productivity (and thus the rate of surplus value extraction) and eventually unemployment.[41] Self-management is then fully integrated into the dynamic of capitalist contradictions as they played out in the past, and as they play out in the current crisis. And, indeed, contrary to governmental hopes for managing unemployment, the generalisation of self-management would

---

40. Négation, *Lip*, 87.
41. Gal Kirn, *Partizanski Prelomi in Protislovja Tržnega Socializma v Jugoslaviji* (Ljubljana: Zalozba Sophia, 2014).

be likely to continue to expand an already sizeable surplus population, blocked from its means of subsistence.

Outsiders to the Workplace

The separation then becomes notable between workers with a strong attachment to a workplace – which can even be their own property – and the expanded masses of workers who are precariously related to workplaces due to casual and temporary employment.[42] Of course, given the precariousness of co-operative enterprises themselves, the separation may not be clear-cut in practice, but it did entail very different practices of struggle and, occasionally, conflict with workers in more stable positions and the consciousness associated with those.

This was evident in the grassroots labour struggles. As already mentioned, the formation of grassroots unions grew in the 2000s to defend the rights of precarious, temporary or outsourced private sector workers whose issues were not addressed by the major unions. These tended to be located in the service sector (postal, catering, private tuition, cleaning, publishing, retail) and to be run by relatively small numbers of workers, who worked hard to encourage their colleagues not to be intimidated by employers. I have witnessed discussions on this issue among grassroots labour activists in a variety of sectors and contexts.[43] Because of this problem, in some cases labour struggles were not even run by workers themselves, but by 'solidarity committees' that organised protests on their behalf.[44] Nevertheless, with increasing numbers of workers left unpaid for several months, grassroots unions have been able to organise actions of withdrawal of labour in protest. Facing difficulties in organising strikes, and left unsupported by major unions, which mostly represented permanent workers, grassroots unions frequently

---

42. Between 2011 and 2013, part-time work and flexible shift work contracts increased by 31.83 per cent and 35.73 per cent respectively, and, according to statistics by the Ministry of Labor given out to the press, in 2014 undeclared labour was assessed to be at 13.85 per cent. S.EP.E., *Ekthesī Pepragménōn 2013* (Athens: Ministry of Labour, Social Security and Welfare, 2013).

43. For example, in the Attica Union of Postal Workers (SETTEA) discussion on 'Developments in the Postal Sector and Worker Resistance', Labour Centre of Athens, 19/1/2012; and the meeting of grassroots unions and labour lawyers on 'Labour Rights in a Time of Crisis and Memorandums', Athens Polytechnic, 21/1/2012.

44. G.P., E.S. and E.P., 'Empeiríes apó ton Agōna sto Restorán Banquet', O-a-blog.blogspot. com, 8/2/2012.

resorted to practices other than strikes or occupations, occupying a space external to workplaces that mirror their contractual insecurity. The most common of these have been protests by employees outside workplaces such as shops, offices or postal collection centres, where public attention can be grabbed while blocking the flow of incoming and outgoing business (for example, the cases of the confectioner Ble,[45] the unpaid temps of the National Census,[46] ACS couriers,[47] actions of the union of teachers in private schools,[48] actions of the union of waiters and cooks[49] and protests by subcontracted cleaners in the hospitals Dromokaitio and Gennimatas).[50]

The popularity of these forms of action, whose frequency increased over the period of crisis,[51] can be understood as a tendency for workers' struggles to block production or business activity from the outside, and to use methods that appeal to social ethics and positive publicity, often in the absence of labour legislation in their favour, faced with the inability to down tools inside workplaces. This externality, and separation from other workers, was especially pronounced where it involved laid-off

45. Unpaid Dismissed Workers of Blé, 'O Agōnas sta Blé Synechízetai … ', Agwnasble. eu.pn, 2/5/2012. The workers who had been dismissed, while still being owed wages, from the confectioner Blé demonstrated outside the company's high-street shops demanding to be paid. After two months of demonstrations, they received their wages.
46. I.K. and A.P., 'O Agōnas tōn Apograféōn', *I Sfika*, no. 1–2 (2012).
47. Élena Kalīmérī and Kyriákos Dīmággelos, 'Mía Ergatikī Domī, ī Apergía tīs ACS kai to Spásimo tīs Tromokratías', Barikat.gt, 11/10/2013.
48. The grassroots union for teachers in private schools, SEFK, has taken action in support of workplace disputes regarding laid-off workers and unpaid wages, by staging protests outside schools. The union has faced intimidation by employers and dismissals of union members. One of its main priorities was the enforcement of collective agreements with employers (SEFK, 'Dráseis 2012', Sefk.gr). In the summer of 2012, employers of foreign-language schools in South Attica signed a new collective agreement with an employer-controlled union that radically cut the wages of foreign-language teachers to €3.52 per hour. Sýllogos Ergazomeénōn stīn Idiōtikī Ekpaídeusī Nomoú Attikīs – Výrōn, 'Prósklīsī se Diapragmateúseis gia tīn Katártisī Syllogikīs Sýmvasīs Ergasías', EnotikiProtovouliaVyronas. blogspot.org, November 2014.
49. The website and blog of the Union of Waiters and Cooks (Sōmateío Servitōrōn Mageírōn, somateioserbitoronmageiron.blogspot.com) lists a great number of protests and interventions outside workplaces where workers were unpaid or unjustified layoffs had taken place.
50. Panattikī Énōsī Katharistriōn and Oikiakoú Prosōpikoú, 'Agōnistīkame kai dikaiōthīkame', *Pekop.wordpress.com*, 28/7/2014.
51. For an indication, of this, despite the fact that GSEE is unlikely to have collected complete statistics on this type of labour activism, see Dīmítrīs Papanikolópoulos, 'Ī Syndikalistikī Dynamikī 2010–15', *Enīmérōsī: Monthly Edition of INE/GSEE*, no. 232 (2016): 2–28.

workers who demanded compensation, as is obvious in the case of the Metropolis music chain:

> When the Panepistimiou store closed down, there were two general assemblies for the first time with all the employees, where the division between pro- and anti-employer workers became obvious. Since then, those workers who were literally thrown into the street began to meet at various cafés at Benaki, where we discussed. So it became established until now to meet once a week and have a regular assembly.[52]

This externality also entailed increased violence: often workers in withdrawal of labour who had blockaded their workplaces have had to deal with riot police, arrests, legal charges, revenge layoffs, threats, lockouts, bans from protesting outside their workplaces, new staff being hired to replace those protesting and direct aggression from employers (for example, the cases of Chatzis patisseries in Thessaloniki,[53] 3E printing,[54] the Pentelikon hotel[55]). In such a difficult context, the 'pro-employer' mentality mentioned above was not at all infrequent. Given precarious economic conditions, many workers felt that any risk to the commercial health of the enterprise caused by protests could put their jobs at risk. Many workers only became conscious of conflicting interests with their employer after they were laid off:

> [W]e were attached to an enterprise that paid the little money it gave us regularly, we had not developed any resistance or consciousness that in good times bosses are good and in bad times bad, this is why the mobilisation started late, after the large store was closed down.[56]

The increased frequency of such actions in the crisis reflects the way in which workers navigating the space between unemployment and precarity dealt with their renewed, deeper exclusion from a stable wage relation and the workplace. Their position betrays increased vulnerability, but also a complete disconnection from the interests of the enterprise.

52. Polyergaleío, 'Synénteuxī me Apolyménous - Aplīrōtous tōn "Metropolis"', *Ī Sfīka*, no. 5 (2013).
53. 'Eleútheroi oi Syllīfthéntes tou Chatzī', AlterThess.gr, 20/1/2012; Aplīrōtoi Ergazómenoi Chatzī, 'Kai Álla Asfalistiká Métra', Chatzisrevolt.blogspot.com, 25/1/2012.
54. '"Loukéto" stīn 3E Ektypōtikī', Ergazomenoi3eektypwtikh.blogspot.com, 6/1/2012.
55. Amáltheia Karalī, 'Pentelikón: Sfodrī Sýgkrousī', *Amarysia*, 25/10/2012.
56. Polyergaleío, 'Synénteuxī me Apolyménous'.

Here, former or precarious workers merely aim to inflict damage on the enterprise and its owners externally, and are more concerned about their compensation than the company's survival. They come to threaten the privileged relationship to the workplace and the wage of those workers who are still 'inside', as if they demand a more equal distribution of insecurity. The case of the dispute in *Eleutherotypía* above also betrays a similar relationship: those left out of the new rationalised venture did everything to undermine it through bad publicity and litigation. Even in cases where they demand permanent positions,[57] insecure workers' equalisation of status with that of those already 'included' can generate worries that a broader section of staff is now at risk in the case of a restructuring. What is certain is that solidarity, in such cases, is very difficult, given that the insiders and the outsiders often have objectively conflicting interests.

Yet, from another perspective, being positioned on the outside or the periphery of production puts into question the traditional model of the workers who organise themselves and affirm their identity as workers with valued skills and capacities, attached to a certain workplace or enterprise, of which they might potentially aspire to become owners. Labour activism in a time of crisis that produces labour power and the population of its bearers as surplus is not straightforwardly a struggle *of workers*, but one of proletarians who are faced with their superfluity vis-à-vis capital. This means that the forms of struggle contrasted to self-management by the journal *Négation* in 1970s France and the theorists of the Italian autonomia in 1970s Italy – sabotage, absenteeism, the 'refusal of work' and 'self-declared marginal living' by proletarian youth – are also rendered irrelevant in this new context.[58] While the latter also took place in a period of restructuring and factory closures, and while the proletarian condition of precarity was key to class experience in those contexts, the scale of both the restructuring and its implications are of a different order in 2010s Greece, so that lack of work, or risking one's job through absenteeism, cannot be experienced as a form of liberation

57. For example, the struggles of hospital cleaners. PEKOP, 'Pīrame Pisō tīn Axioprepeia Mas', Pekop.wordpress.com, 7/7/2014.

58. Négation, *Lip*; Antonio Negri, 'Capitalist Domination and Working Class Sabotage', in *Working Class Autonomy and the Crisis*, ed. Red Notes (London: Red Notes, 1979); Sergio Bologna, 'The Tribe of Moles', *Autonomia III*, no. 3 (1980): 36–61; Bifo (F. Berardi), 'Anatomy of Autonomy', *Autonomia III*, no. 3 (1980): 148–70, 155. For a nuanced evaluation of the Italian autonomia's concept of the 'refusal of work' and marginality, see Nicholas Thoburn, *Deleuze, Marx and Politics* (London : Routledge, 2003), 69–138.

that can be integrated into alternative lifestyles and cultures. It is not that there have not been alternative economies and political squatting; instead, these have tended to be used as resources for opposition or for mutual support rather than as spaces for a form of life opposed to work. This is not only because the resources for such an imaginary became less and less available, but also because the all-encompassing nature of the crisis and the lack of a vision beyond it produced insecurity about young people's long-term future: better to get whatever 'work experience' one can today than be left with an empty CV at 35 because they spent their youth living a marginal lifestyle.

Thus, while the forms of struggle of the most insecure and unemployed proletarians in the crisis again stand in contrast to a positive relationship to one's workplace and work identity, their position produces ambivalence towards capital, the labour market and work. It can produce an awareness of disinvested capital, on the one hand, as a debt to unemployed workers, and, on the other hand, especially for those who have been unemployed for a long time, as a kind of 'aid' that brings the 'opportunity' of work and a wage. Yet, with the 'aid' never arriving, or arriving in the form of repeated episodes of insecure and low-paid employment, the question of who becomes constructed as the cause of this oppressive condition is a matter of ideological contestation, as we are witnessing everywhere today. Here, 'peripheral' labour activism has an important role to play, both in making gains for workers' compensation, which meets immediate basic needs, and in generating a public discourse and consciousness that reveals the locus of exploitation, in a context where, all too easily, blame is projected out to 'foreign' workers, governments and capital, presuming national unity and national production – self-managed or not – as the solution to crisis and the forms of suffering it has produced.

'Self-Management' and Contestation over Means of Production as Common Resources

The position of workers whose workplaces and their means of production are publicly owned is slightly different than that of other workers, and raises even more powerfully the problematics of worker ownership of enterprise. The struggle around the public broadcaster, ERT (Greek Radio and Television), is an example of contestation between workers with a special attachment to their work specialisms and workplace belonging and those outside it, over access to the means of production as a collective resource.

In June 2013, after a dispute with the public broadcasting labour union, the government abruptly decided to shut down the public broadcasting and radio corporation and lay off all of its thousands of staff.[59] The workers responded by taking over the buildings and continuing to broadcast an oppositional programme in support of their campaign to keep ERT open, while large demonstrations in protest against the closure took place daily outside the ERT studios in Athens and Thessaloniki. Supporters of the struggle formed assemblies, which wanted to enter the studios and collectively manage the programme (broadcast online, since the police had deactivated the transmitters). In the Athens headquarters, the issue of 'ownership' of the means of production then emerged: ERT employees, who hoped to be reinstated into their positions, did not want to allow 'outsiders' to enter the studios, and were protective of the studio equipment. It was clear that, for them, the struggle was about their jobs and wages. The opportunity to transform public television into a broader means of social struggle was secondary. Despite supporters' attempts to convince them, workers refused, and only very selectively presented small parts of the proposed programme.[60] Consequently, the supporters started to grow weary of the situation and their numbers dwindled. In early November 2013, at a weak point, the television building was eventually raided by riot police, who forcibly removed all the workers.[61] On the contrary, the workers at the ET3 studios in Thessaloniki were open to collaboration with the supporters' assemblies and began to broadcast a political programme immediately. ET3 was still broadcasting a political programme by the time SYRIZA reinstated all the stations in mid-2015.

A similar, though very different in practice, dilemma was faced by doctors at Kilkis Hospital, who took over and 'self-managed' the hospital to protest delayed and radically reduced wages.[62] Here, the awareness that the hospital is and must remain a free public resource was high and part of the workers' political agenda. However, given the immensity of capital required to run a hospital, workers' control is out of the question

59. 'Greece Suspends State Broadcaster ERT to Save Money', *BBC*, 11/6/2013.
60. Polyergaleío, 'Ti (Den) Paízetai stīn ERT', SKYA.espiv.net, 13/6/2013. Additional information was gathered from personal participation in the first day of the supporters' assembly in Thessaloniki, and a subsequent discussion with an active participant in the supporters' assembly in Athens.
61. 'Ī Kyvérnīsī Eisévale stīn ERT', ThePressProject.gr, 7/11/2013.
62. 'Greek Hospital Now under Workers' Control', Libcom.org, 5/2/2012.

without the economic contribution of the state. Health workers' democratic management of the hospital and their response to patients' urgent needs for free health care, against governmental reforms that demanded payment, had both a symbolic and a material significance[63] that did not fit into the category of 'self-management' but of solidarity among hospital workers and patients – who essentially represent the entire proletarian population – for both workers' wages and the social wage. The democratic management of the hospital did not go so far as to involve patients in its management, but that is conceivably on the horizon of the socialisation and collective social management of healthcare.

The above episodes reveal that the social position and identity of *workers* under conditions of crisis can be oppositional in its political surface, but not always in its effects. Workers defending their position in a context of mass unemployment and the dissolution of public services can in fact entail a conservative stance of self-preservation of the most sheltered workers against those who are rendered expendable, or openness to the socialisation or expropriation of resources for the purposes of broader social struggles.

The Unemployed

Given the unprecedentedly high unemployment levels in this period – affecting, as discussed, about one-third of the working-age population and over half of those under 25 – one would have expected a surge of activity in new organisations of the unemployed. Yet this was not the case. There have been a few organisations: SYRIZA's Network of Precarious Workers and Unemployed;[64] SOVA, a grassroots union for unemployed and precarious workers;[65] groupings of unemployed from neighbourhood assemblies;[66] Syn.E.Ko.Ch., the assembly of workers in workfare programmes;[67] and a few more local initiatives. These groups recognised the overlap between unemployment and unstable work: the inaccessibility of unemployment benefits, and the lowering of wages

---

63. 'Kilkís: Ypó Katálīpsī to Nosokomeío apó tous Ergazómenous', AlterThess.gr, 20/2/2012.

64. 'Díktyo Episfalōs Ergazoménōn-Anérgōn', diktyo-episfaleias.blogspot.com.

65. 'Sōmateio Vasīs Anergōn kai Episfalōn Ergazomenōn', swbanergwn.espivblogs.net.

66. 'Anergoi/es apó tis Geitoniés tīs Athīnas', anergoigeitonion.espivblogs.net.

67. 'Synéleusī Ergazoménōn se prográmmata Koinofeloús Charaktīra', synekox.espivblogs.net.

to almost the level of such benefits, meant that the condition of a great proportion of the 'unemployed' was one of working temporarily, and usually undeclared, in highly exploitative conditions, or in workfare, as opposed to sitting at home with nothing to do.

Interestingly, and in contrast to the labour struggles of precarised workers, none of their campaigns put forward as primary the demand for the creation of new 'jobs', even though they differed in their politics. The absence of a generalised demand for 'the right to work' by the unemployed given the high levels of unemployment probably demands an explanation. Work was not 'refused' at any level, and activism demanded the re-employment of specific employees in specific workplaces, or tried to create employment through self-management and 'alternative economy' projects. This shows that the demand for work was not posed to the state at a greater social level, but only to employers at a local level, suggesting the delegitimation of addressing such a demand to a bankrupt state in the process of laying off masses of public sector workers.

The unemployed organisations mostly made welfare demands, and, probably, this is what constituted them as 'campaigns of the unemployed', given the experienced overlap between unemployment and insecure employment. SYRIZA's network campaigned against illegal employer practices and demanded free transport for the unemployed. The other groups campaigned for the same demands, but also for wider access to unemployment benefits, and against the new workfare programmes introduced by the government, which institutionalised extremely low-paid work.[68] Still, because of relatively low participation, these organisations could not pose their demands with any significant force. They were mostly limited to relatively small demonstrations outside the OAED (Organisation for Labour Force Employment) and high-traffic areas of public transport (to campaign for free transport).

Prior to 2015, there were disagreements among these groups on whether they should pose demands that seemed ambitious in the given context – as, for example, the removal of workfare programmes and the expansion of benefits to all the unemployed – or aim for modest,

---

68. Three new forms of workfare were introduced. (a) 'Training vouchers' (epitagés katártisïs): one-month training seminars on new technologies for €500. (b) Programmes of public-benefit work (Prográmmata Koinōfeloús Ergasías): five-month employment in the public sector and NGOs for a maximum of €625 per month, reduced to €490 after 2013. (c) Workfare programmes of five-month 'work experience' in the private sector for €400–60 per month. See N. 3845/2010 AK.

seemingly achievable demands, such as free transport and having workfare formally recognised as dependent labour with corresponding rights. The reason for the difficulty in taking a unified position on demands is likely also one of the reasons for low participation in these organisations. The demand for a universal unemployment benefit might have been worth fighting for, but it appeared unfeasible.[69] On the other hand, small achievements, such as being paid on time, required disproportionate campaigning in relation to what was eventually gained. Another important reason for the lack of large-scale organising among the unemployed may have been the very fact that their most pressing need has been employment or alternative ways of obtaining the means to live, and these organisations did not offer pro-active solutions to this problem, unlike, for example, movements of the unemployed such as the *piqueteros* in Argentina.

Nevertheless, this activism led to some modest achievements for workfare workers by 2014 – for example, payment without delays and on public holidays according to national insurance regulations.[70] After SYRIZA's first election victory in 2015, free transport was instituted for the unemployed, but no improvement was made to unemployment benefits beyond their expansion to include ex-business owners who became unemployed. On the contrary, workfare projects were expanded and, amid increasing NGO involvement in the management of the 'migrant crisis', and the shrinking of secure public sector employment, much of this workfare employment was used to plug gaps and make savings in these sectors.[71] Campaigning around workfare has thus continued, now contesting the status of workfare 'beneficiaries', which deprives workers of labour rights.[72]

It is evident that, under conditions of economic collapse, and when movements – localised within a nation-state – are not capable of halting the neoliberal form of crisis management, the idea of posing ambitious welfare demands becomes delegitimised and easily abandoned, precisely when it would seem to be most needed. Even with a purportedly radical left party in power, it has not been possible to shift this delegitimation. At best, struggles of workfare 'beneficiaries' aim for recognition as 'normal' exploitable labour with corresponding contracts. It is no

69. SKYA, 'Apologismós tou Agōna Enántia sta Koinōfelī', *I Sfika*, no. 7 (2014).
70. Ibid.
71. SKYA, 'Den Eínai Anthrōpismós! Eínai ī Anadiárthrōsī Ilíthie!', *I Sfika*, no. 10 (2017).
72. For example the group Nofeloumenoi (No Beneficiaries), nofeloumeni.gr.

wonder, then, that the fallback form of collective action in this context has been to organise alternative economies and form co-operatives, which, despite not being able to fully meet needs, can at least provide a social support network that combats the individualised suffering of unstable employment. The broader participation in the latter compared to the former should thus be understood as a practical choice and not as primarily driven by an ideology committed to the 'commons' or 'autonomy' that would in principle reject dealings with the state. On the contrary, it is the state that has become radically impervious to the posing of demands and which has promoted these 'co-operative' forms of managing unemployment alongside the workfare model.

7

Solidarity, Charity or Exchange?

Neighbourhood Assemblies

The movement of the squares, as already mentioned, had the ambition to expand its practices of self-organisation into neighbourhood and workplace assemblies. This was not a novel ambition, as neighbourhood assemblies had already been set up during the December 2008 uprising, and some even earlier than that. While the expansion of workplace assemblies hardly materialised,[1] several new assemblies were set up in neighbourhoods around Attiki, and a few in other cities around the country. In Attiki alone, by Autumn 2011 there were around 50 local assemblies. The new assemblies differed to those of December 2008, in that activists of the left – as opposed to those of the anarchist-autonomous political milieu – were central in them, emphasising political openness and 'addressing wider society'.[2] 'Direct democracy' and 'taking our lives into our own hands' were their slogans, following on from the squares.

Autumn had brought a rapid slashing of indirect and direct wages in both the public and private sectors via cuts and emergency taxes. The assemblies attempted, in a variety of ways and selecting different priorities, depending on their particular composition, to address these problems, as well as local problems involving urban space. Despite the varied composition and variations in the political discourse of each of the assemblies, it can be said that their activities broadly included: collective non-payment of taxes and fares ('self-reduction': for example, blocking ticket validation machines in Metro stations as a way of demanding free transport, campaigning against the entry fee to public health centres and hospitals);[3] solidarity actions and demonstrations with organi-

---

1. Self-organised grassroots unions date back to the early 2000s. However, the notion of 'workplace assemblies' in square discussions envisaged a spreading of self-organisation with wide participation in workplaces. This did not happen, since the squares had very few and indirect links with labour.

2. I have translated the term 'koinōnikī apeúthynsī' as 'addressing wider society'.

3. Such actions of self-reduction had been popularised a year earlier by the 'I Don't Pay' (Den Plīrōnō) campaign of the leftist ANTARSYA party (later the campaign split off).

sations of workers and the unemployed; the defence of public urban space from privatisation; occupations of buildings and/or urban space;[4] anti-fascist action; participation in demonstrations; a variety of forms of self-organisation and sharing of resources (collective kitchens, clothes exchanges, 'social groceries' giving out donated goods); and alternative economy projects (time banks, alternative money, getting cheaper agricultural produce direct from producers).

The older neighbourhood assemblies with a more anti-authoritarian composition were the first to initiate many of these actions, particularly those of self-reduction, over 2010–11, and for many of them those forms of activism had already reached various limits by 2011. According to an account of the movement against transport fares in Athens, which had been run by a coordination of neighbourhood assemblies and involved daily interventions in buses and Metro stations, the movement was unable to promote the generalisation of a *politicised* refusal to pay (as opposed to quietly passing used tickets to one another, which did seem to generalise). Such politicisation was thought of as essential to legitimise free transport at a time of high unemployment and shrinking wages. After several months of daily action, the activists became tired. In retrospect, they realised that they had neglected to take into account the needs of their own group members who may have been unemployed or had fines to pay, through an overemphasis on the political-ideological aspect of their actions.[5] In other words, these groups saw themselves more as an almost immaterial knowing vanguard in an edifying relation to their outside, neglecting the reality of group members as also equally and materially immersed within the social relations they were fighting against.

In comparison, the second wave of neighbourhood assemblies functioned more directly *for* their members, although this was coloured by slightly more mainstream left-wing types of political discourse. Organising against the new 'emergency' property tax attracted a lot of the attention and energy from many assemblies. This tax, which amounted

---

Campaigners intervened at highway toll stations and Metro stations to allow free access. Currently, these campaigns are defunct, even though the highway tolls have continued to rise.

4. For example the campaigns around Navarino park in Exarchia and the Kyprou park in Patision, both of which were spaces occupied and turned into parks by groups organising locally.

5. 'Koinótīta Agōna kai Synántīsīs Foitītriōn, Anérgōn, Episfalōn kai Chaménōn Paidiōn', *O Agōnas gia ta MMM stīn Athīna tīn Período 2010–11* (Thessaloniki, 2014).

to hundreds of euros annually, was charged via electricity bills, with the accompanying threat of electricity cut-offs should it not be paid by the deadline. This was a harsh mode of imposing taxation at a time of high unemployment, and particularly for elderly owner-occupiers, so the reactions against it were strong. The new neighbourhood assemblies facilitated ways to avoid paying this tax, by collectively protesting and getting legal help for impacted residents, as well as reconnecting the electricity for those who could not pay. This attracted many local property owners to the assemblies. The campaign against the tax was eventually partially successful, in having the tax at least disassociated from electricity bills.

While this campaign had, by its nature, an interclass, citizenist and legalistic character, it also did not shirk from taking action that openly defied the law and advertised its doing so. Electricity reconnections, which were not only carried out for those affected by the tax, but for anyone who had been unable to pay their bills, were acts that questioned the commodity status of electricity – that is, the inaccessibility of a basic necessity unless one can pay. Along with other similar acts of self-reduction, these practices at the same time revealed even more strongly the inability to make direct wage demands. With the labour movement officially defunct, these practices reclaimed a fraction of the wage indirectly and in defiance of the normal laws of exchange.

Still, there was also a limiting aspect to the anti-tax campaign, as many assembly participants often recognised.[6] The issue of the property tax monopolised the meetings in many assemblies for several months, marginalising other issues like closing hospitals, unemployment and unpaid wages. In some cases, local property owners did not even actively participate in all the organising efforts around the tax, leaving that responsibility to the more 'activist' members, and merely attending in order to catch up with developments. Some assemblies questioned themselves as to why they were treated as a support service, as this, at times, produced disagreements with participants who did not own property. While it would be unfair to say that the property tax campaign exhausted the assemblies' activities, it did bring to the surface the pattern of a problem that appears to be specific to neighbourhood assemblies as a form of organisation.

---

6. This was an observation reported repeatedly by the newer assemblies in the first countrywide coordinative meeting of neighbourhood assemblies (old and new), 13/1/2012.

Since the peak of participation during the movement of the squares, neighbourhood assemblies' numbers had begun to dwindle by the first months of 2012. The complaint that local participants had surrendered to a 'logic of delegation' and did not actively participate was common to both newer and older assemblies. To the extent that assemblies put any effort into 'addressing wider society', and attracting a broader public to their campaigns, they were repeatedly let down, with the exception of the tax issue. While it seems plausible that there is a socially widespread habit of delegating responsibility, and not only accepting, but feeling safest within, structures of leadership, perhaps there were additional reasons for the depopulation of the assemblies.

The attempt to form a community on the sole basis of living in proximity to one another may not be unproblematic in itself. This type of community seems to have brought to the surface the differences among individuals, as much as it brought them together to solve common problems. The limits of organising on the basis of a locality and a simple democratic principle become more evident if we consider that a connection to a *place* as small as a neighbourhood is stronger when small property ownership is involved than when someone is a tenant and is forced to move frequently as rents fluctuate. The distribution of small property in Greece is broad enough to guarantee the numerical dominance of property owners in many neighbourhood assemblies. The absence of local migrant residents from the assemblies may be related both to the fact that most of them are tenants and to the naturalised racism and social segregation they face. There were several material ways in which the residents of the same neighbourhood would have been affected by the crisis in different and deeply unequal ways. Some could be young and unemployed with difficulty in paying their rent; others could be owner-occupier pensioners unable to pay their bills and taxes; some others could have a business that is failing; yet others may have been affected by the reduction in property values. Only within limits can these differences be formally negotiated within the democratic form, which, by its very premise of bringing together formally equal individuals (citizens), fails to go very far beyond the contentlessness of bourgeois equality. The inability of the form to recognise and challenge social hierarchies arising from property ownership (the co-presence in assemblies of landlords and their tenants, who were often the ones at risk of electricity cut-offs while their landlords were refusing to pay the tax, or who may have sometimes been in a dispute with the landlord)[7] while giving priority to the problems of owners, confirmed that, unless questioned, the relationship to a locality can by default be dominated by the property relationship to the land. To the extent that assemblies assumed a universality to already exist within them, this universality disguised the material inequalities to which bourgeois society is designed to remain blind.

The activities that, on the contrary, acknowledged and attempted to question class and other social hierarchies, such as solidarity actions in coordination with workers and unemployed groups, or solidarity with immigrants in areas where openly racist groups were active, were outward facing. Exploitation and social domination were clearly understood to exist, but there was a wish to expel them from the assembly itself, while at the same time allowing the assembly to be democratically inclusive. This amounted to a tension between a questioning of structural forms of power in capitalist society, and a desire to create a space of universality identical to that of bourgeois democracy: equality is 'for all', everyone is treated 'the same'. The particularity, in capitalist society, of being part of class, race and gender relations, remained unrecognised in the organisation's form, until it was expressed in internal conflict.

The attempts of neighbourhood assemblies and other groups to overcome internal differences and cope with the crisis through the creation of co-operative structures, alternative economies and other self-organised projects have similarly faced internal limits, which I discuss below.

Solidarity Initiatives and 'Alternative Economies'

[E]xchange value or, more precisely, the money system is in fact the system of equality and freedom, and ... the disturbances which they encounter in the further development of the system[,] disturbances inherent in it, are merely the realisation of *equality and freedom*, which prove to be inequality and unfreedom.[8]

With the shrinking or complete absence of both direct and indirect wages, and with basic state services such as healthcare and education becoming both dismantled and less accessible, there have been several

---

7. For example, my own landlord, who participated in the local neighbourhood assembly to contest the tax, later refused to return my deposit of two months' rent.
8. Karl Marx, *Grundrisse* (London: Pelican, 1973), 248–9.

attempts to create alternative structures to support forms of subsistence. This self-organising activity presented itself as a necessity in the crisis, and was itself shaped by it. It ranged from simple initiatives like collective kitchens, to collective gardens for agricultural goods, to the formation of alternative local economies and distribution networks, to the establishment of co-operatives and self-organised health services. In most cases, these activities had the ambition to not merely be a means of subsistence, but part of broader struggle and to effect a social critique. The targets of this criticism ranged from capitalist social relations as a whole to money as a mediator of social relations, to the lack of social solidarity and 'monetary diversity'.[9] Money and the form of exchange, including the exchange of labour, are central concepts that these practices have been concerned with.

Commodity exchange was the core social form that mediated community relations in 'solidarity' economy initiatives, alternative currency networks, exchange networks or time banks, whose numbers rapidly increased in the crisis, and have been promoted in mainstream media as effective survival strategies. Communities based on alternative forms of exchange have been multiple,[10] the idea behind them being, on the one hand, to create economic activity where there is little and, on the other, to create communities and relations of solidarity among the residents of a local area. The benefit of localised currencies has been that, whether time-based or not, they restrict options for exchange to the interior of the exchange community, and protect their members from external competition. It could be said to be a form of micro-protectionism that aims to form a material community among its members.

These two aspects of these initiatives — the emphasis on micro-production and exchange on the one hand, and the concern with fostering a community of solidarity on the other – are closely interlinked and create the potential for an internal tension. The first thing to note

9. Andreas Roumeliotis, 'Antallaktikī Oikonomía', *Eleutherotypía*, 28/3/2011.
10. Examples are the alternative currency exchange network Fasouli (fasouli.wordpress.com); the non-profit Co-operative for Solidarity Economy, Syn-Allois (synallois.org), inspired by the practices of the Zapatistas and also participating in international solidarity; the shop for the exchange of used clothes and other items, Skoros (skoros.espiv.net); Dyo Dyo, a network of exchange in Chios (dyo-dyo.org); Kourseva in Paros-Antiparos (kourseva.gr); Stakraeli in Achaia (stakraeli.gr); The network DIANA in Argolida (ilianthos.wordpress.com); Votsalo in Korydallos (votsalo.org); The alternative currency network in Kerkyra (mpoutsouni.blogspot.com); the moneyless exchange network Peliti (peliti.gr) and many others.

is that these projects, while they imagine themselves as autonomous, are not materially independent from the wider economy, nor is the socioeconomic status of its members defined by relations within the community. Even at the simplest level of exchanging the products of home-based production, there is an external dependence for basic raw materials that an individual urban household is not able to produce. These raw materials or property that, in each community, each member already has or does not have is a given that the community does not seek to alter. This means that the members of an exchange community do not begin on an equal footing, even if they begin with the same number of 'credits'. The community is penetrated by existing inequalities that are exacerbated in the crisis, and it is hard for it to remain unaffected by, and avoid taking part in, the devaluation of labour power at a broader social scale. Thus, in websites where moneyless community exchanges take place, one can encounter requests for day labourers or domestic services in exchange for food and accommodation.

Similar, then, to the case of neighbourhood assemblies, the universality and equality presupposed here by 'equal' or 'fair' exchange, using a medium that is uncontrolled by the state (a 'moneyless' website or an alternative currency), is a formal equality founded on equivalence, no different to that facilitated by the state, which is in tension with the notion of 'solidarity'. What is taken as given, left unquestioned, is property, taken as a defining and unalienable asset of every individual:[11] what each individual 'has to sell', what each 'can offer'. Whether one person 'owns' nothing but their own body and can only 'offer' their labour power, while another person owns a house with a garden that needs gardening, or several hectares of fields with fruit that need picking, or hotel rooms that need painting, is theoretically of no concern to such a 'solidarity economy', as long as the alternative currency is used according to the rules and is not counterfeited. Here, one has to ask whether the members of the community benefit in the same way by entering into such a relation. Through an alternative exchange network, the painter-decorator who paints hotel rooms can get 'credits' that they can only spend at a limited number of local outlets, in order to cater for their basic means of subsistence. The hotel owner, in contrast, is able to

11. Pashukanis' critique of the bourgeois legal form and the link between bourgeois individuality and property is particularly relevant here. Evgeniï Bronislavovich Pashukanis, 'The General Theory of Law and Marxism', in *Selected Writings on Marxism and Law* (London: Academic, 1980).

rent the newly painted rooms, perhaps now at a higher price, for profit in *real* – i.e. state-guaranteed – money. This can be even worse for the worker in the case of moneyless exchange, where only food and accommodation is offered, effecting an even deeper type of dependency. The exchange community is not formally concerned about this. But since the act of exchange takes place in the same way as it does in the rest of the economy, one wonders exactly at which point an act of 'solidarity' took place. Even if, in a great proportion of cases, alternative currency exchange takes place between persons who are in similar economic hardship, the social principle remains the same: a formal equality that has the sole effect of perhaps increasing the total amount of money circulating in an economy, without questioning the material inequality of participants.

This principle can also be seen in time banks,[12] where the general equivalent is time, and labour time is exchanged with labour time only: ostensibly there are no employers, but only people who work for each other. While in other micro-markets a general equivalent measures exchange value, and the value of abstract labour is defined in exchange, time banks attempt to define the value of abstract labour on the basis of *concrete* labour time. Different types of labour are not freely equalised in the act of exchange, but rather their value is predefined by the length of time that each concrete act of labour consumes. In this way, the qualitative aspects of labour, such as productivity, intensity and complexity, are ignored. According to this definition of equality, all types of skills and all levels of capacity and productivity are *formally* worth the same. The ideal time bank exchange is when two persons agree to do something for each other in equal lengths of time, they get to know each other, and create a sense of community. Still, the formal mediation of this give and take by the time bank, the very principle of this temporal equality, restricts rather than facilitates what individuals could do for each other in the name of *solidarity*, as, for example, helping each other when in need without asking for something in return. While the time bank allows for informal free decisions as to which types of labour are exchanged with which, allowing some space for time *gifted* in relation to what this time might earn in the official currency (for example, a lawyer helping out an older woman in a rent dispute with her landlord, while she mends socks

---

12. Examples: the Exarchia Time Bank 'Syn-Chróno' (syntwxronw.org); the Solidarity Time Bank in Moschato (mesopotamia.gr); the Bank of Free Time set up by the local authority of Lamia (lamia-city.gr).

for him), the time bank also restricts the meaning of this act to equivalence (one hour of legal work = one hour of mending socks). It disguises
its meaning as a potential act of solidarity, or of the free sharing of one's
resources, which may have taken place regardless.

This reduction of acts of solidarity to equivalence has the potential
to also produce the opposite result, if the participants of the time bank
begin to make demands on it to guarantee a 'fair exchange'. This would
immediately raise the issue of the qualitative differences of concrete
labour, so that standards may be instituted as to how much work has
to be done within an hour, or as to whether highly skilled labour can be
exchanged with less-skilled labour. The effect of this would be not only
to cancel out the principle of solidarity, but also to make the time bank
increasingly similar to the official form of money.

The perspective, popular in the squares as well as mainstream media,
that has promoted alternative or moneyless exchange relations as a radical
'solution' to poverty and unemployment supposes that money itself is a
type of domination instead of what it is: an abstract equivalent, a function, the most efficient medium of exchange.[13] Commodity exchange
necessitates money, it is not 'dominated' by it. Exchange, the division
of labour, abstract labour, are presupposed by the production of surplus
value, in other words, by exploitation. They are not 'genuine' relations
that then come to be appropriated or corrupted by the form of money
and capitalists. 'Monetary diversity' might then increase the number of
exchanges that take place in an economy at a time of crisis,[14] and it might
create a limited sense of independence from mainstream banks and the
state, but their very principle reproduces existing social relations that are
based on formal equality, going against, instead of promoting, relations
of solidarity that would go beyond it, to establish relations not based on
a logic of equivalence but on social needs and desires.

Other projects do not criticise the form of money, but rather they
criticise 'intermediaries': those traders who mediate between producers
and the shops, and profit from the process of distribution. They thus
attempt to circumvent supermarket profits and enable cheaper access to
local produce while also benefiting producers. Examples are the collective
Kypseli, which aims to link small agricultural producers of ecological
products with urban consumers; the network To Ntoulapi, which

---

13. Roumeliotis, 'Antallaktikī oikonomía'.
14. Ibid.

aims to broach similar links, and to share resources on producing and exchanging quality affordable food, and Zīkos, a self-managed grocery in Exarchia, which promotes the 'horizontal and solidarity trade of food products'. This structure comprises a 'Market Without Intermediaries', which links urban consumers with small producers from non-urban provinces. Many street markets 'beyond intermediaries' have been organised by neighbourhood assemblies or other local 'solidarity' associations. This type of activity began to attract attention in February 2012, when potato producers from Drama, in protest against low wholesale prices and the destruction of 70 per cent of their production, gave away for free ten tons of potatoes at the 24th Agrotica Trade Fair in Thessaloniki.[15] Their act highlighted the disjunction between the hardship of producers and overpriced produce in supermarkets, caused by the artificiality of demand, when such a great proportion of agricultural products never makes it to market. While this campaign operates within the rules of the capitalist economy, it also questions the irrationality of the profit motive, which artificially prevents excess food supply from reaching those in hardship. But the emphasis on the criticism of intermediaries could be exaggerated. In Greece, daily street markets, where agricultural producers can set up stalls, are well-established institutions and this is not an innovative activity. These initiatives increase the number of outlets and opportunities for producers to sell directly, and so they increase the pressure for lower prices. While these types of networks do not effect any kind of radical criticism of social relations (for all we know, the 'small producers' could be employing immigrant labour under the slave-like conditions that have become a norm in Greece), they can be understood as a collective attempt to increase the average wage indirectly, by pushing for price deflation.

Alongside projects centred on exchange, there have been some initiatives that expand to the sphere of sustainable eco-production, such as Nea Guinea and Spithari, aiming to create autonomous networks for the self-managed household and collective production of food (urban gardening), health (production and use of herbal remedies, yoga), clothing (knitting, etc.), building and even energy (offering seminars on building small sustainable energy generators). This vision aims for households or collectives to be able to produce all or most of their needs independently of capitalist networks, although Nea Guinea does

---

15. 'Patátes Moírasan Paragōgoí stī Thessaloníkī', *Vīma*, 4/2/2012.

not specify the cost of raw materials for the most complex types of production or how the products of home production are to be exchanged or distributed. Indeed, these groups do not primarily present themselves as an immediate answer to subsistence in the crisis, but they are more interested in disseminating relevant knowledge for those who are so inclined and have the basic resources to live an 'off grid' eco-friendly lifestyle, whether in urban or rural environments.

Activities of 'solidarity' or charity have been more popular, particularly via neighbourhood assemblies. These have involved collections of donated food ('social groceries'), unwanted clothes (usually promoted as 'clothes exchanges') and unexpired medicine to give to locals in need. This extends to the provision of free services such as free nurseries and lessons for children, and free self-organised primary health services provided by volunteers.[16] Although these services can also be provided by the state, it is relevant to note an important difference. Where local authorities have become involved in such projects, they have turned 'social groceries' into administered food banks, access to which requires proof of identity, residence and income.[17] Thus the relationship between giver and taker is here much more direct and personal, involving trust rather than a concern to administer societal resources. But the debate has frequently emerged regarding whether these are charitable activities or acts of 'solidarity'. Local organisations tend to insist that what they do is 'solidarity', but what is the difference from charity? According to its definition, charity is the voluntary giving of help to those in need. The Greek word used in these discussions is 'philanthropy', which literally means 'love for humanity', a word that belongs to the Christian ethical tradition. In this relation, the recipient is not expected to give back to the giver, who will instead be rewarded by God. In a less religious context, the history of bourgeois philanthropy, the giver helps because of pity for the recipients, or, more cynically, for publicity or social control over them. On the contrary, solidarity, in the English language, suggests not one-sided giving but mutuality, common interests, interdependence

---

16. For example, the local assembly of Vyronas-Kaisariani-Pagrati has offered free music lessons, and the assembly of Kolonos-Sepolia-Akadimia Platonos has offered free school support lessons. 'Archizoume Mathīmata Ekmathīsīs Flogeras', *Syneleysikatoikwnvkp. squat.gr*, 2/10/2013; Laïkī Syneleusī Kolōnou-Sepoliōn-Akadīmias Platōnos, 'Mathīmata Allīleggýis kai Fétos apó tī Laïkī Synéleusī', Akadimia-platonos.blogspot.com, 9/10/2014.
17. For example: Dīmos Peiraia, 'Koinōnikó Pantopōleío, Tmīma Koinōnikōn Drastīriotītōn, Dikaiologītiká', Pireasnet.gr.

and trust. The Greek word is *allīleggýī*, whose etymology similarly means 'mutual reliance'. Solidarity is mutuality, but not a formally 'equal' exchange. Rather, it is a mutuality based on interdependence and the ability to recognise and respond to one another's needs.

The question then is whether solidarity defines the characteristics of an act itself, or if it is a subjective ethical position or moral attitude that can merely be declared. What is the difference between charities collecting bags of surplus goods at supermarkets and neighbourhood assemblies collecting donated bags of food in social centres? Perhaps the only non-subjective difference is the context and the lack of mediation. To the extent that a neighbourhood assembly organises campaigns, alongside its food and medicine collections, which themselves question social power relations and in which the members support one another, it can speak of solidarity. The limits to the creation of such a context of solidarity are yet again the unrecognised effects of interclass composition in assemblies and other local associations. If the members' interests are at odds, and they seek to overcome this democratically instead of addressing existing inequalities and social hierarchies, how can they form a relation of mutuality?

The discourse opposing charity and voluntary work to solidarity has also been very prominent in self-organised initiatives for health. There are many such local health initiatives. The most well known of those that see themselves as acts of solidarity and as parts of social movements are the Social Solidarity Health Centre in Thessaloniki – which began in the context of the 300 immigrants' hunger strike in 2011 – and the Social Space for Health in Petralona, Athens.[18] A similar initiative also began in Exarchia. The necessity for these centres arose as increasing numbers of people lost access to healthcare due to unemployment, while most immigrants never had access. The centres are run by volunteer health workers, and all space, equipment and medicine is donated. They are often openly politicised and part of doctors' struggles against the dismantling of public healthcare and campaigns for free universal healthcare, attempting to enact its decommodification in practice.

Here, participants have often been criticised about the possibility that they could be replacing state provisions by volunteering and thus enabling the dismantlement of public healthcare. Health workers have

---

18. Forum Metanastōn Krītīs, 'Keímeno gia to Symplīrōma Enós Chrónou apó tīn Apergía Peínas tōn 300 apó tous Giatroús tōn 50 tīs Thessaloníkīs', Fmkritis.wordpress. com, 26/1/2012.

questioned how solidarity health centres distinguish themselves from charity projects such as Médecins du Monde and whether they remain independent from the state, NGOs, the church, corporations and political parties.[19] Indeed, there is a basis for such criticism, given that many initiatives for 'social health centres' have not particularly hidden their acceptance of donations from pharmaceutical companies and NGOs, accompanied by a relatively untroubled discourse of volunteering.[20]

Those who have been aware of these issues and contradictions, as, for example, the Social Solidarity Health Centre in Thessaloniki, have tried to negotiate a balance between the symbolic or political meaning of their activity and its actual effectiveness, which, due to the way the health industry is organised in capitalism, is impossible without a major source of funding. The decommodification of 'health' is faced as a task that is enormous and far beyond what a small group of health workers can achieve. The point then becomes not so much to provide a complete service, or to save the lives of all those neglected by the state healthcare system – which would amount to directly replacing previously paid labour with unpaid labour – as it is to help others, to the degree that one can, using one's skills and limited time and resources, and to create an example of how access to healthcare *could* be free.

Since healthcare has existed historically also as part of the state's management of the population – with this becoming particularly evident in the overlap between the securitisation of health and the biopolitical management of migration and sexuality (see Part III) – health workers' practices are defined by the knowledge produced by the modern science of medicine, which is itself premised on a power relation between doctor and patient (typically mediated by the state), the researcher and the human body as object, and on a social definition of health and illness that is itself a form of power.

This type of critique is not necessarily new to health practitioners in solidarity centres, as demonstrated by the texts written by those involved at the Social Space for Health, which runs in the occupation of a closed down health centre in Petralona, Athens.[21] In this project, participants

---

19. For example, the pamphlet titled 'Oi Kairoí Allázoun' circulated in Thessaloniki in February 2012, signed by 'health workers and local struggle assemblies'.

20. 'Thessaloníkī: Koinōnikó Iatreío gia Karkinopatheís apó tis Archés tou 2013', *Prōto Théma*, 11/12/2012.

21. Koinōnikós Chōros gia tīn Ygeía tīs Laïkīs Synéleusīs Petralōnōn, Koukakíou kai Thīseíou, *Ī Diarkīs Diadikasía tīs Autoorgánōsīs tīs Ygeías sta Petrálōna (Méros 20)*, pamphlet (Athens, 2013).

have attempted to question the power relation of doctor and patient, by creating a space for the sharing of information on health in place of a specialist's desk. The focus there is on learning and helping one another rather than the provision of service. Indeed, the Health Space at Petralona did not form itself in order to meet needs but in order to enact an example of a different form of relating. In this sense, it differs from the Solidarity Health Centre in Thessaloniki, which was originally set up to support the immigrants on hunger strike in February–March 2011, who had no access to public healthcare. Very few immigrants use the service at Petralona, and its participants in the health space mostly belong to the same local social network. In every case, the validity of the word 'solidarity' depends on the way social networks negotiate the social inequalities within its composition.

Yet the limits these efforts can face are not only internal but also external. Freely sharing healthcare and knowledge – or even better, co-producing health knowledge – is both a critical and a necessary act addressing hardship in the crisis, and producing relations of solidarity. It is, however threatened by 'healthcare' being systematically commodified *everywhere else.*

Here we should note that healthcare is an area in which the SYRIZA-led government intervened, not completely letting down its members involved in healthcare campaigns and social health centres. They abolished access charges for the uninsured and instituted access for immigrants without requiring asylum or legal residency status (but other forms of documentation are required). The system is now closer to offering universal healthcare on paper, although not in practice. For one, the healthcare budget has continued to shrink under the government's Memorandum commitment to budget surpluses, and so the system's resources have not kept up with increased demand. Pharmaceuticals also do not come free under this scheme except in cases of exceptionally low incomes. But even those covered by public insurance funds encounter barriers to free, high-quality healthcare. Given the uncontrolled penetration of private practice into public hospitals, many patients with serious illnesses end up paying for extra medical attention and risky operations, feeling insecure in an under-resourced system. It is also notable that, despite nominal accessibility, the solidarity health centres are still a necessity for many who cannot afford their medicines or who are caught up in bureaucracy or waiting lists. Thus, a formally 'universally accessible' system is essentially inaccessible and even promotes the growth of a private health sector when underfunded. In this context, do solidarity health centres offer anything more than plugging service gaps for the most vulnerable?

Here we come to the question of 'alternatives' and the possibilities that alternative practice can open up. Insofar as its practice does not come into confrontation with what it wishes to overcome (in this case, the principle of exchange, health as a form of power, the hierarchical division of labour, health service as a commodity), but, instead, merely coexists with it, the object remains intact, and the activity remains circumscribed. In the cases examined, as in health centres, where *uncalculated* exchange, or even giving without return, were practised, mutual support was circumscribed by the scarcity imposed by the restructuring, and the inability to meet one another's needs. The members of such communities have almost no access to surplus wealth (except through donations), but only to surplus labour power, often that of surplus proletarian populations thrown out of production. The energies of this population can be, and are, given away in the form of free labour, but again this cannot guarantee anyone's subsistence. Solidarity will continue to be circumscribed by poverty, unless it questions more directly the rules of economic rationality and the social form of value and equivalence that governs capitalist social relations.

There is, then, a difference between the generalisation and convergence of ruptures that come into conflict with existing social relations, and the enlargement and spreading of alternative autonomous collectively managed spaces, or, even, the multiplication and enlargement of what have been called 'the commons':[22] collectively obtained or occupied spaces (buildings or land) to be used as social spaces and resources for subsistence.[23] Occupied, as opposed to owned or rented, spaces tend to be more politically driven and have been strongly attacked by the state,[24] not only under the ND-led government but, as we will see, under SYRIZA as well. Occupying spaces that are private or about to be privatised begins by challenging private property and coming into

---

22. Caffentzis, 'Future of "The Commons"'.

23. Collectively managing land for agriculture became popular in the crisis, as for example in the project 'Periastikés Kalliérgeies' (PER.KA.) in the peri-urban region of Thessaloniki (perka.org).

24. Several squatted social spaces in the centre of Athens were raided and closed by police in early 2013 (Villa Amalias, Lelas Karagianni, Skaramaga, ASOEE). Anta Psarrá, 'Katalīpseis, ī Émmonī Idéa tou N. Déndia', TVXS.gr, 3/9/2013.

conflict with the state. Yet, collective spaces can also quickly come into conflict with their outside in another way. The form of the autonomous, spatially delimited community is at the same time grounded on a form of common ownership, whether it is legally recognised or de facto claimed. The fact that such ownership is in common does not stop it being a form of ownership which sets up certain boundaries. These boundaries are often policed according to certain criteria set by the community, and it is important to ask what those criteria are. Obviously, there is a difference between actively excluding the police from an occupation and inadvertently establishing social and cultural norms that exclude immigrants from it, or making the space unwelcome to women and non-hetero/cis-normative people. Thus the multiplication of communities alone does not necessarily entail the overcoming of boundaries to produce a kind of universality. Communities are constituted by various forms of conscious or un-thought exclusions, which may or may not advance their critique of existing social relations.

The tension of a community with its outside is most evident in projects that aim to 'liberate' public space from privatisation but also to maintain its internal political integrity. If a lovingly planted occupied park, intended as a haven of community and solidarity in the middle of the city jungle, is as much a public space as any other in the city, it will inevitably be a locus of the same social tensions that exist in the rest of the city. To the extent the community defends the space from the police, it then also finds that it has to protect itself from the petty crime (mostly selling counterfeit cigarettes, drug dealing and drug use, usually carried out by immigrants) that has discovered a new safe haven. In Athens, this tension has led to the policing of such spaces by its members, often culminating in violent expulsions.[25] Here a new, autonomously instituted rule is imposed, and the invaders who disrespect it are expelled. Evidently the new social principle of harmonious coexistence in the occupied space has limited means to negotiate the fact that those invading 'criminal elements' often belong to the most systematically oppressed, racialised and even dehumanised sections of capitalist society.

Self-organised communities and initiatives have been the most creative aspect – in the sense of producing new social groupings or organising communities – of the struggles against the restructuring. Yet

---

25. In particular, the campaigns against drug dealers and drug users in Exarchia led to the formation of 'Groups for Popular Defence' (Omádes Laïkís Autoámynas). These groups also actively expel members from the area.

this creativity faced a core ambivalence, between a practice of exchange between equals/equivalents, and practices of unrestrained or unquantified solidarity, that is, a mutuality beyond the principle of equivalence. For projects that prioritise the principle of exchange, 'solidarity' is a misnomer. An interaction based on a formal notion of equality that presumes an abstract individual cannot be solidarity, because this perpetuates precisely the forms of exploitation and domination to which formal bourgeois justice is blind. In the cases where forms of equivalence were surpassed, as in some neighbourhood assemblies, solidarity health centres, or in collective kitchens, this practice was circumscribed by proletarian dependence upon the wage relation and the so-called 'real' economy under crisis, in which the calculation of value has been continually reimposed.

8

The Forest Against Work,
Workers Against the Forest

Local struggles against development projects may at first sight appear not to be related to the crisis and the anti-austerity movements, and to occur in this period contingently. But the fact that two such local struggles of unprecedented intensity took place in the crisis is not a coincidence. These struggles share the core characteristics of the anti-austerity movements of this period: they are interclass, and in them the themes of community and property reappear in full force. These two struggles are the movement in Keratea, Attiki (early 2011) against the creation of a new landfill site, and the struggle in Skouries, Chalkidiki (2012 and continuing), against the opening of a goldmine. In both cases, the concerns of the residents were ecological (living conditions, the quality of their water and the fate of the area's woodlands would be affected) and economic (in that property values would collapse, the quality of the soil would become unsuitable for agriculture and, in the case of Skouries, the local tourism industry would be negatively affected).

Keratea

The case of Keratea is particularly interesting because its practices of interclass, cross-ideological self-organising, involving blockades, the occupation of spaces and confrontations with police, preceded and anticipated the movement of the squares.

The residents of Keratea have faced the question of waste management since 2001, when the government's waste management project for the Attica region selected locations near Keratea and Grammatiko as landfill sites. Since then, the project had not got off the ground because of the towns' legal challenges to the government's project.[1] The residents'

---

1. 'Ī istoría Archízei to 2003 kai Akóma Den Échei Teleiōsei', *Kathīmerinī*, 8/7/2009; Nántia Vasileiádou, 'Néa Epeisódia sto Sírial tou Grammatikoú', *Eleutherotypía*, 24/10/2009.

objections have been that a more technologically advanced and envi-
ronmentally friendly waste management system is possible, and that,
in the case of Keratea, the chosen location on the hill of Ovriokastro is
inappropriate. First, the position is close to a recognised archaeological
site.[2] The entire region of Lavreotiki is of archaeological interest, partly
because of the ancient ruins of mining tunnels running underneath the
region, dated back to the fifth century BC. These tunnels also pose risks
that toxic wastewater could easily find its way to Lavreotiki's popular
coast. Second, the Lavreotiki region has been formally recognised as an
area of special natural beauty.[3] Third, the landfill site is close to local
farmland and houses, which will be subject to compulsory purchase.
The farmland partly receives water from a spring on Ovriokastro, so the
development is expected to deteriorate the quality of local land as well as
devalue properties in the area.

In December 2010, the government outsourced Attica's waste
management from local authorities to private companies whose owners
have held powerful positions in the Greek economy,[4] and a few days
later it announced that landfill works were authorised to begin. The EU
had given the Greek government an ultimatum to close down existing
unregulated landfill sites and begin operating the new, more technologically advanced ones by 28 December, or pay a fine.[5] Meanwhile, Keratea
residents blockaded the nearby Lavriou avenue to stop machinery
reaching the site. In the early hours of 11 December, large numbers of
riot police, accompanied by a government prosecutor and vehicles for
the landfill works, attempted to reach Ovriokastro. A large number of
residents came to support the blockade, arguing that private land in the
area had not yet been purchased by the state, that the Archaeological
Council had not approved the project and that fresh litigation on the
project was pending in the courts. The prosecutor sent the police away,

---

2. FEK B' 1070/29.12.1995.

3. FEK B' 852/03.09.1980.

4. Specifically, the management of the landfill at Grammatiko was undertaken by Helector
S.A., owned by George Bompolas (also the owner of a major television channel, MEGA
TV, and the high-circulation newspapers, *Ethnos* and *Imerisia*). Helector collaborated
in the project with Mesogeos S.A., which contains capitals owned by Spyros Latsis via
Eurobank, as well as the ship-owning Laskaridis Group. Mesogeos then undertook the
works at Keratea, via a joint venture with Proet S.A. and Edraco S.A. Gelantali, M., 'Látsīs
kai Adelfoí Laskarídī sto Paichnídi tōn Skoupidiōn', *Eleutherotypía*, 27/2/2011.

5. Hará Tzanavára, '28 Dekemvríou: Teleutaía Désmeusī gia tous Skoupidótopous',
Eleutherotypía, 13/12/2010.

but they returned in the evening. The encounter escalated into severe clashes between the residents and riot police who attacked them with teargas, trapped and assaulted older residents, including the mayor, and humiliated arrestees by taking their clothes off. They responded by rioting against the police.

The clashes continued in the following days on the highway and in the town of Keratea, and descended into a kind of vendetta between residents and riot police, which lasted 128 days. Police made first-time use of rubber bullets and water cannons in Keratea. According to residents, the riot police were gratuitously violent, threw teargas into their balconies and yards, damaged private cars and other private property, demolished the huts in which they met to organise and even stole private items. They avenged this by attacking the local police station and burning police officers' cars. Residents also sabotaged the machinery at the landfill site. Transit through Lavriou avenue was closely policed throughout this period, with residents finding it difficult to access their farmland.[6] After the first few months, police themselves began to voice objections about being asked to carry out such a fruitless and dangerous operation for such a long time.[7] Meanwhile, the Lavrio County Court issued repeated decisions to prohibit the continuation of the landfill works, until the outstanding procedures were carried out (compulsory purchase orders, archaeological and other official studies, planning permissions).[8] On 18 April 2011, riot police forces withdrew from the area and no further efforts were made to continue the works.[9] Although there has been no attempt to continue the works at the time of writing, the ND-led coalition government did attempt to restart the process in 2013–14.[10]

Fighting against the landfill and against the police forces united the residents of Keratea beyond prior political or class-based divisions and age differences, and changed their views about oppositional practice. The town's unity was evident: every time riot police attempted to break the blockade or make arrests, the church bells would ring, alerting residents

6. Aris Chatzigeorgiou, 'Ī Máchī tīs Keratéas', *Eleutherotypía*, 13/12/2010; Aléxandros Kyriakópoulos, 'Doliofthorá ta Xīmerōmata', *Eleutherotypía*, 18/12/2010; Aléxandros Kyriakópoulos, 'Keratéa: Matōména Christoúgenna', *Eleutherotypía*, 20/12/2010.

7. 'Policemen Ask to Be Removed from Keratea', *Kathīmerinī*, 13/4/2011.

8. 'Keratéa: Anastolī Ergasiōn Kataskeuīs CH.Y.T.A. sto Ovriókastro', Skai.gr, 1/3/2011.

9. '"Anakōchī" stīn Keratéa', *Eleutherotypía*, 18/4/2011.

10. N.M., 'Keratéa – A. Liósia: Prochōroún oi Monádes Aporrimmátōn', *Eleutherotypía*, 18/6/2013; Argyris Demertzis. 'Prásino StE sto Vounó-Ch.y.t.a.', *Eleutherotypía*. 22/10/2014.

to bring reinforcements. According to the police, more than a thousand combative demonstrators confronted them on a daily basis.[11] Those who participated in the fight say that the entire town was up in arms every day, and through the struggle they began to meet their neighbours and improve their relationships with each other forming a kind of community that did not exist before. But this community of struggle was loosely and thus flexibly organised. Most of the actions were not pre-organised, but were decided and enacted by small groups on the spot, which was widely accepted as an effective aspect of the movement. Rioting also became an accepted practice, among older residents as well, justified by what they saw as gratuitous police violence.[12]

Residents were particularly outraged by the hostility with which television channels portrayed their struggle. One TV presenter even claimed that the rioting at Keratea was 'led by a bunch of Albanians' in an attempt to stir racist sentiment among Keratea residents and against the movement. 'News' of this kind was cultivated by the police authorities, who spread to the media the story that 'Albanians' in the movement 'smuggled rockets' from the neighbouring country.[13] Indeed, many Keratea residents were of Albanian background, but they did not stand out in the movement.[14] The government's attempt to stoke racism to its advantage and the broader role of mainstream television channels as opposition to movements would provoke a generalised anti-media stance, which later became particularly evident in the movement of the squares.

The movement in Keratea, indeed, had several common elements with the squares, and so it should be seen as part of parallel sociopolitical or ideological trends, despite the fact that its aims were local. It could even be seen as a precursor, and perhaps one of the inspirations, of the squares, given that opposition to the memorandum and to austerity was already building up, and Keratea residents, understanding themselves as part of such opposition, often wondered what would happen if militant practices like theirs invaded the centre of Athens. This self-understanding of being part of a broader, as-yet undeveloped citizens' movement was

---

11. Ibid.
12. Konstantinos Katrios, Afroditi Babasi and Nondas Skarpelis, *128 Days at the Roadblocks*, video, full HD, colour (2013). The information in this paragraph is based on residents' views and accounts as expressed in this documentary. Available with English subtitles at www.youtube.com/watch?v=dWdfWpdalgo.
13. Lambropoulos, B. G. 'Ī EL.AS. Fovátai ... Vomvardismó stīn Keratéa', *Vīma*, 23/3/2011.
14. Katrios et al., *128 Days*.

evident in the use of anti-IMF slogans and Keratea residents' under-standing of their local problem as the result of the country being under IMF control.[15] Anti-political notions that politicians were self-interested and corrupt, favouring corporate interests, were also prevalent, as in the squares. These two points of reprobation – political corruption and national 'betrayal' – were mainstream responses to the crisis of citizen-ship, which deepened as the restructuring progressed.[16]

As in the squares, the movement's discourse and practices went beyond left- and right-wing traditions to form a configuration of both, combined with unprecedentedly combative street practices, and spontaneous, decentralised organising. Over this period, increasingly violent practices of riot were legitimised within movements, when back in December 2008 such practices were limited to minorities of mostly young people. In Keratea the broadening appeal of such practices became evident for the first time.

Despite the participation and solidarity of an anarchist contingent within the movement, its combative, seemingly anti-state practice cannot be taken at face value. Keratea residents acted combatively against the state's disciplinary apparatus, often breaking the state's laws while also seeking its recognition. The state's violent rejection of demands led it to escalate its own violent practice and destroy property, in defence of 'smaller' property and collective territory. The movement's discourse was not anti-capitalist, but against 'bigger' capitals, international insti-tutions and their power to affect government decisions, which they saw as having a disastrous impact on small property and 'ordinary citizens'. In these respects, the movement in Keratea, like many of the movements that followed it, produced a community of citizens grounded in territory and property relations. Its composition could not have avoided being interclass, given the universal ecological impact on the area and the wide spread of property ownership in smaller towns. Locality suggests not only the defence of private property but also of common territory. In this respect, the formation of political identity on the basis of locality paralleled the neighbourhood assemblies that sprung out of the similarly interclass squares. And, similar to the way in which the squares were territorialised as spaces *for* the movement, Ovriokastro had also become a space where the movement could meet and organise, a space to be defended also for its function as a collective resource for struggle.

---

15. Katrios et al., *128 Days*.
16. Ibid. See also Chapters 12 and 13.

The community of struggle, however, was frequently imagined as a community of national citizens and property owners.

The conservative tendency in the movement was thus expressed in its defence of property, a militaristic-territorial orientation to riot, its unproblematic interclass unity and the attribution of the problem to 'corruption', which, similar to the squares, reduced the broader problem of the 'unviability' of ecological waste management under conditions of capitalist crisis to a matter of 'self-interested' and 'unpatriotic' politicians. The concept of 'betrayal' has a clear nationalist connotation. Waste management becomes a question of patriotism rather than being linked to its universal dimensions of human health and the destruction of nature. It conveys a fetishistic fixation on the national state's obligations to national citizens and a self-protective stance: the root of the problem is thought to be the *national* leaders' subservience to the *international* IMF. Land and territory are conceived as private and, at best, national property rather than as nature. It is no wonder that anger against 'the lying (mainstream) media' was similarly frequently framed by the figure of the traitor, opening the way for wider acceptance of minor far-right media spreading conspiracy theories in which Greeks *as Greeks* were the target. In this ideological context, the level of violence was justified on the basis of betrayal: a government that has performed high treason is no longer legitimate and any form of violence against it is acceptable.

Thus, while the struggle in Keratea was able to break through divisions among atomised citizens, cultivating the idea and practice of a community of struggle that appropriates and defends common resources, and questioning the limits of legality that signal the end of struggles each time they are heavily policed, at the same time it was limited by and reproduced a limited narrative of struggle that opposed the self-protection of local and national community against a threatening, destructive and predatory international outside.

Skouries

Like Keratea, the movement in Skouries was a locally based territorial struggle against a development project – a goldmine – that would affect the ecology of the local area, and by extension local private property and agricultural, recreational or touristic uses of the land. Similar to Keratea, local residents' acts of sabotage were followed by riot police invasions into the town of Ierissos and arrests. The struggle in Skouries was not as successful, considering that the goldmine has begun works and has already destroyed a large area of woodland, even though locals continue to protest at the time of writing.

Skouries is the location of a contested open pit and underground goldmine on Mount Kakkavos, in the north-east of the Chalkidiki peninsula (Municipality of Aristotelis) in northern Greece, near the coastal towns (and summer resorts, given their magnificent beaches) of Stratoni and Ierissos. The area already hosts two other mines, also owned by Hellas Gold since 2003,[17] when the state sold the assets to the company. The sale has been a significant point of criticism, given that it took place without economic assessment of the assets' value or an open competition process, and relieved Hellas Gold of taxation and royalties to the state. On 23 February 2011, the EC decided that Hellas Gold ought to repay the Greek state €15 million in illegal state subsidies.[18] But beyond the costs to the state, residents of the region who oppose the mine are primarily concerned about the environmental impact of the project. The goldmine in Skouries is set to be the largest of the three mines, involving deforestation of an area larger than 2.5 square kilometres, and open pit mining of 24,000 tons per day.[19] The impact of existing mines is already visible, as the Stratoni coast has often become bright orange with heavy mineral deposits from the mining, and researchers from the Greek Centre for Marine Research have claimed that much of marine life has disappeared from the Stratoni coast.[20] Campaigners, having collected a series of critical reports from sympathetic Greek scientists and metallurgy specialists, criticise Hellas Gold's environmental impact assessment (EIA) for proposing a metallurgical method that is not recommended on soil composition with high percentages of arsenic, as is the case in Skouries.[21] They also claim the EIA underestimates the scale

---

17. Hellas Gold was owned by George Mpompolas' Aktor S.A., until it was transferred to the Canadian El Dorado Gold in exchange for a significant proportion of shares in El Dorado Gold. This means that, in this case too, the interests of major media outlets were also implicated (see note 4 on the companies that undertook landfill works in Keratea). Vasilis Georgas, 'Se Kanadoús Ólos o Ellīnikós Chrysós', *Eleutherotypía*, 20/12/2011.

18. European Commission, 'State Aid: Greek Mining Company Ellinikos Xrysos Needs to Repay Around €15 Million in Illegal Subsidies', Europa.eu, 23/2/2011.

19. ENVECO S.A., *Meletī Perivallontikōn Epiptōseōn Metalleutikōn – Metallourgikōn Egkatastaseōn tīs Etairias Ellīnikos Chrysos stī Chalkidikī* (Athens: Hellas Gold, 2010).

20. Sakis Apostolakis, '"Galázia Sīmaía" stī Nekrī Thálassa tou Stratōníou', *Eleutherotypía*, 24/6/2014.

21. Georgios Psychogyiopoulos, 'Scholiasmós tīs 1492/2013 Apófasīs tou StE se Ó,Ti Aforá tīn Efarmosimótīta tīs Metallourgikīs Methódou Akariaías Tīxīs', Iekemtee.gr, 3/7/2013.

of deforestation that will result from mining, the depletion and pollution of water resources on Kakkavos mountain, the amount of mineral dust (arsenic) that will be unleashed to the atmosphere and the impact on the soil and ecosystems.[22] These impacts, they fear, will also destroy local tourism and agriculture.[23] The impact on water resources is a special cause of worry, since the company plans to deposit mining effluent into two water streams that pass through Skouries. These two streams end in the Kryonerio-Kampos basin, which supplies water to all the settlements in the southern Aristotelis region.[24]

Although residents in the region have opposed mining for decades, the crisis deepened the conflict, as the governments over 2011–14 promoted mining as a mode of 'development' that could help the national economy out of the crisis. Over this period, local legal campaigns against Hellas Gold's rights to exploit the region were able to repeatedly halt works at the mine. When the company was finally given permission to begin works in 2012, demonstrations and blockades at Skouries escalated, culminating into clashes with riot police and arrests with the charge of 'revolting against the state'.[25] This coincided with a period of heavier state policing of movements under the ND-led coalition government.

Five days after the Forest Inspectorate approved the deforestation of 1,754 square kilometres, on 17 February 2013, 40 masked persons broke into the mining site and set fire to containers, generators and other machinery belonging to Hellas Gold.[26] The movement had declared in a blog article that the approval was a *casus belli* against the mining works.[27] After the sabotage, heavy police forces arrived in Ierissos and Megali

22. Theochárīs Zágkas et al., 'Oi Epiptṓseis sto Fysikó Perivállon apó tī Leitourgía Metalleíōn (Exṓryxīs Chrysoú) stis Skouriés Chalkidikīs', report by the Scientific Committee of Teaching and Research Staff (Thessaloniki: Faculty of Forestry and Natural Environment, Aristotle University, 2013).

23. Coordinating Committee of Stageira-Akanthos Against Gold Mining, *Social, Economic and Environmental Impacts of Gold Mining in Halkidiki*, 2012, https://soshalkidiki.files. wordpress.com.

24. 'Sávvato 27/4/2013: Néa Parémvasī Katoíkōn gia Stamátīma tōn Ergasiōn tīs Ell. Chrysós sto Réma tou Karatzá', Antigoldgr.org – *Hellenic Mining Watch*, 28/4/2013.

25. An indicative article with videos from a particularly violent police intervention in a demonstration that ended in 14 arrests: 'Skouriés: ī Eirīnikī Diamartyría pou Metatrápīke se Kólasī', Antigoldgr.org, 22/10/2012; 'Martyría apó Skouriés', *Thessaloniki Today*, 28/2/2013.

26. Costas Kantouris, 'Masked Intruders Raid Greek Gold Mining Company', *Associated Press*, 17/2/2013.

27. Tolis Papageorgiou, 'Agōnas gia tī Zōī ī to Thánato. Ta Psémmata Teleíōsan. Sīmera Sympatriṓtes, na Petáxoume apó ton Tópo Mas tīn Eldorado Gold kai to Mpómpola', *Hellenic Mining Watch*, 11/2/2013.

Panagia and made over 50 arrests across local towns, even apprehending high-school students for interrogation.[28] Residents demonstrated daily outside police stations, and organised motorised demonstrations across the region.[29] Three weeks later, riot police surrounded Ierissos, blocking the two entries to the town to carry out arrests. They tried to disperse protests with teargas, which spread into a local school, causing further outrage. Only four arrests were eventually made, and only two of these persons were indicted for misdemeanours due to lack of evidence.[30] In response, on 11 March, one of the largest demonstrations ever against gold mining took place in Thessaloniki with over 15,000 people – a significant number for the northern city.[31] On 10 April, protesters attacked the Ierissos Police station and set police property on fire outside it. At 3.00 am, riot police raided the homes of two prominent campaigners and made arrests. Ierissos residents, with church bells ringing as in Keratea, gathered at the police station, broke in and wrecked the interior. Protests followed through the next day in Polygyros and Thessaloniki.[32] Yet the size and militancy of the campaign did not pay off. Over 2013–14, Hellas Gold carried out the deforestation of Skouries, amid protests which continue, much subdued, at the time of writing.

The movement in Skouries is special in that it opposed a capitalist investment in the middle of crisis, questioning the meaning of 'development'. What was presented as a universal good – increased economic activity and employment, advanced industry – was contested from the perspective of the land's prior condition and use. On the one hand, the movement resisted the privatisation of land and the damage of woodlands, waters and coasts as essential to biodiversity and recreation, and criticised the fact that there was no significant benefit to residents to counterbalance such damage. On the other hand, this was also a defence of smaller private property and business, its value and its worth as a source of subsistence, as in Keratea. But because 'big business' presented itself in the form of an investment, the issue was much more contro-

---

28. Stavroula Poulimeni, 'Chalkidikī: O Agōnas Synechízetai', AlterThess.gr, 26/2/2013.

29. Struggle Committees of Chalkidiki and Strymonikos Gulf, 'Viázetai ī Alītheia, Viázetai o Tópos kai ī Zōī mas', *Coordinating Committee of Associations of Stageira-Akanthos Against Gold Mining*, 20/2/2013.

30. Dina Batzia, '"Empólemī Zōnī" ī Ierissós', *Eleutherotypía*, 7/3/2013.

31. Sakis Apostolakis. 'Poreía – Stathmós stī Thessaloníkī katá tou Chrysoú', *Eleutherotypía*, 11/3/2013.

32. 'Pólemos stīn Ierissó: Eisvolī tōn MAT se Spítia stīn Ierissó. Dýo Syllīpseis gia tīn Epíthesī stis Skouriés', Iefimerida.gr, 10/4/2013.

versial. Even though Hellas Gold made no promises of any other form of social investment beyond offering jobs to a proportion of the local residents, the offer of 'jobs' was enough to produce internal conflict.

Thus, the conflict was from the very beginning not only between the region's residents and Hellas Gold, but also between residents themselves. While residents of Ierissos, Nea Roda, Ouranoupoli and Ammouliani have been mostly against the goldmine, the residents of Stratoni, Stageira, Paleochori and Neochori, from which most goldmine employees have been recruited, have been in favour. The residents of Megali Panagia have been divided in half.[33] Mine workers and anti-mine campaigners have engaged in a vicious feud that has divided towns and communities in the area.[34] Demonstrations and blockades at Skouries against the mine have invited frequent counter-demonstrations by Hellas Gold employees, which have often escalated into clashes,[35] and scuffles have broken out in the towns' cafés.[36] The active supporters of the mine argue in favour of 'development' and the 'right to work', accusing anti-mine campaigners and 'hypocritical ecologists' of exaggerating the damage caused by mining.[37] According to residents who had participated in previous campaigns against mining in the region, this conflict is not merely based on a difference of opinions and interests, but the mining companies have strategically recruited staff in order to split communities. Over the period 1989–2001, the regional alliances in relation to mining were continually reconfigured, depending on the mining companies' recruitment strategies and the location of the mines, so much so that villages whose majority was against mining on previous occasions support the mining this time, and vice versa.[38]

To be sure, the net number of new jobs to be created by the company has been disputed, considering the predicted loss of jobs and income

33. Alexandra Tzavella, 'Dekaeftá Chiliómetra Chōrízoun dýo Kósmous stī Chalkidikī', *Eleutherotypía*, 6/7/2013.
34. For example, the members of an initiative that opposes the mines at Megali Panagia has accused the mine employees of drunkenly defacing anti-mine materials and beating two women who were part of the campaign. Prōtovoulía Enántia stis Vlaptikótītes, 'Ótan o Ánthrōpos Chásei tīn Axioprépeiá tou Chrīsimopoieí Álla Mésa', Proevla.blogspot.com, 1/6/2012.
35. 'Éntasī se Diamartyría Katoíkōn Enántia sta Metalleía stis Skouriés', TVXS.gr, 20/3/2012.
36. Tzavella, 'Dekaeftá'.
37. Prōtovoulía Politōn Dīmou Aristotélī, 'Gia Poia "Oikologia" kai Poious "Oikologous" Milame stī VA Chalkidikī?', Politesaristoteli.blogspot.com, 23/12/2013.
38. Ntópios ex' Apostáseōs, 'Sto Veloúdino Chrysōrycheío tīs VA Chalkidikīs', *Ī Sfīka*, no. 5 (2013).

in tourism and agriculture. By July 2013, it had been announced that 3,025 workers would be hired by Hellas Gold via an EU and state-funded training programme, and, out of those, 866 would receive contracts lasting a minimum of four months. The latter would continue to be paid partially via state funding.[39] So much, then, for the development's supposed contribution to overcoming the sovereign debt crisis. Not only was the mine sold for an amount detrimental to the state budget, not only would taxes not be collected, but even the workers' wages would be paid by the state, and workers would not even get permanent contracts. Despite this, the Labour Centre of Chalkidiki (a local branch of GSEE) has also openly supported Hellas Gold, bringing legal action in its favour when the Aristotelis Regional Planning Authority ordered the company to cease construction because it had no planning permission.[40] Government ministers and MPs, as well as mainstream media, which, unsurprisingly, supported the mine, have promoted this particular workers' campaign – probably the only workers' campaign they have ever supported – in order to present the anti-mining campaign as minoritarian.[41]

The internal community conflict around mining is important in the context of the crisis for bringing to the surface and rendering problematic the politics of workers' identity and its relationship to capital, when workers are integrated as surplus in the wage relation. The miners – previously a symbol of the traditional working class – actively supported the goldmine, the central state authorities and the police, in order to save their jobs, often helping out in violently policing the movement. They also frequently appeared in the media to support a pro-mining policy. Interestingly, in response to criticism against the Labour Centre of Chalkidiki for supporting Hellas Gold, a defender of the miners showed off his socialist credentials: 'Lenin, writing in 1899, about the development of capitalism in Russia, argued that "on this particular matter, the latter (the interests of labour) coincide with the interests of big industrial capital".'[42] It is this precise coincidence that comes to the surface as the

39. Marios Aravantinos, 'Ellīnikós Chrysós: Théseis ergasías me xéna "kóllyva"', Koutipandoras.gr, 8/7/2013.
40. 'Prosfygī sto StE apó tīn Ellīnikós Chrysós kai to Ergatikó Kéntro Chalkidikīs gia tīn diakopī tōn kataskeuastikōn ergasiōn', Hellenic Mining Watch, 26/6/2013.
41. The ND MP Adonis Georgiadis has been particularly supporting of mine workers' mobilisations. 'Sygkéntrōsī ypér tōn metalleíōn stī Chalkidikī', Voria.gr, 2/3/2013.
42. My translation of both comment and quotation: Vladimir, 'Thoughts on "Prosfygī sto StE apó tīn Ellīnikós Chrysós', blog comment, Hellenic Mining Watch, 27/6/2013.

inevitable element of workers' identity at a time of crisis, revealing the politics of work (secure integration into the wage relation) as dependent upon the continuation of exploitation along with the forms of environmental damage that this entails. The miners' movement in Chalkidiki is a living example of the fact that to affirm 'labour', in these circumstances, is to affirm a category of capital.

Doing so, however, is far from being as simple as making a political 'choice'. As discussed previously, the politics of subsistence in the crisis mystifies the fact that 'subsistence' can have opposing meanings not only for different social groups, but it can be contradictory within the same social group. For the miners, on the one hand, having a job is essential in order to buy the means to *live*; on the other hand, perhaps living on polluted land and breathing polluted air will not exactly improve their life expectancy. 'Choosing' a precarious job and, at the same time, defending capitalist 'development', ignoring the destructive effects such development can have, is founded on a condition where having a job and a wage at all is experienced as a privilege of such proportions that it is worth allowing the destruction of the physical environment on which one's life depends. Thus, miners face two equally undesirable options: either economic difficulty because of unemployment, or health and economic difficulty because of the destruction of the resources for living. The depth of proletarian dependence on capitalist reproduction can translate into support for employers' interests instead of opposition to exploitation – a condition taken advantage of by GD in its attempt to create its own pro-employer labour unions.

The conflict over Skouries was clearly not one between capitalist reproduction and a non-capitalist mode of living that it attempted to subsume. The property relationship of locals to the land is precisely the dimension that would prohibit any depiction of the movement as one between 'local communities' and 'capital'. At the economic level, it could be described as a conflict between the interests of small property and small capitals (small agribusiness, small businesses dependent on tourism and hospitality) on the one hand, and those of 'large' capital on the other, together with the workers dependent on it. Yet such an economic description of the conflict would still be missing the dimension of access to the physical resources of life, such as air and water. The picture would also be incomplete without mentioning the dimension of a certain attachment to this region of Chalkidiki as a *place* for what is called its 'beauty', experienced by its residents and by regular visitors from the broader area of northern Greece. Admittedly, the theoretical tools required to analyse this aesthetic and emotional aspect of the conflict are not sufficiently developed here, and would require a further exploration of the links between identity, a sense of place and the sensual experience of the non-human-made (but always human-affected) world.

9

Care, Vulnerability and Gender Politics

Significantly, there was also a gendered dimension to the conflict in Skouries: while the miners' campaign in support of the mine has been male dominated, women were disproportionately represented in the anti-mine movement. If the reasons for this are not simply to be taken as an essential connection between femininity and nature, one ought to ask how women's sense of themselves, their social roles and their position in the division of labour in the affected Chalkidiki communities are linked to this struggle. An interview with women from the movement, which was published in *I Efimerída tōn Syntaktōn* alongside an open letter inviting other women to get involved, is revealing.[1] In this interview, women from Ierissos presented their role in the movement, particularly after multiple arrests had taken place, as that of providing emotional support to their children, parents and partners who suffered stress from the riot police forays into the town. The close relationships between these women in the small community of Ierissos meant that they all shared that suffering. They campaigned for the release of arrestees and against what they saw as a lack of justice and the violation of the right to the presumption of innocence. The reasons they quoted for fighting against the mine were the familiar ones – pollution of the air and land, the destruction of agriculture, the 'selling out' of state assets – but with an emphasis on their caring social role, particularly as mothers. They expressed concerns regarding the social integration of children after their frightening experiences with the police. The 'Women's Open Letter' described their own encounters with the police and their methods of crowd control, but emphasised their worries about the authorities beating, arresting and imprisoning *men*: their 'grandsons, sons, fathers, and brothers'. Strategically using the emotive weight and drama of the figure of the 'mother' in Greek culture, their letter attempted to appeal to the feelings and gain the solidarity of other women in the country *as carers of men and children*.

---

1. "'Eláte na Palépsoume Óloi Mazí'", *Efimerida Ton Syntakton*, 25/4/2013.

Another interview with women from Ierissos shows that not only did they present themselves in this way, but that, through the movement, they practised a sort of collective responsibility for the struggle, both through women's protest marches in Skouries, where they had to face police repression, but also by sharing everyday tasks of childcare, cooking, cleaning and other types of household maintenance: 'When there is a mobilisation and we have to be away, groups are organised for cooking and collective baby sitting. We no longer worry what will happen to our children.' 'We carry out lots of tasks together: writing collective texts, organising actions. The first serious collective act of solidarity we did was in 2010: Stratoni had been flooded [n.b. the mine workers' village, where El Dorado Gold is based] and we cleaned houses and cooked collectively.'[2] Despite the fact that most of these are typically gendered tasks, these women still felt that something had changed in their social role through the struggle, because they were now engaging in a *public* affair instead of only taking care of private affairs in the home. They were out in the public sphere, fighting politically and through their street actions: 'In this struggle our very role as women has changed. Previously we were just women of the household; now we have transformed into guerrillas.'[3]

Women's self-definition, or at least their self-presentation, in these interviews and open letter, did not challenge cultural norms – what Sherry Ortner has described as the norm of women's 'intermediate' status between nature and culture – but instead reinforced and utilised them to justify the value of their struggle to other women, who were presumed to also identify with these norms.[4] The women of the struggle themselves identified with their position as 'mediators' between nature and culture through their naturalised caring roles:[5] socialising children, nurturing and giving voice to emotions and ensuring that the basic natural resources (air, land) are there for the future generation.

But beyond explaining women's concerns as a 'connection' to the wildness of nature and as a criticism of the destructive calculating reason of capitalist development, women's arguments proposed an *alternative*

---

2. Dina Daskalopoulou, 'Ierissos: To Chōrió pou Émathe na Moirázetai ta Pánta', *Efimerida Ton Syntakton*, 28/4/2013.

3. Stavroula Poulimeni, 'Skouriés: MAT Enantíon Gynaikōn', AlterThess.gr, 13/5/2013.

4. Sherry B. Ortner, 'Is Female to Male as Nature Is to Culture?', in *Readings in Ecology and Feminist Theory*, ed. Mary Heather MacKinnon and Marie McIntyre (Kansas City: Sheed and Ward, 1995), 52–3.

5. Ibid.

rationality of care, of which they presented themselves as the guardians, and which they promoted into the public sphere, beyond their traditional confinement in the privacy of a household. It is then *through* their self-identification as carers, and as the guardians of the physical and emotional well-being of the persons under their care, that women tended to position themselves publicly against the mine. To a notion of proletarian reproduction through the wage and the ability to purchase the means to live, they opposed a notion of reproduction that prioritised a more immediate concern with the body and emotions. Yet, in affirming the side of 'care' in this opposition, women attached it to themselves as a natural responsibility, instead of insisting on its generalisation and the denaturalisation of its gendered character.

This self-positioning of women in struggle was not limited to Skouries or to environmental struggles. Women in female-dominated occupations have similarly tended to emphasis their caring social roles as part of their publicity campaigns. The struggle of the 595 cleaners of the Economics Ministry, which lasted for over 20 months and was successful, is another example.[6] The cleaners were fighting to be reinstated into permanent positions, after they were dismissed in September 2013 to meet bailout requirements and to outsource the ministry's cleaning services. That they were the first to be targeted for dismissal attested to both the attempt to further devalue their 'feminine' labour, and their being perceived as easy targets, given that most of them were middle-aged women of low social status. After they were fired, and despite the announcement of outsourcing, in a great many public sector offices workers were asked to do the cleaning themselves, relegating cleaning to the category of unpaid work. For cleaners, it was thus relevant to emphasise the value of their work, and resist what they saw as unfair targeting of their gender and age, which, for them, meant that it would be very difficult to find new employment and finally get pensions. They reacted with daily protests outside the ministry and at Syntagma Square, drawing attention to the value of their cleaning and caring labour at work and at home, carrying brooms, mops and buckets, and cleaning public sector offices, even though they had been laid off, for publicity.[7]

---

6. The cleaners received support by SYRIZA campaigners, and were reinstated by the SYRIZA government in June 2015. Panagióta Mpítsika, 'Se Nées Théseis sto Ypourgeío Oikonomikōn 421 Katharístries', *Víma*, 23/6/2015.

7. Pétros Katsákos, 'Oi Apolyménes Katharístries Pīran Skoúpa kai Farási', *Augī*, 30/9/2014.

Alongside all this, however, they also stated in all possible ways that they were 'above all mothers'. Their solidarity snacks for Syrian occupiers at Syntagma Square similarly pointed to the social value of their ability to care for others.[8] They frequently pointed at the way in which their gender and age were disregarded by riot police, with whom they clashed repeatedly.[9] Here, despite the outstanding strength shown by those who were targeted for their womanly 'vulnerability', the demand for reinstatement into a permanent position called for a tactic of revalorising 'feminine' caring work both as commodity and as a natural capacity. Thus, fighting against the devaluation of the category of the gendered division of labour into which they were cast left little space for questioning the naturalness of the category itself.

As seen in Part I, the politics of motherhood and its valorisation as women's primary contribution to the community is nothing new in Greek feminism. However, it has always been contested, not least by the movements of the 1970s, so its uncritical and emotive re-emergence in the crisis did seem regressive. How can this be explained? First, the women who gravitated towards this kind of discourse did not mobilise as feminists and do not seem to have been aware of feminist debates on this issue. This, in turn, reflects the failure of feminist critique to penetrate the mainstream discourse of gender in Greek society and, even more importantly, to significantly reconfigure everyday gender relations. Thus the naturalisation of women's caring role in the discourse of movements merely reflects an everyday reality in which such care work is unquestioningly naturalised.

Nevertheless, if, under the conditions of crisis, there are efforts to valorise this gendered caring activity, it is precisely because its social value, which in capitalist society is primarily understood in monetary terms, is ever more harshly denied, relegated to the category of non-value through decommodification, as in the case of the cleaners: it becomes an activity that is no longer worth being waged. Naturalisation goes hand in hand with this condition – the notion that women, as 'naturally' caring, will perform this work regardless – and thus for women to concede to this through references to themselves as mothers is self-defeating. On the other hand, this is not so surprising in a context where motherhood and generational reproduction itself are discouraged, having been made

8. 'Allīleggýī stous Sýrious Prósfyges apo tis Agōnizómenes Katharístries kai Scholikoús Fýlakes sto Sýntagma', 595katharistries.wordpress.com, 20/11/2014.
9. 'Oi Apolyménes Katharístries Diīgoúntai ton Efiáltī tous', *Éthnos*, 7/6/2014.

prohibitively unaffordable. Being a mother under such conditions acquires an almost heroic aura, representing the kind of sacrifice in which struggles invest their imagination. But this same 'heroic aura' of motherhood also appeals to the valorisation of familial normality and its 'breakdown' in the crisis as one of the hegemonic narratives in anti-austerity movements, whose implications were becoming evident.

Marxist feminists, mostly of the autonomist current, have been referring to this condition as a 'crisis of social reproduction'.[10] The term is a misnomer in that, in its effort to produce a generalised ontology of labour and labour struggle into which to fit 'feminine' caring social activity, it fails to distinguish between social relations mediated by value and those that are excluded by its circuit.[11] It is, in fact, the reproduction of bodies whose labour cannot be commodified (the surplus non-worker, the aged, the children and the disabled, the migrant who 'burdens' the labour market) that is in a crisis and not the reproduction of the value-mediated social as such. Human life is, of course, social, and premised on care, relationships and dependence upon others prior to its dependence on the wage (for proletarians). As Judith Butler has argued, the generalisation of precarity pushes to bring into more immediate awareness this social relationality, interdependence and vulnerability.[12] But our dependence on the wage does not figure as dependence or vulnerability; instead, in the fetishism of bourgeois society the wage contract makes itself appear as individual free choice and independence. It is as if the function of the contract is precisely to deny social interdependence. Thus, the loss of the wage, and, secondarily, of the social wage, which again functions though the impersonal atomised relationality of 'right' (another kind of contract) leaves social interdependence 'naked' and voluntary, no longer mediated by economic and political logics of equivalence. Motherhood and childhood are signifiers for this 'naked' need and interdependence: motherhood alleviates it, and childhood is the state of need. Anyone who is forced to live after having lost the illusory security of equivalence-logics might be aware that they have also lost their masculinity and adulthood, their supposed independence.

---

10. See for example: George Caffentzis, 'On the Notion of a Crisis of Social Reproduction', *The Commoner*, no. 5 (2002); Emma Dowling and David Harvie, 'Harnessing the Social', *Sociology* 48, no. 5 (2014): 869–86.

11. See also *Endnotes*, 'The Logic of Gender', *Endnotes*, no. 3 (2013): 56–91.

12. Judith Butler et al., 'Precarity Talk', *The Drama Review* 56, no. 4 (2012): 163–77.

The politics of gender in the crisis could be said to have a lot to do with this dynamic, and certainly not only in Greece. Any careful attention to the discourse of the 'men's rights' movement, 'alt right' forums in 4Chan and even Jordan Peterson's lectures will detect a desperate need to banish vulnerability as the undercurrent of misogynistic discourse. In Greece, GD's projection of invulnerable masculinity is likely to be partly what attracted so many young men to its activism.

Conversely, a renewed feminist and gender discourse began to find a little more public recognition, especially after 2015 when the 'left hegemony' of SYRIZA allowed a bit more public space for it, which is likely to have been inspired by similar trends in the USA and Western Europe travelling through news and social media. But it would be techno-fetishistic to attribute this turn to communication technologies. It is significant that the politics of gender began to be more earnestly discussed in political milieus and activist groups after the anti-austerity movements had been usurped by the fascistic backlash emanating from 'above' (the government) and from 'below' (the growing popularity of the far right) alike, and after the gendered dimensions of this backlash became too obvious to deny. LGBTQI+ networks already highlighted the abuse their members suffered by the police and far-right groups in 2012–14,[13] and feminists expressed alarm at the misogynistic treatment of marginalised women, transgender women and sex workers. Their reactions were strongest after the compulsory arrest and HIV testing of women (including trans women) suspected of sex work in May 2012: a mass sweep operation that led to charges and the imprisonment of 27 women found to be HIV-positive, along with the humiliating exposure of their names and photos in the mass media.[14] The sweep was accompanied by a blatantly misogynistic governmental discourse for the 'protection' of the male-citizen-family-man from the 'health threat' these women represented, along with immigrants who were also quarantined as part of the operation. At the time, feminist responses to these developments were drowned out by a masculinist manifestation of anti-fascism. A queer and feminist critique of the dominant anti-austerity movement and its conservative content was thus overdue. The (now inactive) collective

---

13. 'Prosagōgés Trans Atómōn stīn Epicheírīsī Xénios Zeus', Transgender-association.gr, 16/8/2012.

14. I discuss the context of this campaign in Part III. See also Dimitra Kotouza, 'Biopolicing the Crisis', in *Biopolitical Governance: Race, Gender and Economy*, ed. Hannah Richter (London: Rowman & Littlefield, 2018).

Queericulum Vitae (QV) expressed this critique most forcefully and succinctly at the time:

> Perhaps more space should be given to what the anti-memorandum mobilisation of the 'indignants' meant, but we choose to concentrate on what was left out of the critique. And we are specifically referring to the Greek citizen male head of family as the absolutely victimised (and simultaneously heroised) subject of the crisis, the only subject worth mentioning. The focus of political discourse on this specific subject is problematic, to the degree that it sentences those left outside it, that is non Greeks / non heads of family, to insignificance. There is nothing revolutionary to supporting this version of the citizen as the only political subject. These discourses, even when they are presented as part of the movement, in essence call upon the state to perform its paternal role, asking for a return to a pre-crisis normality. In this way they disguise (or bury) social antagonisms and conflicts (of gender, race, class) that for us were and are important.[15]

The reference to pre-crisis *normality* is key: it refers to the norms of the sanctified patriarchal 'Greek family', the oppressive character of which queer subjects have always felt most strongly and have had to fight against in their everyday lives. It also refers to the middle- and lower-middle-class experience of crisis, an experience of this family having lost its bearings founded on a patriarchal stability linked to economic stability or success. This 'success' was a reality, or a previously conceivable neoliberal fiction, founded on an exclusive social contract between the citizen of *this specific content* – linked to privileges of 'skin colour, sexual identity, physical ability, property' and the state.[16] As I will show in Part III, governments up to the end of 2014 attempted to deal with social discontent against the restructuring by culturally and materially – through the policing and quarantining of marginalised bodies – reinforcing the most fascistic dimensions of this desire for self-protection of the patriarchal family household.

In such a context, SYRIZA presented itself as the anti-fascist alternative and allowed a sprinkle of feminism on its platform. By 2015 – overdue by EU standards – legislation on same-sex partnership was introduced, and the LGBTQI+ movement gained more visibility, along with the conflicts

---

15. QV, 'Krísī Mī Oratī kai Allókotī', Qvzine.net.
16. Ibid.

within it. This was expressed in the fact that many groups publicly refused to participate in the Athens Pride of 2015, citing lack of transparency in the organising committee and its refusal to include representatives from the trans community. The request to include trans representatives in the committee had first been made in 2014, when Athens Pride organisers were elusive in response to LGBTQI+ community requests to disallow participation in the event of HCDCP/KEELPNO (Hellenic Centre for Disease Control and Prevention), the health agency that had been pivotal in the HIV arrests.

Thus, a mostly mild and minoritarian escalation of conflict around gender, which emerged post-2015, was partly a response to insufficient recognition by dominant tendencies in movements of the needs, concerns and hardship that more marginalised gendered groups have been suffering. Indeed, this is corroborated by my own experience of participating in a discussion organised in 2014 by the (now dissolved) queer feminist group Mov Cafeneio on the HIV arrests.[17] The climate of the discussion felt frozen, giving the sense that the majority of the, mostly male, participants had not given much thought to issues around the biopolitical control of female bodies, sex work and bodily autonomy. But even among some feminist groups, sex work had been framed exclusively through the lens of sex trafficking and the forced labour of sex workers. At the time of the incident in 2012, political posters were circulated by the group miyaδa that reversed government propaganda with the slogan 'terror is the Greek porn clients and their state protectors!' The sex clients cause 'terror' because 'they generously fund the slave trade in women', they 'fuck without protection' and 'constantly demand "new blood" in the markets'. In another poster referring to forced sex work, Greek women are called upon to 'stop porn clients' who are our 'fathers, husbands, sons, brothers, friends and co-workers', and not let 'the males roam over the bodies of undervalued women'. While forced sex work and sex trafficking are indeed a frightening reality for many women, representing sex workers as necessarily the passive victims of punters and reducing all sex trade to trafficking and the forced 'looting of female bodies' neglected the fact that the women affected by the arrests were mostly Greek, and it was unknown if they worked independently or for a boss. This simplification of the issue into a dichotomy between female victim and male

17. Mov Cafeneio, talk at the 6th Political Documentary Festival, Fabrica Yfanet, 15/1/2014.

perpetrator betrayed an assumption that only if we present sex workers as absolute victims can we possibly be on their side. If any degree of agency was involved in their sex work then things become too complex: why did they then not protect themselves from HIV? The drive to take an uncompromising stance on the issue has the opposite effect of relativising it. It leaves open the possibility that having made a conscious – however economically constrained – decision to engage in the sex trade, and in that process contracting HIV, justifies the mass arrests and vilification of sex workers. The sex trade itself is demonised to such an extent that it justifies the criminalisation sex workers currently suffer. The ability of women to increase their degree of power and freedom *even as* they engage in sex work and to demand recognition as workers becomes inconceivable. On the contrary, the assumption that they could not knowingly have become sex workers stigmatises them further and delegitimises their experience, rendering it unintelligible.[18]

These feminist issues – sex work, bodily autonomy, the biopolitical control of sexed and gendered bodies, gendered violence – are complex, calling for thought and discussion that cannot be disconnected from honest, non-defensive reflection upon the contradictions of our own gendered experience, sexuality and everyday encounters, which tend to be compromised and not morally pure. This is a process that the third wave of queer feminism is known to have engaged in, represented in Greece by groups like QV, which produced a transformative experience in its members. Through their discussions and the pages of their publications, they questioned their own gender identities, what 'family' and 'household' might mean to them and how to organise their lives, along with a critique of the patriarchal and hetero/cis-normative society, whose norms they have inevitably internalised. The self-awareness emerging from such a process was evident in my discussion with an ex-member of the collective in the summer of 2017, along with her sense that in the past few years there appear to be fewer spaces for such reflection, and that the politics of gender, especially those that oppose abuse and harassment, have tended to become more reactive than reflective.

Indeed, newer autonomous feminist and LGBTQI+ groups have tended to take a more combative stance to their outside, which is linked to their increasing focus on the issue of rape and other forms of sexual

---

18. An extensive critique of the posters by miyaδa and other collectives, including their own, was published in the fifth and final issue of QV. QV, 'Gia mia (Auto)Kritikī tōn Lógōn Allīleggýis stis Diōkómenes Orothetikés', *QV*, no. 5 (2014): 71–96.

aggression. Beyond feminist groups, within political collectives, more women have also been raising issues of harassment and abuse much more actively than they had done previously. These reactions could be seen as a positive breakthrough, given that autonomous political milieus are generally male dominated, creating patriarchal spaces where it is not only the norm for most female voices to be drowned, but where there is little space for women themselves to reflect on gender dynamics, as they are socialised to cope patiently with normalised everyday sexism and gendered forms of humiliation. This trend parallels developments in autonomous left-wing milieus elsewhere in Western Europe and the USA, as well as the 'mainstreaming' of speaking out enacted by the wave of sexual abuse revelations in Hollywood and the #MeToo hashtag. Given the patriarchal norms of political collectives, instances of women accusing male 'comrades' of harassment or abuse have often escalated into conflicts, often formalised through the exchange and circulation of 'position texts' on the incidents. In such exchanges, positions have tended to become polarised between: (a) a stance that presents itself as moderate, makes reference to patriarchy as a structural issue from whose effects groups are not exempt, and looks to ameliorate tensions through diminishing the seriousness of the incident and eliciting an apology from the accused; (b) a stance advocating the validation of the woman's experience through charging the former stance with 'apologism' and demanding action against the accused. The second, more militantly feminist stance, tends to adopt a discourse of 'victim' and 'perpetrator' and to demand a form of punishment for the latter, usually a temporary or long-term exclusion from collectives. Feminists seek in this way to take an uncompromising position against a dominant culture that permits rape and discredits the victims of rape. They draw attention to the vulnerability of the victim and the trauma experienced, as well as the position of power of the male perpetrator. Effectively, they put forward a new moral principle, to be exercised within collectives as a form of law beyond bourgeois law, according to which patriarchal social structure, gender socialisation and the 'misunderstandings' it might produce are no longer tolerated as mitigating factors. Instead, the new principle emphasises the violence of the sexist act, the harm caused by those who would try to minimise it, and the role of both in reproducing the patriarchal structure and its norms.

These developments have raised questions among the members of collectives, including feminists, on whether this uncompromising, accusatory and quasi-legalist approach (evident in the individualised terms 'victim' and 'perpetrator' and the demand for sentencing) might cause a backlash that, drawing attention to the complexity of the matter, would provide an opportunity for men to completely dismiss the issue, in the usual sexist way, as a kind of hysterical overreaction. The debate indeed raises not only this, but a series of other questions. First, why has this kind of anti-rape feminist militancy emerged in the aftermath of crisis alongside the rise of a masculinist neo-conservatism and neo-fascism? Is there a relationship between these? Second, is this militancy likely to be effective in transforming a culture of sexism, harassment and rape? And, finally, can it, despite its uncompromising discourse, open up possibilities for self-reflection across the sex–gender spectrum, or does it close down such possibilities?

I could not claim to answer these questions through the experience of collectives in Greece or through logical argumentation at this stage. It is difficult to say if the dominant masculinism in anti-austerity movements, along with the normalisation of fascist violence and discourse, was what caused feminists to become more alert to the issue of rape, given that they do not themselves, usually, draw such direct connections. At the same time, it is hard to see it as a mere coincidence, given that this conflict has now escalated into a kind of 'gender war' across many countries. As to the likely outcomes of militant feminism, I have witnessed it bring about forms of backlash, but also deeper reflection among men who begin to question their perceptions and theoretical tools, as well as among women who question both their own often patriarchal lens of seeing, and what it means politically and psychologically to valorise the experience of victimhood. What it is possible to say with a bit more certainty is that the opposition between victim and perpetrator on which much of the militant discourse is founded, as well as the notion that the slogan 'no means no' can resolve the problem, does not seem to be sustainable in the long run. The reason for this is that it artificially erases the experience of ambivalence and the element of exploratory or playful mild aggression in flirting and sexual encounters, constructing sexual desire as if emanating from a conscious deciding subject. The female subject is constructed as always at the receiving end of male predatory aggression and as consciously 'deciding' whether to receive that desire or not. In the drive to paint the male as violent predator, her own desire and agency is purified, in the fear that recognition of her desire would serve to justify the violence against her. In doing so, it reproduces the very logic it tries to argue against: if she is not merely a 'victim', if her lack of desire can be questioned, then the violent act is mitigated. Given that these encounters, and our sexual desire itself, are social and thus hued by patriarchal dynamics, it may not be enough to criticise, as feminists, the socially sanctioned solipsism of masculine desire – one that so often leaves female desire no room to exist as anything other than a mere projection of the male perspective, and is thus erased and violated psychically and physically. It is even more urgent to explore how feminine desire is shaped by these dynamics: how it reproduces or escapes from patriarchal patterns and motifs, and how we can fight to create space for this exploration and our potentially subversive sexual expression.

PART III

Nationalism, Biopolitics and Struggle at the Borders

10

Everyday Racism, Crisis Nationalisms and Migrant 'Autonomy'

It would be hard to communicate the depth of social marginalisation that immigrants are subjected to in Greece, and the reproduction of this relation in movements, without mentioning some vignettes of banal, everyday racism. This racism is pervasive, intense and taken for granted to such an extent that it has become invisible and hard to confront in its multiple manifestations. It is normalised to the level of casual small talk, and seems to have a social and emotional function of bringing 'us' together as if talking about the weather. It is an act of 'friendship' to the 'fellow Greek' who has supposedly become a stranger in their own country. It is active race-making.

Having recently arrived in Athens to carry out fieldwork I spent a week looking for somewhere to rent. One landlord I met was eager to have a Greek tenant. 'An unbelievably filthy Thai woman was renting here before', he told me, presumably to make me feel valued and welcome in the potential new flat. Taking a walk near Victoria Metro station, I stopped to buy a coffee. 'It's so rare these days to have a Greek customer!' the young women who served me said warmly. It did not matter that the majority of passers-by were white and Greek, besides two or three people of North African and South Asian appearance. After finding a place to rent, I wrongly expected my landlady, who was both economically and culturally middle class, to have developed more 'educated' opinions. It only took a day before she turned our conversation from high culture to the 'dreadful state of affairs' in the country: the police in Athens was letting black criminals roam around, and it was unacceptable that in Mykonos there was now an 'Albanian mayor'. She, nevertheless, partici-pated in one of the local popular assemblies, among the other property owners organising against the property tax, and saw herself as doing her bit in the fight against austerity. There was no contradiction: we've seen that the dominant subject invoked in this period's interclass movements was that of the politically independent, active national citizen.

The presence of nationalist tendencies within movements, described in Part II as part of an internal distance within the movement of the squares, soon greatly exceeded what was initially dismissed as 'mere popular patriotism'. Elsewhere in Europe, right-wing nationalist politics also gained strength: the victories of the UK Independence Party and Front National in the 2014 EU elections, the questioning of 'multiculturalism' in light of the May 2013 riots in Sweden and the later empowerment of the Swedish Democrats. This fact placed the Greek situation in the context – if not at the edge, given its geographical location – of anti-immigration discourse in the EU more broadly. As already hinted at in the preceding discussion on gender politics, after the elections of May and June 2012, the right wing of this tendency, which up to that point had mainly been visible through the presence of flags and nationalist slogans in demonstrations, was taken over, at least at the level of the spectacle, by a national-socialist party, GD, which entered the parliament for the first time with 18 seats (6.92 per cent). The empowerment of GD and the formation of a three-party coalition government led by ND with PASOK and DIMAR (Democratic Left), alongside the impressive empowerment of SYRIZA, which came second with 27 per cent, brought an end to the succession of mass demonstrations that had culminated in the riots of 12 February. This development was concurrent with the strengthening of a shift already underway in the dominant governmental discourse towards openly racist anti-immigration statements and policies.

This shift involved heavier policing and spectacular forms of biopolitical social control against immigrants and those pushed to the gendered social 'margins' such as sex workers and gay and trans people, as well as those addicted to drugs and suffering homelessness. This was added to the heavy police repression of demonstrations, strikes, local grassroots campaigns, anti-fascists, anarchists and the broader left. Police action was often accompanied, and sometimes even spearheaded, by GD vigilantes who physically attacked immigrants and political opponents. With electoral empowerment and sympathisers within the government, GD got away with the murder of Shehzad Luqman,[1] an immigrant from Pakistan. However, the murder of a Greek anti-fascist, Pavlos Fyssas,

---

1. Antōnía Xynoú, 'Otan oi Dolofoníes den "Mýrizan" Chrysī Augī', *Eleutherotypía*, 20/10/2013.

would not be tolerated and a process towards the criminalisation of GD began.

Yet, clearly, GD's propaganda was not the *source* of the rise of nationalism in this period. Nationalism did not even just come from the right. Left-wing anti-imperialist nationalism also became strengthened, particularly after the haircut of bank accounts in Cyprus in July 2013, which it attributed almost exclusively to German interests and hegemony.[2] To make things even more complex, the 'anti-fascist' resistance to neo-Nazi violence and influence was contradictory, both in its references to historical anti-fascism, and to the extent that it became part of an 'alliance' that (eventually) included the government itself. All too frequently, the 'moderate' liberal wing of this alliance extended its democratic discourse into a 'theory of the extremes' that criminalised protests and social struggles. Thus, the questions of immigration and fascism produced a polarisation between right and left politics at the same time as distinctions between left and right had become blurred both in the populist discourse of movements and that of political leaders.

Paying little attention to left-wing nationalism, most of the analysts of this period's nationalism have focused on the rise of GD. They have not linked this rise to the state's crisis management strategies, but have attributed it to a rise in popular xenophobia in response to high levels of immigration, and to the delegitimation of PASOK, ND and the moderate far-right party LAOS.[3] GD voters are said to have tended to be a 'precarious' section of the population who wanted to punish the major parties for their policies of austerity.[4] This narrow focus on voting behaviour offers a limited perspective as to social processes and the basis for the political discourses that emerged in the crisis. Conversely, the analyses of the left have ranged between exposing GD as the 'long arm' of the repressive state apparatus,[5] making historical analogies

---

2. One of the most moderate examples around that time was Alexis Tsipras' statement that 'Europe today is becoming autarchic, becoming anti-democratic, it is becoming the Europe of big capital and bankers, it is becoming – if you can allow the phrase – a German Europe.' 'Al. Tsípras sto Russia24', Left.gr, 6/8/2013.

3. Antonis A. Ellinas, 'The Rise of Golden Dawn', *South European Society and Politics* 18, no. 4 (2013): 543–65; Vassiliki Georgiadou, 'The Rapid Rise of Golden Dawn in Crisis-Ridden Greece', in *Right-Wing Extremism in Europe*, ed. Ralf Melzer and Sebastian Serafin (Berlin: Friedrich-Ebert-Stiftung, 2013), 75–102.

4. Vasilikī Geōrgiádou, 'Ī Eklogikī Ánodos tīs Chrysīs Augīs', in *2012: O Diplós Eklogikós Seismós*, ed. Giánnis Voúlgarīs and Īlías Nikolakópoulos (Athens: Themélio, 2014), 185–219.

5. Dīmītrīs Psarrás, *Ī Maúrī Vívlos tīs Chrysīs Augīs*, (Athens: Pólis, 2012).

with the Greek civil war and the Weimar Republic,[6] or explaining the subsequent arrest of GD leaders and the criminalisation of the party as proof that democracy is the ideal political form for capitalist reproduction.[7] These perspectives have often sidelined an analysis of the broader rise of nationalism in the crisis, which also affected left-wing discourse. Looking for patterns in historical precedents has also often forestalled a more complex understanding of the particular social dynamics of the present period. While there are indeed many parallels with the great crisis in 1930s Germany (extremely high unemployment, weakness of labour struggles, a large petit bourgeoisie, the rise of fascism, increased state repression),[8] the differences are also enormous (a different global configuration of forces, in a Europe of ferociously competing nationalisms, with establishments facing the threat of organised working classes and an international communist movement). As for the political forms that might facilitate capitalist accumulation, given that Greek capitalism has previously seen very high levels of growth during authoritarian and dictatorial regimes, it is hard to argue for a necessary link between liberal democratic political forms and accumulation.

In contrast, the approach adopted here will discuss nationalism and its role within the movements as a powerful political discourse and practice opposing the restructuring, while at the same time being used to repress such opposition. The strengthening of nationalism poses the problem of ideology in the analysis of struggles, and reveals the limits of a vulgar materialist approach that aims to explain all political and cultural developments on the basis of economic interests. The concept of fetishism introduced in Part I provides an avenue for analysis beyond a simplistic opposition between materiality and ideology. The nationalist response against external control and intervention, the fear of migrants and their labour, are not based on mere ideological fiction, but they find validity in the way capitalist society is reproduced, as well as the way it produces crises. The existence of national separations is not the mere *appearance* of capitalism, the instantiation of a capitalist essence, but its historical material reality, involving past and present power relations among nation-states and capitals, and racialised hierarchies of labour.

---

6. On the civil war as a 'remnant' in the present, see Sávvas Michaïl, *I Fríkī mias Parōdías* (Athens: Augī/Nicos Poulantzas Institute, 2012), 5–10.

7. Cognord, 'When the State Turns Antifa', Neucognord.wordpress.com, 26/10/2013.

8. Sergio Bologna, 'Nazism and the Working Class, 1933–93', trans. Ed Emery (Camera del Lavoro Metropolitana di Milano, 1993).

Crisis calls for a reinforcement of these national hierarchies. In Part I, I linked the emergence of this nationalism to the fetishism of capital. With debt at the core of the Greek crisis, international finance has appeared as the parasitical element that sucks the life out of the 'real' local capitalist production and economy. A fetishistic anti-capitalism that exclusively opposes this most 'abstract' branch of capital can be recognised in the ultra-nationalism grounded on the concreteness of 'blood' (or 'DNA'), favoured by GD, standing against a range of 'foreigners' and 'local collaborators' who conspired against the nation. But the fetishistic criticism of finance also appeals to left anti-imperialism, which has traditionally defended 'concrete' national (ideally industrial) production and its workers. The existing hierarchy of European political and economic powers, which the crisis of globalised and financialised capitalism placed at the helm of European crisis management, similarly reinforced the narrative of Greece as an oppressed nation.

Looking at nationalism as presupposing a specific nexus of asymmetrical power relations, which are part of the process of capitalist reproduction, entails examining not only the relation between labour and capital, but also the relations produced or shaped by the capitalist division of labour, the relation between the dominant subject of the citizen and its (selectively inclusive) exclusions, as well as relations produced through processes of racialisation and the reproduction of gender. One of the effects of the crisis that upset these social relations was the production of previously socially integrated citizens as a part of surplus populations who could not be securely or formally integrated as property owners or workers. In this context, state repression was geared towards policing the balance of power in the social relations that were disturbed by the crisis and producing a – necessarily insufficient but politically potent – sense of security in the dominant subject of the citizen as configured prior to the crisis, one founded on property, race and the patriarchal family.

Thus, the state's biopolitical concern to manage populations in the sense proposed by Michel Foucault, the concern 'to rationalize the problems posed to governmental practice by phenomena characteristic of a set of living beings forming a population: health, hygiene, birthrate, life expectancy, race',[9] was not indiscriminate. The population was produced as internally hierarchised, maintaining the difference

---

9. Michel Foucault, *The Birth of Biopolitics* (Basingstoke: Palgrave Macmillan, 2008), 317.

between the section of the national population to be 'protected' and that section constituted as a 'threat' – a difference structured by race, gender, sexuality and their intersection with class (but not by class alone). This form of social management partly responded to the 'grassroots' concern to reinforce the social status of a 'surplus' citizen in crisis, who is proto-typically a Greek male head of household. The unsettling of hierarchies, which are to a great extent coextensive with the capitalist division of labour, provoked a reaction towards their reconsolidation, one not merely imposed 'top-down' by the state or merely a result of state-led ideology.

Nevertheless, governmental practices along with the ideological division between left and right that emerged in this context shifted the question of borders – in the broader sense encompassing the external and internal borders of the nation and the affective-imaginary borders of identity – from the periphery to the centre of what defines and separates political positions and practices of resistance. Thus, the later shift to a 'left-wing' management of crisis under SYRIZA presented itself as more permissive in its management of borders and detention camps – which in their campaigns they had condemned as dehumanising – but, at the same time, it reproduced a nationalist narrative of doing so. The refugee crisis was responded to in a less self-protective and more charitable and humanitarian mode, portrayed as emanating from the virtuousness of the Greek spirit. The figure of the migrant then continued to oscillate within a range of roles that denied its subjectivity: from inhuman threat to object of pity.

The analysis of nationalism and biopolitics in this chapter provides the context for interpreting the anti-fascist movements, the struggle of migrants – including their labour struggles – and the forms of solidarity and transnational encounter that developed during the 'refugee crisis'. As the struggle of migrants has been moving from invisibility to forcing a recognition of immigrants as complex subjects, it questioned more radically the constitution of the community of struggle around citi-zenship. This was precipitated, above all, by the 'refugee crisis', which I interpret as a form of migrant border struggle, without, however, placing the sole source of agency in migrants as sovereign subjects. Indeed, people emigrate out of need; but, in doing so, they fight collec-tively to override the racialised structures of the border, which are both objective and subjective, material and ideal, operating through concrete barriers and everyday practices enacted by the state as well as citizens themselves, using both legal and extra-legal methods. In the closure of the European borders that followed in 2016 and the deal with Turkey, the racism of these borders, hidden from their formal legal structure, was again blatantly revealed. The EU thus had to 'violate' both international human rights law and the Schengen Treaty in order to prevent the movement of racialised non-European migrants.

I also argue here, following on from Part II, that the key question is *not* how to strategically produce unity by organising a common struggle between Greeks and migrants, or, for that matter, among migrants themselves. I disagree with authors like Sandro Mezzadra and Brett Neilson or groups like SKYA (Assembly for the Circulation of Struggles) who, based on an Italian autonomist-influenced analysis of labour composition (pertaining to the concrete experience of citizens and migrant workers as well as migrant detainees understood from the point of view of their labour power), seek to identify forms, processes and instances of 'translation' between struggles, which would negotiate our 'differences'.[10] Mezzadra and Neilson, while offering an extremely rich analysis of contemporary borders, look to the creation of transnational 'commons' and 'alternative economies' through such mechanisms of translation, while SKYA have suggested that, strategically, the most promising struggle in Greece could now emerge through an alliance between NGO support workers and immigrant detainees.[11] In both cases, not enough attention is paid to the fact that 'translation' and solidarity cannot take place unproblematically among subjects constituted within asymmetrical relations of power, without directly addressing those asymmetries. Doing so presupposes conflict against forms of unity that reproduce domination, because what divides us are not mere 'differences' that can be assumed to be in any way equivalent. 'Translation' cannot be conceived in advance as a theoretical project on behalf of the subjects of struggle but has to emerge from the practices and conflicts that emerge in struggles – their 'negative' moments – and the self-critique that is provoked by this process. This is, first, because well-meaning attempts at solidarity with migrants can easily lapse into forms of patronage and control, precisely because the relation between Greek and immigrant workers, as well as, very often, that between different ethnicities of immigrants, is structured by relations of domination and state methods of classification. Second,

---

10. Sandro Mezzadra and Brett Neilson, *Border as Method, or, the Multiplication of Labor* (Durham, NC: Duke University Press, 2013).
11. SKYA, 'Den Eínai Anthrōpismós!'.

as argued in Part II, 'labour power' is not a transhistorical essence that precedes its 'capture' by capital, as assumed by the autonomist perspective,[12] but a commodity constituted by capitalist reproduction, one deeply devalued during capitalism's crisis. If labour is not the defining living activity from which all agency emanates, it follows that we cannot reduce our analysis of subjects of struggle and relations between them to an analysis of their concrete labour experience and their common property of being 'living labour', or the mere fact that they come into some sort of contact in their daily work.

Despite highlighting the migrant as a *subject* of struggle and not a mere object of circumstance, pity or charity, we can also not assume, as the closely associated 'autonomy of migration' perspective does, that the dialectic of border struggle *is driven* by the ungovernable migrant-worker-subject in 'flight'.[13] The subject of the 'migrant' itself is constituted by the border as a relation, and it is not homogeneous or inherently challenging of borders, even if the migrant is defined by the desire to cross borders. Instead, it is internally divided by nationality, ethnicity and religion, not to mention class, through not only prior histories of conflict along those lines but also, more importantly, in the context of migration, through the legal governmental distinction between economic migrants and refugees. The privilege this affords some war refugees and not others (Syrians over Afghans, for example) produces forms of separation, competition and conflict. Yet, even when this is overcome, it often does so under a concept of 'brotherhood' in which women are absent or subject to male control. Thus the dimension of gender is another line of contradiction and division within the migrant as a subject of struggle, especially when women's absence weakens the struggle itself, and when female and queer migrants begin to explore new ways of life and come together to contest these forms of subjection. This part of the book thus explores these processes of contestation in more detail, in the broader context of crisis, Greece's economic restructuring and rising nationalisms.

---

12. For example, Mezzadra and Neilson (*Border as Method*, 264) state that 'there is a need to approach labor power as precisely a form of power that exceeds, and in a certain sense precedes, processes of discipline and control, dispossession and exploitation'.
13. Manuela Bojadžijev and Serhat Karakayalı, 'The Autonomy of Migration Today', *e-Flux*, no. 17 (2010).

11

Surplus Population Management by a Nation-State in Crisis

The Greek Far Right and Its Growth after 1990

In investigating the relationship between governmental crisis management strategies, the rise of right and left nationalisms and the confluence of such tendencies from 'above' and from 'below', I will begin by presenting a very brief history of the far right in Greece and its links with the repressive state apparatus. This is to help the reader unfamiliar with Greek history and with the specificities of the country's state apparatus understand that the police abuses and the relative free rein GD enjoyed up to 2013 was not the result of the Greek state's incompetence, as it was represented in the international media. As discussed in Part I, an authoritarian form of state was dominant in Greece up to the Meta-politeusi. Yet, after the Metapoliteusi, authoritarian far-right politics did not disappear from the state but were retrenched into the repressive state apparatus, while also participating in politics through formal parties. I will therefore discuss the gradual empowerment of these parties from the 1990s onwards, and GD's genealogy. Yet, it is worth pointing out again that, while the political and social role of the far right cannot be fully appreciated without considering its historical relationship with the state, its recent empowerment must also not be understood as the mere result of state strategy and positive media coverage, but rather as an expression of the embedding of racism in the formation of Greek national identity, a racism that has been inseparable from what Gramsci might have called the national-popular 'common sense'.

The Greek far right and its influence within state mechanisms has a history that runs back to the mid-war period, from the Metaxas dictatorship, through to the civil war and the colonels' dictatorship.[1] The

---

1. For a history of the Greek far right in the 1920s and 1930s, see Spýros Markétos, *Pōs Fílisa ton Moussolíni! Vol. 1* (Athens: Vivliórama, 2006).

most recent part of this history interests us here. After the fall of the anti-communist colonels' regime in 1974 (a regime for which today's GD is deeply nostalgic) and the reinstatement of a right-wing Karamanlis government, there was a trial of the main functionaries of the junta, who were convicted to life imprisonment. However, not all of them were prosecuted. Meanwhile, attacks on immigrants and left demonstrators by far-right gangs who supported the junta regime with the assistance of the police were reported as early as 1975,[2] despite the fact that back then the number of immigrants in Greece was negligible. The situation was polarised, as the 17 November organisation was also then formed, and carried out assassinations of dictatorship functionaries that the Karamanlis government had failed to prosecute.[3] Nikolaos Mihalo-liakos, the founder and current leader of GD, was arrested in 1979 for deadly bombings in cinemas that screened Soviet Russian films.[4] Soon after getting away with only a 13-month sentence, Mihaloliakos founded *Golden Dawn* as a political journal.

With the rise of PASOK in 1981, the attempt for reconciliation, after the intense class struggle that preceded it, also involved the legitimation of communist parties and their role in World War II 'national liberation', alongside the (brief) integration of workers' unions and some of their demands within state policy and a series of nationalisations. Politically, the opposition between communism and ultranationalist right-wing anti-communism was replaced by the opposition between the right and what has been termed the 'anti-right',[5] on which the influential discourse of PASOK was based. Despite these changes, many junta functionaries were still not prosecuted and were allowed to re-enter parliamentary politics, while the depoliticisation of the state apparatus did not go far enough into parts of the army, the police forces and the security services.[6]

---

2. Mpétty Vakalopoúlou, 'O Neofasismós stīn Elláda', in *O Neofasismós stīn Európī*, ed. Giussepe Gaddi (Athens: Néa Sýnora, 1975), 374.

3. Giõrgos Karámpelas, *To Ellīnikó Antartikó tōn Póleōn 1974–1985* (Athens: Grafés, 2002), 26–34.

4. 'Ī Ellīnikī Akrodexiá ston Drómo tou Lepén', *Vīma*, 17/5/1998.

5. Gerásimos Moschonás, 'Ī Diairetikī Tomī Dexiás-Antidexiás stī Metapolíteusī (1974–1990)', in *Ī Ellīnikī Politikī Koultoúra Sīmera*, ed. Níkos Demertzīs (Athens: Odysséas, 1995).

6. A recent interview of Giorgos Bertsos, one of the two journalists who investigated the Lambrakis assassination before the Colonels' dictatorship, is indicative. An insider of PASOK, Bertsos was placed in a top position within KYP, the Central Intelligence Agency, under the first PASOK government in 1981. He was very disappointed, however, when the prime minister, Andreas Papandreou, personally attempted to stop him from dissolving the agency, which was still staffed by functionaries of the colonels' regime.

This apparent omission might be understood in the context of the Cold War that still influenced policy decisions across Europe,[7] as well as in light of the legacy of the Greek civil war.

Through the 1980s, GD was a marginal organisation, reduced to printing its openly neo-Nazi magazine. The far-right parties of the time (EPEN,[8] ENEK[9]) also received tiny electoral support. Yet, by the 1990s, with the arrival of Albanian and other Eastern European immigrants, GD and a number of the neo-Nazi youth groups it supported became increasingly active. They engaged in organising offensives against immigrants and left and anarchist demonstrators, and organising small protests regarding Greece's territorial disputes with Turkey and the issue of Macedonia.[10] Some members of GD also participated in the Serbo-Croatian war on the side of Serbia.[11] This increased activity was timely, as the 1990s was a period of heightened nationalism in mainstream political and cultural discourse, which combined a sense of pride for Greece's business expansion to the rest of the Balkans with a xenophobic stance towards impoverished, usually paperless, immigrants from Balkan countries, who were heavily exploited in construction and agriculture. The issue of the naming of the Former Yugoslav Republic of Macedonia, and sensational media attention to crimes involving Albanian immigrants, exacerbated that nationalism and xenophobia. In

---

Bertsos managed to dissolve it eventually, but the agency was very quickly reformed as EYP, the National Intelligence Agency. Giorgos Bertsos, 'Thessaloníki: To Staurodrómi tōn Praktórōn', interview by Stelios Kouloglou, National Greek Television (NET), 'Reporters Without Borders', TVXS.gr, 21/5/2013.

7. It was not a rare occurrence in countries of the 'Western bloc' for security services to hire members of the far right for their anti-communist strategy, as was revealed by the wave of investigations into the Gladio operation, after the revelations of the Italian prime minister, Giulio Andreotti, in 1990. In Greece, a similar 'stay-behind' operation codenamed 'Red Sheepskin' had been admitted by the then defence minister, Giannis Varvitsiotis, to have been active up until 1988, seven years into PASOK's government. Clyde Haberman, 'Evolution in Europe: Italy Discloses its Web of Cold War Guerrillas', *New York Times*, 16/11/1990.

8. Ethnikī Politikī Énōsis (National Political Union): a party led by Georgios Papadopoulos, the imprisoned leader of the junta regime, who appointed Nikolaos Mihaloliakos as a leader of its youth branch. Makis Voridis, infrastructure minister in the Papademos government in 2011, and health minister in Samaras' government in 2014, had been the secretary of EPEN's youth branch.

9. Eniaío Ethnikistikó Kínīma (Unified Nationalist Movement).

10. Athanásios Theofilópoulos, 'Koinōnikós Apokleismós stīn Elláda' (Panteion University, 2008), 128.

11. Chárīs Kousoumvrīs, *Gkremízontas ton Mýtho tīs Chrysīs Augīs* (Athens: Érevos, 2004), 21–4.

the cultural mainstream there was a renewed trend for a 'return to the roots', a glorification of ancient culture and an exaggerated reverence for the Greek language, together with a condemnatory stance towards any attempt to deconstruct simplistic nationalist narratives.

With the liberalisation of television frequencies in 1989, several new private television channels opened. One of these new television channels was Telecity, which openly promoted far-right ultranationalist, xenophobic and antisemitic propaganda. Its owner, Georgios Karatzaferis, an ND MP who was later expelled by ND leader Kostas Karamanlis in an attempt to appeal to the centre, managed to build his political career and empower his new party, LAOS, through his television appearances.[12] Telecity, true to its owner's far-right affiliations, increased the media coverage of Mihaloliakos, senior GD members and other personalities of the far right, such as Kostantinos Plevris.[13] This coverage served to legitimise, if not popularise, their xenophobic and antisemitic discourse. The growth of nationalism through the 1990s was initially capitalised on electorally by ND and later by LAOS, although GD retained close links to those parties and benefited as well.[14]

Through the 1990s and 2000s, reports presenting evidence of GD's collaboration with the police reappeared numerous times.[15] Some members of GD even left the party in the late 1990s, disappointed about this collaboration, reporting that the police frequently asked them to stage riots against student demonstrations.[16] The most significant of these reports was the leaking of internal police documents regarding the case of 'Periandros', a GD member who was sought by the police for the

---

12. From 1993 to 2000, Karatzaferis was elected MP with ND. In 2000 he launched his own party, LAOS (Popular Orthodox Rally). In the 2007 elections his party entered parliament for the first time, and in November 2011 LAOS participated in the technocratic Papademos government obtaining two ministries. In the elections of May 2012, LAOS lost most of its voters to GD while several of its prior MPs had already joined ND.

13. Konstantinos Plevris was the founder of the 4th August far right organisation in 1960 (named in the memory of the Metaxas dictatorship) and a KYP agent during the colonels' dictatorship. He is also the author of numerous antisemitic and homophobic books.

14. Georgios Karatzaferis, when still in ND in 1998, famously suggested a coalition between GD and ND a in one of his television shows. GD members were also hired as armed bodyguards for ND MPs. Vasílīs Nédos, 'Ellīnikī Akrodexia', Vīma, 11/9/2005. Aretī Athanasíou, 'Astynomikoí Kályptan ton "Períandro"', Néa, 17/4/2004.

15. A list of reported police assaults on immigrants and leftists are listed by Psarras, for many of which GD members supported police operations, and, if arrested, they were readily released. Psarrás, Ī Maúrī Vívlos, 85.

16. Kousoumvrīs, Gkremízontas ton msýtho, 26.

attempted murder of a leftist student, but had not been captured for eight years because of the unwillingness of 'half of the police force'.[17]

The increase in GD's police-assisted attacks could be said to have coincided with the gradual ending of the short-lived 'social democracy' in Greece, when the two main parties, PASOK and ND, began to pursue policies of privatisation, labour flexibilisation and the restructuring of higher education and social security, against which significant protest movements had been formed. GD was then apparently sanctioned by the police to act as an additional vigilante force and assist the policing of the most defiant sections of those movements.

GD's visibility increased further in the 2000s with the arrival of immigrants from Asia and Africa.[18] As with the policing of social movements, GD has had a special role to play as the vigilante branch of the police, whether in collaboration or proactively, since 'cleansing Greece of illegal immigrants' is one of its utmost aims. Its members and supporters began to appear alongside police operations, presenting themselves in the media as 'indignant citizens' (*aganaktisménoi polítes*, cf. the name of the movement of the squares) who helped the police's sweep operations.[19]

Crisis Policing and the Far Right

By the onset of the debt crisis in 2009, a tendency towards the escalation of policing was already under way. The December riots of 2008 already indicated that all was not well on that front, not only for Greek youth, but also for immigrants. From the perspective of the state, the riots called for increased policing and a relegitimation of police authority.[20] Demonstrations were policed more forcefully immediately after the riots, on occasion with the support of GD.[21] Heavier policing in areas with high concentrations of immigrants was also in order,[22] again with the

---

17. Athanasíou, 'Astynomikoí Kályptan'.

18. See Dīmītrīs Psarrás, 'To Pogkróm katá tōn Metanastōn Schediazótan Īdī apó to 1997', *Eleutherotypía*, 22/5/2011.

19. Athanasíou, 'Astynomikoí kályptan'.

20. The deputy minister of public order, Christos Markogiannakis, declared that disorder would be combated by hiring military staff as special guards, creating the Delta team of motorcyclist police and installing more surveillance cameras. Níkos Chasapópoulos, 'Chr. Markogiannákis: "Den Kánō Písō. Me Ópoio Kóstos, Den Tha Gínei Mpáchalo ī Chōra"', *Vīma*, 4/4/2009.

21. Psarrás, *Ī Maúrī Vívlos*, 185–8.

22. 'Entonóterī Astynómeusī ston Agio Panteleīmona Yposchéthīke o Chr. Markogiannákis', *Vīma*, 22/1/2009.

assistance of GD, which had just formed its first 'residents committee' in Agios Panteleimonas, composed of its own members and a number of local shopkeepers. Residents committee 'demonstrations' involved physically abusing any immigrants encountered in the street and ejecting their children from the local playground.[23] Soon, Agios Panteleimonas and nearby Attica square became no-go areas for immigrants.[24] On the basis of this activism, GD was successful in the municipal elections of 2010, with Nikolaos Mihaloliakos gaining a seat in Athens.[25]

The entry of the far right in the Greek parliament was already a fact a year earlier when LAOS gained over 3 per cent of the vote in both the European elections and the national elections of 2009 on an anti-immigration agenda. The pre-election period was favourable for LAOS, as it coincided with the first ever combative demonstration by Muslim immigrants, in response to a police officer tearing an immigrant's prayer book to pieces.[26] This event, and the clashes with the police that followed, was presented in the mainstream media as particularly alarming in terms of immigration policy.[27] The punishment on Muslim immigrants for their defiance came immediately: the next day, a prayer room in Agios Panteleimonas was set on fire.[28]

Police violence and its far-right politicisation began to be increasingly overt as the crisis deepened and the economic restructuring gained pace. In each of the large anti-Memorandum demonstrations, riot police used abundant teargas and stun grenades, attacked demonstrators – the worst attacks involving motorcycle-mounted police riding into the crowds – and carried out arrests with the assistance of undercover officers.[29] On several occasions, police officers revealed their far-right affiliations,

---

23. Geōrgía Dáma, 'Ménos MAT, Akrodexiōn', *Eleutherotypía*, 20/1/2009.

24. George Kandylis and Karolos Iosif Kavoulakos, 'Framing Urban Inequalities', *The Greek Review of Social Research*, no. 136 C (2011): 157–76.

25. See also: Vassilis Arapoglou and Thomas Maloutas, 'Segregation, Inequality and Marginality in Context', *The Greek Review of Social Research*, no. 136 C (2011): 135–55.

26. Souliotis, 'Ī prōtī anoichtī sýgkrousī EL.AS'.

27. Aléxīs Papachelás, 'Ston Ag. Panteleīmona', *Kathīmerinī*, 24/5/2009.

28. 'Epidromī Koukoulofórōn ta Xīmerōmata se Autoschédio Tzamí stīn Plateía Attikīs', *Vīma*, 23/5/2009.

29. There are photographs and videos documenting such incidents in most of the demonstrations that took place since 2010. Some examples from Athens: 'Omáda Dolofónōn Mīchanokínītōn Mpátsōn', Athens.indymedia.org, 16/12/2010; 'Choúnta stīn Plateía Syntágmatos', 29/6/2011, https://youtu.be/S2o_JuaX8gg; 'Efodos Delta ston Pezodromo Mītropoleōs', 29/6/2011, https://youtu.be/b_jocIIboGA; 'Athens Warzone', 12/2/2012, https://youtu.be/aWEVNGcwInE.

either through wearing ultranationalist symbols, or by offering special treatment to members of far-right organisations.[30]

While the protests themselves included right-wing nationalist tendencies as well as left, the right wing of the movements was not connected to GD. In the summer of 2011, while an anti-police stance was developing in the squares, GD would be concerned exclusively with its anti-immigration campaigns and retained friendly relations with the police. As mentioned already, only a few days before the first occupation at Syntagma, on 10–14 May 2011, GD launched a deadly four-day pogrom against immigrants in central Athens, which resulted in 25 hospitalisations and one death by stabbing. Police ran casually behind the attackers, capturing 45, but releasing all of them later on without charges.[31] Still, there was definitely a congruence and ideological continuity between the conservative tendency in anti-austerity demonstrations and GD's 'anti-systemic' oppositional discourse, which rejected 'corrupt, traitor politicians' and the 'status quo', while defending 'the Greek people'.

The governments implementing the restructuring suffered a radical loss of legitimacy, the first in line being George Papandreou's PASOK government that was dissolved in November 2011. It was followed by the caretaker technocratic Papademos government with the support of PASOK, ND and LAOS. By the time of the May 2012 elections, the conditions were already there for the electoral success of GD, but they were made even more favourable in the pre-election period, when racist anti-immigration discourses again became the main strategy of the incumbent parties. Amid criticism of the government for disarray in the public health service and a shortage of medicines for cancer patients, the Ministry of Health launched a campaign to 'protect' citizens from HIV and other viruses attributed to immigrants in overcrowded accommodation and immigrant sex workers.[32] This was called a 'hazardous health bomb', to be contained through mass arrests, building evacuations and forced medical examinations of immigrants, injectable drug users and sex workers, supported by an order for the compulsory treatment of 'at

---

30. 'Akrodexioí Próïn Syndikalistés oi Koukoulofóroi Synomilītés tōn MAT', *Ethnos*, 30/6/2011.
31. 'Pogkróm katá Metanastōn sto Kéntro tīs Athīnas', TVXS.gr, 12/5/2011; Sunderland et al., *Hate on the Streets*, 45–8.
32. 'I ELAS Xekiná tis Ekkenōseis Ktiríōn Ópou Zoun Lathrometanástes', *Vīma*, 25/4/2012.

risk' populations.[33] Women found seropositive, most of whom turned out to have been Greek, were charged with 'intentional grievous bodily harm' against 'family men' – whose responsibility for the transmission of the virus to sex workers was disregarded as irrelevant.[34] The women's photographs and personal details were then publicised by the police and shown on prime-time television and mass-circulation newspapers, with the stated aim that the 'family men' who had sex with them would also go for HIV testing. The women were detained for a year, and released when it became clear that there was no basis to the charges against them.[35]

In the same pre-election period, opening new detention camps for irregular immigrants was also presented as a matter of urgency. Overnight several army barracks were turned into detention camps that lacked even basic amenities, amid protests by locals against immigrants being brought into their area.[36] Clearly, the strong emphasis on the policing of immigration and marginality and the active cultivation of racism in the pre-election context was a subject that privileged the incumbents, as policing was all that the semi-bankrupt state could offer to appease its discontented citizens at that point, in place of responding to the demands for an end to austerity. Their main opponents, the left parties, were at their weakest on this subject, as their discourse of human rights could not be heard amid an already deeply ingrained popular xenophobia and the patriarchal 'common sense' of mainstream conservatism.

The May 2012 elections marked an unprecedented shift in the Greek political scene. Greece's two biggest parties, ND and PASOK, lost an enormous proportion of their traditional voters, while SYRIZA, going from a mere 4.6 per cent to 27 per cent, became the main opposition party, and GD rose from 0.3 per cent to 7 per cent. Despite their losses, ND and PASOK formed a coalition government with the Democratic Left (a small centre-left party).

The electoral empowerment of GD was not surprising, as it was one of the few remaining vessels for disillusioned right-wing nationalist voters, after LAOS had approved austerity policies under the Papademos

---

33. G.Y. 39a, FEK B´ 1002/02.04.2012; 'Greece, Compulsory Health Checks for Immigrants', Ansamed.ansa.it, 2/4/2012.
34. Elena Fyntanídou, 'Epidīmía tou Ioú HIV sto Kéntro tīs Athīnas', Vīma, 6/5/2012; see also the documentary about the women's arrests, their public shaming, the sexist discourse surrounding the entire case: Zoe Mavroudi, *Ruins: Chronicle of an HIV Witch-Hunt*, documentary, (2013).
35. 'Athōes oi Orothetikés Katópin Diapómpeusīs', *Eleutherotypía*, 17/1/2013.
36. 'Oi Prōtoi 56 Metanástes Metaférthīkan stīn Amygdaléza', *Vīma*, 29/4/2012.

government. Yet the size of this empowerment, gathering support from voters of other parties, even the KKE, was unforeseen. At the same time, seen in perspective, most spectacular in those elections was the rise of SYRIZA, which explained the almost anachronistically anti-communist discourse of the new government against its new major opponent.

GD, according to exit polls, was most attractive to young unemployed men.[37] The old theory of petit bourgeois conservatism is then not sufficient to explain its rise, because its lower-class and gendered appeal also demands an explanation. An anti-political sentiment was the main stated reason for this voting choice, and immigration the second.[38] Unsurprisingly, GD was also extremely popular among the ranks of the police.[39] It then appears that GD gained votes by selectively reproducing the nationalist anti-establishment discourse popular in the demonstrations that preceded the elections, redirecting this anti-political sentiment into formal politics and into the policing operations they had been involved in for decades, financially supported by protection racketeering, vigilante services, sex trafficking and other similar activities.[40] Much was made in the media at the time about GD's 'socially beneficial' activities:[41] helping terrified old ladies walk through the mean streets of Athens,[42] offering free meals and collecting blood donations 'for Greeks only',[43] ejecting immigrant vendors from street markets, intervening in hospitals to remove immigrant carers who 'took away Greek jobs'.[44]

The electoral success of GD would not have been such a significant event had it not been followed by the steep increase, during and immediately after the May 2012 elections, of the numbers of racist assaults, stabbings, murders and destruction of homes and shops of immigrants,

37. Exit poll, June 2012, in Vassiliki Georgiadou and Lamprini Rori, 'The New Right-Wing Extremism in Greece', *Anuari Del Conflicte Social* (2013), 322–39, 326.

38. Georgiadou, 'Ī eklogikī ánodos', table 3.

39. In the constituencies where large numbers of police officers vote, obtained as much as 17.2 per cent to 23.04 per cent. Vasílis G Lamprópoulos. 'Enas stous Dýo Astynomikoús Psīfisan Chrysī Augī', *Vīma*, 11/5/2012.

40. Civil Action Memorandum, AVM F2013/3990, AVM F2012/979, 979A Trim.Dioik. Prot.Ath; 'Apórrītī Ékthesī tīs EYP gia ton Lagó', *Néa*, 1/10/2013.

41. Christína Pántzou, *Metanásteusī kai Ratsistikós Lógos sta MME* (UNHCR Greece, 2013).

42. This turned out to have been entirely manufactured by the newspaper *Proto Thema*. Psarrás, *Ī Maúrī Vívlos*, 380.

43. 'O Ýmnos tōn Nazí sto "Syssítio Móno gia Éllīnes"', *Eleutherotypía*, 25/7/2013; 'Epicheírīsī-Fiásko to "Aíma Móno gia Éllīnes"', *Augī*, 5/5/2013.

44. Elena Fyntanídou, 'Apopompī tīs Dioikītoú tou Nosokomeíou Trípolīs gia tīn Éfodo Chrysaugitōn', *Vīma*, 9/2/2013.

which remained at an extremely high level for the following year.[45] The collaboration between police officers and GD in those attacks, as well as those against gay men and left or anti-racist protesters or organisers, was, by early 2013, well documented.[46] The police have not only been inactive when witnessing racist assaults, but they have even joined in, while actively discouraging immigrants from filing complaints and even destroying their legal documents.[47] Migrants often found it hard to distinguish between GD and plain-clothed police officers. Yet no police officer was prosecuted,[48] and evidence linking GD and police officers with racist attacks was ignored by government officials.[49]

Instead, the government negotiated its fragility by following an aggressive strategy of putting the issue of immigration centre stage and targeting social movements along with its major political opponent, SYRIZA. Post-election governmental discourse and policing strategy consistently targeted 'the left', unionised workers and other activists. In October 2012, anti-racist protesters were detained and tortured by police officers who, according to the arrestees, boasted about their GD membership.[50] In December and January 2013, three occupied social centres were evicted in the area near Agios Panteleimonas, the central GD stronghold, and 100 people, anarchists and anti-fascists, were arrested.[51] In the same month, strikes by transport workers were strongly repressed

45. Over sixty racist assaults were reported by the Pakistani Community of Greece within the first two weeks after the elections and over 700 up to 17 January 2013, when Shehzad Luqman was murdered. Pakistani Community of Greece, 'Anakoínōsī gia tī Dolofonía tou Sechzát Loukmán', Antiracismfascism.org, 18/1/2013.

46. A total of 148 incidents were recorded from May 2011 to September 2013 in the 'Map of Attacks on Immigrants in Athens', *The City at a Time of Crisis*, map.crisis-scape.net.

47. Sunderland et al., *Hate on the Streets*; Racist Violence Recording Network, 'Findings (1.1.2012–30.9.2012)', UNHCR.gr, 23/10/2012.

48. Vasílīs G. Lamprópoulos, 'Ī EL.AS. Vgázei Ládi to Dikó tīs "Ampou Gkráimp"', *Víma*, 30/5/2013.

49. Aris Chatzistefanou, 'Golden Dawn Party Infiltrates Greece's Police, Claims Senior Officer', *The Guardian*, 26/10/2012.

50. The torture of anti-fascists by police was publicised in *The Guardian* (9/12/2012). There were also attacks and threats against lawyers supporting immigrants. Kínīsī gia ta Anthrōpina Dikaiōmata Allīleggyī stous Prosfyges, 'Enīmerōtiko Deltio – Samos', Omadadikigorwn.blogspot.com, 30/5/2013.

51. Villa Amalias occupiers were charged under the anti-terrorist law for collecting bottles for recycling, and rubber bullets were used in all of the raids. Dionýsīs Vythoúlkas, 'Víla Amalías: Astynomikī Epicheírīsī metá apó Kataggelía gia Narkōtiká', *Víma*, 20/12/2012; Vasílīs G. Lamprópoulos, 'EL.AS.: "Emfánise" Ópla pou Ríchnoun Sfaíres Kaoutsoúk', *Víma*, 10/1/2013.

and declared illegal.[52] The same policy was followed towards strikes by secondary education teachers against school closures and staff reductions in May.[53] Through the spring, campaigning residents of Skouries were arrested in a series of dawn raids. In June, unpaid seafarers on strike were also arrested for blockading ships,[54] and the public broadcaster ERT was forcibly closed with all of its 2,700 workers summarily dismissed within a day.[55]

This strategy was temporarily favourable. No more major demonstrations and social movements were formed, despite the continuation of the restructuring. The question of immigration directed attention away from the burdens and social disintegration caused by austerity, and projected these problems outwards to an 'external' element, one that did not 'belong' to Greek society, and which, if eradicated, would solve the problem. Meanwhile, small businesses, property owners and even the owner of the Perama shipyard began to enlist GD vigilantes against labour protests and unions,[56] or to threaten immigrant tenants who had not paid their rent.[57]

The government's permissive stance towards GD and its heavy repression of left movements fits not only with its aim to implement the restructuring and manage the resistance to it, but also with the main governing party's own political history and composition. A section of the members of ND have traditionally come from the far right. That Vassiliki Georgiadou's discussion of the strategies ND has historically been used in order to position itself favourably vis-à-vis the far right in different political conjunctures is revealing.[58] Up to 2009, ND followed various strategies of incorporating far-right politicians and ideologies or demarcating itself from them, as it did in 2000–9 in order to appeal to the centre. Under the leadership of Antonis Samaras, from 2009 onwards, the far right was reincorporated into the party and the same strategy was

52. Achilléas Chekímoglou, 'Paránomī ī Apergía se Metró, ĪSAP kai Tram', Víma, 21/1/2013.
53. 'Epistráteusī tōn Kathīgītōn Apofasízei ī Kyvérnīsī', TVXS.gr, 11/5/2013.
54. 'Dýo Nautergátes Synelīfthīsan gia to "Mplóko" stī Rafína', TVXS.gr, 07/6/2013.
55. 'YPOIK: To Nomikó Prósōpo ERT A.E. Échei Katargītheí', Nautemporikī, 11/6/2013.
56. GD had set up an employer-supported union at Perama shipyard that launched assaults against left-wing union leaders. Members of the Union of Waiters and Cooks also fought against GD members in June 2013, after the employer at a Thessaloniki fast food outlet enlisted them as his private police force. Giórgos Paganīs, 'Oi Vrómikes Mpíznes tīs Chrysís Augís sto Pérama', Real News, 29/9/2013, 32–3.
57. It is indicative that two old friends of my left-wing mother joined GD specifically to make use of its 'services' against their immigrant tenants.
58. Georgiadou, 'Ī Eklogikī Ánodos', 7–10.

followed after GD's ascent, by making friendly openings to the party.[59] Some very vocal ex-members of LAOS (Adonis Georgiadis and Makis Voridis) were given prominent positions and ministries, while another far-right politician, Failos Kranidiotis, was the prime minister's special adviser. In this configuration, ND opposed same-sex civil partnership and an anti-racist bill that would criminalise hate speech.[60] Most glaringly, only a week before the murder of Pavlos Fyssas, an ND MP stated that his party would consider a coalition with a more 'serious' version of GD.[61]

ND's government policy, accordingly, appealed to ultranationalist and racist concerns. Almost immediately after taking power, the ministry of public order unleashed an anti-immigration operation, called Hospitable Zeus, which involved indiscriminate arrests of 'foreign-looking' people to certify their documents. On several occasions this resulted in unlawful detentions and beatings of unsuspecting non-white tourists.[62] Once more, the vigilante participation of GD members proactively 'assisted' the police, by delivering immigrants into police stations. There were also government efforts to purge immigrant children from kindergartens,[63] to take away the right to citizenship from second-generation immigrants and to limit recruitment in the police and the armed forces to those who are Greek 'in genus'.[64] Adding to GD's rising homophobic assaults,[65] the police embarked on arresting and humiliating transgender women in the streets of Thessaloniki.[66]

At the same time, and despite ND's pre-electorally expressed doubts about the restructuring, the ND-led government took a hard line in implementing privatisations, austerity and layoffs by bypassing parliamentary procedure. They did this by issuing emergency legislative acts,

59. Panagiotis Psomiadis, a northern ND MP, stated that GD was a 'sister party' in June 2012. 'Antidráseis gia tis Dilōseis P. Psōmiádī perí Chrysīs Augīs', *Nautemporiki*, 13/6/2012.

60. Helena Smith, 'Greek Laws "Fall Short" as Racist and Homophobic Violence Surges', *The Guardian*, 7/9/2014.

61. 'Mp. Papadīmītríou: Giatí Óchi mia Sovarī ChA stīn Kyvérnīsī?', TVXS.gr, 12/9/2013.

62. Chloe Hadjimatheou, 'The Tourists Held by Greek Police as Illegal Migrants', *BBC*, 10/1/2013.

63. 'Seirá Paírnoun ta Nīpia sto Stóchastro tīs Chrysīs Augīs', TVXS.gr, 12/10/2012.

64. Lámpros Staurópoulos, '85 Vouleutés tīs ND Théloun Móno Éllīnes to Génos na Katatássontai stis Stratiōtikés Scholés', *Vīma*, 25/2/2013.

65. 'Aúxīsī stis Omofovikés Epithéseis me tīn Ánodo tīs Akrodexiás', *Eleutherotypía*, 21/1/2013.

66. Marína Galanoú, 'Ótan ta Trans Átoma Proságontai, gia na "Veltiōtheí ī Eikóna tīs Pólīs"', Left.gr, 18/7/2013.

as for example in the case of the ERT closure, or by banning strikes. The executive repeatedly bypassed the state's own laws in the name of a 'national emergency'. This practice, combined with sanctioned police abuse and a friendly stance to GD, had the advantage of being nominally democratic, while in effect resembling authoritarian forms of rule. This was a systematic temporal and spatial expansion of what could validly be called a state of exception as part of the state's crisis management strategy. The state increasingly resorted to extra-legal (permissiveness to GD, police collaboration) as well as legally exceptional (emergency legislative acts) means of imposing the restructuring. On one hand, the state covered up GD's collaboration with the police, allowing and politically legitimising its violence, which was, to a significant extent, a vigilante service to Greek employers, small businesses and landlords. On the other hand, the state intensified both legal police repression as well as the use of emergency powers to ban strikes and impose mass layoffs.

An additional strategy that strengthened the far right was the promotion of a 'theory of the extremes', which equated left and right 'extremism' and placed the government in the moderate, democratic and law-respecting political centre, supposedly *beyond* political conflict. The theory of the 'extremes' had the function of downplaying GD's racist violence and garnering support for heavily policing the other 'extreme' – demonstrators, strikers and anti-fascists. 'Violence' lost its context and became detached from the power relations of which it was part, so that riots in demonstrations were as 'extremist' as the murder of immigrants, using the deaths at Marfin (see Part I) as a continual reminder. Only 'legitimate' state violence ought to be acceptable, regardless of its scale or context. But, framed in this way, GD's own racist violence was also partially legitimised, since it was on the side of the state and sought to 'enforce the law' in a vigilantist way. On the contrary, the political bank robberies carried out by a group of anarchists,[67] and the escalation of the street conflict between GD and anti-fascist groups, were used as evidence for the 'lawlessness' of the left in this conflict between 'extremes'.

The government's appeals to democracy and moderation were, nevertheless, not particularly convincing, until, in September 2013, the anti-fascist Pavlos Fyssas was killed by a member of GD, Giorgos

---

67. The case was highly publicised because the group included Nikos Romanos, the friend of Alexis Grigoropoulos who witnessed his murder in December 2008. 'Profylakistéoi oi Syllifthéntes gia tī Diplī Līsteía ston Velventó', *Vīma*, 6/2/2013.

Roupakias, during one of the party's intimidation offensives in Nikaia.[68] The murder of a *Greek* man was too embarrassing for the government to ignore, and the evidence against GD was overwhelming, so processes began for the arrest of GD members. Friendly openings to GD were abruptly stopped, and the government used the opportunity to criminalise the party and gain back a small section of their voters through a renewed strategy of demarcating itself from the far right. The government could now present itself more consistently as the upholder of rationality and legality in the chaos. GD was named a criminal organisation and its main leader and several MPs were arrested. A series of raids that revealed evidence of systematic police collaboration and participation in GD's protection rackets, and senior officers of the police and intelligence services were fired.[69] The investigation even reached a head of ship-owning business, Anastasios Pallis, suspected of having funded and provided GD with weapons.[70] This was an unprecedented move by a state that had tolerated GD's activity for almost 30 years. Strangely, GD's supposed popular base (up to 15 per cent countrywide in some polls) hardly showed up to support its leaders who were being prosecuted, at a time when its very survival on the political scene was at stake.[71]

The government's U-turn took the anti-fascist movement by surprise, and leftist analyses debated whether it was intended to neutralise a political enemy, to avoid new riots, or if it simply submitted to pressure from EU partners. Yet the spectacular legitimising effect of this reaction should not be underestimated.[72] With GD's extra-legal vigilante contribution to repressive crisis management expelled, the empowered discourse of legality could open the way for the formal legitimation and normalisation of the emergency restructuring measures. The spectacular rejection of the extra-legal could be seen as part of a process of normalis-

---

68. Helena Smith, 'Greek Golden Dawn Member Arrested over Murder of Leftwing Hip-hop Artist', *The Guardian*, 18/9/2013.

69. According to the Civil Action Memorandum, a large number of police officers who acted as security of GD MPs joined in vigilante actions. The deputy police commissioner at Agios Panteleimonas police station was also charged with dealing drugs and weapons and running a protection racket in collaboration with GD, and the commander at Nikaia police station, known for the routine torture of immigrants, was accused of supplying information to protect GD members from prosecution.

70. Argyrō K. Mōrou, 'Dyo Karaviés Ópla kai i Chrysí Augí', *Eleutherotypía*, 13/10/2013.

71. Only around 200 people turned up to protest the arrest of GD's leader, Nikolaos Mihaloliakos. Later, on 26/10/2013, a larger protest managed 2,000 people at the most.

72. For two weeks, an enormous proportion of mainstream television time was taken up with detailed coverage of the police operations against GD.

ing the exceptional. At the level of political discourse, it also neutralised the *political* anti-fascism into which left parties and anti-authoritarian groups had invested so much of their energies – to be discussed in Chapter 13.

The War Discourse of the Restructuring

The unresolved debates over immigration that had appeared in the squares had by now broken out into a conflict between 'fascism' and 'anti-fascism', with the most conservative part of the movements becoming attracted to GD's anti-immigration anti-Memorandum discourse. The government, in turn, portrayed both of these sides, including SYRIZA, as 'extremist', while benefiting from the externalisation of the problem offered by GD's anti-immigration tirades. The discourse of 'extremes' was apposite from a liberal perspective, given that, as already discussed, the level of violence in social movements had escalated from 2008 onwards. Yet the accusation of 'extremism' against the left also harked back to a dated anti-communism.[73]

The re-emergence of a renewed 'right versus left' polarity that had gradually become marginalised in the post-dictatorship era was then another function of this discourse, which did not stop at the issue of immigration. The government utilised a typical trope of the far right, in identifying the entire post-dictatorship era as one of left extremist disorder and 'left ideological hegemony'. This notion exonerated the governments of the period and favoured the implementation of the restructuring, since the return of 'order' was now overdue. Homogenising the multifarious forms of anti-neoliberal resistance in the 1980s, 1990s and 2000s as a strategy of 'the left', the latter was said to represent the 'vested interests' and the 'old corrupt status quo' that had led the Greek state into a semi-default status. In a phenomenal logical inversion, it was no longer governments but social movements that were responsible for the crisis. The government presented itself as comprising bold and innovative leaders who were finally bringing progress and development to the country. The more authoritarian the imposition of the measures, the more valiant their promoters were said to be.

This might seem like a familiar Thatcherite ideological trick, but in Greece this narrative gained an additional dimension of *historical*

---

73. Arīs Ravanós, 'Ī Ideologikī Īgemonía tīs Aristerás, o Néos Echthrós tou Samará', *Vīma*, 29/2/2012.

revisionism, which has had multiple manifestations. It encompasses an academic revisionism that reconsiders contested moments of Greek history, such as the civil war, from a 'corrective' point of view that, despite its right-wing perspective, presents itself as the long-awaited return of objectivity in Greek historical science,[74] and a 'lay' revisionism that portrays the dictatorships of the twentieth century as the golden ages of Greek history.[75] The history of the civil war and the colonels' dictatorship carry an enormous weight in the definition of political identities in Greece, and the shift in the 'official' narrative attempted to reconfigure history and memory as part and parcel of the economic restructuring. These historical narratives, which are not really new, but are actually a repackaging of the state narratives of the civil war period and the dictatorship periods, are to a great extent directed towards 'reassessing' and vindicating (a) the pre-war openly fascist dictatorship of Ioannis Metaxas of the 1930s which is credited with 'introducing' social security, (b) those who fought on the side of the Germans and the state against the communists in the civil war and (c) the anti-communist 1966 colonels' dictatorship, credited for the economic growth of the 1960s.[76]

This 'reassessment' of the past was more than an apologetics for the historical predecessors of the right. These examples of 'successful' authoritarianism in the past served a present where the heavier repression of workers and social struggles ought to be legitimised. Erasing the history of the opponent – the labour movement and other social movements associated with the history of the left – was clearly a war tactic. In combination with the use of extra-legal and legally exceptional means, heavy police repression and the theory of the extremes and racialising practices, this was part of the reconfiguration of reality necessitated by an economic, social and political restructuring. In the new reality,

74. An example is Stathis Kalyvas's revisionist work on the Greek civil war. A member of the right-wing Konstantinos Karamanlis institute, Kalyvas has built his career by counting civil war victims based exclusively on right-wing accounts, and producing a new historical narrative on 'red terror', which he presents as free from 'ideological fixations'. Stathis Kalyvas, 'Red Terror', in *After the War Was Over*, ed. Mark Mazower (Princeton: Princeton University Press, 2000). For one of many critiques see: Hagen Fleischer, 'Ī "Kókkinī" kai ī "Maúrī" Vía', *Vīma*, 10/1/2010.

75. *Kathimerini* published a popularised biography of the dictator Ioannis Metaxas in its 'leaders' book series alongside personalities such as Aristotle, Alexander the Great and Ioannis Kapodistrias. Marína Petrákī, *O Iōánnīs písō apó ton Metaxá* (Athens: Kathīmerinés, 2014).

76. Countless far-right blogs make this argument, e.g. see '"Junta", G. Papadopoulos: The Full Truth You Are Not Told!!!!' [In Greek], Alithiastofos.blogspot.com, 25/10/2012.

labour ought to recognise that it is no longer an equal 'social partner' represented within the state, but a mere cost in the production process, which must be shed when superfluous. The re-emergence and redefinition of those histories of war signalled a state that openly now took a political *position of war*,[77] by openly adopting a new, *partisan* stance in relation to the history of those wars. This contrasted with the stance of the post-Metapoliteusi state, which aimed for 'democracy and reconciliation' and condemned prior dictatorships while remaining neutral and silent towards the civil war.

Yet the discourse against the Metapoliteusi (seen as a period from 1974 onwards) was not initiated by ND or GD. It has been particularly influential since the late 2000s and was manifest in the movement of the squares, interpreted both from a libertarian-democratic perspective (the revolution against the dictators did not go far enough, expressed in the slogan 'bread, education, freedom, the junta did not end in 1973') and in reactionary ways that were nostalgic of the junta (a new junta was needed to punish traitor politicians and promote economic growth). Again, this criticism united radically opposed viewpoints under similar oppositional practices. After the 2012 elections, this split became more obvious and openly politicised.

Interestingly for this conjuncture, while the 'enemy' in the state's war discourse was effectively a class enemy – those at the bottom of social stratification (illegal immigrants), the remaining labour unions that decided to act at all, the militant left and those who opposed development projects – it was rarely identified as such from either of the two political sides. Instead, both the right and the left side of the conflict strove to define themselves as representatives of 'the Greek people'. The left narrative of the past wars – the civil war, the struggle against the junta – did not present its history from the perspective of the Greek labour or communist movement, but as a history of anti-imperialist national liberation. The anti-fascism that was reawakened in this conjuncture was an anti-German anti-Nazism, identifying GD as the descendants of German collaborators. In framing politics in this way, for the left also, national sovereignty was at stake first, and class struggle was again understood through the anti-imperialist lens. Both sides of the conflict then produced narratives of national unity and of 'collective national interests'.

---

77. Cf. Foucault's discussion of historico-political discourse and its use as a weapon of war in its claim to truth in *Society Must Be Defended* (New York: Picador, 2003), 53.

As I discuss in more detail below, the left parties – as well as parts of the anarchist/anti-authoritarian scene – attempted to oppose the restructuring by putting forward an anti-imperialist discourse against 'the Germans' that was not that dissimilar in its externalising function to that of populist far-right discourse. Particularly after the bailout of Cyprus in March 2013, they attributed this – and by extension the Greek bailout – almost exclusively to 'German interests and hegemony'. In this case, too, the left-wing response to the rise of far-right nationalism was unable to distinguish itself from that which it supposedly sought to oppose.

Crisis Biopolitics Meets Crisis Fascism

Beyond the level of political contest, however, this war of narratives was also part of a crisis management strategy that aimed to manage the surplus populations produced in the crisis, by reseparating and reclassifying them through biopolitical processes of racialisation and abjection. These processes correspond to existing asymmetrical social relations that were unsettled by the crisis. GD activism and the state's policing mediated already inflamed class and intra-class antagonisms, defending the threatened relative status of parts of Greek capital, the Greek petit bourgeois ravaged by the crisis and, crucially, unemployed or underemployed Greek surplus proletarians, against internal and external 'threats'. This state offensive was a spectacular defence of the status of the Greek citizen, which underwent a crisis, in the dissolution of the prior social contract between civil society and the state.

This crisis management strategy is most intelligible in the context of the crisis of state sovereignty. The role of government, particularly in a conjuncture of crisis, is not only concerned to maintain its own political legitimacy, but also to facilitate social reproduction in its broadest sense of ensuring the continuity of existing social relations, as well as in the Foucauldian sense of 'enhancing' the population's productivity by managing it socially and biologically. Yet, in financialised capitalism, states face restrictions in how they carry out this management. As discussed in Part I, after the 2008 financial crisis it has become more than evident that national states are subject to a financial type of governmentality, which radically limits their autonomy in governing a territory and ensuring capitalist accumulation within it. In the EU, the interdependence among states effected by the common currency has also meant that Eurozone states cannot make independent decisions on managing and stabilising the local economy. This can draw the national state, particularly a deeply indebted state, into a severe political crisis. It can no longer avert social struggles and problems of legitimation, because it no longer has the flexibility to manipulate state policy in order to achieve a balance between ensuring the servicing of debt, continuing accumulation, as well as ensuring that populations can be integrated productively.

As discussed, social movements identified this as a problem of sovereignty and national independence, giving rise to a strengthening of nationalist ideologies. On their side, Greek governments until the end of 2014 responded to this problem by resorting to heavier policing, inventing new political discourses to legitimise this repression and allowing the operation of extra-legal and vigilante forces of social control. This discourse of legitimation attempted to reconstruct a national narrative, with preference to a parochial, inward-looking and xenophobic anti-immigrant discourse, at the same time as the national state appeared to collaborate willingly with a wider regional crisis management project overseen by supranational institutions. We could call this a kind of compensatory practice that reaffirmed the nation-state in its interior at the same moment of its inability to do so at the level of international relations.

This nationalism's most distinctive characteristic is that it emerges as part of the crisis of the nation-state. At the same time, this recourse to nationalism is not an anachronism but is also actively reproduced in today's international capitalism and its crisis. 'Globalisation', financial governmentality and supranational institutions may have challenged the integrity of national economies, but they also reinforce national boundaries through the creation of a stratified global labour market,[78] already marked by a history of colonial racialisation. (Re)racialising immigration controls reinforces this stratification by preventing the global mobility of populations who are integrated as surplus into the wage relation. Controls intensify as the crisis deepens and expands these populations.[79] Immigration has been discouraged, and the low value of migrant labour has been reproduced, through militarised border regimes, mass internment into camps, racialising discourses and keeping immigrants in a status of illegality or a legally low status, often even preventing them accessing formal justice, for as long as possible.[80] At the

---

78. Castles, 'Migration, Crisis'.
79. ILO, *World Employment 2015*.
80. See Matthew Carr's extensive journalistic fieldwork along the borders of Europe. Matthew Carr, *Fortress Europe* (London: Hurst, 2012).

borders of the EU, this population management strategy escalated as the austerity imposed in Southern Europe also produced European surplus populations in these border areas.[81]

In the case of Greece's immigration policies, this has played out in the preference for 'fencing' as opposed to 'gatekeeping' external and internal immigration controls.[82] In the policing of its eastern border with Turkey, from 2011 onwards Greece strengthened its fencing practices with increased EU funding and the contribution of Frontex. Inside the country's territory,[83] immigrants have been managed exclusively through spectacular 'fencing' measures such as mass arrests and placement in detention camps. On the contrary, 'gatekeeping' measures that would control immigrants' informal employment or prosecute their employers have not been actively enforced.[84] Immigrant workers have been prey to employers who have alternately mobilised GD or the police to terrorise them into tolerating unpaid work and squalid living conditions. Another section of irregular immigrants, who attempt to make a living as street vendors, have been similarly forced to operate under the terror of the police and GD vigilantism. Greek immigration policy has actively created the conditions for a proletarian segment in the labour market that has few resources to resist the violent and openly racist methods by which its labour power is devalued. The control of proletarian migrants into the EU has thus not been a mere matter of law enforcement, but existing laws and human and refugee rights conventions have been frequently overriden in order to prevent their mobility and to manage their labour power. This was most spectacularly evident in the EU's deal with Turkey to control the so-called 'refugee crisis'.

These policies signal the radical stratification of surplus populations and their differential management by national states. The domestic surplus population, which exploded in the crisis with extremely high rates

---

81. Greece's immigrant population as a proportion of its native population was 8.9 per cent in 2013. It increased from 1990 to 2013 by 119 per cent. In this latter statistic, Greece is exceeded by Finland, Spain, Serbia, Italy, Norway, Iceland and Ireland. United Nations, Department of Economic and Social Affairs, Population Division, *Trends in International Migrant Stock* (United Nations, 2013).

82. Anna Triandafyllidou and Maurizio Ambrosini, 'Irregular Immigration Control in Italy and Greece', *European Journal of Migration and Law* 13, no. 3 (2011): 251–73.

83. According to Eurostat data, 72,420 were found to be illegally resident in Greece with deportation orders in 2012, but only 15,746 were deported. A very small proportion, 9,575, were able to make asylum applications.

84. Triandafyllidou and Ambrosini, 'Irregular Immigration Control'.

of unemployment, is differentially managed, through workfare and other attempts to integrate it economically by reducing the price of its labour power. To understand this differentiation it is also important to keep in view the constitution of citizenship in the modern Greek nation-state, which defines *racially* the Greek nation and national identity. Even today, granting citizenship to long-term immigrants is scandalous: it corrupts the entire narrative that constitutes Greekness, because its identity is not one of empire (incorporation) but one of liberation (separation) in its relation to other ethnicities. As discussed in Part I, this biological notion of the nation and citizen based on 'blood' has been linked, historically, politically and conceptually, to the patriarchal household as a unit of generational reproduction, and thus to the oppression of women and the policing of gender and sexuality. This policing has been common to right- and left-wing traditions, even if feminist and LGBTQI+ movements have fought for space and recognition within the left.

Most exemplary of this biopolitical crisis management strategy and its reproduction of a stratified surplus population is the 2012 'public health' campaign that entailed the quarantining of immigrants and the arrests of HIV-positive women, along with the Xenios Zeus immigration policing operation that followed it. It is not sufficient to understand these operations as a hegemonic ideological project to cultivate a 'moral panic' and a conservative 'common sense', as a Gramscian analysis, influenced by the work of Stuart Hall and others, might suggest.[85] This is because such an approach does not explain why specifically the *border* and *sexuality* have been the major points of concern of governmental management and discourse in this moment of crisis. It is, at the same time, not sufficient to use a straightforward biopolitical paradigm that would read the motivation of 'enhancing the population' as the core premise of these strategies. When the economic measures pursued blatantly diminish the population's means of life, it is unsatisfactory to explain these strategies as the performance of the governmental function of 'making live' in a straightforward way.

We might begin by looking at the broader context of how neoliberal governmentality has, in recent years, shifted its focus from a 'rights-based' management of public health to a risk management approach that fits within a *dispositif* of security.[86] As Julia Smith notes in a survey of recent

---

85. Stuart Hall, ed., *Policing the Crisis* (London: Macmillan, 1978).
86. Michel Foucault, *Security, Territory, Population* (Basingstoke: Palgrave Macmillan, 2009), 16–20.

governmental responses to HIV in the EU, the passage from 'rights' to 'risk' entails moving from the universal provision of healthcare that attempts to prevent social marginalisation, to the separation of populations between those who are the 'threat' and do not have access to free healthcare, and those who are to be protected on the basis of their citizenship and economic status.[87] 'Risk' is thus tied up with the othering of populations whose illness is only of interest to the government insofar as it is infectious. This risk management approach even defines the research questions that come to be posed by a section of medical science: the geographic profiling of the 'origins' of HIV infections, and their attribution of the problem to immigration,[88] is politically motivated insofar as citizenship itself is political. We are thus not simply seeing a cover-up of public health cuts. Instead, a specific *logic* of managing public health becomes merged with the policing of borders and sex work, founded as it is on the hierarchisation of populations.

While the security *dispositif* takes place in the context of a neoliberal restructuring, its deepening of racialised and gendered segregations raises the question of whether it represents a tendency towards an anti-liberal, or even fascistic, departure away from the neoliberal paradigm. This is not a new question; the continuity between liberal biopolitics and totalitarianism – especially Nazism – already concerned Foucault, and more recently Giorgio Agamben and Roberto Esposito.

Giorgio Agamben has identified strong continuities between totalitarian and liberal democratic state practices, and has drawn attention to the increase in the powers of the executive in liberal democracies over at least the past half century.[89] This resonates with the mode of crisis management pursued in the period we are discussing. Under the conditions of legal exception, sovereign biopower facilitated the spreading of terror by allowing citizen vigilantism against life that did not belong to or was undesirable in the body of the citizens. Agamben's analysis is based on the Schmittian notion of the sovereign exception, but the arbitrariness embedded into this notion leaves us unable to explain *which* bodies fall into the exception and for what purpose. It leaves out of its purview ongoing historical patterns which suggest that *specific*

---

87. Julia Smith, 'Europe's Shifting Response to HIV/AIDS', *Health and Human Rights Journal* 18, no. 2 (2016): 145–56.

88. D. Paraskevis et al., 'HIV-1 Outbreak among Injecting Drug Users in Greece, 2011', *Euro Surveillance* 16, no. 36 (2011): 2–5.

89. Giorgio Agamben, *State of Exception* (Chicago: University of Chicago Press, 2005), 18.

social categories, defined by gender, race and class, tend to be affected. It also cannot explain historical shifts in the degree to which the state of exception is exercised and the forms it takes.

A more historicised account of the relationship between liberal and fascist biopolitics is provided by Roberto Esposito, who has analysed the modern liberal nation-state as constituted by a 'paradigm of immunisation'.[90] His analysis has identified a shared biopolitical lexicon between the immunisation of the liberal propertied individual – and thus the transposition of the meaning of liberty into protection and security – and the immunisation of the community in its most self-destructive, 'auto-immune' form in Nazi biopolitics. Here, the absolute immunisation of the national body from the 'threat' of the foreign becomes auto-immune: it destroys the national community itself, by coming to justify the mass murder of 'life unworthy of life' (thanatopolitics), both within and beyond what are taken to be the borders of the community.

Esposito points out the enduring political and etymological link between birth (*nascita*) and 'nation', revealing its inherently racial meaning,[91] and drawing attention to the intimate links between the racialised, sexualised and gendered selectivity of modern biopower through the problem of generational reproduction. Women's reproductive role and thus their pivotal position in the control of health and racialised-genealogical dimensions of populations has historically rendered their bodies into objects of biopolitical control – most paradigmatically in eugenics. The *fraternity* on which the modern concept of democracy rests is related to the objectification of the female body specifically, and, in our relevant case, to the constitution of the sex worker as a threat to men as representatives of the national political body.[92]

But we may need to go beyond the historical constitution of the modern liberal state, and take into account the imperatives of capitalist reproduction in different phases of capitalist development if we wish to understand how and why the imposition of a specifically neoliberal restructuring crosses over into fascistic forms of social control. It is also important to keep in mind how histories of struggle have transformed the meaning of citizenship, given that there has been no linear progress from liberalism to fascism from the nineteenth to the twenty-first century.

---

90. Roberto Esposito, *Bíos* (Minneapolis: University of Minnesota Press, 2008), 45–77.
91. Ibid., 169.
92. Ibid, 172–3.

The contemporary neoliberal state, whose sovereignty is subservient to the multiplicity of risk management calculations that add up to the abstraction of financial governmentality, may *appear* as the fundamental bulwark against the vicissitudes of the market. In practice, however, state power, and, in fact, an empowerment of the executive branch of the state, as Saskia Sassen has noted, is used to impose the imperatives of balanced state finances and flexible labour markets regardless of the human, and often political, cost.[93] States are impersonally 'punished' for sovereign debt and insufficient 'reforms', and this punishment is transferred to individuals, who are impacted differentially depending on their economic position. The punishment is particularly severe when demand for labour power is low and increasing proportions of the population are cast off as surplus to the reproduction of capital.

The subjection of the state to the abstract governmentality of the market deepens already existing social separations, because, from the perspective of financial risk management, the free market, liberated from the moderating restrictions of social democracy, has an immunising function, expelling 'weak' and 'unhealthy' elements and strengthening the rest of the economy. At the level of individuals, the caesurae that distinguish 'unhealthy' bodies-as-economic-units are the sediments of historically interrelated economic, racialised and gendered social divisions and disadvantages.

Under the governmentality of free market competition, the life of those who suffer market 'failure' is not merely redundant but an element that undermines the health of the collective social body as market. The drive to destroy those 'weak' elements eventually becomes a form of auto-immunity, producing a thanatopolitics of the *other* body constituted by property and liberty, namely that of the propertyless proletarian, who, regardless of formal standing under the equal 'protection' of the law, can become 'bare life' in Agamben's terminology. Yet this is not a thanatopolitics of sovereign exception as Agamben would have it, but is instead inherent to the very content of rights (the primacy of negative economic freedom). As Pashukanis has eloquently put it, 'for the proletarian this very "material freedom" means the possibility of quietly dying of starvation'.[94]

---

93. Saskia Sassen, 'The State and Globalization' (Global Jean Monnet ECSA-World Conference, Brussels, 2006).
94. Pashukanis, 'General Theory of Law and Marxism', 105.

As discussed, there is an element of legal exception to the imposition of neoliberal restructuring, but this has an ideological function rather than being necessary to the exercise of sovereign power. While neoliberal governmentality seeks to protect the economic community through the immunising function of the market, as Hayek himself has pointed out, the market does not reward according to any specific principle and, as such, it cannot be made into an instrument of 'collective value or social justice'.[95] But, Hayek reasons, the belief in the 'justice' of the market – its meritocracy – is necessary for social legitimation. Given that market competition disadvantages those who are already disadvantaged, we can see how the reinforcement and moral justification of existing hierarchical social separations can be a neoliberal governmental technique of self-legitimation. In a moment of economic crisis, which, as discussed, is also a political crisis and a crisis of the nation-state's sovereignty, the legitimation of neoliberal restructuring entails the exercise of an exception, whereby those *already* marginalised lose their remaining rights and subjectivity. Social marginalisation becomes concretised into the language of disease, and the marginalised population is reduced to a dehumanised viral threat.

Nevertheless, as I insist in Chapter 12, this form of crisis management does not only emanate from the state. It can be and has been a demand 'from below', driven both by rational motivations based on competitive self-protection, and psychic-irrational anxieties.

---

95. Friedrich A. von Hayek, *Law, Legislation and Liberty, Volume 2: The Mirage of Social Justice* (London: Routledge, 1976); Raymond Plant, 'Neo-Liberalism and the Theory of the State', *The Political Quarterly* 75, no. s1 (2004): 24–37, 36.

12

Nationalism from Below

Abjection and Anxieties of Contagion

I have discussed how, through the demands of neoliberal social legitimation, already marginalised populations become additionally stigmatised
through policing strategies that have an ideological function. But this
ideological strategy cannot succeed unless it can also interpellate a great
proportion of the spectators, who are called upon to consent to this governmental action. The anecdotes in Chapter 10 should be enough to
show the degree to which racism is embedded into the 'common sense' in
Greece across classes, what politicians love to call 'the popular sentiment',
which they exploit to fit their strategies: the targeting of immigrants and
public exposure of women in the government's campaign against HIV
happened as part of a pre-election strategy with the correct expectation
of broad popular approval. The rise in homophobic and transphobic
attacks in this period cannot be attributed to GD gangs either, given
that they rose further after arrests of its members had begun.[1] In any
case, despite the arrests and revelations about its deadly violence and
criminal activities, GD still received 6.28 per cent of the vote in the 2015
elections, becoming the third party and losing less than 1 per cent of its
vote since 2012. The prominence of racism, misogyny and homophobia
in the crisis thus clearly has not been a mere result of state strategy. The
question again emerges of how this racist and misogynistic nationalism
is produced and why it has become so popular in this crisis.

Here is where things often get tricky for critical theorists. Until
recently, and since the Frankfurt School's, and, to some extent, Deleuze
and Guattari's, concern to consider mass popular phenomena of fascism
as also emanating *from below*, popular resistance has been fetishised
as that political element of democracy that is by definition revolution-

---

1. Iōanna Fōtiadī, 'Plīthaínoun oi Omofovikés Epithéseis sto Kéntro tīs Athīnas',
Kathīmerinī, 30/8/2014; 'Meiōthīkan oi Ratsistikés Epithéseis, Auxīthīkan oi Omofovikés',
In.gr, 31/10/2014.

ary. Fascism itself has been equated to totalitarianism, and the fact that fascism was also, historically, a form of mass – though disciplined – insurrection, was almost forgotten.[2] Across Europe and the USA, after the unprecedented strengthening of far-right politics over the past six years, these questions have re-emerged with urgency. Yet, one can still detect a residual tendency, among left-wing commentators and academics, to emphasise the *rationality* of 'working-class' support for politicians like Trump and the discourses of sovereignty and self-protection around Brexit,[3] sometimes even describing the patriotic impulse as a kind of basic human bond, whose questioning emerges from a bourgeois cosmopolitan experience disconnected from the problems and experience of the 'working-class people'.[4] These types of analysis tend to criticise the conception of racism as also an affective phenomenon, rejecting it, again, as a liberal bourgeois perspective that blames the working class and conceals its own more 'sophisticated' racism.

It is no use choosing the side of rationality or irrationality in this opposition. Looking at the case of Greece, it is possible to identify both rational and irrational motivations for popular attitudes that converge with far-right politics. It is also no use taking the side of a sanctified 'working-class experience' avoiding – or uncritically naturalising – the fact that this experience is tied up with its national and racial identity. At the same time, while irrationalism and mysticism have historically been used as concepts with explanatory power in analyses of fascism,[5] racism also contains a strong element of rationalism. In consonance with Marcuse's argument that in 'advanced industrial society … it is the rational rather than the irrational that becomes the most effective locus of mystification',[6] and the preceding discussion of biopolitics, it is evident that capitalist rationality reproduces and remobilises the persisting mystifications of race that also implicate sex and reproductive

2. Beyond some exceptions – see, for example, Marcel Stoetzler, 'On the Possibility that the Revolution that Will End Capitalism Might Fail to Usher in Communism', *Journal of Classical Sociology* 12, no. 2 (2012): 191–204.

3. 'Editorial: President Trump?', *Insurgent Notes*, no. 13 (2016); Freundinnen und Freunde der Klassenlosen Gesellschaft, 'Subtile Härte', *Konkret*, October 2016, English translation available at endnotes.org.uk.

4. Victor J. Seidler, *Making Sense of Brexit* (Bristol: Policy, 2018); Lisa McKenzie, 'The Class Politics of Prejudice', *The British Journal of Sociology* 68, no. S1 (2017): S265–80.

5. For example, Wilhelm Reich, *The Mass Psychology of Fascism* (Harmondsworth: Penguin, 1975); György Lukács, *The Destruction of Reason* (Atlantic Highlands, NJ: Humanities, 1981).

6. Herbert Marcuse, *One Dimensional Man* (London: Abacus, 1972), 194.

bodies (blood, genes, essentialised culture, the common history and fate of a 'people').

The coming together of rational and affective elements can be seen in Balibar and Wallerstein's analysis of nationalism and racism specifically in relation to immigration and crisis, written in the 1980s: racism is the result of, and contributes to, the transformation of rights into 'privileges that have to be protected or reserved for certain "natural" beneficiaries'.[7] The insecurity of subsistence in the classes affected by crisis fuels panic and a clutching on to those taken-for-granted rights, now reconstituted as privileges, which favours precisely this reconstitution promoted by the restructuring. In the more recent case of Greece, there are four perspectives through which the control, policing and violence towards a population of non-citizens, and its ideological and ethical justification on the basis of racialisation, can be understood as founded on the rationality of social administration, the calculation of profit and labour market competition.

First, as discussed at length already, there is the racist rationality of social administration and population management, with which any citizen might identify on the basis that it represents the 'common good' or the 'national interest'. The very posing of immigration as a problem of rational social administration, usually in terms of their usefulness or burden to the domestic economy, objectifies and instrumentalises the bodies of non-citizens who enter a country's territory.

Second, this type of management of the migrant population, the 'fencing' or 'cleansing' of public spaces from migrants through sweep operations or GD vigilantism, clearly benefits the employers, landlords and petit bourgeois competitors of migrants (as workers, tenants, street vendors or small shopkeepers). Indeed, typically, Greece's small business owners have tended to support the policing of migrants, for exploitative or competitive advantage, especially in the crisis. Beyond the pragmatic reasons, the zealousness of such support can be explained by the identification of this class politically and culturally with its integration into the nation-state in the prior social contract that was unilaterally voided with the restructuring.

Third, and in favour of a heavier policing of migrant employment, for unemployed proletarian citizens the control or eradication of illegal

---

7. Étienne Balibar and Immanuel Maurice Wallerstein, *Race, Nation, Class* (London: Verso, 1991), 226.

immigration is assumed to raise the number of available jobs as well as wage rates, through decreasing competition in the labour market. While, in the period before the crisis, the petit bourgeois class was widely seen as the dominant voice of racist discourse, as expressed by 'residents committees' concerned with property prices and the 'cleanliness' of their neighbourhoods,[8] in the crisis, working and unemployed proletarians increasingly joined in, as is evident in the shifting voting patterns for GD, whose electoral results, beyond the traditionally far-right region of Lakonia, came to be highest in traditionally working-class urban neighbourhoods. Though, as mentioned, the scale of racism in Greece goes far beyond voting patterns, and SYRIZA's victory in the 2015 elections should not be considered as reflecting the lessening of the problem.

This element of intra-class competition when immigrants are treated as a threat to status, jobs and wages has been frequently translated into the terms of class struggle by arguing that it is the capitalists who allow the migrants into the country to 'divide the working class', and that 'neoliberal globalisation' favours immigration in order to increase global labour market competition and bring wages down. Beyond the ethnocentric premise of these arguments, which presume that each national working class ought to look after its own interests (and thus does not need the moralising internationalist interventions of academics and militants), they are also inaccurate. First, it is well documented that the neoliberal phase of globalisation has not coincided with an opening of borders (with the exception of the EU) but rather with a tightening of border controls against populations outside the most 'developed' countries with a European lineage – even those who were previously considered citizens of colonial empires.[9] Second, it is not the presence of immigrants that 'divides the working class' but, evidently, the notion that proletarians ought to stay 'each in their own country' is already an argument for them remaining divided. But we should also not understand these tendencies as the result of the disappearance of working-class identity and its replacement by nationalism and racism. The weakness of labour struggles, and the strengthening of nationalist opposition to the restructuring in the name of the interests of a national 'people', signifies the continued validity of a working-class identity, however fragmented and contradictory, which identifies with the interests of the nation and

8. Kandylis and Kavoulakos, 'Framing Urban Inequalities'.
9. Castles, 'Migration, Crisis'.

its capital, precisely because of its relationship of mutual implication with capital – its dependence upon capitalist development for its own existence as a class.

These last two perspectives entail an identification with the first perspective above. The standpoint of 'our economy' is adopted: that of capitalist reproduction, which requires investment, jobs, a solvent public sector, infinitely increasing property values, law and order, and citizens performing their duties and being loyal to the state (the nation). Of course, it does not quite work this way. Eliminating migrants is unlikely to increase wage levels, improve hospitals and kindergartens or increase property values that have bottomed out in the middle of the crisis. Yet the culprit for this failure is not sought in the very premises of capitalist reproduction but, instead, in leaders' mistakes, corruption, laziness and other moral failings that can only be overcome with better law enforcement or their replacement by new leaders. While this perspective is not satisfied with the realities of the present state of things, it is opposed to the restructuring and might join struggles against it, at the same time it entirely identifies with its principles of rational social administration, experiencing them as necessary for the very functioning of society and individual subsistence.

Thus the contradictory character of capitalism, which comes to the surface in its crisis, the tendency of its strict instrumental rationality to turn into irrationality, is reflected in the self-contradictory response to the crisis by proletarians and proletarianised petit bourgeois strata. The weakness of the labour movement and the failure of combative and persistent mass protests to stop the restructuring appears to have strengthened a last ditch position that affirms a *national* proletarian identity (and citizenship), and which, unlike that of the traditional labour movement, and often in a directly hostile stance against it,[10] entirely identifies with capital in its demand to re-enter the wage relation as the only way out of the intolerable proletarian predicament of being surplus. This is an apparently rational, but essentially self-defeating, response to the broader dilemma facing proletarians in the crisis: the wage relation presents itself as the only option for subsistence, but fails to integrate proletarians, meet their subsistence needs or provide any kind of security. In the absence of an alternative imaginary for social life, and

---

10. According to a poll in July 2013, 60 per cent of respondents supported public sector layoffs. Vasílis Chiótis, '"Nai" apó to 60% gia Apolýseis sto Dīmósio', *Vīma*, 21/7/2013.

because life in capitalism outside the wage relation is unsustainable, one's own condition comes to be understood from the perspective of state and capitalist management. The naturalised identification of work and the wage with subsistence is therefore at the core of nationalism.

The self as economic unit is thus instrumentalised along with the migrant other. Yet the apparently rationalist instrumentalisation of the migrant – their usefulness 'for us' – is itself founded on mystifications and anxieties. The fetish of the unified society contained within the nation-state, the imaginary 'national community' of households headed by men, is linked to the myths and concepts of the essential (white) European or Greek supremacy, of the migrant as an invading savage and carrier of disease and crime. The powerful household analogy of 'host' and 'visitor' by which national identification operates in relation to immigration points to a broader concept of *borders* that locates them not only in the territory and in everyday bordering acts and practices, but also in the boundaries of individual and collective identity, as well as the integrity of the national body whose autonomy, health and virility are under threat. It is no wonder that the prime accusation against 'Pakistani' immigrants propagated by far-right blogs is that they 'rape our women', conveying the visceral fear of miscegenation. Meanwhile, when immigrant women are raped, blame is reversed, as in the case of the rape and cyber-bullying of a Bulgarian teenager in Amarynthos in 2006, for which the local community blamed the girl, and local courts exonerated the perpetrators.[11]

'Abjection' may be the most apposite concept to help understand the convergence of racism and misogyny, operating concurrently at social, political and psychic levels of subjectivity in the crisis.[12] Judith Butler has elaborated how 'subjects are constituted through exclusion, that is, through the creation of a domain of deauthorized subjects, presubjects, figures of abjection, populations erased view'.[13] For her, abjection is central to the operation of normative gender and sexuality and the con-

---

11. The local community even organised a violent offensive against feminist and anti-racist demonstrations in their area. Penelope Papailias, 'The Screen of the Migrant Body', *Greek Review of Social Research*, no. 140–1 (2013): 261–73.

12. Although there are also alternative approaches to the psychic operations associated with racism and misogyny. We may mention here Franz Fanon and Wilhelm Reich, as well as recent analyses of nationalism, racism and sexism, in Lene Auestad, ed., *Nationalism and the Body Politic* (London: Karnac, 2014).

13. Judith Butler, 'Contingent Foundations', in *Feminists Theorize the Political*, ed. Judith Butler and Joan W. Scott (New York: Routledge, 1992), 3–21, 13.

stitution of gendered subjectivity, by deauthorising forms of gendered and sexual being that become unintelligible. But abjection does not only produce *invisible* subjects, and is evidently also associated with racial imaginaries. The ideological strategies discussed in Chapter 11 have counted on the extensive media *exposure* of racialised and gendered figures of abjection. As Imogen Tyler has more recently emphasised, it is the active cultivation of social disgust – 'social abjection' – towards unemployed, impoverished and migrant populations that is pursued as part of neoliberal governmental rhetoric.[14]

'Social abjection' interpellates citizens motivated by a 'rational' self-protective impulse by mobilising anxieties over invasion by a contagious other. Contagion is symbolically relevant insofar as the other is vulnerable and socially marginalised, and becomes concretised into a superficially rational discourse of health, bodily integrity and economic functioning. The increase in street violence against immigrants, gay men and trans women fits within this pattern. This fear of invasion, and of the threat to the *borders* of identity, is a central theme in the psychoanalytic concept of abjection as elaborated by Julia Kristeva: it is 'not lack of cleanliness or health that causes abjection but what disturbs identity, system, order'. What threatens is not illness as such but the fact that 'borders, positions, rules' are violated.[15] Those interpellated by the designation of 'family men' in the campaign against sex workers with HIV were said to be threatened by a danger that resymbolised the threat of poverty and unemployment as a fatal viral infection by a (foreign) woman.

At the core of the operation of abjection in the crisis is the abjection of the emasculated, vulnerable self, which is either projected out into a vulnerable other and attacked, or is capable of turning into self-destruction. The affective dimension of self-protective and self-destructive reactions to the crisis and austerity probably begins with this experience of loss of economic autonomy and the associated gender roles of the patriarchal family unit – in Greece this is especially relevant to the proletarianised ex-family business owner. This can also be experienced as loss from a woman's perspective, to the extent that she may have found meaning and comfort in her gendered role as carer and assistant to others within

---

14. Imogen Tyler, *Revolting Subjects* (London: Zed Books, 2013), 46.
15. Julia Kristeva, *Powers of Horror* (New York: Columbia University Press, 1982), 4. Iris Marion Young uses this concept to analyse the psychic dimensions of racism and misogyny in her essay 'Abjection and Oppression', in *Crises in Continental Philosophy*, ed. Arleen Dallery, Charles Scott and Holley Roberts (Albany, NY: SUNYP, 1990).

patriarchal family structures. We saw this sense of meaning among women in the struggle in Skouries. Thus it should not be surprising that the ultra-masculine and violent image projected by GD was not only attractive to men but also to many women. GD's politics drew attention to the *male* victims of the crisis, just as women in Skouries were most concerned about their husbands and brothers being arrested. It was also exclusively men who engaged in public suicides as forms of protest, which in Chapter 9 I linked to the self-abjection of emasculated vulnerability turned into violent reaction. The violence of suicide, in these cases, is not turned only against the self. Most self-immolations were designed to set fire to branches of banks. Dimitris Christoulas' much discussed public suicide sparked an angry demonstration and the beating of a police officer by the crowd. His suicide note read: 'I believe the youth without a future one day will take up arms and, in Syntagma Square, they will hang the national traitors upside down, like Italians did to Mussolini in 1945.' The note is evidence of the imaginary of empowerment through armed struggle as a response to the emasculation of vulnerability and dependence as much as it instantiates the kind of nationalist anti-fascism I discuss in Chapter 13.

The patriarchal culture that associates masculinity with individual independence and autonomy then comes to interact, in a volatile way, with the independence, competitive 'capability' and self-reliance valued by (neo)liberal ideology. The contradiction between the myth of the market as a reward mechanism and the actuality of its arbitrary immunising logic is a source of social and psychic tension. The feminised element within the self at risk of 'failure' is feared and ought to be expelled, in the same way as the market's immunising mechanism expels those no longer essential to the reproduction of capital.

The psychosocial conjuncture of the concern with borders and sexuality can then be linked to the historical form of immunised individuality produced in modern liberal societies, and the tensions this form of individuality is subject to under a neoliberal model in crisis. The operation of abjection in this sense demonstrates how the dynamics of patriarchal misogyny, Eurocentric racism and the stigmatisation of the poor intersect not only in the practices and ideologies promoted by neoliberal and increasingly authoritarian states, but also *within* the subjects produced in such a society. The fear of the marginalised other is also a denial of the self as potentially in need of others, and thus dependent and emasculated. In Kristeva's words, 'There is nothing like the abjection of self to show that all abjection is in fact recognition of the *want* on which any being, meaning, language, or desire is founded.'[16]

Left Nationalism and Anti-Fascism

Beyond producing a militant ultranationalist, anti-immigrant authoritarian camp, the way in which the crisis and the imposition of the restructuring was experienced also generated a left nationalist anti-imperialist camp, which represented a great proportion of the left: not only the left-wing parties SYRIZA, KKE and ANTARSYA (Anticapitalist Left Cooperation for the Overthrow), but also tendencies within the anarchist/anti-authoritarian scene. Beyond the anti-imperialist centre–periphery economic analyses of this camp, which I discussed in Part I, another corollary of this formation was the emergence of a contradictory form of nationalist anti-fascism, associated with the tension between 'right' and 'left' historical narratives of World War II and the civil war.

It is important to point out that, beyond any 'theory of the extremes', the left nationalist anti-fascist camp is not merely a mirror of its enemy. Yet, in frequently deploying the history and historical political discourse of the classic division between left and right in Greece (the civil war), it tended to produce a nation-centred as opposed to a class-based perspective. Despite long-running divisions within this left spectrum on the issues of nationalism, statism and democratism, the dominant anti-fascist discourse tended to favour anti-imperialist theories of 'people's oppression', drawing analogies between the German occupation and German hegemony in the EU, and reawakening a mythical image of World War II communist anti-fascist national resistance. While initially this anti-imperialism was characteristic mainly of the parties left of SYRIZA (and the left wing within it), in the crisis it tended to expand to anarchist/anti-authoritarian groups. Slogans reminiscent of the civil war became more common in anti-fascist demonstrations led by anarchists, despite their traditional enmity towards the KKE. The question of fascism then came to concern less the problem of immigration and more the issue of whether the right or the left was the most patriotic force and could guarantee national sovereignty.

This ideological trend can be understood in the context of the worsening position of Greek labour in the international labour market,

---

16. Ibid., 5.

as the restructuring, imposed by European institutions and Germany as Greece's major creditor, compressed the value of local labour power. Left-wing anti-imperialist analyses interpreted this, as discussed in Part I, in terms of value transfer from 'Greece' to 'Germany', a conception that points to a real relation of economic dominance but risks erasing distinctions between different classes and business interest groups, state property and finances, and common and private land. At the level of popular political discourse, this produces the personification of the suffering looted motherland and the productivist and moralist accusation of betrayal against the upper classes and power holders, who have left the country's productive forces 'underdeveloped'. The living tradition of left civil war discourse concerning bourgeois collaborationism with the German occupation came to match perfectly a contemporary discourse of collaboration with the German-led Troika. The discourse of 'treason' then crosses the boundaries of 'left' and 'right', albeit with different degrees of emphasis to the problem of immigration. Anti-imperialists have been talking about the Troika as a 'German occupation of Greece', and have striven to make the parallel as explicit as possible. In the 9 October 2012 demonstration in protest against Angela Merkel's visit to Athens, members of the POE-OTA (electricity) labour union demonstrated dressed as Nazi officers and swastika flags were set on fire.[17] Immediately after winning the elections of January 2015, Alexis Tsipras made sure he paid his respects at the monument in Kaisariani for local World War II resistance fighters executed by the German occupying forces.[18] This was evidently a populist move, as later, during EU negotiations, it became plain that Tsipras represented the more Europhile branch of SYRIZA.

Left-wing anti-imperialist nationalism (or 'patriotism' as it prefers to call itself) tends to evade criticism in Anglophone and Western left-wing and academic discussions, associated with their experience of a domestic nationalism linked more with imperialism than with anti-imperialism, as well as enduring Marxist traditions from Lenin onwards in support of national independence struggles. From that perspective, the nationalisms of 'oppressed nations' have been typically analysed as 'progressive' and have gained much support. Theories of peripheral populism have similarly remained untroubled by the nationalism embedded in populist

17. Graeme Wearden, 'Merkel Visits Greece as 50,000 People Protest', *The Guardian*, 9/10/2012.
18. 'Sto Mnīmeío tōn Ektelesthéntōn stīn Kaisarianī o Tsípras', *Vīma*, 26/1/2015.

discourses, or have considered the nation-state as the essential and primary political unit of democracy.[19] The critique of peripheral nationalisms is then abandoned to the theoretical contortions of tendencies like anti-Deutsch, whose premises are also nationalist. Consequently, Greek left patriotism is frequently taken to be the representative voice of the 'Greek left', and the intense ongoing debate over the issue remains invisible.

Four tendencies of left nationalism can be identified in this conjuncture. Here I will present their political positions and their contradictions, before describing the limitations in the way they have pursued anti-fascist action and migrant solidarity.

First, and most prominent, has been the spectrum of anti-imperialist left-wing parties and organisations, encompassing KKE, SYRIZA's 'Left Platform' – which, after June 2015, seceded and formed Popular Unity (LAE – Laikī Enótīta) – some small parties participating in the ANTARSYA coalition[20] and Takis Fotopoulos' 'inclusive democracy movement'. This spectrum, despite differences in economic positions, which range from Keynesian-type state management (Popular Unity) to socialist workers' management (ANTARSYA), has always self-identified as 'patriotic', 'anti-imperialist' and 'internationalist'. In the crisis, it has promoted a discourse of 'betrayal', 'collaborationism' and 'colonialism' to describe Greece's status in the crisis, as well as favoured EU exit, debt cancellation and a return to a national currency. The tendency's 'anti-imperialist internationalism' translates into a keen concern about the role of NATO in the Balkans, opposing Greece's participation in NATO-led alliances. A subsection of this tendency – parties currently in Popular Unity and Takis Fotopoulos – view Russia as a power capable of opposing NATO's hegemony through forming a 'Eurasian alliance', and have kept a favourable stance to Russia's military operations in Syria and Ukraine.[21] The 'mission' of a Eurasian alliance opposed to the Atlantic alliance is associated with the Russian far-right theorist Alexandr Dugin,[22] so pursuing these political relationships has entailed entering a

---

19. Laclau and Mouffe, *Hegemony and Socialist Strategy*; Chantal Mouffe, *For a Left Populism* (London : Verso, 2018).

20. However, note that within ANTARSYA there is debate over these issues, though to a much lesser extent within Popular Unity.

21. Andréas Zafeírīs, 'Ī Schésī Koúrdōn me ĪPA-Rōsía kai sto Váthos ... Aigaío', Iskra.gr, 22/2/2018; Dīmītrīs Sarafianós, 'Níkī sto Laó tīs Novorōsías!', Antarsya.gr, 19/9/2014; Tákīs Fōtópoulos, 'Ī Pagkosmiopoíīsī, ī Rōsía kai ī Aristerá', Antipagkosmiopoihsh.gr, 7/12/2014.

22. Aleksandr Gelevič Dugin, *Eurasian Mission* (Milton Keynes: Arktos, 2015).

network of both left-wing and far-right political organisations, including and led by Dugin himself.[23] In practice, KKE and Popular Unity took a nationalist stance on the naming of the Republic of Macedonia. Both parties rejected the resolution proposed by the SYRIZA-led government in 2017 on the name 'North Macedonia', converging with right-wing nationalists on the issue. This lack of distinction with far-right forces led many parties and individuals to depart from Popular Unity.[24]

Nevertheless, these political forces also take an official 'anti-fascist' stance, express solidarity with immigrant workers and refugees, and oppose border controls, formulating their anti-fascism as parallel to their opposition to imperialism. In their doing so, however, they often reduce the question of the freedom of movement to that of imperialist war, as if war is the only reason motivating migration. They tend to prioritise national interests, so that the activities of Frontex and the NATO navy in the Aegean are criticised primarily for violating 'Greek sovereignty' rather than for their role in preventing free movement.[25] To be at the same time 'patriotic', 'internationalist' and 'anti-fascist' is not a contradiction, they claim, by making direct references to the anti-fascist national liberation armies of World War II. But here 'fascism' is reduced, on the one hand, to the strategies of specific countries (Germany, the USA, or more vaguely 'the West') and, on the other hand, to GD's direct racist violence, so much so that Eurasianism fails to provoke worry as a fascist and imperialist project. The belief that an alliance with Russian imperialism and the choice of an 'alternative sphere of influence' would rescue Greece from its current indebted state is taken to justify these relationships. But there is a deeper level of political and economic assumption, as well as of social relationality and belonging, that validates such a contradictory stance. While the identity of the Greek 'people' or 'working class' is capable of opening and expanding to a universal 'internationalist' principle in theory, this is only allowed in the final instance and with the retention of politically separated 'peoples'. In practice, the universal principle is never applicable in the present but is always deferred.[26] 'Greek

23. Kerin Hope and Courtney Weaver, 'Alarm Bells Ring Over Syriza's Russian Links', *Financial Times*, 28/1/2015.

24. An example is the group departure of Turkish minority candidates: A. P., 'Omadikī Apochōrīsī apó tī Laïkī Enótīta', *Efimerida tōn Syntaktōn*, 3/4/2018.

25. 'Oi Théseis tou KKE gia to Prosfygikó – Metanasteutikó', *Rizospastīs*, 6/3/2016; 'Apófasī Politikoú Symvoulíou tīs LAE', laiki-enotita.gr, 18/3/2018; 'ANTARSYA – 3ī Syndiáskepsī, Théseis, Kefalaio -G', Antarsya.gr, 4/3/2016.

26. See also my critique of anti-imperialist analysis by a follower of Fotopoulos, who

interests' are always a priority, linked to the dependence of the working class, as formed in the present, on the national state and its economy, as well as to the centrality of waged labour in these parties' socialist or social democratic programmes. 'Jobs for all', a priority demand in their manifestos, is intimately linked to the strengthening of a national economy, whether state led, worker led or led by a mix of state and private enterprise, based on the fiction that Greece would be able to unilaterally write off its debts without consequences. This drive to build an autarkic, 'independent' national economy with full employment and high wages under conditions of economic war, combined with their inability to even imagine a decoupling of subsistence from the wage, could not only potentially lead to a further deepening of austerity, but leaves open the possibility of a restriction on population, and thus the control of borders, not by 'imperialist forces' but by Greece's own border force.

The second tendency is expressed by a subsection of vanguardist anarchism that favours armed struggle as a strategy. Their repeated references to the National Liberation Front and Army in World War II, the civil war and the massacre of Greek Security Battalion forces in Meligalas – captured by the slogan 'EAM-ELAS-Meligalas: this is the way for the people to win' – are inspired not only by their patriotic 'anti-fascism' but even more by the bearing of arms.[27] This is clearer in the slogan 'EAM-ELAS, Cells of Fire'. The 'urban guerrilla' group Cells of Fire Conspiracy – despite the organisation's own nihilist-anarchist ideology,[28] which would furiously reject patriotism – is imagined by its supporters as continuing the tradition of national-popular armed struggle in Greece, along with other organisations engaged in robberies and bomb attacks in banks, luxury shops and state agencies, such as Revolutionary Struggle and 17 November. The discourse of the last

suggests that internationalism is today a vacuous idea. Dimitra Kotouza, 'Whose Lives Matter?', in *Beyond Crisis*, ed. John Holloway, Katerina Nasioka and Panagiotis Doulos (Oakland, CA: PM, 2018).

27. In September 1944, the communist guerilla forces of EAM-ELAS threw the corpses of defeated Security Battalion soldiers of the collaborationist Ioannis Rallis government into a well shaft in the town of Meligalas. GD organises a pilgrimage to the location each anniversary of the event to commemorate the victims.

28. 'The cherished child of red "anarchists", the proletariat, carries within it the work ethic, the vainglory of patriotism, the worship of small property, the remnants of religious conservatism [...] We uphold the black of anarchy. Chaos, disorder, living dangerously, the nihilism of action, the armed confrontation with all that exists, the fire of permanent anarchist insurrection.' Cells of Fire Conspiracy – FAI/IRF – Cell of Imprisoned Members, 'Kommounistikopoiïsï: Ï Gerontikï Ánoia tïs Anarchías', brochure, June 2015, 16, 20.

two groups on the crisis indeed differs little from that of the patriotic anti-imperialists mentioned earlier, with the same references to 'collaborationism', 'traitors', 'occupying forces' and the 'selling out of the Greek people to the transnational economic elite'.[29] It seeks to spark an armed uprising against the state, but has an individualist-existentialist conception of the 'heroes' of this vanguard. With a large number of its members imprisoned and frequently organising hunger strikes, they have developed a mythology of subjective freedom, commitment to insurrection, self-sacrifice and heroism. What inspires supporters is the strength of the individual anarchist standing up to state violence and the suffering of imprisonment while upholding their anarchist political values against all odds: the revolutionary transcends all obstacles with the intransigence of their internal freedom. The humanist essentialism of this notion, what Adorno criticised as the 'jargon of authenticity',[30] the dogmatic assertion of a heroic, authentic, free and sovereign decision-making subject amid the overwhelming evidence of unfreedom in all aspects of social life in capitalism, might be the least of the problems with this political tendency. More troublesome is its uncritical celebration of war as a means of struggle, not to mention the macho, invulnerable posturing associated with it – the imagery of bearded ELAS guerrillas on horseback, the adulation of their butchery – whose historically national content has led many of the contemporary supporters of 'urban guerillas' in a patriotic direction. It follows that the anti-fascist struggle is reduced to physical violence against individual 'fascists', and 'victory' is judged by the criterion of muscular power in the street, the very criterion upheld by the fascists themselves.

The third tendency is that of anti-Hellenism. Though on the surface anti-patriotic, feminist, anti-fascist and encompassing groups that are active in solidarity with immigrant workers – as, for example, the Autonomous Initiative Against Forgetting (Autónomī Prōtovoulía Enántia stī Līthī), from whose solidarity work I quote in Chapter 13 – this tendency is at bottom nationalist, influenced by anti-Deutsch political ideology originating in German anti-fascism.[31] Beginning with a well-justified

---

29. Politikī Katáthesī tou Níkou Maziōtī sto Eidikó Dikastīrio tōn Fylakōn Korydalloú, Athens.indymedia.org, 29/1/2013; Giannīs Souliōtīs, 'Proklītikī Emfánisī Xīroú', *Kathimerini*, 21/1/2014.
30. Adorno, *Jargon of Authenticity*.
31. One of the earliest introducers of anti-German ideas in Greece was the journal *Terminal 119* (terminal119archive.wordpress.com). *Shades* is a more recent example. 'Gia

motivation to advance a radical critique against a common-sense antisemitism in the Greek left and left-wing popular culture, as well as to unbury the history of genocide of a formerly sizeable Jewish community, these political tendencies have been led to defend the state of Israel as the only nation worth defending. The existence of such a current can seem curious in the Greek context, given that the country does not have a public tradition of processing its role in the Holocaust, and neither can it reproduce the essentialism of the anti-Deutsch discourse that identifies Germanness with the ability to cause genocide. On the contrary, its stance against Greek nationalist anti-imperialism leads its supporters to evade any reference to contemporary German imperialism. Yet, they share with anti-Deutsch ideology the transposition of patriotism to the essentialisation of and identification with another nation, that of Israel. At the same time, as a political identity, anti-Hellenism offers the benefit of being able to claim a unique hyper-radical stance, accusing the entire spectrum of the left of racism and antisemitism, insofar as they criticise Israel's operations in Gaza. What Raphael Schlembach has noted in relation to anti-Deutsch applies equally to anti-Hellenism: 'paradoxically, the treatment of "a people" as a homogenous mass – something that anti-Germans accuse the anti-imperialist Left of – is reproduced in the anti-German discourse of Israel and the Jews'.[32]

As the fourth tendency of left nationalism I would categorise the section of SYRIZA currently in government. SYRIZA has been criticised for its coalition with the populist right – verging on far-right – anti-Memorandum party Independent Greeks. But we might take this as a reflection of the dominant nationalism of popular resistance to austerity. Similarly, the populist nationalism of Tsipras's pre-election discourse, the references to World War II and the claim to German war reparations, as well as the patriotic language that accompanied the June 2015 referendum and the subsequent description of the government's capitulation as a foreign 'coup' is not distinct from the left-wing anti-imperialism described above – despite divergent judgement on whether the 'coup' could be avoided and thus constitutes a national betrayal by SYRIZA. What is distinctive is the form this left-wing nationalism took in the context of their governmental management of

tīn Prospátheia Stīsímatos Ellīnikoú Mpoykotáz (BDS) enántia sto Israīl', TheShadesMag. wordpress.com, 3/6/2018.

32. Raphael Schlembach, 'Towards a Critique of Anti-German "Communism"', *Interface: A Journal for and about Social Movements* 2, no. 2 (2010): 199–219, 212.

the 'refugee crisis' and the dispute with the Republic of Macedonia. In both of these cases we see ethnocentrism presented as solidarity with the foreign other or cross-national 'friendship' framed in ethnocentric terms. During the first phase of the 'refugee crisis' the government promoted a discourse of the ancient virtue of 'Greek philoxenia' – hospitality – to cultivate patriotic pride in offering help to refugees, as well as to enlist the population in the voluntary assistance of large numbers of migrants, which the government had limited resources to manage itself.[33] The latter discourse was successful and it did motivate a form of patriotic solidarity with migrants, whose limits soon became obvious, as we will see. The second example – the government's name deal with Macedonia – is similar in the sense that it has entailed an attempt to reframe as patriotic a decision that the traditional nationalist stance rejects as a form of betrayal. Far from a capitulation, the new naming, the government argued, forced Macedonians to change their constitution and thus 'our fatherland is established as a leading power in the Balkans'.[34]

The examination of these four tendencies I hope shows that problematising left nationalism in the Greek case is crucial, especially in the current conjuncture, considering that it is a country of the *European periphery* – as opposed to one with a direct history of colonisation – located at a European border designed to keep out racialised populations. It is also a country with a significant fascist tradition, which, because of its geopolitical status, has often merged elements of 'Eastern' imperialism and anti-imperialism.[35] An anti-imperialist peripheral perspective is thus not automatically 'progressive', whatever the word might be taken to mean. We ought to ask, in each instance, what the *content* of left nationalism is, and to what degree it is able to avoid reproducing the kind of ethno-racial essentialism and ethnocentrism associated with the fascism it professes to oppose. The examples discussed here show that the 'patriotic' left stance is mired in contradictions, and the credibility of its claim to a simultaneous 'internationalism' is extremely fragile.

---

33. See also an anthropological critical view on this development: Evthymios Papataxiarchis, 'Unwrapping Solidarity?', *Social Anthropology* 24, no. 2 (2016): 205–10.
34. Spýros Rapanákīs, 'Megálī diplōmatikī níkī – megálī istorikī eukairía', *Augī*, 13/6/2018.
35. Consider, for example, the proto-fascist racial ideology of Ion Dragoumis, which stood against French and British influence and economic control over the new Greek nation. Michalis Kaliakatsos, 'Ion Dragoumis and "Machiavelli"', *Journal of Modern Greek Studies* 31, no. 1 (2013): 53–84.

13

Migrant Struggle and Anti-Fascism

The Limits of Political Anti-Fascism

Although the turn to anti-fascism seemed finally to prioritise questions of racism and abuse against immigrants for the left, after the relative sidelining of the issue in 2011, a separation between anti-fascist and immigrants' own struggles remained. Anti-fascist actions carried out by Greek activists had the primary aim of obstructing GD actions, to 'invade' spaces dominated by the party and to promote anti-fascist politics. Local actions encompassed: demonstrations (on foot or on motorbikes) through areas of Athens with large immigrant populations who were systematically intimidated by GD; organising anti-fascist festivals as well as open discussions on fascism and anti-fascism; distributing anti-fascist propaganda material like posters, leaflets and graffiti in streets, schools and other public spaces; pressurising landlords against letting to GD, who were aiming to open new political offices in every neighbourhood through the country; and, finally, creating 'anti-fascist defence groups', which aimed to drive GD gangs out of certain areas through street fights, attacks on GD offices and on shops and cafés that gave them space, as well as by taking over of spaces where GD ran 'black economy' operations.

This form of anti-fascism was primarily a political and territorial fight against GD, leaving aside secondary issues of the racist policing of immigrants, structurally reproduced racism and its cultural-political dimensions, or engagement with immigrants themselves. When anti-fascist demonstrations entered immigrant neighbourhoods, they were content that many immigrants cheered their actions and remained untroubled by their self-positioning as external 'liberators'. While their fight contributed to the creation of spaces where immigrants felt a little safer, this was done without collaboration or discussion with the immigrants living in those spaces. Immigrants did not gain more say or more control over conditions in their neighbourhoods, where they continued to be treated as visitors, as an alien body in a space controlled by its 'real' (Greek) residents. The anti-fascist struggle then materialised as a fight among citizens over the fate of voiceless and nameless 'foreign' non-citizens.

In this, there were a few exceptions, of which two stand out. First, the activities of SEK (Socialist Workers' Party), in organising actions in conjunction with leaders of immigrant community organisations, and, second, the assembly between immigrant street vendors and students at ASOEE (Athens University of Economics and Business). Although I cannot provide evidence on the full scale of SEK's collaboration with immigrant communities, there are some indications that encapsulate the organisation's *relationship* to those communities. In migrant demonstrations organised by SEK, immigrants do not project an independent voice but instead carry SEK banners and shout SEK slogans. An insight about what might be going on in that relationship can be gleaned by the account of a Senegalese interviewee, an immigrant street vendor with experience from both SEK and ASOEE assembly meetings. In the former, immigrants were separated by nationality, each of which had a representative. Only representatives spoke, while the other migrants did not get to know each other. He felt discriminated against and used to organise demonstrations for an electoral purpose.[1]

In contrast, the relationship between students and migrants, and among migrants themselves, built around the ASOEE struggle, grew out of the desire of students to keep the police out of campus, and the migrants' need for a safe space to set up shop and make a living. From 2012 onwards, the new government stepped up its campaign against migrant street vendors, who are accused of being unlicensed and not paying tax. The relationship between street vendors and students had, by then, already begun to be built, with students providing a space for vendors to escape into when police turned up, followed by collective low-level rioting against the police to prevent them from entering the campus.[2] This turned out to be successful, and an assembly evolved from it, in which participating students made a conscious effort not to dominate the discussion. Due to the many languages spoken and translation being needed, the pace was slow. The composition has not been stable, as many migrants have had to leave the country, while

1. Ī Sfīka, 'Synénteuxī me Metanástī Mikropōlītī apó tīn Senegálī', *Ī Sfīka*, no. 5 (2013).
2. Scar, 'Koinoí Agōnes Ntópiōn kai Metanastōn (kai Pank Katastáseis stīn ASOEE)', *Ī Sfīka*, no. 2–3 (2012).

new vendors were attracted by the arrangement.³ Nevertheless, bonds started to form gradually between the participants. 'The assembly has improved our relationships with other immigrants and the development of trust among us. It has also changed the mentality of many, we now feel like a big family. It helped us to learn what each has to say and to exchange opinions.'⁴ Together, participants in the assembly have also planned regular *mikrofōnikés* (actions where political statements are amplified through a microphone), court support and solidarity, as well as demonstrations.⁵ The multilingual polyphony and exuberance of demonstrations organised by the ASOEE assembly were in great contrast to the regimented character of those organised by SEK.⁶

The contrast with SEK became even more obvious when the assembly attempted to organise a demonstration in protest against the police murder of the Senegalese street vendor Babacar Ndiaye.⁷ In the organising meeting, the community leaders of a Senegalese religious sub-community participated. They objected to an immediate *mikrofōnikí* or a demonstration, wanting to arrange a different demonstration with SEK a few weeks later, which would be guaranteed to be 'peaceful'. Between the, perhaps reasonable, caution against migrants being arrested for rioting, and SEK's aims to incorporate migrant protest into its strategy in a controlled manner, both SEK and the community leaders played a role in controlling and dampening the resistance of migrant community members. While the ASOEE environment thrived on facilitating discussion of its members' ideas, both SEK and the community leaders thought it safest to keep those voices under control. Their approach also seems to have been driven by a notion of respecting the intolerant sensibilities of the Greek public: immigrants should not display their cultural difference too provocatively, should not make too much noise or express too much anger and should speak the correct language, one addressed primarily to Greeks.

The case of ASOEE appears to have been an exception, even more so after political anti-fascism faced its own limits when GD members began

3. 'Synenteúxeis me Metanástes Mikropólités', SKYA.espiv.net, 22/6/2013.

4. Ibid.

5. Scar, 'Apó tīn Ntáka éōs to Ntakár Apénanti stous Ntángka Eímaste Mazí', *I Sfíka*, no. 5 (2013).

6. 'Video and Fōtografíes apó tīn Poreía tīs 4.4.2015', Immigrants-ASOEE.espivblogs.net, 5/4/2015.

7. 'Schetiká me tī Dolofonía tou Metanástī Mikropōlítī Babacar Ndiaye sto Thīseío', Immigrants-ASOEE.espivblogs.net, 3/2/2013.

to be arrested for the murder of Pavlos Fyssas. The same government and media that had been defending GD was suddenly perceived to have made a U-turn, appropriating the anti-fascist discourse. But this could only seem to be a paradox and a form of ideological appropriation if one left any change in the *actual* conditions for immigrants out of the picture of 'anti-fascism'. Sadly, this appeared to be more and more the case for a great proportion of the left and the anarchist/anti-authoritarian milieu as soon as the problem of GD appeared to be being dealt with. The party's removal from the political scene did not mean the disappearance of racist discourses, police abuse against immigrants in streets and in camps and employers' racist bullying and violence. Yet these issues became politically secondary after the arrest of GD members, reconfirming the political focus of this anti-fascism. Towards the end of 2014, a certain hierarchisation, or at least a parcellisation, of struggles, whereby each left and anarchist group chose their favoured patch, seemed to result from this condition. This was evident in November 2014, when three important hunger strikes coincided.

First, there was the hunger strike of around 600 Syrian refugees – women, men and children – who had occupied Syntagma Square for 27 days under winter conditions, demanding papers to travel in Europe. Syrians argued that they were penniless in Greece, unable to find work (without a work permit or speaking the language) or accommodation and prey to various mafias. The papers granted to them by the Greek state were six-month permits, after which they would have to leave the country. However, this was impossible: even if they tried to travel elsewhere via normal transport, or even on foot, they would be arrested.[8] Instead of travel documents, the prefecture eventually promised that it would provide accommodation and asylum. The hunger strikers who refused and insisted on travel documents were evicted violently from the square by riot police at 3.00 am on 15 December, and 51 of them were arrested. Some of the evictees were forced to leave behind their personal belongings, including their shoes and identification, and, barefoot and paperless, were threatened with deportation.[9] This struggle was supported mainly by members of ANTARSYA and smaller groups of activists, as for example the cleaners of the economics ministry, but the

---

8. 'Synénteuxī me Treis Gynaíkes Prósfyges apó tī Syría', 0151.espivblogs.net, 15/12/2014; Kinimatini, 'Synénteuxī Sýriou Prósfyga sto Sýntagma', Twitter post, 25/11/2014.
9. Tásos Mórfis, 'Ti Apéginan oi Sýroi Prósfyges tīs Plateías Syntágmatos?', Popaganda.gr, 17/12/2014.

left did not help in any concerted way, as their attention was diverted to another hunger strike.

Second, a new hunger strike began in the Amygdaleza detention camp. Besides the detainees' core demands for shorter detention and better conditions (healthcare, amenities, food quality), the strike also responded to the death of a detainee. Muhammad Ashfaq had been beaten heavily by guards during one of the uprisings in the Korinthos detention centre, which caused him respiratory problems. The guards refused him access to treatment for over two weeks, and he eventually died during his transfer to hospital. After only four days of hunger strike, 30 detainees were released and another 150 were to be considered for release, which led most detainees to end the strike.[10] This case received minimal support and only a very brief mention in most left-wing and anarchist media.

Third, a hunger strike was started by Nikos Romanos, the friend of Alexis Grigoropoulos who witnessed his police murder in December 2008. Romanos was imprisoned for taking part in a bank robbery along the lines of 'anarchist robberies' carried out by groups like Cells of Fire Conspiracy and Revolutionary Struggle. As a prisoner, he was successful in his university entry exams, and when he was refused permission to attend classes, he began a hunger strike. Romanos' case was highly publicised by all media, accompanied by the classic discourse of the heroism and subjective freedom of anarchist prisoners, and enjoyed mass support and concern about his well-being from the anarchist scene as well as the left, including SYRIZA. His hunger strike lasted 31 days, until, eventually, with much pressure from SYRIZA in parliament, he was permitted to leave on condition that he would wear a surveillance bracelet.[11]

It is not surprising that the overwhelming majority of the anarchist and left scene were most moved and mobilised by the case of Romanos. Both his 'principled anarchism' and his link to December 2008 sparked the imagination of anarchists, who occupied the GSEE offices in memory of the uprising – although this time with the support of GSEE itself, and only for the duration of Romanos' strike.[12] There was also

10. Tásos Mórfis, "'O Mocháment Asfák Épasche apó Ásthma: Den ton Pīgan Poté se Nosokomeío, Gi'Autó Péthane'", Popaganda.gr, 21/11/2014.

11. Anta Psarrá, 'O Níkos Más Édōse Anáses Eleutherías', Efimerída tōn Syntaktōn, 11/12/2014.

12. 'Līxī tīs Katálīpsīs GSEE', KatalipsiGSEE.espivblogs.net, 10/12/2014.

sympathy for his trauma due to the police murder of his friend. SYRIZA could deploy its discourse about the fundamental rights of prisoners, and pro-armed-struggle anarchists would add another name to their list of heroic personalities. This prioritisation, however, had another meaning. It meant, unequivocally, that some people's lives matter more than others'. As with Pavlos Fyssas, so with Nikos Romanos, the lives of *Greek* comrades – if immigrants in struggle are called 'comrades' at all – matter the most. There was neither a scandal nor a riot after the multiple murders of immigrants at the hands of the police and GD. The names of victims and hunger strikers are rarely widely known. Certainly not only in Greece, the deaths of immigrant victims of police and racist violence are 'ungrievable', as Judith Butler has noted,[13] and this ungrievability is so normalised that it takes hold even within the political communities of those who consider themselves anti-racist. The degree of invisibility of hundreds of Syrian migrants in Syntagma Square, the inconsequentiality of the police sweeping the square for Christmas shopping, at the same time as the great majority of the left focused exclusively on a single Greek person's hunger strike, revealed the depth of unaware racism among the most politically 'progressive' sections of Greek society.

This separateness and marginalisation of immigrants' struggles and voices was symptomatic of the unquestioned national essence implicit in the forms of political and social identification characteristic of both anti-Memorandum and anti-fascist discourse. The *patriotic* anti-fascism of civil war references failed to question the givenness of Greek unity. In effect, the fight between fascism and anti-fascism dominantly presented itself as a fight between two forms of nationalism. Anti-fascist nationalism paid lip service to the rights of migrants, while reproducing their otherness through its political practice.

Migrant Struggle and Invisibility

Migrants' struggles were then the other side of this period's dominant nationally unifying opposition to the restructuring as well as the activity rendered invisible by dominant anti-fascism. Immigrants demanded the most basic of things, most of which 'citizens' took for granted: freedom from detention; to walk in the street without the fear of a deadly assault; freedom of movement; or, even less audaciously, humane treatment

---

13. Butler, *Precarious Life*.

by guards, healthcare and meals that do not cause malnutrition when in detention. The very presence of immigrants in the country by itself criticises the naturalised birthrights of citizens, and extreme violence against them has aimed to reaffirm the community of citizens as ethnically uniform and the nation as a protector of its 'natural' subjects. It is when migrants' struggles entered the street, the squares and privileged university space (the 300 hunger strikers, the Pakistani workers in Lakonia, Syrian refugees at Syntagma) that they appeared to challenge the racism of a 'Greek public' most, terrified by masses of dark faces in the streets. These struggles, left with very little room to move, have had to struggle, to a great extent unsuccessfully, against invisibility.

The subject of the 'immigrant' is, of course, not a unitary one, and immigrants' experiences have varied in Greece depending on economic conditions at the time of their arrival, as well as their 'ethnic origin'. As discussed in Part I, the experience and status of Albanians and other immigrants from Eastern Europe who have managed to integrate economically and culturally to some degree is very different from that of more recent immigrants from outside Europe, despite the racialised discrimination and violence the former suffered since the 1990s. But racialisation based on colour, the notion of 'civilised Europeanness' and the corresponding restrictions on immigration expose African and Asian immigrants immediately to repeat police arrests, racist street attacks, detention and deportation. The management of immigration and asylum has also changed since the 2015–16 'refugee crisis', along with the broader political discourse and practice of movements, which I discuss in the next section.

Over the period of crisis and beyond, immigrant's struggles have been the least visible not only because they were neglected by the 'Greek public' but also because immigrants without papers find safety in clandestinity. Many confrontations have therefore taken place not because immigrants sought them out, but because they became police targets as part of governmental crisis management strategies. The great majority of their actions responded to racist police abuse, detention, street violence and murders, but also to unpaid wages. Actions encompassed demonstrations, camp uprisings, hunger strikes and labour strikes.

The first immigrant struggle of this period, and one of the most significant, most publicised and most written about, was the hunger strike by 300 immigrants from January to March 2011 demanding legal permits to stay in the country.[14] The first 250 North African immigrants, who came mostly from Crete, approached parties of the left for help to obtain a space for a hunger strike, and were supported to occupy a space at the Athens Law School. As soon as the occupation and hunger strike began, the racism of the response defied expectations, foreshadowing the escalation of racist discourse in the years to follow. Hunger strikers were presented, particularly by right-wing students, government politicians and mainstream media, as elements bringing dirt and disease,[15] ruining the reputation of the Law School and turning it into a 'bomb that threatens public hygiene and security'.[16] Within four days, after forcing the university deanery to close down the Law School and lift the university asylum, which was then still nominally in force, the government issued an ultimatum that the police would raid the university unless the hunger strikers were rehoused.[17] Left-wing supporters were accused of 'politically exploiting humanism', and they, in turn, conceded to the rehousing.[18]

While government politicians continued to complain that strikers should be moved out of the centre of Athens,[19] because their presence might allow 'various forces that are invested in social conflict to "cross ways"',[20] 50 more immigrants began a hunger strike in Thessaloniki on 14 February.[21] After 44 days of hunger strike, and after several strikers had been hospitalised, the relevant ministers agreed to discussions.

---

14. The immigrants also demanded 'that residence permits are no longer connected to work credits; that all of those who lost their permits for the above reason are re-legalised; the vindication of everyone whose application was rejected in 2005, after their application had originally been accepted and after they had been forced to pay thousands of euros each; the establishment of a permanent and open procedure for complete legalisation, which will process applications continually; an end to the criminalisation of our comrades in solidarity with us, who have been treated as suspects of criminal acts by the authorities'. Anoichtī Prōtovoulía Allīleggýīs stous 300 Metanástes Apergoús Peínas, 'Hunger Strikers' Assembly Decision: 21/02', Allilmap.wordpress.com, 22/2/2011.

15. Níkos Mastoras and Stelios Vradelīs, 'Mazikī apergía peínas apó 300 paránomous metanástes', Néa, 25/1/2011.

16. 'Kataulismós Lathrometanastōn ī Nomikī', Éthnos, 25/1/2011.

17. K. P. Papadiochos, 'Kérdī kai Zīmíes metá tī Nomikī', Kathīmerinī, 30/1/2011.

18. Apostolos Lakasas, 'O Anthrōpismós, Vorá stīn Politikī Ekmetálleusī', Kathīmerinī, 25/1/2011.

19. Autonome Antifa, 'Tésseris Méres pou Den (Thélei na) tis Thymátai Kanénas', Autonome Antifa, no. 22 (2011): 6–7.

20. Ibid.

21. 'Message by the Assembly of Fifty Hunger Strikers in Thessaloniki to the Mayor and the Members of the City Council', Allilmap.wordpress.com, 14/2/2011.

Eventually, the protesters were offered legal permits to remain, which included the right to travel to their country of origin as well as the right to work. The ministers also agreed to reduce the number of years required to achieve legal status from twelve to eight, as well as reduce the national insurance contributions required to renew permits and access public healthcare.[22] However, this did not last. Over the following years, the strikers were involved in continual wrangles with bureaucracy and street protests to have this agreement implemented. Most urgent, for them, was that work permits had not been given, and they had lost their jobs for participating in the strike.[23] In 2014, the new minister of public order, Nikos Dendias, put an end to the renewal of their six-monthly renewable permits. Strikers were subsequently charged with illegally staying in the country and were convicted to four months imprisonment and €1,500 in fines each.[24]

Despite this eventual defeat, this was a significant step forward for immigrants in Greece in general, who, for the first time, initiated and carried through a major struggle, placing their issues centre stage of a racist political scene. The hunger strike, according to the migrants, was used as a tactic of last resort, after the failure of other forms of protest.[25] They directly addressed the state, which was seen as the only authority able to solve the problem of clandestinity and continual police persecution realistically. Yet, the distance between the immigrants and their politically motivated supporters became clear even in this relatively successful collaboration between them. The political mediation of the struggle by the left alienated anarchist/anti-authoritarian supporters, who were against the negotiations around rehousing and wanted instead to defend the university asylum.[26] Conversely, left supporters viewed anti-authoritarian supporters as disruptive. Both sides, while contributing practically to the struggle, appear to have continued to operate in ways that reflected their groups' and organisations' political objectives rather than the practical and social benefits that this struggle would entail for immigrants.

---

22. 'Apergía Peínas tōn 300 Metanastōn Ergatōn', Diktio.org, 30/3/2011.
23. 'Apó tī Synénteuxī Týpou Prōīn Apergōn kai Allīléggyōn tīn Pémptī 26/1 gia ton éna Chróno apó tīn Apergía Peínas tōn 300', Fmkritis.wordpress.com, 26/1/2012.
24. '4 Mīnes Fylakī kai 1.500 Eurō Próstimo', Fmkritis.wordpress.com, 16/11/2014.
25. 'Apó tī Synénteuxī Týpou', 26/1/2012.
26. Kýklos tīs Fōtiás, 'Allīleggyī ston Agōna tōn 300 Metanastōn-Ergatōn Apergōn Peinas', Maúri Sīmaía, no. 59 (2011).

This stance can be seen even in a text that is self-critical about the tendency of the struggle's supporters to prioritise questions of ideology and consciousness and their failure to build lasting social bonds with immigrants.[27] Despite this self-critique, the author contends that the Law School should not have been occupied because it resulted in another university asylum violation. He also argues that the method of hunger strike was inappropriate, because the state was only pressurised by it on the basis of a humanitarian logic of international human rights laws and institutions, as well as because it signalled to other immigrants that they can only achieve anything by risking their lives and well-being. But while the hunger strike is indeed an appeal to the vague discourse of human rights, it is worth noting also that, in this specific context, human rights signify a universality that comes into contradiction with the logic of citizenship, which justifies the political and economic exclusion of immigrants, as well as the violent methods by which this exclusion is enforced. We may also wonder whether there are many alternative methods left for immigrants to demand things that Greek citizens take for granted, considering that they are a population treated as 'surplus', casually racialised and dehumanised, talked of as a 'threat to hygiene' and suffering frequent police abuse. The degree of violence immigrants typically face means that the hunger strike may actually be a safer form of struggle than, say, demonstrating and exposing themselves to riot police in the street. The assumption that 300 people had an easier option of struggle but that they gratuitously chose to risk their lives in order to evoke humanitarian sympathy, is, perhaps, filtered by the lens of the Greek activist whose own struggle faces much lower risks. Besides, the argument against human rights is rarely advanced when those conducting a hunger strike are imprisoned Greek anarchists. Why is it that the latter are perceived as heroes, while the former as oppressed people seeking sympathy? Could this also be the lens of racialised privilege and white guilt?

The location of the hunger strike in the Law School is also assessed from the perspective of the citizen. Locating the hunger strike in that space threatened the right of citizen students themselves to the university asylum precisely because it questioned the asylum as the privilege of a citizen. Here were persons whose place of birth is used as an excuse to devalue their lives and labour power, demanding that

---

27. Symeōn Vátalos, 'Gia tīn Apergía Peínas tōn Metanastōn ...', SKYA.espiv.net, 10/5/2011.

the asylum should also protect them and their struggle. That was the biggest controversy, revealing the racist logic that maintains such a distinction. The state's agreement to negotiate, however mediately, with persons that it previously treated as a 'threat to public hygiene' – that is, as subjectless bodies – did question the imposition of invisibility and voicelessness, despite the fact that the ministers' promises later proved to have been false. Only a few of the texts written in the aftermath of this struggle partially recognised these achievements.[28] The movement was an example of what Butler and others have called 'acts of citizenship', constrained, nevertheless, in its demands by the logic of inclusion in an institution that is itself by its definition exclusive. It is only, perhaps, the universal corporeal dimension of the hunger strike itself that transcends, symbolically, the limits of a citizenship.

After 2012, amid the escalation of racist street attacks, abusive policing, work exploitation under the threat of GD vigilantes and increasingly long-term incarceration in camps, immigrants responded through organising forms of self-protection, protests and sometimes rioting. Attempts at immigrant self-defence against GD attacks remained mostly clandestine.[29] Most took practical measures such as walking in larger groups at night.[30] More well known have been the defensive attacks against GD by members of the Roma community in the Athens suburbs of Ano Liosia – a community whose members have always faced racism, and whose formal citizenship status has rarely entailed equal treatment in practice. In June 2012, Roma residents responded to a GD attack by rioting, setting a bus on fire and even firing shots against the police.[31]

At a more organised scale, there have been demonstrations against the racist murder of Shehzad Luqman,[32] and the police murder of Babacar Ndiaye,[33] led by community leaders (Pakistani and Senegalese respectively). These demonstrations did not sustain a momentum despite

---

28. Migrants' Forum in Crete, 'To FMK gia tīn Apergía Peínas tōn 300 – Mia Prōtī Apotímīsī', Fmkritis.wordpress.com, 24/3/2011.

29. Aside from a second-generation immigrant from Kenya, Michael Chege, stating publicly on Channel 4 that he was part of a self-defence group nicknamed the 'black panthers', no visibly organised self-defence groups are known, although there are many anecdotal accounts of night-time street clashes. Jamal Osman, 'Standing Up to Golden Dawn in Greece', *Channel 4 News*, 28/5/2013.

30. Ī Sfīka, 'Synénteuxī me Metanástī Mikropōlítī apó tīn Senegálī', *Ī Sfīka*, no. 5 (2013).

31. '"Pólemos" Autī tī Stigmī sta Anō Liósia', Athens.indymedia.org, 18/6/2012.

32. Antōnía Xynoú, 'Otan oi dolofoníes'.

33. Immigrants-ASOEE, 'Schetiká me tī Dolofonía'.

the importance of the issue, possibly because the community leaders and parties involved (SEK and SYRIZA) were successful in preventing the full expression of anger, as discussed above. But it also shows that immigrants in the centre of Athens rarely had the confidence to contest their marginalised and vulnerable status in public space without the support of Greek political parties and organisations. Contestation by immigrants organising independently nevertheless did take place in rural regions where they were subject to extreme segregation combined with extremely exploitative work relations.

Two such cases became more widely known. The first is that of strawberry pickers in Nea Manolada (Ilia Prefecture, Peloponnese). The conflict between workers of various nationalities and bosses in Nea Manolada has continued for over a decade, involving extreme abuse and terror against workers. Despite frequent strikes through these years, workers' living conditions – residing in greenhouses without basic amenities for which they pay a high proportion of their wages in rent – have not improved. Nevertheless, strikes and protests have continued, despite bosses' drastic measures to prevent them. In April 1999, a Bangladeshi worker was reported to have been shot in the hand.[34] In June 2001, there was arson of the greenhouses where Bulgarian workers stayed, with more cases of arson continuing to occur through to 2009.[35] On 19–20 April 2008, thousands of strawberry pickers went on strike and were assaulted by locals and the police.[36] In June 2009, two local livestock breeders tied two Bangladeshi workers to a motorcycle and dragged them through the street, accusing them of cattle theft.[37] The catalogue of abuse is endless, and it became worse during the crisis, when wages started to be paid less and less frequently. In April 2013, Bangladeshi workers collectively confronted their supervisors after having worked unpaid for six months; in response, the supervisors shot and injured 30 of the workers.[38] A local demonstration of about 3,000 people was soon organised in protest by the Immigrant Workers' Union and the Movement against Racism and the Fascist Threat (KEERFA) (both

---

34. Autonome Antifa, 'Péftontas apó ta Sýnnefa (gia Kamiá Dekariá Chrónia): Manōláda', *Autonome Antifa*, no. 9 (2008): 6.
35. Mákīs Nodárou, 'Fōtiá stous Kataulismoús tīs Ntropīs: Fráoules kai Aíma', *Eleutherotypía*, 4/6/2009.
36. Mákīs Nodarou, 'N. Manōláda'.
37. Mákīs Nodarou, '"Kou Kloux Klan" stī Manōláda', *Eleutherotypía*, 20/6/2009.
38. 'Migrant Workers Shot by Bosses in Manolada Farm', *Kathīmerinī*, 17/4/2013.

supported by ANTARSYA) along with other local unions and collectives. This was followed by smaller immigrant workers' demonstrations at the courts in Patras where the employers underwent trial.[39] Yet, beyond the help offered by the human rights lawyers of the Council for Refugees, the level of active solidarity the workers received could not help them access basic justice against insurmountable odds. In court, the supervisors only received suspended sentences for the shooting, the employer was acquitted and it was not considered a case of systematic labour trafficking, after a series of procedural 'errors' that favoured the defendants.[40] Many of the workers were consequently detained or deported, and the rest were blacklisted by their ex-employer.[41]

The second, similar case is the struggle of Pakistani agricultural workers in Skala (Lakonia Prefecture, Peloponnese – a region with a strong far-right tradition). In this case, workers appear to have been better able to organise, despite enduring weekly police raids in the crowded shacks where they had to reside, as well as an apartheid regime imposed by the town's mayor, which has prevented them from renting properties inside the town and entering spaces including cafés, shops and beaches.[42] In response to the police raids, and in demand of unpaid wages, the workers organised a five-day strike from 1 July 2014, accompanied by demonstrations in the town centre.[43] This was their second mobilisation since September 2010, when they organised a two-day square occupation, an extremely brave action in a town without a tradition of workers' or left-wing politics. The occupation had temporarily stopped the raids,[44] but the situation had again worsened, and workers were continually threatened that they would be deported or that GD would be brought in. On 8 July 2013, GD demonstrated in Skala against 'illegal immigrants' in a show of strength.[45] The strike of July

39. 'Megáli Diadílōsī Kóntra sto Ratsismó kai tīn Ekmetálleusī', *Eleutherotypía*, 29/4/2013; 'Poreía MetanastÓN gia tī Manōláda', Thetoc.gr, 29/7/2014.

40. Greek Council for Refugees (GCR), 'Manolada: The Chronicle of a Judicial Failure', GRC.gr, 7/8/2014. According to the GCR, which brought the action to court, a case of labour trafficking should have been examined for all of the 119 employees and not only for those who had been injured by the shooting.

41. 'Apeláseis Ergatōn gīs sta Fraoulochōrafa tīs Manōládas', TVXS.gr, 17/3/2014.

42. 'Mia Prōtī Katagrafī tīs Syzītīsīs me tous Pakistanoús Metanástes stīn Skála Lakōnías', Skalalakonias.wordpress.com, 23/7/2014.

43. Kōstas Zafeirópoulos, 'Ī Manōláda tīs Lakōnías', *Efimerída tōn Syntaktōn*, 9/7/2014.

44. Autónomī Prōtovoulía Enántia stī Līthī, 'Ī Sýntomī Istoría tīs Pakistanikīs Koinótītas Stīn Lakōnía', *0151*, no. 3 (2014).

45. Ibid.

2014 was significant in empowering the Pakistani workers, although it brought them face to face with the fierceness of local racism: 'we did not anticipate so violent, so unprovoked and so vehement a reaction against us. When the demonstration got near Skala police station, the mayor ran towards us shouting that we should all get out of Skala, that he does not like any of us, and he yelled at the police to arrest us all.'[46]

Despite their sense of empowerment, some of the workers felt that, because their demonstration provoked further abuse, they were unsure whether further mobilising would be a good idea.[47] Indeed, in a few weeks' time, police again raided the Pakistani area and arrested 35 people, of whom 21 have been detained and are to be deported.[48] The daily raids and arrests escalated into an elimination campaign well into 2015 under the SYRIZA government.[49] Nevertheless, despite the arrests and expulsions, a Pakistani community of workers remains today in Skala, and, according to them, wages are now a little better and life a bit more peaceful. In response to segregation, they have also been able to open some of their own shops, making space for themselves in the town.[50]

These two cases show that the struggles of migrant workers are, necessarily, qualitatively different than those of Greek workers, because they directly confront practices of bordering and the policing of immigration within the country's territory. It is not surprising that Greek workers and unions are not up in arms when migrant workers are victimised in this way, and are not convinced by the argument that they will also one day suffer what the immigrants are suffering. The expectation that migrant and Greek workers are anywhere close to uniting in their struggle will be unrealistic until the division of labour in Greece stops being structured on the basis of race and immigration status. Immigrant workers' organisations, such as the Immigrant Workers Union, are right to respond to every such incident by demanding, first and foremost, identical rights for immigrant workers. This is a necessary premise for a material basis of cross-ethnic solidarity among workers, but it goes radically against current popular trends for national economic protection, as well as

---

46. 'Mia Proti Katagrafi', Skalalakonias.wordpress.com.
47. Ibid.
48. Autónomī Prōtovoulía, 'Sýntomī Istoría'.
49. Autónomī Prōtovoulía Enántia stī Līthī, 'Ī Orgánōsī tōn Metanastōn Eínai to Móno Prógramma Diásōsīs Tous apó ton Ellīnikó Voúrko', Skalalakonias.wordpress.com, 13/2/2015.
50. 'Stous Drómous tīs Skálas #12: To Pakistanikó Kommōtīrio', Skalalakonias.wordpress. com, 2/10/2017.

the commonplace governmental 'good sense' of border controls as a mode of managing the labour market. This 'good governmental sense' is blemished each time immigrant workers manage to make gains that question this racist division of labour, but, again, visibility matters in this case far more than it does for any other workers' struggle, because the racism upon which this division is based is also reproduced through racist representations. The degrading treatment of immigrant workers by employers is not only a violent mode of control but it has the symbolic effect of normalising the image of the immigrant as a suffering body, not so different from the effect of images of dark-skinned migrant bodies drowning in the Mediterranean.

Between mid-2012 and 2014, the escalation of police sweep operations, which led greater numbers of immigrants to detention camps, and the increase in detention periods from three months to a year or longer,[51] provoked more mobilisations and riots in detention camps. These are too many to discuss here analytically, but I will enumerate some of them indicatively, before dedicating a little more space to the uprising in the Amygdaleza camp. In September 2012, 45 migrants went on hunger strike in the Xanthi detention camp.[52] On 17 November 2012, migrants in the Korinthos camp went on hunger strike to protest the abuse of Navit Yaser and demand that he received medical treatment. They also protested against beatings by guards during prayer. The next day a riot broke out, which was repressed with ten injured and 24 arrested.[53] On 23 November 2012, immigrants detained in the Police School of Komotini started a riot in protest against the prison conditions.[54] On 4 December, there was a riot in the Amygdaleza camp which ended after negotiations with authorities.[55] From December 2012 to March 2013, there were repeated protests and riots in the Fylakio camp in Evros against the length of detention. Many rioters received exemplary punishment.[56] In February 2013, arrestees went on hunger strike in Nikaia Police Station

51. Omáda Dikīgórōn gia ta Dikaiōmata Prosfýgōn kai Metanastōn, 'Kéntra Krátīsīs Metanastōn – Apothīkes Psychōn kai Sōmátōn', Omadadikigorwn.blogspot.com, 14/8/2013.
52. 'Se Apergía Peínas 35 Metanástes sto Kéntro Fýlaxīs tīs Xánthīs', XanthiPress.gr, 27/9/2012.
53. KEERFA, 'Symparastasī stīn Exegersī Metanastōn sto Stratopedo tīs Korinthou, Diamartyria, Tritī 20/11 4mm', Antiracismfascism.org, 19/11/2012.
54. 'Exégersī Metanastōn stī Scholī Astynomías tīs Komotīnīs', XanthiPress.gr, 23/11/2012.
55. 'H "Ágnōstī" Exégersī stīn Amygdaléza', Zougla.gr, 4/12/2012.
56. 'Exégersī Kratouménōn to Kéntro Fýlaxīs Metanastōn sto Fylákio', Evros 24, 8/2/2013; 'Chronológio', NoLager.espiv.net, 31/10/2013.

(Pireaus), which has been notorious for its links with GD. The strike was violently repressed.[57] In April 2013, around 1,800 immigrants detained all over Greece participated in a hunger strike.[58] In the same month, there was another riot in the Korinthos camp.[59]

Amygdaleza was one of the new camps opened by the new ND-PASOK-DIMAR government in 2012. It was converted from an old army barracks with the simple addition of modified shipping containers, aiming at creating more space for more detainees. The conditions in the camp were said to have been wretched, but of more concern for immigrants was the formal extension of the detention period to 18 months.[60] On 10 August 2013, guards apparently felt it necessary to add insult to injury by trampling on immigrants' plates of food. That day, a large-scale riot broke out, during which prisoners set the containers on fire, attacked the guards with stones and managed to break through the gates and escape. Out of the escapees, 56 were recaptured and imprisoned, further extending the length of their incarceration.[61] The uprising in Amygdaleza was the most violent action of resistance by immigrants in the country to date. Immigrant participation in rioting during demonstrations is not comparable, as it has typically been low key. This action powerfully rejected the unfreedom and debasement migrants were forced to endure, as well as its legal justification on the basis of national integrity. In a sign that this wave of protests was not going to end soon, and a few days later 400 immigrants in the Orestiada camp went on hunger strike.[62]

While the uprising in Amygdaleza was a powerful action, it is worth considering, in the case of camps too, the relationship between the hunger strike and the riot as means of migrant struggle and asking if it is as clear-cut a contrast as it seems. Hunger strikes appear more passive. From the point of view of citizens, they appeal to compassion and are a reminder of the strikers' devalued humanity. From the point of view of government, they are an embarrassment and have the potential to draw attention to abuses. Hunger strikes, insofar as their publicity is

---

57. 'Apergía Peínas Metanastōn gia Xylodarmoús sto AT Nikaías', TVXS.gr, 12/2/2013.
58. 'Apergía Peínas 2.000 Metanastōn gia tis Synthíkes Krátisis', *Eleutherotypía*, 8/4/2013.
59. 'Exégersī sto Stratópedo Metanastōn stīn Kórintho', *Eleutherotypía*, 10/4/2013.
60. Omáda Dikīgórōn, 'Kéntra Krátisis Metanastōn'.
61. 'Exégersī Metanastōn, Sovará Epeisódia kai Syllīpseis stīn Amygdaléza', *Vīma*, 10/8/2013.
62. 'Apergía Peínas 400 Metanastōn stīn Orestiáda', *Vīma*, 28/8/2013.

not overshadowed by competing events, are a forceful negotiating tactic for abused detainees, enabling their demands to be heard more widely. Yet these demands, which usually follow a series of abuses or detainees' deaths, do not imply that detainees are naïve about the system of negotiations. Besides, as we have seen, riots can also be accompanied by demands. While more physically passive, the hunger strike is ethically aggressive, a form of blackmail that places direct blame on authorities for one's potential death, in response to a degrading situation. Riots might be a more explosive enactment of anger, but, while they sometimes promise the possibility of escape, they can also carry the risk of longer imprisonment – if not beatings and death – when caught. The alternation between the two forms of struggle by the same prisoners in quick succession suggests that the choice of one over the other form is not ideological but may instead depend on the energies, capacities and feelings of protesters in each instance.

When migrants appear passive in the face of cruelty, it is only because their actions are violently restricted and their voices are systematically silenced, often even by their supposed supporters. The representation of incarcerated immigrants either as passive victims when on hunger strike or as an irrational, out-of-control menace when rioting is a racist representation, pervasive from TV screens to the language of their supporters. Even when given access to publicity, immigrants' stories are frequently turned by supporters into stories of victimhood. As Imogen Tyler has so eloquently demonstrated in her book, *Revolting Subjects*, the modes of resistance under conditions of abjection frequently utilise that very abjection – for example, the seeming passivity of stitching one's lips during a hunger strike – to reveal and at the same time refuse, the kind of dehumanisation immigrants are subjected to. Their image communicates where communication is blocked. So it is important for those of us who seek to offer solidarity to be able to see and listen differently, questioning our habitual ways of perceiving and avoiding the projection of what we know from our own conditions of life.

After the 'Refugee Crisis': Migrants as Multiple and Complex Subjects

From 2015, the enormous rise in migration from Syria, Afghanistan and Iraq added a new dimension to the relationship of Greece's new 'left-wing' government to the rest of the EU, and produced a context that caused a shift in the relationship between citizens and migrants. The vast number of people crossing through Greek territory, their struggles at the borders and in camps and the diversity of this population, could be said to have, to some degree, questioned their invisibility, their representation as mere bodies suffering violence and death, and forced their recognition as complex subjects. Though certainly only to a limited degree, this process did challenge the common-sense constitution of the community of struggle around citizenship.

Through it has been extremely important, in the context of a hostile European immigration and asylum policy, to point out that these particular migration flows consisted predominantly of war refugees, and thus that they could not be treated as 'illegal' (i.e economic) 'immigrants' in the usual militarised manner, it is also important to alter our perspective on this issue and question also the humanitarian representation of refugees as mere victims of circumstance. It was also clear, since they were coming from Turkey, that they were seeking a *better* place to viably settle and build a new life. This was the scandal, for those who claimed that they, therefore, were no longer refugees, based on the most ideological liberal conception of freedom: if entering a labour contract is a choice, emigrating in order to obtain one, or a better one, is little more than capricious shopping around. From that perspective, it was incomprehensible that people would take deadly risks in order to reach that 'better' place. The migrants' penetration through intra-European borders was another scandal, questioning the premises of free movement reserved only for Europeans. In crossing each of these borders, they revealed the fragility of the notion that the human misery caused by wars in which European powers participate must leave Europe unaffected. They revealed the racist selective applicability of the Geneva Convention and the Schengen Treaty, both of which had to be violated to stop people of non-European ethnicities and religions crossing borders. In continuing to cross and demanding the freedom to travel to their country of choice, they challenged the notion of the refugee as someone who has no other needs and desires than merely to stay alive with some food and shelter. Given the legal, ideological and moralistic loading of the terms 'immigrant' and 'refugee', here I will nevertheless use the term 'migrant' in order to signify the act of mobility, regardless of its causes or motivations, which are usually more complex than these categorisations allow.

The 'refugee crisis' reached its peak over the summer of 2015, at the time of the most intense phase of the SYRIZA–EU negotiations over austerity. This coincided with the imposition of capital controls, the referendum on the EU deal and the second elections of September 2015, in which SYRIZA was again able to form a government despite its capitulation and departure of the Left Platform. This coincidence, and the Greek government's seemingly loosened border controls – which rejected detention camps, stopped the practice of refoulement and aimed to unblock the asylum system – led many to argue that a 'crisis' was intentionally caused as a negotiation card, although it is hard to find evidence for such a claim. The Greek government was represented in international media as refusing to take action to stop the flows, but the issue was less ideological than it was practical. What is certain is that migrant numbers towards the Greek islands, attracted by the opening of the Macedonian border, peaked to more than 1,000 per day at a time of governmental vacuum and lack of preparation and resources for reception and processing. In fact, Tsipras's statements at that time repeatedly demanded EU assistance and recognition that the Greek border with Turkey is a 'European border', and insisted that Turkey be involved in discussions to stop the flows, start a reallocation programme and even establish camps and hotspots on Turkish rather than Greek territory.[63] Framed in a humanitarian language that spoke exclusively of 'refugees' to legitimise the flows, this was nonetheless an approach not at all different to the one the EU finally pursued in the deal negotiated with Turkey, which violated refugee rights.[64] The main point of contention was the involvement of the NATO navy, which was seen as a geopolitical problem in that it mediated the management of Greece's sensitive border with Turkey and was seen – across Greece's political spectrum – as a loss of sovereignty. This was not opposed on the basis of an open border policy.

There has been much international reporting on the generosity and hospitality of the 'Greek people' who, though ravaged by the crisis, supported refugees with assistance and provisions, even taking them into their homes.[65] The image of such action subverted the nationalist-racist protection of the European household from dirty and uncivilised 'others'. But the broader context of crisis can help understand how this happened and the meanings it acquired. The cash-strapped government sought to

---

63. Prime minister's parliamentary address on the refugee issue, Primeminister.gr, 30/10/2015.

64. The deal violates the Geneva Convention by recognising Turkey as a 'safe country', even though Turkey is only a partial signatory to the convention and excludes recognition for non-European refugees.

65. Benjamin Dodman, 'Greece's Tale of Two Crises', France 24, 12/4/2016.

make the most of grassroots capacities for volunteering, until it received allocated EU funds and support, as well as defuse the racist reactions that had been systematically cultivated by the prior government. They thus not only encouraged the operation of NGOs and grassroots activism in immigrant governance, assistance and processing, lifting laws that crim- inalised such assistance as 'people smuggling',[66] but they also promoted a patriotic notion of 'a duty of rescue' and 'solidarity' to refugees. Making references to 'the stories of our grandfathers and grandmothers' of the Asia Minor catastrophe, Tsipras, with the enthusiastic input of state media, insisted on the notion that 'as Greeks we know what it means to be a refugee' and can 'give a lesson of sensitivity and humanity' to the rest of Europe.[67] 'Greek philoxenia' (hospitality), a concept with references to ancient national heritage, the 'Greek psyche' and the national tourism industry were also enlisted through subsidies to 'Greek families' that would rent accommodation to refugees.[68] Thus, taking refugees into one's home was not always a form of genuinely spontaneous hospitality, but it was also a state-led scheme meant to be lucrative for the Greek households that participated. Writing on the biopolitics of humanitarian refugee governance, Luca Mavelli draws attention to the pastoral aspect of biopolitics, which also involves the government of *host* populations, promoting their well-being by restoring a national self-understanding as moral, caring and compassionate.[69] In this case, 'refugees' in need, especially when there were 'women and children' among them, and while their fleeing through Greece was the norm, became valuable for the emotional life of a host population and counterbalanced their humil- iation vis-à-vis the rest of the EU.

Nevertheless, however cynically one wishes to interpret the phenomenon, many people, especially locals on Aegean islands who had not previously been involved in pro-migrant activism or charity, came to experience a greater proximity with migrants than they would have done otherwise. As Euthýmios Papataxiárchis observes, based on his ethnographic work in Lesvos, the meaning and concrete reality of

66. 'UNHCR Warns of Growing Asylum Crisis in Greece and the Western Balkans Amid Arrivals of Refugees from War', UNHCR.org, 10/7/2015.
67. Prime minister's message at ET3 Channel on refugees, Primeminister.gr, 27/11/2015.
68. Prime minister's parliamentary address on the refugee issue, Primeminister.gr, 30/10/2015.
69. Luca Mavelli, 'Governing Populations through the Humanitarian Government of Refugees', *Review of International Studies* 43, no. 05 (2017): 809–32.

the use of the term 'refugee' was pivotal in 'humanising' migrants, for a series of reasons.[70] First, the 'illegality' of the migrant was no longer of relevance because the 'refugee' came to carry connotations of fleeing, passing through, not even really demanding 'hospitality' because one is not a visitor. Indeed, out of almost a million people migrating through the Aegean border since 2015, only a small fraction have remained in the country, most of them involuntarily,[71] after the Macedonian border closed and the EU–Turkey agreement came into action in March 2016. Second, the large number of people, women and children among them, provoked identification both at the level of national memory (the 'Asia Minor catastrophe') and at a level of the value of motherhood and family in local communities, which provoked the 'duty of rescue' that Tsipras also referred to. Third, the island's economy was boosted by the arrival of a wide diversity of small and large international NGOs, and activists and volunteers from the Greek mainland and across Europe, creating complex systems of humanitarian governance and 'solidarity structures' in which locals also came to be involved.

These events, and particularly the large-scale involvement of NGOs, reignited, for the more politicised activists, the debate over the meaning of 'solidarity' and its distinction from charity and humanitarian aid and management. What came to eventually distinguish 'solidarity' in this context was action that supported migrants in their struggle to surpass the categorisations of immigration law (migrant versus refugee) and the limitations of humanitarian refugee management, which tended to provide the bare means of survival and removed the element of choice as to where and how migrants would live their lives. At the camp of Idomeni, migrants pushed to cross the Macedonian border through rioting, clashes with border police and identifying new routes. The solidarity pursued by activists there, including those based in Thessaloniki as well as members of the international No Border network, actively supported these actions, and even helped large numbers cross a river near the border.[72] By that time, the state management of flows had already begun to again criminalise such activity as 'people smuggling',

---

70. Euthýmios Papataxiárchīs, 'Ī "Eurōpaïkī Prosfygikī Krisī" kai o Neos Patriōtismos tīs "Allīleggyïs"', *Sýgchrona Thémata*, no. 132–3 (2016): 7–28.
71. UNHCR Mediterranean Situation, unhcr.org.
72. Nick Squires, 'Activists Helped Thousands of Migrants Illegally Cross the Greece–Macedonia Border', *The Independent*, 15/3/2016.

and the 'duty of rescue' at sea would be turned into an offence, even when carried out by previously recognised NGOs.[73]

The relationships and networks forged in Idomeni through collective struggle, both between migrants and activists and among migrants themselves, appear to have played a role in how relations of solidarity developed in squatted housing projects for migrants in Thessaloniki. One of the Thessaloniki activists who squatted Orfanotrofeio in 2016, a large empty old orphanage that belonged to the church, told me that they chose to emphasise the dimension of building a community of struggle in the space, as opposed to simply providing housing, and for this reason they avoided having many temporary residents. This helped provide a degree of stability for migrant residents, build relationships and ensure that migrants were not dominated by locals in the assemblies. Migrants came to take the initiative in the administration of the space and in its becoming a centre for struggle linked to migrant mobilisations in regional camps. The 'open camps' were created as part of the evacuation of Idomeni and migrants there faced problems with crowded, unsanitary and unsafe conditions, expensive transport to and from the city, and road safety around the camps.[74] Many protests took place, and these mobilisations came to coincide with the No Border Camp in Thessaloniki in July 2016, in which migrants participated actively, fronting demonstrations. These networks came to be a threat to local and national government and its projects of managing migrant populations, which is probably the reason why Orfanotrofeio, along with two other Thessaloniki squats that housed migrants, were evicted soon after, with the Orfanotrofeio building even being immediately demolished. The state's intervention did much to damage these networks of struggle, not only through the evictions but also by dispersing migrants to refugee housing. Yet the experience is said to have been transformative for many, not least in breaking down barriers of ethnicity that have tended to produce mutual suspicion and sometimes conflict in camps.

A story has been recounted to me more than once to indicate the difference between the role of migrants in solidarity projects in Thessaloniki as opposed to Athens. Two migrant activists representing Orfanotrofeio travelled to an assembly for all migrant squats at City

73. J. J. Gálvez, 'Greece Arrests Three Spanish Aid Workers Trying to Assist Refugees', *El Pais*, 15/1/2016.
74. E Karavasíli, 'Ta Dromológia kai ta ... Chiliómetra tōn Prosfýgōn stī Thessaloníkī', Karfitsa.gr, 15/6/2016. 'Ston Kataulismó Prosfýgōn sta Diavatá', *Vice*, 20/7/2016.

Plaza, Athens. There, they discovered that they were among very few migrants participating, and the only ones who had a leadership role and were scheduled to speak. Indeed, I have witnessed the relationships between local activists and migrants in one of the squats in Athens, and, despite the commitment and hard work of activists, it was easy to see that dynamic play out. While the assembly formally followed an anarchist process of collaboration and horizontality, it was clearly led by the Greek activists, who were keen to enforce the rules of the house, and expressed frustration with people not doing their fair share of work. Communication was mostly unidirectional in this way, with interpretation from Greek into Arabic and Farsi, and residents responding, if at all, in either defensive or apologetic ways. Micro-conflicts between individuals of different ethnicities also existed, in the form of seemingly minor everyday annoyances and cultural misunderstandings. The local activists took the role of administrators, protectors and mediators, and none of the immigrants had roles of leadership even though a few of them seemed to have a motivation to do so, especially those who spoke fluent English.

It does seem that the willingness of 'hosts' to relinquish control of a solidarity project to their 'guests' is contentious. Athens activists in particular tended to assess the 'success' of such housing projects in terms of the ability of 'hosts' to establish rules and garner the respect of resident migrants. As it turns out, the experience of Thessaloniki migrant activists who visited Athens did not reflect the ecology of of squatted housing projects in Athens. In fact, a few were initiated by a Syrian activist long settled in Athens and others are led by European, mostly Spanish, activists who arrived specifically to engage in such projects. But the latter cases, in which the distinction between 'hosts' and 'guests' becomes unclear, have a reputation of disorder among Greek activists.

For 'guests', and even more so non-European immigrants in Europe, to be able to take control of a space and the means of communication is a radical move, which crosses a usually very rigid boundary. It is not merely a process of translation, to refer back to Mezzadra and Neilson's proposal – it is not even merely a rejection of voicelessness and invisibility – but it directly challenges the dominant voice and language of the citizen within the territory they are supposed to rule. It is a form of 'heterolingual address', in which the host's language becomes just one among others,[75] beyond the space of a solidarity project, in *public* space. Before the 'refugee crisis', this only happened in exceptional situations, as in the case of ASOEE demonstrations with immigrant street vendors. Since then, political posters, banners and slogans in Arabic and Farsi are becoming more common. These do not only violate the linguistic norms of Greek public space, but they indicate the existence of political communities that are beyond the control of the citizen 'hosts'. The added factor that these are languages associated with 'Muslim' cultures, and are claiming presence as languages of social struggle, poses a threat to European self-understanding, as long as intentional misconstruals can be prevented.

There is, still, another dimension to this. Whether led by Greek, Spanish or Syrians settled in Greece, it matters whether the relations developed within those spaces develop into a form of collective action or a form of service provision. This is where the experience of Orfano-trofeio seems to have produced a much deeper distinction between the meaning of solidarity and the type of activity NGOs are engaged in. It did not simply fixate on horizontality – or on enforcing the rules of the space – but it provided resources for resistance and empowerment, as opposed to merely meeting housing needs. In other words, in its space migrants emerged as subjects with complex desires that they pursued actively.

Yet migrant leadership can sometimes itself reproduce limits and borders. Some migrant-led squats in Athens have segregated Syrian and Afghan migrants because of conflicts between them. Conflicts between these two ethnicities, which are also common in camps,[76] reflect the governmental categorisation of different types of refugees, which from the start prioritised Syrians' needs and asylum applications. A greater proportion of Syrians also has a middle-class background and better access to resources, an additional cause for envy. Thus the creation of a 'mobile commons' – the ideal of resource sharing and collaboration among migrants, which Papadopoulos and Tsianos suggest is the essence of a politics of migration – does not always take place, as resources are not, or cannot be, always shared on the ground.[77] Contrary to their

---

75. Naoki Sakai, *Translation and Subjectivity* (Minneapolis: University of Minnesota Press, 1997) quoted by Mezzadra and Neilson, *Border as Method*.

76. Giannīs Souliōtīs, 'Exichniástīke to Aimatīró Epeisódio me Énan Nekró sto Kéntro Filoxenías stī Malakása', *Kathimerini*, 1/10/2018.

77. Dimitris Papadopoulos and Vassilis S. Tsianos, 'After Citizenship: Autonomy of Migration, Organisational Ontology and Mobile Commons', *Citizenship Studies* 17, no. 2 (2013): 178–96.

contention, inspired by an 'autonomy of migration' perspective, that 'the heterogenising effects of power should not be confused here with the multiplicity of mobile subjectivities and struggles', mobile subjectivities and struggles can and do reproduce the *segregating and hierarchical* effects of power. This is often not a question of merely overcoming 'heterogeneity' but of fighting against the logic that produced the hierarchy in the first place. It is a logic that, at bottom, brands Syrians as more 'desirable' migrants than Afghans – an issue about which the latter have been actively protesting despite NGOs attempting to prevent them from doing so.[78]

Another separation among migrants is that of gender. Indeed, traditional gender roles became an obstacle to protests in camps. Often, women were expected not to participate and remain 'house-bound' in the camp, effectively weakening those struggles. On the other hand, migrant women and men in solidarity spaces do take advantage of opportunities to explore different gendered ways of being. I have encountered young women who have abandoned traditional modest femininity, men displaying non-masculine forms of vulnerability and genderqueer individuals demanding recognition and respect. Queer migrants have found one another and formed communities and movements, demanding the right to asylum based on gender discrimination often with support from Greek LGBTQI+ organisations.[79] It is not necessarily Greek activists who facilitate this process of questioning gender roles. On the contrary, solidarity spaces are male dominated and there is little reflection about gender within them, even though they do allow various forms of gender expression. As for Greek public spaces, they continue to be far from safe for those visibly transgressing gender norms.

While projects and struggles in cities fight to normalise the visibility, voice and complexity of migrant subjects, a much more violent process is taking place on Aegean islands where 'hotspots' now operate. With the 'refugees welcome' phase long over, the language and practice of distinction between 'refugees', 'immigrants' and 'illegal immigrants' has returned in full force. The processing of asylum applications, which can take more than a year, determines whether one will be deported or be allowed to live in Greece. In the meantime, thousands of migrants, including a high

---

78. Are You Syrious? 'Ngos Prevent Camp Residents from Joining Protests', Medium.com, 22/8/2017.
79. Marianna Karakoulaki and Dimitris Tosidis, 'Transgender Refugees in Greece Reclaim their Dignity', *Deutsche Welle*, 8/7/2018.

proportion of children, are trapped in overcrowded 'hotspots', living in tents and lacking access to basic hygiene and heating. The camp in Moria, Lesvos, is one of the most notorious, in which frequent detainee protests, hunger strikes and uprisings have taken place, the most forceful by migrants from sub-Saharan Africa. This was a struggle that directly addressed the racialised dimension of the migrant/refugee distinction, given that skin colour determined their very ability to apply for asylum, as well as their violent treatment by guards and police.[80] We see, again, how the subject of the 'migrant' itself is constituted by the border as a relation, in this case a subject fighting directly against its racial categorisation, intimately linked to the ability to cross borders.

---

80. Coordination of Collectives and Persons Against Detention Camps, 'Conversation with A. One of the Migrants Prosecuted for Incidents at Moria on 17–18 July 2017, [in Greek], Ssaekk.espivblogs.net, 4/4/2018.

Conclusion

Through its analysis of social struggles in Greece, this book has taken an approach that reveals tensions, arguing that negative moments and points of seeming disintegration are at the same time 'productive': they allow reflection and reveal forms of exclusion, blind spots, unintelligibility, contradictions and denial that need to be dealt with if movements are to move towards greater universality. I hope I have shown that even though this seems like a very abstract idea, it is also very concrete. Movements have dissolved repeatedly because their imagined universal and inclusive identity contradicted their composition and failed to recognise social questions of class, gender, race, differential resources and needs. They have met limits by reproducing the very relations they fought against. Their nation-centred identity gave a stepping stone to far-right discourses and political formations. Their taking for granted of normative family structures and gender roles as something to uphold in the whirlwind of crisis gave space to misogyny and violence against non-normative genders and sexualities. Their assumption of the spontaneous revolutionary content of class and labour experience has been blind to how workers' and class identities can be mobilised to reactionary ends.

But pointing out these issues is not intended to cultivate a view of the future as a fascist apocalypse. Recognising these weaknesses creates spaces for critique and transforms social action and political orientations. For example, migrant solidarity, despite its limits, has now become an ethical norm, even among left perspectives that flirt with a protectionist attitude. Lessons were drawn both from the way GD appropriated the nationalist impulses of the squares, and from the activity of migrants who have made their complex experience and perspectives more publicly visible. Gender, in its broader problematisation not only of women's social position but also the deadly link between the patriarchal family, property and the violence of hetero-cis-normativity, is at the very least an issue that most movements now feel compelled to recognise. The political response to the lynching of LGBTQI+ and HIV activist Zak Kostopoulos, who was murdered by shopkeepers and police after an alleged theft, is a significant example of this shift.[1]

Of course, there are limits to this. Kostopoulos's murder was far from a cause for national mourning, and some forms of dogmatism are unshakeable. The leader of Popular Unity, Panagiotis Lafazanis, recently gave an interview at Konstantinos Plevris' far-right TV channel Rehellenisation, as the party continues to pursue a left–right nationalist coalition. If movements, though their experiences of failure, can produce and are capable of spreading new forms of social awareness, this awareness does not emerge automatically but it becomes part of the political, activist and theoretical work of the movements that succeed it. Critical awareness can be stunted, however, by retreat into identity and identity-thinking, which combine an assumption of an inner unity and plenitude with the paranoid projection of internal contradictions to external figures of ill will. Whether it is 'cosmopolitan elites', betraying governments, US imperialism or inherently evil 'fascists', they all allow the avoidance of hopelessness through the denial of our own failures and limitations, they all help us draw strength from the imaginary virtue and radicalness of our politics, eventually risking the repetition of the same failures. The courage to face our own contradictions is empowerment through the recognition of weakness, and is our strongest defence against the emergence of fascisms nearer to 'home' than we ever thought possible.

The proponents of strategy aiming at state power will be unsatisfied by this analysis, asking 'what is to be done' beyond focusing on reflective processes of struggle. Srnicek and Williams have recently mounted a critique against 'folk politics', referring to struggle that is local, aims at limited wins, creates alternative communities and turns away from 'major' politics.[2] Self-organisation, horizontality and lack of a grand strategy are thought to be some of the main failings. Movements are said to be in fear of gaining power and unable to imagine a non-capitalist future, let alone formulate transformative economic policies and demands. They propose instead that intellectuals ought to construct 'solutions' for urgent problems, and inspire broad movements including grassroots groups, hierarchical organisations and political parties. Yet, given that this is what has already been happening at the organisational

---

1. 'Hundreds March to Protest Circumstances of Death of Zak Kostopoulos', *Vīma*, 26/9/2018.
2. Nick Srnicek and Alex Williams, *Inventing the Future* (New York: Verso Books, 2015).

level, for example around SYRIZA's electoral victory in Greece, why is it that not much has been transformed?

Srnicek and Williams might argue that the demands put forward were not what they propose: universal basic income and the reduction of work hours on the basis of the acceleration of automation. But nowhere do the authors consider the *structural* constraints of their policy ideas. If universal basic income was to actually reduce dependence on work and thus raise wages, inflation and capital flight would likely follow, which is why no government, despite its politics, would implement it in a capitalist economy at any level above the basic level of welfare that exists today. The 'decommodification' of labour is not only opposed because of ideological fixation on the work ethic, but also because pro-letarian dependence on the wage is a basic principle of labour market operation in capitalism. Similarly, the demand to accelerate the development of current capitalist industrial technologies so that more work can be automated fails to consider the environmental impact of energy use and raw material extraction, supposing that the reduction of work hours would alone solve these issues. This focus on production technology as the driver of transformation is not far from what Postone has criticised as the major pitfall of twentieth-century communist revolutions: the notion of 'liberating' the productive forces 'fettered' by the relations of production. Directly addressing forms of social domination becomes a secondary, subsequent stage of struggle.[3]

The Leninist question of 'what is to be done' implies that transformation is only feasible via existing political forms and institutions. The response is that transformative agency is most severely limited when demands and imaginaries are restricted to policy transformations within a nation-state. The Gramscian insistence on gaining national-popular hegemony first is flawed, not because of its verticality, but because it fails to address urgent problems that current movements are grappling with: environmental destruction, global warming and extractivist exploitation; the dependence of national economies on global financialised capitalism; and exclusionary, racist and fascistic national politics driven to secure welfare for narrowly bounded communities, and the patriarchal backlash that accompanies this.

Deprioritising these problems in favour of a 'domestic' strategy, left populism finds increasingly common ground with the right. Across

---

3. Ibid., 175–6.

Europe, current popular-nationalist narratives against 'globalisation' overlap with a discourse of defending the interests of a national 'working class'. In Greece, GD, in its peak moment of growth, attempted to form their own labour unions and prevented migrant workers from taking jobs. Many attribute these phenomena to the inability of the left to organise the working class after decades of defeat and diminishing ranks in the labour movement.[4] The leader of Germany's left-wing party Die Linke, Sahra Wagenknecht, has interpreted this to mean a tougher stance on immigration.[5] Some left-wing critics have defended her discourse, arguing that 'a party that follows its moral imperatives without recognizing citizens' concrete experience cannot hope to win new supporters'.[6] Others have similarly attributed the electoral victories of Donald Trump and Brexit to the left's lack of appeal to working-class experience and its overemphasis on 'identity politics'.[7] Even left-wing academics have argued against criticising 'popular "feelings of patriotism"' and working-class complaints about immigration.[8]

The case of Greece has frequently fed into these discussions. After SYRIZA's difficult negotiation and eventual compromise with the austerity and privatisation agenda pushed by EU creditor countries, the 'return' to economic and political sovereignty has been seen as even more urgent.[9] Oppositional imaginaries see the sovereign nation as a precondition for democracy and a refuge from exploitation, or, more accurately, as a way to protect the value of a national labour power – in Greece and elsewhere – against international competition and what is often called the 'race to the bottom'. It is also a demand to return to national production, thought to be stifled by international finance. The Brexit vote in the UK, and the subsequent empowerment of Jeremy Corbyn's Labour Party, were accompanied by a similar imaginary of protected economy, welfare state and borders.

Despite SYRIZA's capitulation, its 'left victory' continues to inspire hope for left populist projects. Its failure is attributed alternately to its

---

4. Nancy Fraser, 'The End of Progressive Neoliberalism', *Dissent*, 2/1/2017.
5. Guy Chazan, 'German Political Shift Favours Hard-Left Icon Sahra Wagenknecht', *Financial Times*, 24/2/2017.
6. Volker Schmitz, 'The Wagenknecht Question', *Jacobin*, 5/2/2017.
7. Paul Mason, 'Britain is Not a Rainy, Fascist Island', *The Guardian*, 25/6/2016; 'Editorial: President Trump?', *Insurgent Notes*, no. 13 (2016).
8. Seidler, *Making Sense of Brexit*, 14; McKenzie, 'Class Politics of Prejudice'.
9. For example, Costas Lapavitsas, *The Left Case Against the EU* (Medford: Polity Press, 2018).

'betrayal' of the 'Greek people' – a moral failure that other parties can avoid – or the dogmatic neoliberal policies of the EU, which can be avoided by prioritising 'national sovereignty'. Accusations of betrayal forget that SYRIZA never had a programme of EU or Eurozone exit, and, in fact, their rejection of exit gave them credibility as a 'government party'. The referendum itself came with reassuring statements that a 'No' vote would not lead to 'Grexit'.[10] Besides, SYRIZA's economic principles were always social democratic, with internal division between the mainstream and the Left Platform bearing only on the questions of the Eurozone, sovereignty and the role of foreign investment. The party's EU negotiating team, including Varoufakis, believed in transforming the EU from the 'inside'. Thus, SYRIZA's choice to agree on the bailout and avoid 'Grexit' followed an already openly declared orientation. It is similarly unsurprising that the party's programmatic statements after winning the September 2015 elections focused on attracting investment, rehabilitating banks from debt through repossessions, removing 'corruption' and rationalising the state.[11] The pension cuts demanded by the bailout were 'balanced out' by only a slight increase in benefits, while lip service to immigrants' human rights and workers' dignity have turned into the EU–Turkey migration agreement and new restrictions on the right to strike. The latter fits within a very rational centre-left political concern: the undermining of its left opposition. Thus the right to strike is restricted only at the 'primary' enterprise level, so that strikes can be controlled top-down by the large compromised unions and GSEE. The policing of movements has similarly continued, targeting pro-migrant activism, the Popular-Unity-led campaign against repossessions, anarchist insurrectionists and others.

While SYRIZA's 'turn' highlighted the impossibility of democracy even when it came to very moderate social democratic concessions, and has made the conflict appear convincingly as one between weak Greece and hegemonic Germany in the EU, I have insisted that such an interpretation remains on the surface. Supranational control is not only located in the EU, but in complex forms of financial governmentality, associated with international capitalist competition to which all states are subject. The demand for democracy and national independence would then not come to fruition after a potential Grexit, but it would make it clearer than

10. Public address by the Prime Minister A. Tsipras, Primeminister.gr, 3/7/2015.
11. Prime minister's speech on government's programmatic statements, Primeminister.gr, 5/10/2015.

ever that democracy can only be realised when the forms of exploitation and domination that its bourgeois form disguises in the figure of the citizen are abolished.

Even so, the Grexit route remains unpopular in Greece, despite the supposed betrayal of the 'No' vote. This is why pledges of 'solidarity with the Greek people' by left Brexit supporters are misplaced, in denial of the UK's dominant international position.[12] Few in Greece really ever wanted to exit the EU. On the contrary, Greece was threatened with being 'thrown out'. Greece's precarious belonging in the EU, beyond certain economic benefits, is critically tied to its belonging to 'the West', and an exit would entail demotion to an even more peripheral position. Moreover, while Brexit demands closed borders and an end to free movement (including that of Greek immigrants), Grexit had nothing to do with immigration. In fact, because Greece is not a preferred destination for migrants, it is the closure of internal EU borders favoured by Brexit that entraps immigrants there. As to external borders, Europe's *racial* project of preventing migration from Africa, Asia and the Middle East supplants the Greek national one, which would favour letting people pass through the country's territory. But if the peripheries of Europe are ever to be recognised as truly European, they ought both to embrace 'modernisation' and to keep the Barbarians outside the gate. Finally, while, for Greece, entering the EU has entailed a wave of neoliberal reforms since the 1970s, the UK has always been far ahead of the rest of the EU in its drive to marketise all aspects of economic and social life. In fact, the UK's withdrawal from the EU opens the way for further labour market deregulation.[13]

Given these contradictions, we seriously ought to ask if a nationally self-protective stance is the best response to the present conjuncture, and reflect on the violence of regulating labour markets by rendering racialised proletarian populations expendable through a system of lethal border controls. Is this ideal image of left-wing sovereignty – sometimes also imagined as 'inclusive, multiracial, multicultural, welcoming'[14] – even possible in the current configuration of the global economic and financial system, or could its impossibility, along with its intro-

---

12. See T.J. Clark, 'Where Are We Now? Responses to the Referendum', *London Review of Books* 38, no. 14 (2016): 8–15.

13. Sandra Fredman et al., 'The Human Rights Implications of Brexit' (Human Rights Hub, University of Oxford, 2015).

14. Stathis Kouvelakis, 'An Open Letter to the British Left', *Jacobin*, 7/5/2016.

spective and nationalist premises, intensify proletarian suffering and cross-national hostility? We already see the answer in left populist positions on Greece's relations with Macedonia and Russian imperialism, which stoke the flames of ultranationalist paranoia and promote a bellicose bipolar international system driven by racial imaginaries ('Atlanticism' versus 'Eurasianism').

Conversely, we may ask if building political solidarity in Europe through a movement to democratise the EU – Varoufakis' Democracy in Europe Movement 2025 – is a good response. Here, taking a stance against a 'retreat into the cocoon of our nation-states'[15] leads to constructing the larger cocoon of the 'European economy' and the racialised unity of 'European peoples'. 'A historically minded Europe that seeks a bright future without hiding from its past' means also not hiding from Europe's colonial history, its internal north–south east–west hierarchies, and death at its borders.[16]

If utopian imaginaries are to even begin to flourish in the current conjuncture, transnational forms of organising ought to expand beyond Europe and its ethnicities. Doing so can be informed by the limits of the alter-globalisation movement, whose most populist currents constructed the narrative of a vilified global financial elite and a 'new world order' conspiracy, falling into the trappings of antisemitism.[17] The alter-globalisation imaginary of only 15 years ago failed to such an extent that anti-globalisation discourse is mobilised today almost exclusively to defend the nation-state from the incursions of finance capital. The movement frequently confused social inclusivity with political diversity,[18] ignoring the degree to which the latter could contradict the former, so that right-wing nationalist tendencies were sometimes included insofar as they had a common enemy.[19] This is another pitfall of the populist priority to construct the biggest movement possible on the basis of the lowest common denominator, especially if this 'common enemy' is as

15. Democracy in Europe Movement 2015, 'Manifesto, Long Version', Diem25.org.
16. Ibid.; Peo Hansen and Stefan Jonsson, 'Bringing Africa as a "Dowry to Europe"', *Interventions* 13, no. 3 (2011): 443–63.
17. See Werner Bonefeld, 'Nationalism and Anti-Semitism in Anti-Globalisation Perspective', in *Human Dignity*, ed. Werner Bonefeld and Kosmas Psychopedis (Aldershot: Ashgate, 2005), 147–72.
18. Elizabeth Betita Martinez, 'Where Was the Color in Seattle?', *Colorlines*, Spring 2000.
19. Eric Krebbers and Merijn Schoenmaker, 'Seattle '99, Wedding Party of the Left and the Right?', De Fabel van de Illegaal – Savanne.ch.

vague as 'neoliberal globalisation', or conversely, as narrowly concrete as 'global elites' and 'transnational corporations'.

A more reflective alternative for today might be to develop transnational networks mediated through migrant-diasporic movements. Transnational encounters could enable struggles and subjects to produce – through conflict and challenging one another – new imaginaries, action and critique that question relations of domination and subjectivated identities, and create new grounds for alliance. On this reflective basis they would aim for new forms of organisation to effect structural transformations that transcend national territories. To succeed, transnational struggles ought to be able to produce a 'multiversal' perspective, an identity that affirms non-identity and engages in self-critique, based on which social, production, class, gender, racialised and intercommunity relations would be negotiated.

Social struggle, especially when it substantially challenges existing social relations, political institutions and establishments, is likely to face an ideological media war, militarised police, surveillance, prisons, torture and even armies. To survive such attacks, it ought to, above all, avoid turning itself into its own enemy by becoming a paranoid self-destructive formation or a populist bureaucratic machine. Even if this is not what would appear, at the most critical moment, to be the easiest way forward, it is probably the only way for utopian imaginaries themselves to grow, survive and not disintegrate into fascist ones.

Index

The Pluto Press Newsletter

Hello friend of Pluto!

Want to stay on top of the best radical books
we publish?

Then sign up to be the first to hear about our
new books, as well as special events,
podcasts and videos.

You'll also get 50% off your first order with us
when you sign up.

Come and join us!

Go to bit.ly/PlutoNewsletter